D1004103

International Political Economy Series

Series Editor: **Timothy M. Shaw**, Visiting Professor, University of Massachusetts Boston, USA and Emeritus Professor, University of London, UK

Titles include:

K Ravi Raman and Ronnie D. Lipschutz (*editors*)
CORPORATE SOCIAL RESPONSIBILITY
Comparative Critiques

Ben Richardson
SUGAR: REFINED POWER IN A GLOBAL REGIME

Marc Schelhase
GLOBALIZATION, REGIONALIZATION AND BUSINESS
Conflict, Convergence and Influence

Herman M. Schwartz and Leonard Seabrooke (*editors*)
THE POLITICS OF HOUSING BOOMS AND BUSTS

Leonard Seabrooke
US POWER IN INTERNATIONAL FINANCE
The Victory of Dividends

Timothy J. Sinclair and Kenneth P. Thomas (*editors*)
STRUCTURE AND AGENCY IN INTERNATIONAL CAPITAL MOBILITY

J. P. Singh (*editor*)
INTERNATIONAL CULTURAL POLICIES AND POWER

Susanne Soederberg, Georg Menz and Philip G. Cerny (*editors*)
INTERNALIZING GLOBALIZATION
The Rise of Neoliberalism and the Decline of National Varieties of Capitalism

Kenneth P. Thomas
INVESTMENT INCENTIVES AND THE GLOBAL COMPETITION FOR CAPITAL

Helen Thompson
CHINA AND THE MORTGAGING OF AMERICA
Economic Interdependence and Domestic Politics

Ritu Vij (*editor*)
GLOBALIZATION AND WELFARE
A Critical Reader

Matthew Watson
THE POLITICAL ECONOMY OF INTERNATIONAL CAPITAL MOBILITY

Owen Worth and Phoebe Moore
GLOBALIZATION AND THE 'NEW' SEMI-PERIPHERIES

Xu Yi-chong and Gawdat Bahgat (*editors*)
THE POLITICAL ECONOMY OF SOVEREIGN WEALTH FUNDS

International Political Economy Series
Series Standing Order ISBN 978–0–333–71708–0 hardcover
Series Standing Order ISBN 978–0–333–71110–1 paperback
(*outside North America only*)

You can receive future titles in this series as they are published by placing a standing order. Please contact your bookseller or, in case of difficulty, write to us at the address below with your name and address, the title of the series and one of the ISBNs quoted above.

Customer Services Department, Macmillan Distribution Ltd, Houndmills, Basingstoke, Hampshire RG21 6XS, England

---

The Future of US Global Power

Delusions of Decline

Stuart S. Brown

Maxwell School, Syracuse University

© Stuart S. Brown 2013

All rights reserved. No reproduction, copy or transmission of this publication may be made without written permission.

No portion of this publication may be reproduced, copied or transmitted save with written permission or in accordance with the provisions of the Copyright, Designs and Patents Act 1988, or under the terms of any licence permitting limited copying issued by the Copyright Licensing Agency, Saffron House, 6–10 Kirby Street, London EC1N 8TS.

Any person who does any unauthorized act in relation to this publication may be liable to criminal prosecution and civil claims for damages.

The author has asserted his right to be identified as the author of this work in accordance with the Copyright, Designs and Patents Act 1988.

First published 2013 by
PALGRAVE MACMILLAN

Palgrave Macmillan in the UK is an imprint of Macmillan Publishers Limited, registered in England, company number 785998, of Houndmills, Basingstoke, Hampshire RG21 6XS.

Palgrave Macmillan in the US is a division of St Martin's Press LLC, 175 Fifth Avenue, New York, NY 10010.

Palgrave Macmillan is the global academic imprint of the above companies and has companies and representatives throughout the world.

Palgrave® and Macmillan® are registered trademarks in the United States, the United Kingdom, Europe and other countries.

ISBN 978–1–137–02315–5

This book is printed on paper suitable for recycling and made from fully managed and sustained forest sources. Logging, pulping and manufacturing processes are expected to conform to the environmental regulations of the country of origin.

A catalogue record for this book is available from the British Library.

A catalog record for this book is available from the Library of Congress.

10   9   8   7   6   5   4   3   2   1
22   21   20   19   18   17   16   15   14   13

Printed and bound in the United States of America

In memory of Allen Kaufman, friend and mentor

Contents

Illustrations

Tables

Figures

Acknowledgments

I am indebted to many people who helped during the writing of this book. First, I want to express sincere thanks to the following colleagues who provided critical commentary and advice on parts of the manuscript: George Abonyi, Yubraj Acharya, Arnold Bascombe, David Bennett, Jim Bennett, Peter Bova, Steve Brechin, Arthur Brooks, Jim Bruno, Len Burman, Keith Bybee, Mihaela Carstei, Selina Carter, Ryoichi Hayashi, Dave Shana Kushner Gadarian, Jonathan Gupton, Peg Hermann, Diana Hollman, Nassim Jose Alemany Isaac, Linda Jirouskova, Philipp Kapl, Nancy Lee, Ortrun Merkle, Eric Morris, John Palmer, Grant Reeher, Billy Register, David Reidy, Dave Richardson, Al Roberts, Robert Rubinstein, Rory Shannon, Jennifer Snyder, Enis Tanner and Hongying Wang. Appreciation also extends to an anonymous reviewer who provided detailed and perceptive comments. My greatest appreciation and gratitude go to David Levey, who read the book in its entirety at each stage of revision. He has been an indispensable fount of wisdom and counsel throughout the research and writing of this book.

I gratefully acknowledge the outstanding efforts of research assistants with whom I had the pleasure to work at the Maxwell School of Syracuse University while this book was being written. In particular, I would like to express particular appreciation to Charles Deluca, Frauke Hentz, Mathew Lazare and John Mayernik. Thanks also go to Jie Dai, Max Glikman and Caroline Rose Nielsen for their assistance. My utmost gratitude goes to my graduate assistant, Ryan Rommann, whose dedication and diligence in the final stages of research and writing proved invaluable.

This book was made possible by Palgrave MacMillan's series editor, Tim Shaw, who believed early on in the importance of the topic and encouraged me all along the way. My gratitude extends to Christina Brian and Amanda McGrath of Palgrave who patiently shepherded this book through the production process. I also wish to express my thanks to Cherline Daniel for coordinating the copyediting stage of the project. I gratefully acknowledge the support extended by the Maxwell School's Moynihan Institute of Global Affairs and its director, Peg Hermann.

Finally, I could not have persevered without the encouragement and understanding of my wife, Rachel, and my son, Evan. Without their love and support completing this book would have been a far greater challenge.

Part I
Introduction

Delusions of Decline: US Global Power in a Turbulent Era

Consider the following country in the year 2030: Its overstretched military occupies several populous countries. Innovation and productivity at home have stagnated. Prohibitive trade barriers insulate its beleaguered firms from global competition while few still demand its once formidable currency. The former steady flow of immigrants has dwindled to a trickle; and students migrate elsewhere to train. Unmitigated health care inflation has overwhelmed the national finances while reliance on unfriendly creditors reaches alarming proportions. A proliferation of menacing state and non-state actors underscores the country's diminished influence and stature.

Now envision a rather different country: Backed by reinvigorated alliances and supported by adroit public diplomacy, economic statecraft and cultural outreach, an unequaled military skillfully confronts the world's most pressing security threats. The country remains uniquely positioned to lead and coordinate collective solutions to pressing transnational challenges. Aspiring individuals from around the world migrate to its entrepreneurial economy and free-wheeling culture. Buoyant living standards, widespread freedoms and the unwavering optimism pervading this dynamic, multicultural society attract universal envy and respect.

These semi-caricatured portrayals capture two alternative paths for today's preeminent global actor. Which view offers the more plausible forecast? That virtually universal awe over the scope of US power has dissipated in less than a decade seems striking. Four key events seem to have driven this dramatic shift in perception: (i) the 2003 invasion and occupation of Iraq; (ii) the US-centered financial crisis of 2007–2009; (iii) the rancorous debate and political stalemate over fiscal adjustment; and (iv) stagnation in the median real wage. Each, in its own way, has revived competing visions over issues of social justice and concerns over the US political system's ability to reconcile them. Simultaneously, such developments have spurred global spectators to re-question the durability and legitimacy of US power.

Reinforcing doubts about US predominance has been a more gradual re-configuring of global power. The latter has involved re-ascendant states, an expanding influence for various non-state actors and a proliferation of transnational challenges. Such developments have revived perceptions of a re-emerging multipolar world associated with a qualitative diminution in US influence. Although a characteristic resiliency has defied the skeptics over the decades, recent pressures have proven sufficiently pronounced to raise legitimate doubts over the US's ability to rebound in a similarly robust fashion this time around.

The original inspiration for this book grew out of an article titled the "Overstretch Myth" co-authored with David Levey for the journal *Foreign Affairs*. Levey and I argued that the implications of running chronic current account deficits – the annual difference between what US residents spend and earn abroad – depend on how one interprets the associated stock and composition of the US's (net) liabilities to the rest of the world. In response to economist Larry Summer's quip – "there is something odd about the world's greatest power being the world's greatest debtor" – we replied that alarm over US "foreign debt" seemed exaggerated. One sentence elicited particular attention: "If anything, the world's appetite for US assets bolsters US predominance rather than undermines it" (Levey and Brown, 2005a).

This book sets out to defend the latter statement within a broader context than international trade, capital flows and "dependence on the kindness of strangers" (Levey and Brown, 2005b; Setser and Roubini, 2005). It seeks to identify and challenge core claims underlying a more general presumption of US secular decline. This requires reassessment of the full spectrum of US economic, military, political and cultural power assets: Does the US still enjoy a sufficiently superior global position and influence to justify its status as the predominant actor within the international system? Is any other single player or unified group of actors willing to assume the mantle of global leadership and offer a viable alternative to the US-led liberal world order?

Examining the arguments and evidence advanced in the ever-expanding literature on US decline, this book answers these two core questions with an emphatic yes and no, respectively. The book's central claim can be stated more definitively: The US retains a qualitative predominance across the principal dimensions of global power. Its state and civil society continue to exert a pivotal influence on world affairs. The US remains, in a word, hegemonic. Under what conditions such hegemony can be maintained is the central theme explored in this book.

In analyzing the rise and fall of the great powers neither Yale historian Paul Kennedy (1987) in his classic account nor most subsequent commentators have distinguished with sufficient clarity between primary and more secondary underpinnings of global power. This book's effort to systematically differentiate between the (primary) determinants of national decline, on the one hand, and the (secondary) underpinnings of "imperial overstretch," on the other, supports a more bullish assessment of longer-term US prospects.

In particular, the underlying microeconomic and macroeconomic pillars of US global power remain robust. Owing to a durable dynamism and relatively auspicious demographics, the US appears poised to outperform other developed economies over the longer term. The internal dynamics of US productivity and labor force growth, and their myriad determinants – notably an endemic entrepreneurial spirit of innovation and broad openness to transnational movements of people, capital and ideas – continue to buttress its relative economic prowess. In contrast, any tendency toward military overreach – insufficient boots on the ground relative to the demands of (self-assumed) foreign entanglements, and/or resource over-commitment in foreign campaigns – represents a more reversible phenomenon.

Along with other advanced countries, the US faces formidable budgetary challenges and a macroeconomic imperative to progressively delever. Critical to macroeconomic stability therefore will be broad public support for the sacrifices needed to restore longer-term fiscal solvency alongside healthier household and financial institution balance sheets. Forestalling the onset of decline will require summoning a systemic capacity to surmount the current political gridlock over national resource allocation priorities. Still, Americans have met momentous challenges before; and some encouragement can be taken that the country's upward debt trajectory has been thrust to the center of public policy debate. In the meantime, the book argues that much of the current handwringing over the dollar's diminishing status and the role of US macroeconomic policy in driving global economic imbalances reflects misinterpretation or hyperbole.

An underlying theme of this book concerns the enhanced stability and prosperity, and hence legitimacy, garnered through leadership in the provision of global public goods. Such services provide core benefits to the world community while consolidating the leading state's position atop the global power structure. For example, the US Navy secures the strategic sea lanes and chokepoints through which key commodities like oil flow to all regions of the world.[1] The US has also led in the creation and reinvigoration of institutions that promote and safeguard multilateral trade and finance. Meanwhile, in key strategic regions the US presence as a counterweight to aspiring regional hegemons is tolerated if not always enthusiastically embraced. Although Americans have heretofore shared in the economic and security benefits, will tightening resource tradeoffs and growing insecurities at home render the country less willing to tolerate international free riding of (largely) US-financed global services?

Powers that are perceived to export insecurity or exploit other nations tend to spur the formation of countervailing coalitions to clip the leading state's wings. In this context, for example, the invasion of Iraq and the squandering of moral stature in locations like Guantanamo and Abu Ghraib have dealt a blow to US prestige. Such setbacks, however, have not translated *pari passu* into any broad-scale repudiation of US liberal and democratic values. Nor, as this book will attempt to argue, can any other single development be persuasively claimed to pose an insurmountable challenge to the US's overall global position. Despite much scholarship that predicts concerted state balancing against the US, the evidence marshaled to date has proved underwhelming (Brooks and Wohlforth, 2008). Moreover, no viable alternative to a US-based liberal trading and security order has been on offer, nor does any other actor or even group of actors appear to offer a comparable assemblage of assets for projecting global power.[2]

Notable among the structural developments buffeting US power today is the relative shift in the locus of economic and geopolitical gravity from the "West" to emerging Asia. Alternatively, one can characterize this shift as North to South, favoring a more geographically diverse set of emerging states, anchored by the so-called BRICs (China, India, Brazil and more controversially Russia) but supplemented by other important regional players, such as Turkey, Mexico, Poland, Indonesia and South Africa. Meanwhile, are we migrating from a world of multilateral rules and institutions, where the US has stood as the ultimate arbiter and guarantor, to one of competing regional economic blocs and spheres of influence?

The unprecedented pace of economic growth in China in particular raises a central geopolitical issue – how can China's decisive re-emergence on the global stage be accommodated without subverting the existing international "rules of the game"? That China's re-ascendancy and the takeoff experienced within the emerging world more broadly would have been unimaginable without globalization may be cause to celebrate US influence. But such acknowledgment glosses over the palpable anxiety, in advanced and developing economies alike, over competition from emerging countries, particularly those featuring pervasive state direction of the economy.

As the champion of a progressively integrative and liberal global economy, particularly one encompassing formerly semi-autarkic but still largely dirigiste economies, it seems reasonable to ask whether the US has unwittingly created a Frankenstein that threatens the future well-being of American workers. As discussed in succeeding chapters, the specific policy response to foreign economic statecraft (and more generally, foreign country success under US-led globalization) is integral to the broader debate over hegemonic decline.

The more general diffusion of power to other state and non-state actors raises equally fundamental questions about the residual scope of US influence. The challenge of asymmetric warfare to the US's conventional military prowess, for example, has been vividly displayed on the hot and dusty battlefields of Afghanistan and Iraq. The nuclear ambitions of an aspiring regional hegemon like Iran, and the limitations of US-championed sanctions to materially slow its march, raises doubts about the enduring utility of US hard power assets. Can US and allied power be wielded to preclude the acquisition of nuclear materials by al Qaeda and fellow travelers? Can the US consistently galvanize collective action to ring fence a capricious North Korea? More generally, does the world still look presumptively to the US for leadership that meets the material and security needs of the global community? And once again one needs to pose the question in reverse: Do Americans perceive sufficient benefits from the more secure order delivered largely at their expense; or is the burden of US global activism increasingly perceived as exceedingly exorbitant (Mandelbaum, 2010)?

Several principles guide the analysis throughout the book: First, as a rule, competitive markets represent a superior mechanism for economy-wide resource allocation and wealth creation. Capital misallocation will still periodically recur. The sub-prime bubble, for instance, exposed long-incubating systemic distortions, incenting reckless risk-taking by an inadequately regulated financial sector. "Unfettered" markets guarantee neither efficiency nor equity, especially when economic and political control becomes concentrated or corrupt and where markets de-anchor from core societal moorings. The recent economic crisis likewise confirms the critical role of the state, the decisive intervention of which can limit wider fallout from incipient instability.

While the constituent categories of "market failure" – where market prices and social costs diverge – make a presumptive case for governmental intervention,[3] against this must be weighed the prospect of governmental failure.[4] Striking the right balance between the market and government thus involves a delicate balancing act, and reasonable people can agree to disagree over the efficacy of specific government correctives to private decision-making. Yet, some tradeoff appears to exist between the scale of governmental redistribution and intervention in markets, on the one hand, and economic dynamism on the other.

Second, while interstate cooperation is usually preferable, a disparity of capabilities among states, differences in national values, a proclivity toward "free-riding" and obstacles to effective coordination suggests a predominant state may sometimes be required to take the lead in "putting out fires." Collective action may either not occur or materialize too slowly in the absence of an activist, leading power.

Just as "corporate social responsibility" is not mainly about altruism, the provision of core global public goods serves to reinforce hegemonic legitimacy while upholding national economic interests.[5] Meanwhile, predominant states can be vulnerable to a hubris that encourages an injudicious application of power (Beinart, 2010). Whether inciting opprobrium or praise, periodic unilateral action in response to perceived crisis significantly defines what it means to be hegemonic. While some are anxious to transcend such a system in favor of a more progressive post-nationalist world, for now the hierarchical distribution of state power continues to matter.

Finally, in terms of the principles guiding the analysis, hegemony transcends the confines of the state. It involves releasing the creative energies of households, non-profits and corporations domiciled in the leading state, allowing them not only to transact internationally but also to transfer financial resources, skills, ideas, norms, technologies and security (and undoubtedly, sometimes insecurity) globally.[6] In addition to its policymakers and the organs of government, a hegemonic power, by definition, features a broad array of such influential, globally oriented non-state actors including philanthropies, foundations and religious charities, professional associations, transnational non-governmental organizations, universities and corporations. Their collective impact and ability to contribute to the solution of pressing global problems can often rival that of the state itself (Brown, 2012).

This book offers neither a partisan political perspective nor does it seek to defend a specific ideology.[7] As much as possible it avoids normative categories; thus, for example, no systematic effort is made to weigh the impact of the US on global "welfare." Moreover, this is not another book on US foreign policy. Rather, through a critical synthesis of debates in the economics and international relations literatures, the book strives to offer a template for evaluating the state of US power and the prospective challenges to it. The book's core remit thus lies in outlining objective preconditions for sustained US primacy versus secular decline. It is hoped that non-Americans as much as Americans will find much here that stimulates new ways to think about the evolving nature and exercise of global power today.

My first encounter with concerns over US decline came growing up in suburban New Jersey. My father, a salesman of computer-controlled machine tools – sophisticated presses, lathes and grinders required to produce the country's advanced manufactured products – would regale the family at the dinner table with tales of US technological superiority. Years later he would speak with resignation about stiff competition from cheaper imports. Much has changed with the structure of the US economy and with the world writ large since the late 1960s and 1970s. Successive waves of pessimism and optimism concerning US "competitiveness" and influence have accompanied this revolution. Against the backdrop of today's turbulent pace of economic and geopolitical change, are the latest claims of waning US power more on target than similar, prior claims? Against the rapidity and complexity of global developments, is it quaint to continue to view the world through the lens of US hegemony? If not, for how much longer and under what circumstances? These are the main questions this book explores.

Part II
Global Power: Key Issues

1
US Power: Past and Prologue

Evidence for US primacy used to be less contestable. Financial and strategic support from the US notwithstanding, Europe and Japan required decades to rebound from the devastation of World War II. Their later economic "challenge" eventually would succumb to the US revolution in information and communication technology (ICT), in the one case, and a protracted economic stagnation in the other. While sleeping giants India and China had self-selected out of global capitalism, US-headquartered transnational corporations roamed the world uncontested even as US manufacturing exports boomed. Systemic defects spelled, first, implosion, then dissolution, for the US's main strategic rival, the former Soviet Union. As long as a looming threat from Islamist extremism remained beneath the radar, the Western state-centered international system appeared unassailable. The US seemed to straddle this world like a colossus – militarily, economically, politically and culturally. Yet the world, and the US's position within it, looks rather different today compared to 1950, 1991 and 2001. Do recent shifts in the global system's tectonic plates augur secular decline for the world's preeminent power?

The rest of this chapter is organized as follows. To help situate the perspective advanced in this book, the section "The popular literature on 'decline' " provides an overview of today's controversy over US decline. The section "Globalization and global power" discusses the relationship between global power and globalization, and its implications for the nature and scope of US power today. Against this analytical and historical backdrop, the section "Maintaining primacy in a turbulent era" introduces the basic contours of the argument advanced in the book. The section "Structure of the book" concludes with a brief overview of the remaining chapters.

The popular literature on US "decline"

National "decline" for a preeminent global power refers to a (composite) reduction in economic dynamism, military prowess, political-cum-diplomatic clout and cultural impact.[1] Influencing the argument in this book have been scholars and pundits who have addressed the question of US decline directly or indirectly, partially or comprehensively, and from varying vantage points. Leading credit in particular goes to Yale historian Paul Kennedy for his magisterial *The Rise and Fall of the Great Powers*. Certain core constructs he invoked a full generation ago continue to frame the contemporary debate (Kennedy, 1987). Still, Kennedy's "imperial overstretch" construct and much of the subsequent commentary it spawned can sound mechanistic and over-determined today.

Less celebrated but more persuasive is Harvard political scientist, Joseph Nye, in his 1990 publication *Bound to Lead* (Nye, 1990). Nye's argument, that overstatement of US power in the immediate post-war period inflated perceptions of its subsequent descent, remains a cautionary tale on biased historical comparison. His early analysis also captures core qualities that still differentiate the US from lesser "great powers." Yet, much has changed in the 20 years since its publication, notably the dissolution of the former Soviet Union, prolonged stagnation in Japan, the rollercoaster of European monetary integration, September 11th and the invasions of Afghanistan and Iraq, the sub-prime financial crisis, macroeconomic stabilization and take-off in key emerging markets, and the marked re-ascendancy of China. Since much of this change lies at the intersection of economics and international affairs, an updated analysis of today's global economic forces and their implications for national power is needed.

In the writing of this book, the wide-ranging reflections of historian Niall Ferguson have proved especially thought-provoking. For example, Ferguson has been ahead of the curve in locating a major constraint on the exercise of US power in its ominous fiscal trajectory (Ferguson and Kotlikoff, 2003). Still, he may be overzealously stretching an otherwise sensible description of US vulnerability through analogies with the likes of much smaller, endemically profligate states such as Greece (Ferguson, 2010). For the time being at least, the Eurozone sovereign debt crisis reaffirms the US dollar and treasuries as uncontested sources of reserve currency status.

Ferguson's (2008) skepticism about the sustainability of US global power is epitomized in the metaphor "Chimerica." The latter views the global financial system through the lens of an unstable co-dependency between the US and China (Ferguson, 2008). "Global imbalances" appear to capture the coexistence of macroeconomic overstretch on the one side and systemic mercantilism on the other. As the discussion in Chapter 4 outlines, however, alternative, structural explanations for global payment imbalances have moved the discussion well beyond simple caricatures of over- and under-consumption.

Ferguson's (2004b) admonition that a world deprived of an activist, predominant state remains vulnerable to a generalized anarchy merits deeper reflection. The latter theme lies squarely in the tradition of hegemonic stability theory, as pioneered by economic historian Charles Kindleberger. In the spirit of Mancur Olson (1971) on collective action problems, Kindleberger maintained that global economic stability requires the backing of a singularly powerful state architect and defender of global trade and financial institutions. Central to this role was setting the trading and monetary rules of the game and the use of its reserve currency as the leading medium of exchange, unit of account and store of value (Kindleberger, 1973). This notion of hegemonic stability can be extended beyond economic regimes to areas ranging from nuclear non-proliferation, through the protection of vital sea lane traffic, to maintaining the balance of power in strategic regions. Yet, it remains an open question as to how indispensable hegemonic leadership of the Kindleberger variety in fact is and whether enhanced cooperation can substitute in a situation of hegemonic decline.

Moreover, those who highlight how the US furnishes core governmental-type services on a global scale (Mandelbaum, 2005) increasingly question what the US can afford given mounting fiscal pressures (Mandelbaum, 2010). An unresolved tension therefore pervades this literature. Is US coordination and financing so critical to render a more collective furnishing of public goods inadequate or unlikely? If so, what motivates the US to assume this burden? The paradox is explained if the US can be shown to gain, sometimes disproportionately, if not always economically *per se* then in terms of global clout and leverage.

The example international trade provides is instructive. Classical trade theory posits that countries can benefit from trade even when trading partners resort to export subsidies and other trade barriers. This perspective in effect recommends setting out a welcome sign to (cheaper) imports without requiring reciprocity for the country's own exports. The US has not generally adopted this "liberal unilateralist" position. US trade policy has instead often mirrored the assumptions of more recent trade theory, which includes an element of rivalry in addition to the more traditional focus on mutual gains from trade. Utilizing its leverage as the reserve currency country and the single largest goods market, the US has deployed its bargaining power to wrest trade concessions on behalf of its industries and firms. It has leveraged its military clout to enhance the protection and perquisites afforded its corporations abroad while lowering the effective risk premium on foreign investment in the US through credible protection of the homeland and its assets (see Norrlof, 2010, pp. 67–72).

The US has hardly been laissez-faire toward aggressive import pricing or foreign state promotion of market share for national champions. And US officials have vociferously condemned such foreign practices as intellectual property infringement, discriminatory government procurement practices, "currency manipulation" and "endogenous innovation." It has readily resorted to administered protection – including World Trade Organization-sanctioned non-tariff barriers, notably the anti-dumping and countervailing duty laws.

The upshot is that the hint of altruism underlying the metaphor of "benevolent hegemon" can mischaracterize or exaggerate US practice. In certain contexts the "selfish hegemon" (Bhagwati, 2008) seems a more apt description of US behavior. Crucially, however, the US commitment to broadly open trade among other core rules of the liberal global order ostensibly benefits other actors sufficiently to forestall any broadside against the US-led system.

Yet, among the underlying themes of the current debate over decline, is a widening perception that US leverage has weakened in recent decades. The end of the Cold War, in particular, marked a diminution in the need for US-provided security and economic services. This coincided with a decline in inter-state violence and accelerated growth in key emerging countries, lowering dependence on US markets and military prowess. Is the US less advantageously positioned as "privilege taker" today owing to a less prominent role as global public goods provider (Mastanduno, 2008)? Have we entered a world in which core transnational challenges demand greater multilateral problem solving efforts? If progressive diminution in US leadership effectiveness is a reality, the less than stellar recent track record of international coordination under the auspices of the G-20 and other multilateral organizations is cause for concern (Frieden et al., 2012).

Nobel laureate Paul Krugman's insights have significantly shaped the central argument advanced in this book. In particular, his 1994 article "Competitiveness: a Dangerous Obsession" appropriately questions the meaning and utility of ranking countries – as opposed to individual companies – according to an aggregate competitiveness score built up from disparate and wide-ranging micro-criteria (Krugman, 1994). National performance need not reflect uniformly high rankings across such minutiae as per capita cell phone usage or median mathematics scores.[2] Sustained predominance presupposes rather a robust level and sustained pace of national (average) productivity growth underpinned by entrepreneurial innovation and a skilled and flexible labor force. As argued more systematically in later chapters, the preoccupation with national competitiveness seems more often a subtext for a "national security" view of the world rather than one premised on ongoing improvements in living standards.

Early on, Krugman also warned sensibly against hyperbolic parallels between the US and other fiscally challenged countries, like Greece (see e.g. Krugman, 2010a). In other contexts, however, he plays down US resiliency, invoking comparisons instead with the lost decades of Japan (Krugman, 2010b). While drawing certain warranted parallels, such comparisons underemphasize the decidedly distinct structural underpinnings of these two national economies. Meanwhile, Krugman's (2010c) preoccupation with Chinese exchange rate "manipulation" downplays the global structural factors that, arguably, better explain payment imbalances. Yet he is hardly alone here. Influential analysts, ranging from Fred Bergsten at the Peterson Institute of International Economics to Martin Wolf of the *Financial Times* and numerous others, have overplayed the significance of yuan undervaluation, even if such views continue to represent the conventional wisdom (see e.g. Wolf, 2008).

Already foreshadowed in this introduction to the debate over US decline is the tug-of-war between, on the one hand, traditional systemic advantages the US has enjoyed – including rapid technological progress, entrepreneurialism and flexible markets – and, on the other hand, the macroeconomic instability associated with mounting indebtedness and chronic underemployment that are currently buffeting the country. Some would contend that the national debt overhang threatens to overwhelm or dissipate the country's endemic microeconomic strengths. Alternatively, an erosion of microeconomic foundations – reflected in structural "headwinds" such as longer-term unemployment and an impaired credit system – may be impeding macroeconomic adjustment, threatening a protracted Japan-like stagnation.

In recent years, for example, Bill Gross and Mohammed El-Erian of leading bond firm PIMCO have invoked the metaphor "the new normal" to describe a prolonged decline in trend growth based on a future of deleveraging, re-regulation and heightened protectionism (see e.g. Gross, 2010). In their facetiously titled *This Time is Different*, economists Carmen Reinhart and Kenneth Rogoff (2009) cite ample precedent for prolonged sub-par recoveries from financial crisis-triggered debt overhangs. Meanwhile, the fallout from the debt-fueled housing and consumption boom–bust cycle leads Nobel laureate Joseph Stiglitz (2010), among others, to question whether a bloated, under-regulated financial system has added anything of value to the national economy in recent years.

In a succession of accessible works, Kevin Phillips (2006, 2008) argues that the onset of secular US decline was triggered by a confluence of distinct structural developments. These include a crisis of petroleum import dependency, necessitating an exorbitant military apparatus for securing oil supplies and requiring a costly campaign in Iraq to counteract the stranglehold of state-owned oil companies over global petroleum reserves and pricing. Phillips then links this energy security theme to an impending dollar crisis: a de-invoicing of oil from US dollars approaches, he argues, to be accompanied by widespread currency de-pegging and accelerated diversification out of dollar foreign exchange reserves. The oil-cum-dollar equation is then linked up to endemic financial instability via current account deficit financing, excessive financialization (declining manufacturing), the concurrent explosion in economy-wide indebtedness and the onset of the sub-prime credit crisis.[3] A complicated and bold thesis indeed, albeit with many analytical holes (see Chapter 4).

On the other side of the intellectual barricades are stalwart defenders of US-style capitalism, such as Nobel laureate Gary Becker and Judge Richard

Posner, who worry about heightened impediments to growth emanating from overzealous regulatory reform. Their preoccupation lies with maintaining the characteristic dynamism of the US economy based on flexible labor markets, lower marginal tax rates, less intrusive regulation and a more limited welfare state compared with the US's European peer group (see e.g. Becker, 2010).

In *Seeds of Destruction*, Glenn Hubbard and Peter Navarro argue that the key to overcoming secular stagnation and returning the US to the path of robust growth is the removal of core structural imbalances perpetuated in the main by overreaching federal public policies combined with foreign (Chinese) mercantilism. Such policy-induced distortions are reflected in overconsumption, underinvestment and trade deficits (Hubbard and Navarro, 2011). These stalwart believers in lightly regulated capitalism see the US as dangerously close to a "tipping point" unless core market-friendly reforms are adopted in the areas of taxation, financial regulation and macroeconomic policies. Other staunch believers in the underlying virtues of "Anglo-Saxon" capitalism, such as Nobel laureate Ned Phelps, have grown increasingly skeptical about the prospects for regaining dynamism in the midst of long-duration unemployment and stagnant investment.

While such reflections provide a cautionary tale concerning the strengths and weaknesses of alternate models of modern capitalism, the analysis of Amar Bhidé of the Columbia Business School appears particularly insightful. In contrast to the usual preoccupation with "overconsumption," he stresses the continual feedback and stimulus of the "venturesome" American consumer to US corporate innovation (Bhidé, 2008).[4] Moreover, his work highlights the important distinction between innovation and invention, capturing the misconceptions surrounding preoccupation with growing technological competition from the East.

Adam Segal (2010), Senior Fellow at the Council of Foreign Relations, writes perceptively about the growing Asian challenge to the US's traditionally commanding lead in innovation. While hardly underplaying the gains in Asian innovativeness over recent decades, his book, *Advantage*, provides a sober antidote to exaggerated claims that the US confronts an across-the-board assault on its dominance of the technological frontier. No one should question that the US has much to improve in the areas of education, taxation, immigration and health care, to mention a few central reform priorities to maintain robust productivity growth. As discussed at length in Chapter 3, however, much of the US public discourse on "competitiveness" is marred by misguided notions about what is most needed to maintain a dynamic, innovative and entrepreneurial economy. The debate over competitiveness would likewise benefit from a more careful assessment of the benefits and costs of state capitalism, Chinese-style, specifically as it impacts global standing, national security and the innovation process.

Another recent book that focuses on a core secular advantage favoring the US is Joel Kotkin's *The Next Hundred Million: America in 2050* (2010). He lasers in on the US's relatively buoyant demographic outlook with its comparatively stable fertility rate backed by projected immigration trends. These relatively bullish demographics should attenuate the old age-dependency challenge confronting the US among many other (advanced and certain emerging) countries today. Kotkin reminds us of the enormous welfare gains garnered from foreign students, on the one hand, and immigrant workers and entrepreneurs, on the other. This emphasis stands in contradistinction to those pundits who decry the dangers of US openness (see e.g. Buchanan, 2002).

Such structural advantages as emphasized by Becker, Bhidé, Kotkin and Segal notwithstanding, the conventional wisdom appears to favor the declinist over a more primacist perspective on US power. The anemic economic recovery from the sub-prime credit crisis despite significant macroeconomic stimulus has fueled a deep-seated pessimism. Superimposed on the cyclical realities, moreover, are longer-standing concerns: notably a "hollowing out" of the middle class reflected in stagnant median wages, increasing income and wealth inequality, the unmitigated rise in medical and education costs and an increasing average duration of unemployment and underemployment. Nor does the sense of endemic gridlock in Washington help to instill optimism concerning the political capacity to meet the country's core challenges, such as stabilizing the ominous public debt trajectory. Such sober observations provide ample grist for the declinist mill.

In terms of their impact on public opinion – both American and non-American – the declinists also appear to hold the upper hand on geopolitical and other extra-economic dimensions of the power debate. A representative example is Boston College professor Andrew Bacevich (2002, 2008). Speaking with authority from some 20 years of experience in the armed forces, he makes a cogent case that the US suffers from military overstretch, reflecting a structural disequilibrium between the supply and demand for boots on the ground in Iraq and Afghanistan among myriad other global assignments. Bacevich would resolve this imbalance not through expansion of military personnel but by scaling back most military commitments. He argues persuasively that nation building efforts lie beyond the core capability and justifiable deployment of the armed forces and that the George W. Bush-initiated "long war" against Islamist extremism represents an unlimited, hence wholly unrealistic, war posture. According to Bacevich, the utility of military power today has receded relative to other instruments of power, and US military power is overstated in any case. He favors rolling back what he deems to be US imperial adventurism.

When he moves beyond the appropriate deployment of troops to a more generalized Kennedy-esque macroeconomic overstretch argument – for instance, the US faces a cultural "crisis of profligacy" – Bacevich's argument stands on shakier grounds. While it is justified to raise the twin (trade and fiscal) deficits and military "expansionism" as legitimate policy concerns, relating them to the broader question of national decline requires a more careful economic analysis. Still, his contention of a deep-seated crisis of citizenship merits closer scrutiny in the context of strains on the US political system as it copes with the twin pressures of globalization and global power. Bacevich's antidote to ostensible national decline is to arrest chronic (as distinct from cyclical) debt-financed overconsumption, conscientiously pursue energy independence and scale back US power projection.

Another contribution from the popular declinist literature comes from the New America Foundation's Parag Khanna (2008a, 2008b). His *The Second World* is one of a spate of publications heralding the arrival of a multipolar world, in which US geopolitical stature has already irreversibly plunged. Khanna views the US in decline across virtually every dimension, throwing it into competition with Europe and China for influence in the "second world" in Latin America, the former Soviet Union, the Middle East and Asia. In acknowledging the rising clout of would-be regional hegemons as well as other, populous powers, Khanna is on to an important development. Yet he overstates the influence exercised by China today and almost certainly exaggerates the power of Brussels, even prior to the onset in 2010 of the debt crisis in the European Monetary Union's (EMU) southern periphery. The criteria for judging who is rising and who is falling can sometimes be puzzling. For example, while rightly highlighting Russia's disastrous demographics, Khanna's low expectation for (a much younger) India seems surprising. While showcasing the increasing influence of certain regional powers, such as a Brazil, Turkey and Iran, has merit, Khanna, and others of similar persuasion, arguably lack a sense of proportion in situating countries along the spectrum of geopolitical influence relative to the US.

Comparably bullish outlooks on US hegemony in the more popular literature seem somewhat more difficult to locate. A notable exception is the view of historian Robert Kagan (2012), who, like Joseph Nye, cautions against exaggerating the global influence and autonomy the US exercised at the supposed height of its power (e.g. immediately after World War II or the Cold War). Referring to the "mythical past of overwhelming dominance," Kagan seems on point in arguing that in the past the US often failed to "get others to do its bidding." Moreover, he asserts: "During the first three decades after World War II, great portions of the world neither admired the United States nor sought to emulate it, and were not especially pleased at the way it conducted itself in international affairs."

Among others who reject the claim of hegemonic decline are geopolitical strategists George Friedman and Thomas Barnett.[5] In an iconoclastic forecast of the next 100 years, Friedman (2010) stresses geographical certainties. Among these is the unrivaled spatial position of the US as a trans-continental superpower bordering two oceans – the Atlantic and the Pacific. Given a confluence of developments, namely ongoing disunity in the Eurasian continent[6] and the shift of commercial gravity to the Pacific Rim, US naval power affords virtually unassailable protection for the US homeland while perpetuating East Asia's reliance on US patrolling of the sea lanes. Friedman's overall assessment of US power is captured as follows:

> Whatever passing problems exist for the United States, the most important factor in world affairs is the tremendous imbalance of economic, military, and political power. Any attempt to forecast the twenty-first century that does not begin with the recognition of the extraordinary nature of American power is out of touch with reality. But I am making a broader, more unexpected claim, too: the United States is only at the beginning of its power. The twenty-first century will be the American century.
>
> (2010, p. 18)

Another uncompromising prediction of sustained predominance comes from Thomas Barnett (2009). His is an unwavering belief in the power of globalization, backed by the US "military Leviathan," as the leading antidote to failing states and anti-modernist forces. He welcomes China's more active role in Africa and Latin America, "simply because America cannot hope to govern the emerging global security environment on its own" (2009, p. 69). Moreover, given their inability to replace the stabilizing and security role of US military power, ample scope exists for strategic co-dependency between the US and emerging states. For Barnett, European enlargement also plays an important role in integrating countries on the periphery of the European Union (EU). Although Barnett worries about military overstretch, unlike Bacevich, he embraces large-scale stabilization and nation building in conjunction with European and Asian allies. His reflections (Barnett, 2004, 2009) stand out as a systematic effort to relate US power to ever-expanding globalization. In contrast, the thesis to be developed in this book describes a more complicated dialectic between US power and globalization with the necessarily positive correlation presumed by Barnett less assured.

Former Council on Foreign Relations president Leslie Gelb (2009) employs an illustrative pyramidal metaphor with the US singularly occupying the "Penthouse" and with remaining states situated on successive rungs below.[7] The US remains the sole power with the global reach to play an indispensable role in resolving transnational problems, backed by an equally necessary coalition of allies. Channeling Bacevich, Gelb decries the increasing disutility of military solutions to regional and global problems while citing the rising centrality of economic power. The US still leads other singular states economically even if the financial crisis has diminished its former luster.[8] Yet, according to Gelb, expanding crevices in the US power arsenal are evident in the squandering of resources, including international goodwill in hopeless nation building efforts while neglecting investment at home. An increasingly fractious and deadlocked political system completes this sobering picture. "The US is at the point of declining as a nation and as a world power...I count myself among those who think the situation is serious but reversible..." (Gelb, p. 278).

Notable among accessible, constructive accounts of US power is Fareed Zakaria's *The Post-American World* (2008a). As a highly successful immigrant to the US, he keenly appreciates the opportunities that US society affords. He is equally mindful of the US economy's enduring structural strengths. He finds much less to admire, however, in the US political system's glaring ineffectualness in addressing fundamental challenges.[9] While such arguments resonate in today's polarized political climate, Zakaria walks an exceedingly narrow tightrope in highlighting the residual assets of the US alongside the striking advances among emerging states. He sometimes seems to want it both ways by heralding "the rise of the rest" while denying US decline, even as he relegates the US to the less-than-predominant rank of "first among equals."[10] Precisely where the US stands in Zakaria's view arguably remains fuzzy.[11] After all, even as a mere "chairman of the board," the US retains an outsized capacity to reshape global institutions (2008a, 2008b).

So much of today's debate over US decline centers on the prospects for China to eventually challenge the US for global predominance. The literature is voluminous and covers a wide spectrum of opinion about China's potential to rival the US. One end of this spectrum sees China eventually supplanting the US as global hegemon (see e.g. Fishman, 2005; Jacques, 2009). Arvind Subramanian (2011a) provides a more rigorous economic defense of this claim. In contrast, in her *China Fragile Super Power*, Susan Shirk portrays China as a rising economic power, albeit one with significant internal political tensions.[12] A decidedly less optimistic view is captured in Jonathan Watts' *When A Billion Chinese Jump* (2010).[13]

Coming full circle with our panoramic critique of the more popular literature on US decline, Nye's (1990) early, even-handed portrait of the range of US power assets still seems particularly prescient, even if the internal and external forces buffeting US power have evolved significantly since its publication. In his latest in a lifetime of work exploring the nature of power, Nye concludes:

Because globalization will spread technical capabilities, and information technology will allow broader participation in global communications, American economic and cultural preponderance will become less dominant than at the start of this century. But that is not a narrative of decline. The United States is unlikely to decay like ancient Rome or even to be surpassed by another state, including China. The first half of the twenty-first century is not likely to be a "post-American world," but the United States will need a strategy to cope with the "rise of the rest" – among both states and non-state actors. The United States will need a smart power strategy and narrative that stress alliances, institutions, and networks that are responsive to the new context of a global information age. In short, for success in the twenty-first century, the United States will need to rediscover how to be a smart power.

(Nye, 2011b, p. 234)

Globalization and global power

US power in historical context

Historians of empire have analyzed the succession of great Western powers beginning in the 15th century, including Venice, Spain, Holland and the UK. While her global position today exceeds the reach of any prior historical precedent, the US arguably confronts a more complex and intractable world. For example, the awesome British Empire for which "the sun never set" still coexisted with a Germany that dominated continental Europe, a rising US that had surpassed it in industrial productivity, and a Russia that hamstrung British maneuverability in Asia. Yet, notwithstanding such powerful rivals, the British presided over the crumbling of the Ottoman Empire; and (initially at least) walked all over a fragmented Indian sub-continent.

With the collapse of its principal rival, the Soviet Union, in 1991, the US appeared to face only one potential peer challenge in the distant future – a still developing China. Meanwhile, a rich, albeit inwardly focused Europe, exhibited scant inclination to project extra-regional power remotely comparable to that of the US. Meanwhile, the much heralded economic challenge from Japan had begun to recede.[14] Yet, the world has changed significantly in the two decades since the end of the Cold War. While enjoying fewer resources and lacking anything approaching the US's strategic superiority, in its heyday the British Empire arguably faced nothing approximating the cluster of regional and transnational trials roiling the US and world today.

Citing just one example among multiple regional and transnational challenges, the ever turbulent (Greater) Middle East comprises an aspiring regional nuclear power in Shiite Iran, an extremist Sunni global jihadist movement in al Qaeda and its offshoots, and an Israeli-Palestinian stalemate that at any point could explode into renewed violence. More recently, there has been the democratic promise but also greater turbulence wrought by the Arab Spring. Punctuating this revolution is the sectarian civil war and human tragedy in Syria. As the deaths of US diplomats in Benghazi and recent protests elsewhere in the region remind one, anti-American terrorism remains a threat. Nevertheless pockets of regional support for the US remain, notwithstanding its historical backing of Middle Eastern dictators. Add to this equation the protracted wars and expensive state building exercises in Iraq and Afghanistan. And if this were not enough, there remains the ever present threat of an Islamist takeover of nuclear Pakistan and renewed conflict with its "mortal" enemy, India.

More generally, the global system has altered profoundly since the seemingly simpler days of bipolar US–Soviet rivalry. Power has increasingly dispersed from West to East and North to South, to non-state or supra-state actors including non-governmental organizations (NGOs), regional and international organizations, transnational corporations, and terrorists and drug traffickers, plus aspiring regional hegemons and other emergent powers (Haas, 2008). The ICT revolution and the rise of key emerging markets have transformed a globalization process hitherto identified almost exclusively with the US. States like Venezuela and Russia wield energy as a foreign policy weapon. And last but certainly not least, there is the re-ascendancy of China.

In sum, while it boasts historically unprecedented resources and an outsized power differential with other actors, the gamut of capabilities the US ostensibly requires to confront today's strategic challenges also seems to have proliferated exponentially. This confluence of unparalleled capacity, on the one hand, and the scale of strategic predicaments it confronts, on the other, epitomizes the underlying dialectic that so complicates the assessment of US power today. Its unprecedented material wealth, military power, and cultural and political sway aside, can the US withstand the mounting pressures from a burgeoning number of challengers and challenges? Can US predominance survive the forces that threaten to spawn a new "anarchic" phase of global history (Ferguson, 2004b)?

In contrast to herculean attempts to stretch the notion of "empire"[15] beyond recognition, "hegemony" offers a more value-neutral construct for capturing the underlying character of US global power. In international relations theory, a hegemon represents a disproportionately powerful state capable of imposing some order on an otherwise "anarchic" system – that is, a world in which neither global government nor advanced global governance prevails. Hegemony reflects a qualitative state in which one power gets its way somewhat more often than not and whose positions on key global concerns carry a preponderance of weight. Although a hegemon can lead in the provision of global public goods, in acknowledging the numerous ways in which the US has supported the global system since World War II, one need not accept the expansive claim that it "acts as the world's government" (Mandelbaum, 2005).

For (global) hegemony to be interpreted meaningfully, predominance in one dimension does not suffice. Hegemony presupposes disproportionate influence across multiple spheres – military, political/diplomatic, economic/technological and cultural/ideological. Militarily this presumes "command of the commons" (Posen, 2003), especially control of the oceans and the ability to project power into any region – in a word, global reach. It means serving as the "go to" power, uniquely positioned to provide troops, naval power and airpower to stabilize a war-ravaged hotspot or to credibly broker regional conflict resolution. At a minimum, it implies the ability to credibly function as an "outside balancer."[16] While precluding the subversion of sovereignty implied by empire, hegemony can neither be wholly de-territorialized. A residual quasi-imperial element is reflected, for example, in the network of US military bases, carrier battle groups, expeditionary force capability, Special Forces and military trainers in client states ("imperial grunts")[17]; as well as a periodic willingness to interfere in the internal affairs of "sovereign" states.[18]

In addition to its military dimension, hegemony presumes disproportionate clout within multilateral institutions created to manage leading global challenges, such as development and financial crisis. A hegemonic role involves the assumption of leadership in alleviating the suffering from natural disasters or to combat global threats to human security, such as HIV-AIDS, ethnic cleansing and international terrorism. Hegemony thus incorporates a vanguard role in stemming the regional and global fallout from ungoverned regions.

In today's globalized economy a leading feature of hegemony involves the guardianship of relatively free product and services trade, and broadly mobile capital, buttressed by widespread circulation of the leading state's currency that serves as the anchor and numeraire for the international monetary system.[19] A vital cultural and ideological dimension also underpins hegemony. A hegemon exerts influence through the "soft power" reflected in the attractiveness of its institutions, belief systems and cultural trappings (Nye, 2004). A world that embraces the predominant state's values more likely will be one in which the international community considers it, despite all of its warts and missteps, fundamentally legitimate.

A further requirement underpinning hegemony is that the predominant state can broadly reconcile the international "rules of the game" with its own "national interests" (Ikenberry, 2002). The sustainability of hegemony depends on other national governments believing that their interests are broadly advanced under such (hegemonically safeguarded) international conventions (Mead, 2004). In the absence of global government, the security, economic infrastructure and values espoused and underwritten by the predominant state can help provide the glue cementing enhanced global stability. And yes, this involves an overriding effort on the part of the hegemon to secure its own predominance by thwarting the efforts of aspiring global powers, particularly those that seek to overhaul the rules of the game underpinning the liberal hegemonic order.

Last but not least is the material foundation of hegemony. Since this dimension receives detailed attention throughout this book, it will suffice here to say that material prosperity and the technological dynamism, entrepreneurialism and openness with which it is closely allied provides the *sine qua non* of latent US power.

In sum, as defended more expansively in Chapter 2, given the pervasive influence it exerts across multiple facets of power today, the US represents history's most complete global hegemon. The likes of Venice, Holland, Spain, Napoleonic France and even the UK at its apex possessed far more limited degrees of influence. Thus, notwithstanding its long-standing application to previous great powers, global hegemony is only fully realized with the rise of the US and most evidently in the aftermath of the Cold War.

Globalization and US power

When the history of the late 20th and early 21st centuries is written, two overarching themes are likely to dominate. The first involves the evolution of US global reach. The second concerns a qualitative change in the contours of globalization. Among other features, the latter includes revolutionary advances in telecommunications and transportation, increasingly intricate global supply chains and a shift in the locus of economic activity and influence toward Asia and emerging markets more generally. After World War II, globalization constituted a principally US project and one which continually reenergized and reinforced US influence. Do globalization and US power remain compatible and mutually reinforcing today?

According to one school of thought, having long since exported its patented "marketplace society," the US triggered forces that are now exerting economic "blowback" on an ill-prepared American society (Agnew, 2005). Values the US has long promoted – free trade, capital mobility and liberal immigration – have come home to roost. The integration of China, India and the former Soviet Union into the global economy produced "three billion new capitalists," flooding the global labor pool and pressuring workers throughout the industrial West with super-competitive manufacturing costs (Freeman, 2005a, 2005b; Prestowitz, 2006). Flush with financial wealth, these rising economic powers, according to many, will prove increasingly reluctant to subsidize US "overconsumption" (Faiola, 2009).

Others who envision a growing incompatibility between globalization and US global power forecast ongoing political blowback, reflecting payback for a cumulative history of neo-imperial interventionism (e.g. Bacevich, 2002; Chomsky, 2004; Johnson, 2004). Less a backlash against prior intrusion, other observers would ascribe counter-US opposition to the proclivity of states to exploit any opportunity for gains in relative power to enhance security in an uncertain world (Waltz, 1979). After all, structural shifts in the world economy have placed emergent players in a position to make opportunistic claims on the global system and to more ably ensure their own security. However one spins it, according to this perspective, cumulative economic and geopolitical change over the past half-century now spells the eclipse of US predominance. In globalization the US created its Frankenstein; the tidal wave it spawned now engulfs the country: "...Globalization is not synonymous with Americanization; in fact, nothing has brought about the erosion of US primacy faster than globalization" (Khanna, 2008b, p. 62).

Against this narrative stands an alternative perspective which projects a more synergistic relationship between globalization and US power. In this view, the US remains at once the principal power promoting free mobility and exchange, and the main enforcer of financial and security arrangements that safeguard international transactions. The US continues to constitute the main "go to" power whenever a pressing regional or global threat to the system emerges. Through its provision of core public goods, including maintenance of a liberal trading system, provision of global liquidity and "safe haven" financial assets, securing of strategic commodity flows, and coordination of opposition to "rogue" actors, the US effectively safeguards the economic, technological and cultural interchange that constitutes contemporary globalization (Mandelbaum, 2005).

According to this second perspective on the nature of US power, flexible labor and financial markets, and superior innovativeness and entrepreneurialism allow US policymakers to reconcile competing social demands at home with mounting pressures from globalization and technological change. The intrinsic dynamism and resiliency of US capitalism has allowed it to cope with new structural developments and emerging competitors (Friedman, 1999). Meanwhile, judicious use of US power ensures that globalization can continue. For example, deploying his characteristically evocative imagery, Tom Friedman puts it so:

> The hidden hand of the market will never work without a hidden fist. McDonald's cannot flourish without McDonnell Douglas, the designer of the US Air Force F-15. And the hidden fist that keeps the world safe for Silicon Valley's technologies to flourish is called the US Army, Air Force, Navy and Marine Corps. And these fighting forces and institutions are paid for by American taxpayer dollars. With all due respect to Silicon Valley, ideas and technology don't just win and spread on their own.
>
> (1999, p. 373)

In contrast to the late 19th and early 20th centuries, globalization today involves not simply mobile capital in search of resources or the infrastructure needed to transport resources (e.g. railroads, canals and ports) but a profound fragmentation of the production process itself, creating an intricate global network of production input sourcing. Emerging in the 1950s, for example, was a form of overseas financial investment involving far more than the customary purchases of sovereign and utility bonds, namely direct investment in manufacturing facilities, acquisition of equity positions in foreign enterprises, and creation of truly multinational financial and service

Table 1.1 Emerging market external financing, 2007–2012

	2007	2008	2009	2010	2011	2012
Emerging and developing economies						
Private capital flows	694	264	337	605	503	268
Private direct investment	441	485	317	392	462	394
Private portfolio flows	109	−62	125	241	130	133
Other private capital flows	145	−158	−105	−28	−89	−259
Developing Asia						
Private capital flows	205	80	192	407	303	113
Private direct investment	175	170	104	224	218	167
Private portfolio investment	68	10	58	101	42	42
Other private capital flows	−39	−99	30	83	43	−96

All values are in billions of US dollars; positive figures indicate a net inflow of capital from the rest of the world.
Source: International Monetary Fund, *World Economic Outlook database*, October 2012.

establishments. In the 1980s and 1990s, that process deepened into a new international division of labor in which production, research and marketing were partitioned across enterprises worldwide, creating the geographically dispersed and intricate global supply chains witnessed today.

The direction of capital flows has likewise changed dramatically. Orthodox economic theory predicts that capital will flow from the capital-rich North to the capital-deficient South. On cursory inspection, this is exactly what is happening; in recent years the emerging market countries, as a group, have been net recipients of **private** capital (see Table 1.1). Yet, many such populations still save more than they invest domestically. Their resulting current account surpluses, supplemented by net private capital inflows, have facilitated the amassing of unprecedented stockpiles of **official** capital in the form of foreign exchange reserves and sovereign wealth funds.

This (public) capital has been largely recycled to the advanced industrial countries, mainly through purchases of government and quasi-government securities. A disproportionate share of these resources has flowed to the US as the principal reserve currency and location of the most liquid and sophisticated capital markets. As pointed out by numerous critics, the UK's export of capital – its net creditor status – contrasts markedly with the opposite situation facing the US today. That in addition to this official capital the world's wealthiest country still attracts steady gross inflows of private capital prompts an obvious question: why do foreign investors remain so willing to supplement their dollar-denominated assets in the immediate aftermath of a global economic crisis originating in the US? This counter-intuitive directional pattern of net capital flow has been maintained despite the anemic recovery and ominous longer-term debt outlook in the US. Notwithstanding structural shifts favoring leading emerging markets and despite a worrisome fiscal picture in the US, the persistent preference for dollar assets amid successive flights to quality testifies to the sharply declining volume of "safe" international assets and the anchor role the US still provides within the global financial system.[20]

While the expansion of markets and the rise of transnational corporations in Latin America and developing Asia have also been leading features of globalization, less discussed is the ongoing dominance of transatlantic trade and investment. Although media attention is more often focused on trade balances, worldwide sales by the foreign affiliates of European and US transnational corporations, combined with bi-directional, transatlantic foreign direct investment (FDI) flows, represents a significant multiple of US (and European) exports and imports today. Contrary to common perception, during 1990–2009, 55 per cent of the $2.9 trillion in US FDI outflows went to Europe, while (low wage) China received little over 1 per cent of total US FDI (Quinlan, 2011, p. 150). Yet this reality may be changing. Given the disparities between European and Asian trend growth, a structural shift in dominance from transatlantic to transpacific flows seems likely. More generally, changes in the costs of energy, transportation, and unit labor costs across countries, some post-financial crisis increases in trade barriers and heightened currency volatility, and the reappreciated advantages of agglomeration, customization and closer proximity to product and input markets, may be facilitating some rethinking of MNC location including the prospect for greater reshoring (On Point, 2012).

Another noteworthy structural development in the global economy involves the increase in transnational transfers. Although comprehensive inter-country data are unavailable, it is widely accepted that the US leads the world in "non-state transnational transfers" to developing economies. These generally unrequited (non-*quid pro quo*) flows include, first, remittances and, second, the transfer of money, technical assistance and training services, and goods in kind from a variety of non-state actors, including philanthropies, religious charities, other NGOs, universities and corporations (Brown, 2012). Table 1.2 provides estimates of a sub-set of US transnational transfers compared to that of four other industrialized countries.

Against this selective overview of recent global economic trends, which of our two overarching perspectives appears the more persuasive? Will the secular forces of globalization reinforce US primacy or precipitate decline? Is US society institutionally and culturally positioned to adjust and benefit from the wrenching change wrought by new competitive forces? And is the global system today any more likely to avoid the fate of prior episodes of globalization, when international rivalry reversed a profound economic integration that, as today, had been buttressed by the power of the leading state (see e.g. Friedan, 2006; O'Rourke and Williamson, 2001)? Such are among the core themes explored throughout this book.

Table 1.2   Transnational transfers, 2009

	ODA	Remittances	Philanthropy	Total
		2009		
US	28.8	90.7	37.5	157.0
UK	11.5	13.8	6.3	31.6
Germany	12.1	9.9	1.4	23.4
France	12.6	8.4	1.0	22.0
Canada	4.0	12.2	1.3	17.5
		2010		
US	30.4	95.8	39.0	165.2
UK	13.1	13.3	4.2	30.6
Germany	12.9	7.3	1.5	21.7
France	12.9	8.7	1.0	22.6
Canada	5.3	14.7	1.9	21.9

All values are in billions of US dollars.
Source: Hudson Institute, Index of Global Philanthropy and Remittances 2011, 2012; Based on data from OECD (2011) DAC Aid Statistics, Donor Aid at a glance www.oecd.org/dac/stats/donorcharts.

Maintaining primacy in a turbulent era

That "declinism"[21] has resurfaced so forcefully and so soon following the dawn of the US's "unipolar moment"[22] seems striking. The rapidity of the purported transition from a global system centered on US primacy to one based on a re-emergent "multipolarity,"[23] non-polarity or state de-centered anarchy[24] should thus provide pause for reflection. After all, as the late Samuel Huntington once remarked, already by 1988 "the United States [had] reached the zenith of its fifth wave of declinism since the 1950s" (Huntington, 1988, p. 76). Although a comprehensive overview of what is entailed by hegemonic decline is the focus of Chapter 2, we cannot proceed further here without placing the question of declining US power in broad perspective.

For reasons discussed throughout the rest of this book, any notion of absolute decline in the sense of internal implosion or systemic decay is not at issue. Rather, what remains open to question is the nature and degree of relative decline in the US's global position and reach. Economic convergence remains a powerful secular force that can steadily narrow the gap in average living standards between rich and dynamic, emerging economies. Given this natural process of the "rise of the rest," a meaningful notion of decline for the preponderant state in the system requires one to think in terms of the core conditions for maintaining (global) hegemony. The challenge is to define a qualitative threshold below which the composite (multi-dimensional) power gap narrows to a point where "hegemony" no longer accurately conveys the underlying distribution of global power. While postponing further discussion of this complicated subject here, it bears emphasis that hegemonic decline involves a more fundamental challenge than that involving the (predictable) economic convergence of a few rising states or notable shifts in constellations of regional power.

In the event, the transition to a multi-polar world may well prove less linear than some acute observers suggest. Questioning presumptions of a "post-America" world, this book highlights the relative robustness of US economic, military, political and cultural assets and the country's enduring, composite power potential. Its focus remains on more durable, structural underpinnings of US power in contrast to certain admittedly worrisome but more immediate exigencies that preoccupy US policymakers today.

In assessing the longevity of US power, one can recall precedents when the US engineered more dramatic reversals of fortune. Paralyzed by Vietnam and buffeted by a crisis of political legitimacy (Watergate) and OPEC supply shocks, the US found itself reeling from Soviet expansionism during the late 1970s and early 1980s. Simultaneously, the country faced a ferocious economic challenge as European and Japanese firms out-competed their US counterparts in advanced manufactures. Extending beyond the anticipated post-war (European and Japanese) convergence, this underperformance signaled deep structural weaknesses. By the 1980s the Reagan "twin deficits," the developing-country sovereign debt crisis and unrelenting international competition all seemed to herald a deterioration in the prospects for US prosperity and influence.

While observers fixated on the US productivity slowdown, American scientists, engineers, and "hackers" in the peninsula south of San Francisco were quietly preparing the foundations for the ICT revolution (Markoff, 2005). Much as the UK's burst of creativity in the late 18th century in iron, textiles and shipping had laid the foundations for its political and military power (and the First Industrial Revolution), from US technological creativity came all of the components that would coalesce to launch the (third) ICT revolution.

Having suppressed double-digit inflation, the 1979–1982 "Volcker shock" ushered in a generation-long expansion punctuated by two brief and mild recessions dubbed the "Great Moderation." Meanwhile, the Soviet Union disappeared onto the "ash-heap of history;" and the Japanese economy never exhibited more than tentative signs of sustained recovery from protracted stagnation. Fundamental reforms over decades translated into a pronounced turnaround in US economic performance circa 1995. Investment in information technology proved especially critical in boosting the capital stock per worker and productivity growth. Expanding global market opportunities reinforced the competitive advantages of US firms in innovation-intensive sectors such as advanced services, high-technology products and the licensing of intellectual property. Having converged toward

US per capita income levels, the continental European economies subsequently failed to replicate a US productivity growth acceleration based on extensive ICT application in the workplace, reorganization of production processes, new product development and knowledge-augmenting investment. If the longer-term ICT revolution remains in its infancy, the US may enjoy unique potential to leverage her "first mover" status into successive applications of new technologies for years to come.

This book makes a concerted effort to distinguish more carefully between two concepts – decline and overstretch – that have been misleadingly conflated in many prior accounts of national power. The record of arrested descent and reversal described above complicates any straightforward application of the "imperial overstretch" story to the US today. In Paul Kennedy's account, the history of the rise and fall of great powers reflects first and foremost the inability to maintain equilibrium between national resources and foreign commitments. In this framework, once a country's resources prove inadequate to meet ever-expanding external pursuits, scant prospect exists for priority reassessment, and subsequent realignment of objectives with resources. Instead, national decline ensues more or less inexorably from the presumed, virtual irreversibility of the incipient state of overstretch.

A more fundamental question involves the ability to maintain the systemic capacity for sustainable wealth creation and competent governance. The British Empire's decline, for instance, arguably concerned less an accumulation of excessive foreign entanglements, including exhaustion from two world wars, and more the erosion of internal dynamism and resource mobilization capacity. Likewise, the key issue for the US is less whether it faces temporary overextension abroad and more whether the very engine of economic growth confronts pervasive structural impediments. Concerted national decline would suggest a deep-seated crisis impacting the institutional basis for innovation and investment. Such an economic crisis would typically also be accompanied by erosion in the institutions and levers of governance needed to overcome it.

As the reader no doubt suspects by this point, this work owes considerable debt to the insights of Joseph Nye on key issues: First, hyperbolic assessments of power allegedly achieved in the past can bias notions of the national trajectory today. Cycles of US declinism can involve dangerous extrapolation well into the future from periods of historical anomaly, such as the aftermath of World War II or the downturn triggered by the sub-prime crisis. Second, national power remains an exceedingly complex, multi-dimensional and contextual phenomenon; and resource capacity should not be equated with a capability to realize such potential in the form of specific outcomes. The latter reflects an ability to influence behavior through a spectrum of mechanisms including agenda setting, preference formation, asymmetrical structuring and deterrence. Alliances and networks provide critical, power multipliers for a preponderant state.

Where this book may part company with Nye lies in how hegemony is defined in today's fast evolving context. Nye describes a three-dimensional "chessboard" of global power. On the first dimension of military power, the US stands alone. In the dimension of economic power, he positions the US among several "major players," notably China, Europe and Japan. On the bottom chessboard is a diffusion of players in the realm of transnational relations with no distinguishable sense of order, hierarchy or leadership (Nye, 2011a, p. 3).

Conceding that US preponderance across particular dimensions of power has diminished relative to certain base-periods, this book maintains that the US's singular position at the apex of the global power hierarchy remains qualitatively uncontested. While US influence can prove indecisive in particular instances, no other single actor, or groups of actors, possesses anything approaching the structural advantages that allow the US to influence the broader economic, security and ideological contours of the system. To use Nye's chessboard metaphor, across dimensions of play there may be varying actors jockeying for higher position, yet the US holds the highest position of composite power overall.

History shows that no previous power has sustained predominance indefinitely. A similar fate may well befall the US at some point in the distant future; but meanwhile, the evidence marshaled to forecast the US's steady economic and geopolitical decline seems underwhelming. Contrary to much received opinion, core underpinnings of US dynamism persist; key dimensions of her power projection remain entrenched; and elements of a flagging international legitimacy seem reversible.[25] While complex forces buffet the USA today, glib pronouncements that the BRICs, other ascendant state or non-state actors, or the forces of globalization writ large are poised to displace the US as the predominant power – the global hegemon – are not supported by the evidence.[26]

Structure of the book

This rest of the book is organized as follows. Closing the section "Global Power: Key Issues" Chapter 2 addresses two major themes. First, it reviews the constituent components of US power. In particular, it revisits how the combination of technological dynamism, overwhelming military power, broad political-cum-diplomatic influence and the cultural attractiveness of a uniquely multicultural society has proved to be a potent package underpinning post-war US primacy and leadership. It argues that US hegemony – qualitative predominance across multiple dimensions of power projection – remains a durable feature of the global system today. But it is equally true that the rise of new global actors and forces creates the imperative to adapt perspectives, policies and institutions in order to maintain systemic primacy.

In addition, the chapter offers a fundamental critique of the meaning and relationship between national "decline" and (imperial) "overstretch" that have dominated much of the literature. It argues first that decline is the more primary and less remediable of these two, often conflated phenomena. Second, I argue that attempts to equate overstretch with (fiscal and trade) deficits and energy import dependence, are, misguided. A narrower notion of "military overstretch" is shown to be a more applicable, albeit a more readily reversible, phenomenon.

The section "Material Underpinnings of Global Power" rejects the consensus view that US power rests, shakily, on an edifice of crumbling economic foundations. Highlighting the enduring strengths of the system, chapters 3 and 4 feature the more durable microeconomic and macroeconomic underpinnings of US power, respectively, placing in perspective significant vulnerabilities and challenges to these pillars of strength in the short and medium term.

Chapter 3 examines prevalent concerns that the US risks relinquishing technological leadership, first to advanced country peer competitors and eventually to dynamic newcomers. While challenges remain, the chapter argues that the core institutions supporting superior US innovation, entrepreneurship and productivity remain well entrenched. Central to maintaining US prosperity and power, however, is an ongoing commitment to an open economy, including a progressive immigration policy. A leading theme of this chapter is also that the concept of national "competitiveness" has been poorly construed, encouraging erroneous approaches to reinforcing core US economic strengths.

Chapter 4 focuses on the US current account deficit, and external "indebtedness" as purported symptoms of national overextension and decline. The standard "American profligacy" explanation for US trade deficits and capital flows is dismissed in favor of a more persuasive, global structural interpretation. Examined in this context is the regular drumbeat for accelerated Chinese renminbi appreciation as the key to redressing "global imbalances." The chapter assesses the "balance of financial terror" argument, involving the threatened dumping of US dollars by (unfriendly) foreign creditors. I evaluate the ability of the US dollar to retain its central reserve currency status, particularly in light of the fissures within the EMU and the inconvertibility of the yuan. Finally, I weigh the contribution of foreign capital inflows to the Great Recession and consider whether US foreign debt is likely to engender a future crisis that can significantly alter the distribution of global power.

The section "Global Public Goods and the Re-ascent of China" features the theme of US leadership in the provision of global public goods. This highlights the legitimacy as well as more tangible gains that leading states garner from leveraging their influence to meet the collective needs of the global community. I apply this theme to the perpetuation of a US-led world order founded on such core principles as the safeguarding of human security, an open international trading system and the maintenance of balance of power within core regions of the globe.

Chapter 5 examines US leadership in the protection of human security with a focus on nuclear proliferation. US leadership takes the form of galvanizing international action behind nuclear counter-proliferation and, in particular, keeping weapons of mass destruction out of reach of rogue states and extremist non-state groups. Utilizing case studies on Iran, North Korea and Pakistan, the chapter grades the US on its leadership in the area of nuclear proliferation and examines the latter's centrality to US power in the future.

Chapter 6 adopts a regionalist perspective to US leadership, focusing on dynamic East Asia. US involvement in this region is analyzed through two distinct lenses. The first involves the success with which the US helps to maintain the balance of power within the region. The second assesses the success with which the US has reconciled intra-regional economic integration with its goal of maintaining a liberal multilateral trading and financial order globally.

The discussion to this point leads naturally to confronting a leading policy issue of the 21st century – "managing the rise" of China. Chapter 7 explores this country's prospects for rivaling the US. It recognizes China's achievements to date while weighing its formidable future potential against its principal vulnerabilities. In assessing China's prospective challenge to US predominance, the chapter explores the likely balance between cooperation and confrontation going forward. Will gains reaped from participation in the prevailing world order trump incentives to mobilize resources to scale back US power? Is China positioned to offer a viable alternative to US-championed global rules of the game?

The section "Domestic Constraints on US Power" drives home a central argument of the book: the principal dilemma for the US lies principally in how to forestall (internal) decline and less so in how to avoid succumbing to (external) overstretch. As formidable as they may seem, the array of external challenges confronting the US as discussed earlier in the book ultimately poses a less fundamental risk to US primacy, as compared with two core domestic challenges.

Chapter 8 assesses the strategic implications of US fiscal imbalances. Focusing on the central problem of excess health care cost inflation, other oft-cited contributors to fiscal distress are placed in perspective. While the challenge to the budget from medical care inflation is genuinely worrisome, the US starts with significant advantages that militate against an otherwise more explosive increase in the burden of debt. Still, these advantages can be trumped by a growing preoccupation in global capital markets with unsustainable US indebtedness that appears to defy ready political resolution.

The second of these core domestic challenges, explored in Chapter 9, gauges the ability of an ideologically polarized and gridlocked political system to offer bipartisan solutions to fiscal and other principal policy challenges. The US has engineered dramatic reversals to many economic and social threats in the past. Nevertheless, an increasingly fractious political system may mean that a sovereign debt crisis is required before decisive measures are taken to mitigate this overriding risk. If it comes to that, the edifice of US power would erode significantly. This chapter examines the political debate over fiscal stress and other core underpinnings of hegemony in the context of the 2012 presidential race.

The potential for improved political efficacy is also assessed in light of American public opinion concerning pressures from globalization. The chapter asks whether policymakers face a growing disconnect between national policies and the tolerance threshold of the American people. Have missteps in Afghanistan and Iraq, and aggravation of anti-Americanism worldwide, dampened Americans' appetite for global leadership? Does the flurry of legislative activity over tightening border controls auger a rising fortress mentality? While public sentiment remains fluid, the chapter presents evidence that Americans, with important caveats, continue to embrace the principles of an open economy and an active exercise of US power.

Given the domestic and external challenges reviewed throughout this book, the Conclusion (Chapter 10) defines the core conditions that would allow the US to maintain its qualitative hegemony over the coming decades. In this turbulent era, what steps must the US take to maintain its current predominance?

2
Dimensions of US Power, Decline and Overstretch

Conventional wisdom holds that the US's global stature and impact have decisively, and irreversibly, declined. In much of the world, preoccupation has shifted from an overpowering US "empire" to incapacitating "imperial overstretch." This chapter argues that no such qualitative degradation in aggregate US influence seems so obviously discernible. Rather, the evidence presented here corroborates Paul Kennedy's subsequent recanting of his original thesis: "Nothing has ever existed like this disparity of power; nothing...no other nation comes close" (2002).[1]

This chapter reviews the constituent core assets with which the US projects power in the 21st century. It gauges the extent to which other actors materially constrain the US in translating its latent power into predominant influence.[2] Its aim is to begin the task, pursued to its logical conclusion in the remainder of this book, of reassessing the prospects for sustained US predominance given the main systemic challenges – internal and external – buffeting the US today.

The chapter is divided into two broad segments. The section "Constituent dimensions of US power" delineates the military, political-cum-diplomatic, cultural-cum-ideological and economic assets underpinning US global power. In the section "Decline and overstretch" I differentiate between two popular, albeit often misleadingly conflated, concepts – national decline and national overstretch. Brief summary comments conclude the chapter.

Constituent dimensions of US power

Ever since the writings of Thucydides, Machiavelli and Hobbes, power has been an elusive concept to pin down. Fundamentally, the international relations literature distinguishes between power resources and power conversion capacity. Defined as the command over resources – a function of geography, technology, the stock of physical and human capital, and even more intangible attributes, such as culture– latent power may, but need not, translate

35

into commensurate control over actors and events. The effective exercise of power therefore fundamentally involves the ability to deploy resources in a manner that persuades others to act in one's interests.

This principle sounds straightforward yet the process is multi-faceted and challenging to measure. This is especially true in defining "hegemonic" power. This connotes disproportionate quantitative and qualitative command over global resources and a systematic ability to leverage such advantage into shaping or guiding the decision-making calculus of others. While exerting hegemonic power sometimes requires imposing one's will, it more often entails deftly exploiting dense networks in which one enjoys status, influencing global norms or agendas, and persuading others to embrace one's narrative on securing global welfare. Whether the emphasis is on hard power (the use of military weaponry or coercive economic instruments), soft power (reliance on cultural-cum-ideological attractiveness and diplomacy), or some optimal combination predictably labeled smart power, the goal remains getting others to act or move in a particular direction, to induce behavior deemed desirable, at the lowest cost to one's own wealth and position in the international system (see e.g. Armitage and Nye, 2007; Gelb, 2008; Nye, 1990, 2004, 2011).

Today's overarching security challenges differ fundamentally from the bipolar struggle that preoccupied the US and allies for half a century. While the collapse of the former Soviet Union may have ushered in a "unipolar moment," profound alterations in the fabric of the international system since then vastly complicate the application of traditional levers of power. To gauge the extent to which these new and varied forces have effectively diluted US primacy requires a dispassionate assessment of the US's constituent power assets and their effective deployment, a task to which we now turn.

The military dimension

The most palpable manifestation of US hegemony remains the country's overwhelming military power. The latter grants the US effective command of the global commons – that is, sea, air and space – "that belong to no one state and that provide access to much of the globe" (Posen, 2003). Our purpose here is to summarize only the most salient means through which the US military predominates, recent setbacks notwithstanding.

The US spends more on defense than all the great powers – allies as well as rivals – combined, and on some accounts virtually as much as the rest of the world.[3] Although the defense budget represents some 25 per cent more in real spending than in the late 1960s at the height of the Vietnam War, defense spending as a share of the economy has not exceeded 5 per cent in recent years.[4] The latter can be compared with a defense share of gross domestic product (GDP) of 5.7 per cent as recently as 1988 – three years before the collapse of the Soviet Union – 14 per cent during the Korean War and nearly 10 per cent of GDP during the Vietnam War. Viewed against this standard measure of national economic capacity, therefore, the US defense burden appears decidedly manageable.

Such measures impact potential, but what of actual capability? The bottom line remains uncontestable: the air force, navy and ground forces of the US face no peer competitor, nor is one poised on the immediate horizon. In short, the US military wields clear and unprecedented (conventional and nuclear) superiority, most recently showcased in the invasions of Afghanistan and Iraq.[5]

The following overview underscores only the broadest underpinnings of US military superiority. First, nothing comparable exists anywhere else in the world to the US Air Force. This assessment applies to any critical measure of capability, including advanced systems integration techniques in the production of aircraft, the unequaled training and skill of its pilots, the accuracy of advanced targeting technology and close air support, and the extraordinary improvement in "airlift" capacity:

> Wide-body aircraft construction and improved jet engine efficiency have greatly increased aircraft load and range capacities. C-5As and C-17s can carry M-1A2 tanks, the heaviest ground assault weapon. A fleet of 250 C-17s could pick up all the tanks in a heavy division and move them from the United States to the Persian Gulf in 36-48 hours.
>
> (Odom and Dujarric, 2004, p. 79)

Although the cost of replacing aged aircraft has proven exorbitant, and contracts for fighter planes like the F-22 and F-35 have been scaled back, no other country comes close to matching the technological sophistication and reach of US airpower, given the latter's worldwide bases, refueling capabilities and air management control:

> An electronic flying circus of specialized attack, jamming, and electronic intelligence aircraft allows the US military to achieve the "suppression of enemy air defenses" (SEAD); limit the effectiveness of enemy radars, surface-to-air missiles (SAMs) and fighters; and achieve the relatively safe exploitation of enemy skies above 15,000 feet
>
> (Posen, p. 15).

US air power is perhaps best evidenced by its virtual monopoly of advanced drones and their current deployment in as many as six countries. The Pentagon uses approximately 7,000 aerial drones today compared with fewer than 50 a decade ago, and these numbers will continue to climb (Bumiller and Shanker, 2011). These drones range in size from that of an insect, to wings the length of a football field. The Predator, which can stay in the air for up to 20 hours, is increasingly being replaced by the Reaper, which can carry 3,000 lb of munitions. During the Obama administration's first two years, 85 per cent of those reportedly killed by drones were militants compared with 60 per cent during the Bush administration (Bergen and Tiedemann, 2011).[6] Drones have reportedly killed more than 1,900 insurgents in Pakistan's tribal areas since 2006 (Bumiller and Shanker, 2011). And the CIA used a new bat-winged stealth drone, the RQ-170 Sentinel, to spy on Osama bin Laden's compound. While these technologies have been successfully deployed to target insurgents and terrorists, their accuracy depends critically on boots in the field. They obviously provoke public outrage when they tragically take the lives of innocent civilians. In sum, drones present significant legal and ethical issues (Singer, 2011).

Second, no country can compete with the training and arming of US land forces. With the partial exception of the UK, no army enjoys a comparable class of weapons. Epitomizing this superiority is the tank-destroying effectiveness of the M-1A2 tank (Odom and Dujarric, 2004, p. 72). Reinforcing this ground capability are the highly effective Bradley infantry fighting vehicle (M-2), Apache attack helicopter and multiple rocket launcher system (MRLS). No country can challenge the US Army in tank warfare and the country's air and space dominance renders impotent most enemy advancing ground forces and supporting airpower. As the early phase of the Afghanistan conflict demonstrated, army Special Forces in coordination with comparable units in the navy and air force represent superior US strategic assets. No better example of the contribution from battle-tested US Special Forces can be cited than the mission to capture Osama bin Laden.

Third, the US navy faces no modern "blue water" rival. Building anything comparable to the US fleet exceeds the means of all but the most advanced industrialized countries. They would be decades away from achieving that goal even if they were to make such a commitment today, which they are not. Protecting critical chokepoints from threats that could upset the functionality of global trade has become the province of the US navy.

Epitomizing naval dominance are US nuclear attack submarines and 11 aircraft carrier battle groups capable of launching state-of-the-art aircraft from each of the globe's oceans. Protecting such assets is a formidable fleet of Arleigh Burke-class destroyers, "billion-dollar multi-mission platforms capable of anti-air, anti-submarine, and land-attack missions in high-threat environments" (Posen, p. 12).

This gaping lead in naval power notwithstanding, heavy investment in technological modernization continues. Although no other country currently fields anything close to US maritime power, the US military is increasingly focused on Chinese naval modernization. Designed to blunt US power in the Pacific, China has been developing "anti-access, area denial" technologies. For example, China's new "carrier killing" missile, the DF-21D, can cripple a naval ship 1,700 miles away. Its arching trajectory is designed to foil ship defense guns and missiles, potentially destroying a 97,000 ton carrier and its crew of 5,000 sailors. China is also producing quieter submarines that can stay submerged longer in order to patrol waters farther from China's coastline.

While China's navy remains incapable of engaging the US in head-to head battles, the new anti-access technologies could deter or delay US naval forces from aiding regional allies. Although hesitant to characterize China's naval ambitions as a leading threat, the US military is working conscientiously to counter these advances. In particular, the US is developing unmanned drones and bombers capable of taking off from carriers farther out at sea. In addition, the US is opening new military bases in the Pacific region, beginning in Australia (Barnes et al., 2011). In sum, while US naval dominance remains undisputed, a potential longer-term challenge from China nevertheless looms.

Across the armed forces, manifesting US technological superiority today are global positioning system (GPS) reconnaissance, navigation and communications satellites, the latest generations of precision-guided missiles, stealth technology, high-energy lasers and unmanned drones. Strategic and tactical nuclear superiority, unparalleled ability to project conventional force, combined with the (relative) protection its physical juxtaposition between two vast oceans affords, grants the US unsurpassed strategic advantage. Underlying this overwhelming capability are superior science, technology and industrial know how, and increasingly sophisticated global telecommunications networks.

Six US military commands oversee a globally dispersed million-plus standing army and a string of forward bases housing its personnel and armory. Providing an uncontested ability to repel attack and prevail against any and all armed forces, US forward deployments, mobile heavy combat power projection capability and nuclear deterrent superiority can be said to offer US allies a unique public good.[7] Through defense treaties and an "over the horizon" presence, the US military provides a highly credible deterrent to state aggression in Europe, Asia and elsewhere. Monitoring strategic sea lanes and chokepoints, the US also furnishes the essential security infrastructure to combat blockade and piracy, safeguarding international commerce.

Asymmetric warfare and state building

One knows that no conceivable alliance of nations can defeat the US. But this does not ensure that the US can – at an acceptable political cost – impose its will on a limited area in an asymmetric conflict environment. For instance, had the US put in 2 million troops and invaded North Vietnam, it probably could have subjugated and changed the government of that country. But this was wholly unviable politically and geopolitically.

While the US military enjoys virtually complete nuclear and conventional superiority – particularly where advanced sea-, air- and land-based forces are combined – it has demonstrated less success in the stabilization and reconstruction phases of conflict, particularly when combating insurgency or guerrilla resistance. This can be exasperating and sobering: "How much use is military power in a democratic age? What is the point of being the only superpower, the sole owner of the unipolar moment, if you cannot maintain control of a single medium-sized state, or even a medium-sized town?" (Cooper, 2005, p. 27).

Experience in Iraq and Afghanistan captures the enormous challenge required to wage successful counter-insurgency. Moreover, it reveals how difficult even scaled down ambitions at state institution building and the effective (re)transfer of sovereignty can be. Prolonged occupation inevitably encounters diminishing returns and military campaigns offer no substitute for the fundamental, yet fleeting, political imperative of "winning hearts and minds." Once local opposition mounts, history suggests dim prospects for "victory." Sustaining American and local public support just long enough to leave in place a capable, indigenous army and police force, and establishing the basic environment for lasting security and decent governance, pose a gargantuan task.

In addition to the challenge of waging successful counter-insurgency, it remains unclear whether the US military possesses an effective and calibrated response to the asymmetric tactics of militant non-state actors. For example, while important gains have been made against al-Qaeda and fellow travelers, the prospect of an all-out terrorist campaign with state backing has yet to be tested.

Cyberspace

The Stuxnet worm, which reportedly damaged one fifth of Iran's nuclear centrifuges (Broad et al., 2011), provides a prime example of how the US among a few other advanced technological states can in principle exploit the instrument of cyberwar.[8] Although the US possesses the very best cyber offensive capability, it is itself highly dependent on computer networks for its economic infrastructure and military activities. "If the nation went to war today in a cyber, we would lose," concludes Michael McConnel, executive vice president of Booz Allen Hamilton (Mills, 2010a). Some argue that cyberwarfare is a less likely weapon of choice for terrorist organizations because such weapons arguably fail to deliver the same psychological blow as more visible physical attacks (Nye, 2011). While non-state actors currently lack the capacity to launch sophisticated, large scale cyber-attacks on high value targets, this can change.

While experts agree that the US dominates cyber-offense, it also has a long way to go in building an adequate cyber-defense. Cyber security experts are especially concerned with the ability of the private sector to protect the nation's critical infrastructure. As former White House cybersecurity adviser Richard Clarke (2009) puts it: "America's connectivity to the rest of the world is unlimited and controlled by no plan or agency."

The US has been victim to cyber attacks since 1999. While yet to experience an all-out assault, cyber attackers are stealing substantial information from US firms every day (Mills, 2010a). For example, McAfee analysts report that five major multinational oil and gas companies have been victims of hacker attacks, losing data worth millions of dollars (Homeland Security, 2011). Officials have privately confirmed that "logic bombs have already been placed in America's power-grid control systems, presumably by foreign warriors" (Clarke, 2009). Cyber attacks have also compromised government agencies and public figures. While all were overcome without irredeemable damage, more formidable attacks are likely in the future. In July 2011, the Pentagon released its first "Strategy for Operating in Cyberspace" and declared it will treat cyberspace as another domain of war (US Department of Defense, 2011).

In summary, more than any other dimension, US military capability is synonymous in the public imagination with the global projection of power. That challenges and limits to its military predominance exist in no way vitiates the ongoing reality of US military primacy. Certain state and non-state organizations will work assiduously toward nullifying particular aspects of US military advantage. Evolving forms of asymmetric warfare – of either the low-technology Al Qaeda variety or the higher-technology "assassin's mace" – will also pressure the US military to innovate continuously.

In this time of approaching fiscal austerity, the US military also faces an increasingly difficult dilemma over defense resource allocation priorities. However, given its spending and capability lead, no segment of the US's armed forces will face a credible threat to its overwhelming superiority for the foreseeable future.

The political dimension

An important pillar underlying composite US power has been the legitimacy garnered through its global leadership. The aftermath of World War II marked an extraordinary period in which the US "took the lead in fashioning a world of multilateral rules and regional partnerships – and it put itself at the center of it all" (Ikenberry, 2010). During the Cold War, the US established binding security pacts with Europe and Japan, and threw its political capital behind institutions supporting a liberal trading and security order. It thereby ceded policy autonomy by "locking itself" into arrangements that enhanced global security while allaying concerns over the exercise of US discretionary power (Ikenberry, 2003, p. 50). By minimizing coercion in favor of marshaling consent, the US secured the allegiance of other states.

Notwithstanding its effective ability to dictate the principles underlying multilateral arrangements and exert de facto control over most multilateral bodies, US policymakers were mindful to grant significant "voice" to others. While circumscribing US autonomy of action, in signaling respect for other nations' interests, such institutionalized allegiance and efforts to establish a "shared identity" rendered the US more influential than it would have been based on its superior material capabilities alone (Buzan, 2004). This consensual manner of conducting international relations broke sharply with the classic European tradition of balance of power politics.

Although other states, in principle, can work to deepen such cooperation by further embedding the US within global institutions, US positions on the Kyoto Treaty on Climate Change, the International Criminal Court, the Anti-Landmine Ban Treaty and the Antiballistic Missile Treaty underscore the limits of "binding" when such participation ostensibly conflicts with US national interests. Such examples highlight the inherent tension between effective US enabling and disabling of multilateral institutions (Foot et al., 2003, p. 18; Luck, 2003, p. 48). Key to sustaining US legitimacy therefore is its willingness to lead in the reform of multilateral institutions such as the United Nations (UN), the International Monetary Fund and the World Bank to reflect changing circumstances and to maintain the delicate balance between international cooperation and policy autonomy.

With the collapse of the former Soviet Union in 1991, certain states, including important allies, grew increasingly alarmed over perceptions of "Gulliver Unbound" (Joffe, 2006, p. 60). For example, on top of principled disagreement, French frustration with US "hyper-puissance" and Russian and Chinese anxiety over encroaching US influence played some role behind the vetoes lodged in the UN Security Council against the invasion of Iraq. More generally, a perceived deterioration in US diplomatic effort under the George W. Bush Administration exacerbated distrust in certain circles: "How policy is conducted can sometimes be as important as the substance of policy, and consultation, adroit diplomacy, and tact in working with other countries and institutions are essential in assuaging the sensibilities of foreign leaders and in gaining political and material support for American objectives ... " (Lieber, 2005, p. 6). It would not be unwarranted to ascribe certain shortcomings of US diplomacy to the disproportionate resources allocated to the Pentagon versus the State Department and the United States Agency for International Development.

Aside from dissatisfaction over US state diplomacy, former Defense Secretary Robert Gates, in specific reference to Osama bin Laden, captured the ramifications of the country's recent underinvestment in public diplomacy: "How has one man in a cave managed to out-communicate the world's greatest communication society?" (PRI, 2008). During 1994–2001, expenditures on public diplomacy had declined by over 50 per cent and the annual $1.5 billion public diplomacy budget comprised roughly one day of Pentagon spending (United States, Advisory Commission on Public Diplomacy, 2004). Having honed its communication skills during the Cold War, first with the US Information Agency's Voice of America, Radio Liberty and Radio Free Europe, the US public diplomacy effort began to atrophy. Just when non-US news sources like Al Jazeera were proliferating, this diminished effort to elucidate US policies and values eroded the basis for rallying goodwill and support. While incapable of trumping deeply unpopular policies, by providing a more transparent window on US perspectives exchange and English language programs in earlier years had allowed individuals around the world to acquire a less filtered, first-hand exposure to American life (Hughes in PRI, 2008).

This is one area where the US non-governmental sector has the potential to make a still greater impact. In addition to providing financial and technical assistance, philanthropies, foundations, faith-based charities, universities, think tanks, volunteers, professional associations, a variety of other non-governmental organizations (NGOs) and the media have been instrumental in the diffusion of US values, norms and technologies. In part to bolster their images abroad, US corporations have also made their own contribution through "corporate social responsibility." It is difficult to overstate the potential impact of such transnational transfers – particularly when these are conveyed as part of a dialogue with local populations rather than a (uni-directional) imposition of "universalist values" (Brown, 2012). Promoting the values of democracy and human rights in such a way arguably promises greater success than via the more ambitious and intrusive vehicle of "state building."

Aside from shortcomings in state and public diplomacy, the US has sometimes underperformed on global leadership within realms that would seem the natural province for a hegemon, as with transnational issues like global warming (Mandelbaum, 2005, pp. 105, 217). In this context, the Bush Administration's fixation on "the global war on terrorism" perplexed and alienated many, damaging US credibility (Zakaria, 2004). The Bush and Obama administrations' on-again-off-again efforts toward the Palestinian-Israeli conflict likewise depressed hopes for a more vigilant US stabilization role in the strategically vital Middle East. Although US diplomacy has amassed its share of successes, efforts to "engage" nations such as Iran or Syria, and even Pakistan, have largely failed (Etzioni, 2011, p. 183).

While no nation can contribute equally across all global concerns, structural hegemony provides unique leverage and carries a special burden of responsibility (Obama, 2009). Debates over the future of US global power will continue to rest on varying perceptions over, first, the US's willingness to lead and, second, the willingness of the rest of the world to be US-led.

The US's relative success at global agenda setting, preference formation and as the embodiment of internationally respected norms and values should all prove integral to its sustainability as global hegemon.

That the global diffusion of power occurring in recent years has to some extent at least eroded relative US influence seems hard to deny. Actors whose clout has strengthened resist being "dictated to" by US objectives. Measuring the US's political sway, however, can also be subject to a certain selection bias if one enumerates instances in which US initiatives have been blocked while failing to record where "things are not happening that the United States does not want to happen" (Wohlforth, 2012). The issue is the extent to which US political sway still proves more decisive, more often, across more regions and issues, relative to that of the great powers and to that of actors whose stars have more recently risen.

The cultural dimension

Another important dimension of US hegemony involves the "soft power" inherent in the attractiveness of American culture, values and way of life (Nye, 2004). Notable here is the "universalist" appeal associated with an inherently open society. US popular culture as exported via film, television, music, sports and fashion, as well as modern business practices and the licensing or transfer of cutting-edge technology, finds adherents and imitators across the globe. As such, the words of Max Lerner in his 1957 book *America as a Civilization* continue to resonate: "If he is not admired he is envied; and even his enemies and rivals pay him the homage of imitation. People throughout the world turn almost as by a tropism to the American image" (quoted in Starobin, 2009).

For many years the US has welcomed a steady flow of students and immigrants to its shores. While losing some luster in difficult economic times such as these, the allure of certain core cultural myths – for example, rugged individualism and the "self-made" person – appears to endure for many who continue to migrate to the US in pursuit of opportunity. US cultural influence finds additional expression in the widespread impact of its core, liberal values, including religious tolerance, freedom of speech and assembly, the presumption of innocence over guilt, and the separation of church and state. In training so many of the best and brightest in the physical sciences, mathematics and the social sciences, US universities have played a disproportionate role in diffusing ideas and skills throughout the world. Along with the English language assuming the role of lingua franca for international commerce and diplomacy, the transnational transfer of ideas, norms and values by US universities, media, NGOs and corporations has gone far to frame the discussion and to negotiate the resolution of contentious global issues. Although American patriotism seems quaint to some – notably to a Europe in the throes of consolidating a post-sovereign, transcendentalist vision – much of the world, including Brazil, China, India, Russia and Iran, remains comparably nationalistic.

Also evident, however, is resentment against the invasion of US commercial icons and social mores. This manifests itself in periodic revolts against American "cultural imperialism," even if the international appeal manifest in the products of corporations, like Starbuck's, Apple and Google, and the ongoing penetration of American music and film are difficult to dismiss.

Others deride the American work ethic as extreme and decry the country's weaker social safety net. Yet, increasing numbers of states concede that demographic pressures mandate some scaling back of social welfare commitments in the direction of the US model. The US's impressive record of entrepreneurialism and economic dynamism has inspired adoption of reforms in many countries where aspects of more free-wheeling US-style capitalism are embraced. With the collapse of the Soviet Union, for instance, many of its former republics opted for a less fettered version of capitalism to that associated with much of Western Europe. Today efforts to introduce greater labor market flexibility, more akin to US and UK experience, are evident in the European Monetary Union's "periphery" (Dalton, 2012).

Nevertheless, recent years have witnessed an unmistakable if not irreversible decline in the US's international prestige. Widespread condemnation of the Iraq invasion, revelations of prisoner abuses at Abu Ghraib and Guantanamo Bay, extraordinary rendition to undisclosed foreign centers, notwithstanding disclaimers that "we don't do torture,"[9] reports of civilian massacres by US marines, and illegal domestic wiretapping have inescapably eroded the country's moral stature. Mantras recited *ad nauseum* about the inherent identity of American values and a universal promotion of liberty fall on deaf ears when such claims blatantly conflict with evidence of human rights infringements.[10] The global fallout from the US sub-prime debt crisis has likewise lowered confidence that US free-market orthodoxy has the answers to challenging questions of economic organization and reform.

While some polling suggests that non-Americans differentiate between their feelings about the US government and the American people, anger over US foreign policy can, and does, spill over into attitudes about American society. Indeed, anti-Americanism remains a potent global force. It is striking that a people with a credible claim as leading purveyors of global culture can simultaneously be the object of such widespread hostility. That anti-Americanism, at least within certain circles, may reflect in part redirection of anger against domestic societal shortcomings combined with normal resentment of the powerful makes it no less real (Joffe, 2006).

For example, there is the palpably negative public perception of the US in much of the Middle East. If a goal was to win over "hearts and minds," these findings suggest an uphill challenge ahead in this and other volatile regions. Generic anti-Americanism appeared to soften following the humanitarian and logistical assistance provided to victims of the 2004 Asian tsunami and Pakistani earthquake (Knowlton, 2006). And enough residual goodwill arguably exists to allow American values and ideals to win back erstwhile, albeit disillusioned, devotees. While this may be less evident among certain traditional US allies, pro-American sentiment is often more transparent among younger democracies from Eastern Europe to India. The enduring popularity of American popular culture and values even extends to some unlikely candidates, such as the disproportionately young population of Iran.

Moreover, counteracting resentment of American culture or US foreign policy is the continuing inflow of foreigners voting with their feet. Today, the US is home to some 43 million immigrants or almost 15 per cent of its population. Comparatively, the US has roughly four times the number of immigrants as Russia, the second most popular migrant destination.[11] Of the some 700 million people seeking to relocate globally, some one-quarter reportedly would like to find their way to the US's shores (Gravelle, 2010). For such individuals the US remains a beacon of hope and represents the prospect of a better life. In addition, international students rank the US as the preferred destination for study abroad. In 2009, of the 3.7 million international students studying in foreign countries, 18 per cent choose to study in the US, making it the most popular destination for foreign students (OECD, 2009). In sum, the ability to remain an open, multicultural society – one that welcomes the most aspiring and talented – delivers a powerful counter-example to the anti-American discourse.

Amy Chua has provocatively argued that the key attribute shared among five or six historical "hyperpowers" has been the tolerance exhibited by these societies and their accommodation of cultural diversity (Chua, 2007). This ability to reconcile pluralism with shared national values can largely be ascribed to the US during much of its history. In contrast, concerns that the incorporation of "alien" peoples gradually erodes the integrity of national culture – a minority view ostensibly shared by the late Harvard political scientist Samuel Huntington and conservative pundit Patrick Buchanan – for observers like Chua signals impending decline.

Will the US continue to set an example of broad inclusion as in "what matters is not where one comes from but where one is going"? (Zakaria, 2008a). Or will she succumb to nascent nativism in response to the social pressures attending globalization and technological change? The answer will prove critical to whether the US can harness its traditional embrace of openness to the consolidation of strategic primacy.

The economic dimension

Thus far in this discussion, little has been said about economics, though many would consider it the dominant determinant of national power (Gelb, 2010). This concerns US economic performance but also the institutional basis for global prosperity – the liberal trading order. As global hegemon, the US assumes lead responsibility for safeguarding this system. Promoting openness lends greater stability to weaker states by supporting economic development, encourages the democratization of emerging markets and transition economies, and ensures that the global commons remains unobstructed.

One need not embrace a crude economic determinism to argue that among all discrete dimensions of power the material base exerts disproportionate influence.[12] Today's turbulent headwinds notwithstanding, the underlying pillars and longer-term prospects for the US economy remain comparatively strong.[13] Despite the natural convergence process bolstering Europe and Japan after World War II, the US, remarkably, has maintained a steady share of global GDP during much of the last half-century.

Furthermore the US is likely to outperform other advanced industrial countries over the coming decades. Such outperformance will be achieved through the maintenance of a robust pace of annual productivity growth and a steady increase in its labor force. The US should continue to enjoy a deep resource base, including a skilled and educated labor force, a rich physical capital stock, a dynamic economy embedded within robust market-supportive institutions, and advanced science and technology. Although its dependency ratio of workers to retirees will deteriorate in parallel with other aging societies, the US population and labor force are forecast to grow at a relatively brisk pace, particularly via ongoing immigration of younger populations. The comparative success with which the US acculturates immigrants from around the world thus assumes a significant role in this projected outperformance.

While the political, cultural and military dimensions of US power enjoy an influence independent of material factors, an erosion of US economic fundamentals would significantly dilute the composite impact of these extra-economic variables. For example, US military power rests on the extraordinary resources that the US can commit to national security without eroding civilian prosperity. The innovativeness of US capitalism likewise supports the military's superiority in precision, high-technology combat and the ability to recruit, train and equip an unparalleled professional force.[14]

In addition, the global dominance of US-headquartered transnational corporations and its leading voice in the international financial institutions places the US in the vanguard to uphold and revise the architecture of the global trading and financial system. It also places it in a leading position to orchestrate and enforce, with international cooperation, a crackdown on the financing of terrorists and "rogue" states.

For years, US wealth has supplied the lubricant for world economic growth with the American consumer providing a disproportionate share of global aggregate demand for goods and services. Emerging markets and others have long relied upon a strategy of export-led growth premised on producing for the US and European markets.[15] While especially evident during the record pre-crisis period of sustained global growth, US spending also proved instrumental in containing the fallout from the global financial crisis triggered in Asia, Russia and elsewhere during the late 1990s. While this places arguments about emerging market "decoupling" in perspective, the extent to which the US consumer can assume the role of global locomotive in the future is more questionable.[16]

Furthermore, US public diplomacy – decidedly deemphasized during the early years of the George W. Bush Administration but having made somewhat of a comeback under Barack Obama – presupposes the commitment of meaningful resources to bolster US legitimacy as world leader and enforcer (reviser) of global rules and institutions. The Millennium Challenge Corporation, for example, has pledged assistance to states that combat corruption and promote governance and economic reforms. The US has deployed its logistical capability to deliver supplies to populations ravaged by natural disasters, as with the 2004 Asian tsunami and the Pakistani earthquake. The Bush and Obama administrations made major financial commitments to battling HIV-AIDS in Africa. Finally, the military campaigns and associated reconstruction in countries like Afghanistan and Iraq have involved enormous expenditure, albeit much of it tragically squandered.

However significant, such global transfers by the US government pale against the extraordinary commitment of private individuals, NGOs, foundations, universities and corporations whose collective philanthropy, remittances, technical assistance and export of ideas and technologies trumps that of US official foreign assistance. For example, in 2010, foreign workers employed in the US remitted just under $100 billion to families and communities back home (Hudson Institute, 2012). These private income transfers augment recipient households' resources, smooth consumption, and provide working capital for family-run businesses. Even US cultural exports are often economic in nature, as epitomized by the omnipresence of corporate giants such as McDonalds, Starbucks and Nike, or the special effects of Hollywood blockbusters. Such US transfers or exports mirror the robust system of wealth creation and creativity at home.

The abundant material base provided by a unique agglomeration of natural and sophisticated human resources, a rich capital stock, and an unparalleled system of entrepreneurial-driven innovation has been reflected in and augmented by the "exorbitant privilege" the US enjoys from the dollar's reserve currency status.[17] While the latter facilitates greater macroeconomic flexibility, it also mirrors the "exorbitant burden" the US shoulders in its myriad functions as global hegemon.

Composite US power

In sum, US global influence remains a complicated and fluid equation. The combination of overwhelming military prowess, economic dynamism, political sway and a highly diverse, multicultural society proved to be a potent package underpinning post-war US leadership. By dint of its hard and soft power, the US today retains a superior position from which to balance opposing state interests within key strategic regions, working to bridge them under the umbrella of one integrated global system. The central vision animating that liberal international order is one of free mobility and open society. As such, the US has enjoyed a superior ability to influence the global agenda and to structure the debate on the resolution of key global challenges. One clear test of its ongoing influence lies in its ability to help modify the systemic rules of the game in a manner that preserves its own autonomy while reinforcing the foundations of global stability.[18]

In the final analysis, with no state exhibiting comparable influence across so many distinct dimensions, the US legitimately can be said to represent history's most consummate hegemon, wielding unprecedented "structural power" (see e.g. Beckley, 2011, p. 48). This hegemony presumably could be maintained even were the US, from time to time, to relinquish some ground along one or two dimensions of its composite power. For example, over the coming decades the US will continue to cede aspects of its relative economic clout to dynamic, emerging economies even though it will remain in other respects the dominant and richest economy in the world (see e.g. El-Erian, 2008).

In the event, slippage across a wide spectrum of US power assets would ultimately translate into a loss of hegemonic status. For example, a steady cumulative assault from global terrorist networks and defiant would-be nuclear states, active resistance to US predominance by the leading powers, broad repudiation of US liberal trade and other key norms, and perhaps most of all a marked erosion of internal dynamism, are among the principal factors that could, in combination, precipitate an enduring eclipse of US power. A key question concerns whether the US can surmount the effects of recent setbacks and prolong its qualitative lead over ascendant regional economic and strategic state and non-state players. Comparing the pressures weighing on the US today against the multi-dimensional assets it commands, is it plausible to argue that the US faces a genuine prospect of decline, marking the end of its strategic predominance? We now proceed to address this question in the remainder of this chapter.

Decline and overstretch

More conceptual conundrums

As mentioned at the beginning of this chapter, the exercise of power refers to the ability to persuade, dissuade or compel others to act, more often than not, in accordance with one's core interests or policies. It likewise refers to a capacity to shape the global agenda or "rules of the game." Such ability presupposes possession of important material and non-material assets, but critically the capability to deploy these assets in such a way as to achieve decisive or at least strong indirect, influence on other state and non-state actors. Rather than a treatise about national power per se, this book explores the factors that can perpetuate or undermine the position of the preeminent state in the global system – in other words, the underlying sources of sustaining or relinquishing hegemony.

When various observers opine about national decline, and more specifically the decline of a hegemon, they can refer to very different phenomena. Certain international relations theorists imply, for example, that decline tends to ensue after one state has achieved significantly greater relative power, attaining potentially structural "unipolarity." The mere concentration of power provokes counterbalancing by others, which are inherently threatened by their loss of relative clout.[19] In contrast to alliance building, concerted counter-balancing saps the energy of the predominant state, diverting resources to its defense of the status quo against would-be challengers.

Alternatively, other observers emphasize the likelihood of blowback against the "unilateral" decision-making or otherwise broadly disparaged actions of leading powers. Such unilateralism rather than the mere accumulation of greater power assets makes particular states appear inherently menacing (see Walt, 2005). For example, by unsettling other states over the scope of its ambitions, the 2003 invasion of Iraq encouraged a belief that US power had ceased to be benign. By threatening to undermine its alliances and fomenting more organized opposition to US interests, the erosion of US legitimacy occasioned by actions in Iraq accelerated an ongoing diminution in its relative power.

Some have stretched the concept of national decline by invoking less relevant,or transient factors. Suggested symptoms of systemic decline include, for example, the fall in manufacturing employment, excesses emanating from a bloated financial sector, undue influence over foreign policy from fundamentalist Protestant denominations or a "pro-Israel lobby," and failure to pursue a responsible post-petroleum energy policy.[20] The cumulative impact of these and other largely extraneous or subordinate factors has been advanced by certain observers as portending the eclipse of US hegemony.

Others refer instead to "the rise of the rest," that is the development of new power centers, barely incipient a generation ago (Zakaria, 2008a). The common thread uniting these otherwise disparate states ostensibly lies in having successfully exploited opportunities from US-led globalization. Having narrowed the formidable gap with US levels of prosperity (influence), one can speak of relative US decline by sheer dint of positive developments external to the US but largely attributable to US influence.

Finally, by hegemonic decline one could have in mind a mushrooming of seemingly intractable, geopolitical threats involving increasingly bold "rogue" states, and extremist, non-state actors. Such developments conjure up an increasingly complex and recalcitrant world against which even the predominant state can appear overwhelmed. In Kennedy's (1987) formulation, such a world reinforces the leading power's temptation to expand into new frontiers in order to enhance security. On top of its already formidable responsibilities – the ongoing costs of consolidating existing markets and alliances – newly menacing forces compel a hegemon to make increasingly exorbitant foreign commitments. Strategic overreach inevitably follows.

The "imperial overstretch" paradigm

A core deficiency of the imperial overstretch perspective is that it posits a state inexorably compelled to embrace increasingly onerous responsibilities beyond what would have been chosen based on more rational prioritization linking ends with means. In Kennedy's view of history, once signs of overstretch surface – classically, a bloated military crowds out private civilian and public sector investment – scant allowance exists for policy reversal. The imperatives that would prevent the leadership from reassessing priorities and realigning resources with objectives are rarely specified. Why proactive policy reversals by reasonably forward-looking statesmen cannot stanch incipient overstretch, preventing the underlying sinews of power from unraveling, is left largely unexplained.[21]

Most problematically, the imperial overstretch paradigm confuses overstretch and decline. Properly defined, overstretch involves an assumption of foreign or global commitments beyond what national resources comfortably allow. In contrast, decline concerns a marked deceleration in the state's internal engine of wealth creation, deterioration of the quality of domestic governance, and erosion of the country's social vitality and cohesion.

Involving a reduction in internal dynamism, the onset of decline concerns first and foremost a pronounced erosion in steady-state productivity growth. It likewise can involve the debilitating impact of disadvantageous demographics as reflected in rising old age dependency. But decline also can mirror a domestic political system that is progressively paralyzed by corruption, regulatory capture or the mounting sectarianism of special interests

(Olson, 1984). In addition, decline can reflect a growing gulf between social priorities and the goals of the state, as well as precipitous diminution of soft power, as global culture and ideology progressively diverge from or clash with that of the predominant state.

Decline is thus conceptually more primary than overstretch. While it may accelerate ongoing decline, overstretch remains the subordinate, less fundamental phenomenon. Tactical mistakes, of course, are made and require timely reversal. Stubborn refusal to alter course even where the costs clearly dominate reasonably anticipated, longer-term returns erodes the capacity to act elsewhere. But it should also be acknowledged that ambitious global commitments define, in part, the raison d'être of a leading power.

Generally, great powers do not decline because they find themselves over-committed. They decline when they fail to generate adequate investment to support great power responsibilities. Predominant powers decline because the internal basis for financing their commitments is eroded. Such erosion usually triggers a societal inclination to draw inward, focusing on internal problems and reducing engagement with the outside world. Overstretch does not mainly explain the fall of the British, Spanish or Roman empires; deterioration in resource generation capacity and socio-political cohesion marked the primary basis for their collapse. In sum, decline reflects dissipation in underlying capability.[22] Kennedy and his followers thus have it exactly reversed; decline generally engenders overstretch, not the other way around.[23]

US experience in Iraq and Afghanistan, and earlier in Vietnam, illustrates this fundamental distinction between overstretch and decline. Each of these campaigns involved a substantial commitment of national resources. Although its total cost exceeded that of the more recent wars, the debilitating and recklessly financed Vietnam debacle – a relatively clear example of "imperial overstretch" – did not precipitate a period of protracted national decline. Rather, an apparent breakdown in the country's ability to generate wealth internally – reflected in a discernible deceleration of productivity growth and reinforced by profound social cleavages – marked the onset of incipient decline in the 1970s. Had renewed economic dynamism and a broad restoration of social and political stability not materialized, a collapse of US hegemony would have been virtually assured. Vietnam-occasioned overstretch was not the underlying cause of embryonic stagnation. Likewise, a protracted failure to restore robust economic growth following the Great Recession would mark the eventuality of US secular decline and the loss of hegemony. This would have had relatively little to do with the wars in Iraq or Afghanistan. One overriding lesson seems to be that predominant powers, by definition, can afford to take certain strategic gambles – even ones that appear reckless in retrospect – without risking a secular erosion of national wealth and global impact.

Is the US in decline?

One argument marshaled to substantiate a presumption of secular US decline can be summarized and summarily dismissed at the start. Today the US accounts for a decidedly lower share of world GDP – somewhere between one-fifth and one-quarter depending on the statistical measure employed – compared with a markedly larger share (circa 40–50 per cent) of global output immediately after World War II. Accompanying this shrinking weight in the global economy moreover has been the steady erosion of the manufacturing sector a purported sign of deindustrialization and widely ascribed telltale sign of generalized decline.

The post-war size of the US economy must be understood in the context of the devastation experienced in Europe and Japan during World War II, and the well-documented tendency for poorer (or war-ravaged) countries to subsequently rebound and converge to the income levels of richer countries over time. By the early 1990s, much of Europe and Japan had climbed to some 80 per cent of average US income levels, before steady-state US productivity growth performed an about face, outpacing that of the US's principal allies. Although US manufacturing employment declined steadily for virtually a half-century – paralleling similar trends around the world – manufacturing output and exports retained a steadier share of the global economy, reflecting superior productivity growth. More generally, the transition from a manufacturing-based to a services-dominated economy recalls an equally momentous, earlier transition from an agricultural to an industrial foundation.

While this perspective looks back on the post-war period, a more forward-looking view on the longer-term trajectory of the US economy is instructive. Figure 2.1 compares longer-term economic growth projections for three groups of countries – the G7, the BRICs and the so called N-11 (or aspiring

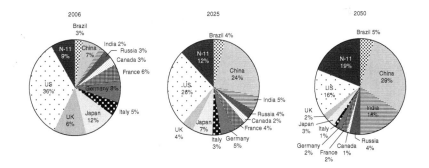

Figure 2.1   GDP: country shares for G-7, BRICs and N-11

Note: N-11 groups Bangladesh, Egypt, Indonesia, Iran, Korea, Mexico, Nigeria, Pakistan, Philippines, Turkey, Vietnam.

Source: Goldman Sachs (2007) *BRICS and Beyond*.

future BRICs). In particular, the emerging Asian giants, India and China, are projected to enjoy relative gains owing to a classic convergence process marked by anticipated faster than average annual growth rates in the coming decades. In this sense, the commercial center of gravity will gradually shift toward Asia, restoring the region's historically larger weight within the global economy.

Yet, forecasted US outperformance – relative to its industrial economy allies in Europe and Japan – remains equally noteworthy. The US is expected to increase its share of aggregate G-7 output from 47 per cent in 2006 to 58 per cent by 2050. Furthermore, US GDP is forecast to exceed all but one country to 2050. More pointedly, the BRIC economies will long continue to be much poorer, with markedly lower per capita GDPs relative to that of the US well beyond 2050 (Table 2.1). While longer-term projections are subject to great uncertainty, by 2050, Americans could remain almost twice as rich as the Chinese and the Brazilians, and a quarter more than the (unweighted) average for the G-8 (including Russia).[24]

Contributing to these comparative economic growth trends is a more favorable US demographic outlook relative to Europe, Japan, Russia and China. The latter accordingly are likely to see their labor force growth rates lagging behind that of the US (see Figure 2.2). According to these projections, by 2050 the US could account for as much as half of the G-8 labor force.[25] In particular, American society's characteristic openness and effective acculturation capacity hold out the potential to continuously replenish the US labor force with a youthful and aspiring immigrant population.

This demographic advantage is further illustrated in Table 2.2, which presents elderly to worker dependency ratios based on 2010 UN forecasts. The data show the number of dependents per 100 workers. The larger the number, the more onerous is the burden on current workers. Projecting

Table 2.1   GDP per capita, 2006 (US dollars)

	2006	2025	2050
Brazil	5,657	12,996	49,759
China	2,056	12,721	49,576
India	823	3,005	21,145
Russia	6,953	26,112	78,435
Canada	38,255	48,857	76,370
France	36,045	48,429	75,253
Germany	34,616	45,069	68,308
Italy	31,328	41,630	58,930
Japan	34,010	46,404	66,825
UK	38,445	52,681	80,942
US	44,386	57,455	91,697

Source: Goldman Sachs (2007) *BRICs and Beyond*.

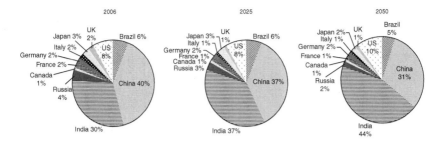

Figure 2.2 Global labor force: country shares
Source: Goldman Sachs (2007) *BRICS and Beyond.*

Table 2.2 Elderly dependency ratios

Number of dependents per 100 persons of working age

	2005	2025	2050
Japan	30	50	70
Italy	30	39	62
S. Korea	13	30	61
Germany	29	41	57
France	25	36	43
Canada	9	33	42
China	11	20	42
UK	24	31	40
Russia	19	26	39
Iran	7	11	37
Vietnam	9	14	37
Brazil	9	17	36
US	18	29	35
Mexico	9	15	31
Indonesia	8	12	30
Turkey	9	14	30
Bangladesh	7	8	23
Egypt	8	12	22
India	7	11	20
Philippines	6	9	16
Pakistan	7	8	15
Nigeria	6	6	8

Note: All ratios are number of dependents (65+) per 100 persons of working age (15–64).
Source: UN World Population Prospects: The 2010 Revision Population Database.

to 2050, as one would presume, the (more youthful) developing countries, with the exception of (rapidly aging) China, fare better whereas the
outlook for members of the G-8 looks considerably worse. Relative to the
advanced countries but also China and Russia, the advantageous US position
is striking.

Another perspective on population aging is given by the forecast median
age. As Table 2.3 shows, by 2050 the US will look younger according to
this criterion than all other G-7 countries, and considerably so compared
to Russia and China. Its aging process will also notably be much slower than
that of India, whose median age will be only moderately lower than that
of the US by 2050. On this criterion, by 2050 the US may look as young as
Indonesia or Turkey and younger still than Vietnam, Brazil and Korea.

Of course, much can happen for long-term forecasts to fail to materialize.
Yet, demographic patterns are largely "baked in the cake" and slow to fundamentally alter course. The ramifications for the outlook of US power have
been aptly summarized: "Global Aging is ... not only likely to extend U.S.
hegemony ... but deepen it ... " (Haas, 2007, p. 113).

Table 2.3   Population median age

	2005	2025	2050
Japan	43.1	50.1	52.3
Korea	35.0	45.1	51.8
Italy	41.7	48.4	49.6
Germany	42.1	48.3	49.2
China	32.2	40.1	48.7
Iran	24.2	36.3	47.2
Vietnam	25.9	35.8	45.8
Brazil	27.0	35.5	44.9
Canada	38.6	42.4	44.0
Russia	37.3	41.5	43.1
UK	38.8	40.8	42.9
France	38.9	41.9	42.7
Turkey	26.4	34.0	42.3
Mexico	25.1	32.2	41.8
Indonesia	26.0	33.3	41.6
Bangladesh	22.4	30.4	41.3
US	36.2	38.6	40.0
India	23.9	29.7	37.2
Egypt	22.9	29.0	36.9
Pakistan	20.2	26.4	34.7
Philippines	21.2	25.7	32.5
Nigeria	18.4	19.2	23.1

Source: UN World Population Prospects: The 2010 Revision Population
Database.

Is the US overstretched?

The deficits

In the first instance, structural[26] budget deficits are more likely to be symptoms of incipient overstretch than *prima facie* evidence of national decline. Overstretch suggests a need to realign commitments and resources, hence spending and revenues. In principle, persistently large deficits demand adjustments that need not materially impact the underlying drivers of longer-term prosperity. In contrast, if fiscal imbalances prove sufficiently chronic, they can eventually trigger growth-inhibiting alterations in microeconomic incentives. In such cases, incipient overstretch **can** mutate into a more primary threat to the system's underlying dynamism.

In its classical formulation, "imperial overstretch" refers to unrestrained and exorbitant foreign military campaigns. The latter can be said to redound to the detriment of great powers by crowding out more productive capital investments. Yet in contrast to widespread impression, the US fiscal challenge does not primarily reflect out-of-control defense spending and the burden of foreign entanglements. If this were the case, then the feasibility of financing an ever-expanding global power projection would be brought into question. This neither minimizes the sizable resources the US commits to military-related spending nor denies that cutbacks in such spending can help facilitate overall fiscal adjustment. Rather, the point is that an endemic failure to rein in explosive economy-wide health care costs with the latter's implications for public sector health insurance programs – the real fiscal challenge – will do more to endanger macroeconomic stability and eventually erode the material foundation of US power (see Chapter 8).

But viewing (health-care driven) fiscal deficits as a necessary manifestation of overstretch is misguided for a more basic reason. The root of the US fiscal problem involves unsustainable commitments – particularly in the area of health expenditure – made by government to its citizens. It is decidedly not a question of any dearth of national resources to adequately meet the health needs of the population at large. As the richest country in the world, the US possesses more than enough resources to achieve this goal. The relevant political and social question is whether the population's basic health requirements are best met via ever-expanding entitlements requiring increasingly higher levels of taxation.

Some have mistakenly stretched the concept of overstretch to apply to current account imbalances – essentially the excess of imports over exports and their impact over time on external liabilities. As discussed elsewhere (Levey and Brown, 2005) and at greater length in Chapter 4, US current account deficits represent a more complicated byproduct of financial globalization and structural underpinnings of today's global economy. It is mistaken to characterize such external deficits as prima facie evidence of over-consumption or overextension. US current account deficits represent a "general equilibrium" outcome driven by microeconomic decision-making and government policy globally.

Energy import dependency

An alternative example of purported overstretch relates to US energy import dependency.[27] In one sense, this could be subsumed under the discussion of current account deficits since oil imports can approach the order of one-fifth of annual US imports. But its contribution to external payments deficits aside, reliance on imported oil is commonly considered a strategic threat in its own right.

Following concerted progress in reducing per-dollar-of-GDP energy consumption after the OPEC oil shocks of 1973 and 1979, US oil consumption fell 15 per cent during 1979–1985, after which the earlier trend of increasing consumption resumed. Coinciding with the secular decline in domestic petroleum production, the share of imports in US oil consumption doubled from 30 per cent in 1973 at the time of the first oil shock to roughly 60 per cent in 2005. Since then, domestic shale oil and gas discoveries combined with a resumption of conservation efforts have helped to decrease foreign oil imports to some 45 per cent of domestic consumption (US Department of Energy, 2012).

Having collapsed in 2009–2010, relative to their peak in summer 2008, followed by a subsequent upward spike owing to unrest in the Middle East, real oil prices are generally expected to see a secular increase, due to robust global energy demand growth in emerging economies and increasing marginal costs of petroleum extraction. Given the Persian Gulf's ongoing centrality to global oil reserves and current production, many decry the tens of billions of dollars flowing to authoritarian Middle East petro-states. They fear that such funds will find their way to radicalized madrassas that indoctrinate disaffected youth in extremist politics. According to these critics, foreign oil dependence perversely impels the US – consuming as much as one quarter of global oil supplies – to allocate disproportionate resources to the military in order to counter a radical jihadist threat fueled by US- (Western-) financed petrodollars.

This US energy overstretch argument reflects some rather questionable assumptions. The first is that US "dependence" on oil imports somehow reflects an exception to the principle of comparative advantage. One of the central tenets of international trade is that countries tend to import those goods or services that are produced relatively more cheaply abroad. Relative production costs thus explain the large share of US oil imports perfectly well. Aside from current technological constraints (e.g. the transportation fleet's reliance on petroleum) or environmental concerns, if other countries represent lower marginal cost providers any concerted campaign to substitute domestic energy sources for petroleum imports would seem self-defeating, at least from an efficiency perspective.[28]

The goal of energy independence has never made much sense unless owing to unstable providers, the US (and the rest of the world) would be unable to secure the physical energy it needs at world market prices (Bryce, 2008). As with most other key commodities, petroleum represents one integrated global market. Thus, if certain foreign suppliers choose to sell their products elsewhere, there are ample alternative locations from which oil can be imported at the prevailing world price.

A second assumption underlying the oil overstretch thesis is that US monopsony power is sufficiently large such that any feasible reduction in US oil demand would lower average world energy prices demonstrably. Yet, even with its 25 per cent share of global oil consumption, a (pronounced) permanent (say) 10 per cent reduction in steady state US oil demand would lower global oil demand by only 2.5 per cent. Such a reduction would exert at most a modest effect on global oil prices. More dominant factors include robust demand growth in China and India, and the expected diminution in spare global (conventional) oil capacity. Any plausible reduction in US oil demand would exert negligible downward pressure on world oil prices with little consequent impact on the revenues flowing to oil producers, whether in the Middle East, Russia, Africa, Latin America or for that matter, the US. In other words, Middle Eastern producers will receive the same petrodollars largely irrespective of US energy consumption.

A third assumption is that independence from foreign oil would insulate the US economy from the vicissitudes of oil price volatility. This is, of course, false. Even in the event of energy self-sufficiency, shifts in global oil prices generally would impact US consumption, investment, output and the price level in a way that is similar to a situation of higher oil import dependency (at least outside of the energy sector itself).

Finally, there is the presumption that lower oil import dependence would significantly trim US defense expenditures, suggesting less "blood for oil." In fact, the US itself sources no more than 10 per cent of its oil imports from the Middle East and here disproportionately from (traditionally reliable) Saudi Arabia. Its remaining top five sources include its North American neighbors Canada and Mexico, plus Venezuela and Nigeria, all of which rely significantly on US sales. Yet, quite apart from its own national economic and security needs, US hegemony for decades – explicitly since the promulgation of the Carter Doctrine in the late 1970s – has involved a military presence premised on ensuring control over the safe flow of oil for the world economy, and not primarily to safeguard US consumption per se.

By ensuring the free passage of oil through the Strait of Hormuz, the Strait of Malacca and other strategic chokepoints, the US navy provides a critical global public good in ensuring an unimpeded flow of oil supplies through the world's sea lanes. Irrespective of changes in its own energy sourcing, the US – across both Democratic and Republic administrations – presumably would continue to regard Persian Gulf stability and the projection of military force into that and other energy-rich regions as vital to global security. Regardless of the pace of reduction in the share of imported crude, it remains a key pillar of US strategic doctrine to protect open navigation as a means to safeguard a healthy global economy. Thus, irrespective of bipartisan paeans to ending "America's addiction to oil," most Republicans and Democrats alike remain avowed hegemonists. It is therefore misleading to conclude that a speedy transition toward energy independence would translate into significant savings on defense expenditure.

The dubious pursuit of energy independence as a primary objective of policy should not be equated with the more defensible goal of achieving greater energy security. Striving to lower dependence on any one group of energy suppliers – foreign or domestic – and achieving greater diversity and balance across alternative fossil fuels and greener energy sources remains prudent (Yergin, 2012). Having dismissed the notion of energy import over-dependency (overstretch) and the related goal of energy independence, there is a notable development in the US (and global) energy outlook that merits special mention for other reasons. The perfection of horizontal drilling technology to unlock large supplies of previously inaccessible oil and gas from shale rock – a process known as hydraulic fracturing or fracking – is rightly seen as a potential "game changer" for the US economy. While the US remains in the technological lead here, similarly promising developments appear to be simultaneously occurring elsewhere. The significance of this (global) energy revolution has less to do with achieving greater energy independence (as often advertised) than with augmenting global energy supply and consequently lowering the costs of energy usage by households and firms everywhere.

According to the Energy Information Administration, discoveries of shale gas in the continental US can provide enough natural gas to last a century (The Economist, 2011b). Unlike oil, whose price is determined by supply and demand on one integrated world market, natural gas prices tend to be set regionally. Hence, the high prospective volumes of US-produced natural gas at relatively low prices are likely to spur investment and employment in energy-intensive US industries such as petrochemicals and steel. A recent net exporter of refined petroleum products, the US may soon be able to export liquefied natural gas. In short, in addition to being among the world's major agricultural and manufacturing producers the US could become a significant net exporter of certain energy products and technologies. These (oil and gas) developments will reduce US manufacturing costs, increasing employment and improving the trade balance. Geopolitically, the greater global availability and improved distribution of natural gas – rendering it more like oil – will depress the leverage of producers over consumers, as with Europe's hitherto reliance on imports from Russia. While environmental concerns over fracking remain, natural gas emits about half as much carbon and CO_2 as coal, which currently occupies a central place in the US energy complex.

The real case for "military overstretch"

On closer scrutiny, most claims of chronic resource "overstretch" involving fiscal deficits, current account imbalances or energy import dependency remain unconvincing. Yet, a compelling case can be made that a more microeconomic state of overstretch plagues the US's defense effort. US military manpower and resources indisputably remain overstretched by extended and repeated tours of duty in Iraq and Afghanistan, in addition to numerous other operational commitments abroad.

That the US faces an acute shortage of active and reserve forces as well as large "reset" (equipment replacement) requirements should be distinguished from arguments relating to any impact of defense spending on macroeconomic stability. While US military spending continues to outpace that of the rest of the world, as we have seen the latter accounts for a smaller percentage of national GDP than in many previous periods. Although it will undoubtedly be asked to share in overall fiscal adjustment, the current overextension of the US military reflects a narrower challenge compared with that inspired by Paul Kennedy's analysis.

Recent deployments have placed enormous demands on military resources, with the Pentagon concerned about its ability to simultaneously meet obligations in Iraq and Afghanistan while maintaining adequate troop levels and equipment to handle new contingencies.[29] Concerns about force exhaustion were raised early on in the Iraq war effort, and later with two key reports released in early 2006, one commissioned by Democratic members of Congress and the other by the Pentagon. These described the military as at a "breaking point," with the congressional report noting that "this strain, if not soon relieved, will have highly corrosive and potentially long-term effects on the force" (BBC News, 2006). Multiple signs of strain on the military are illustrated by numerous indicators (see Appendix 2.A).

While feasible avenues for relieving military overstretch are apparent, Afghanistan and Iraq, like the wars in Vietnam and Korea before them, raise pointed questions about the limits to US military capability. US military planning traditionally has been based on a two-war doctrine, or the ability to fight and decisively win two major, overlapping conflicts, a doctrine which remains fundamentally unrevised. Former Defense Secretary Robert Gates has argued that "the United States is unlikely to repeat another Iraq or Afghanistan – that is forced regime-change followed by nation building." Certain military strategists, however, still foresee a need to focus significant resources in the future on counter-insurgency and state building.

The limits of US military power combined with the possibility of future resource-intensive operations raises the question of allied burden sharing. As evidenced by various NATO campaigns, the Europeans and other allies have much to contribute to peacekeeping and peace building as well as supportive combat operations. However, few allies possess the technological sophistication of US forces, limiting their effectiveness within US-led out of theater operations.

Although there has been much discussion about strengthening unified defense capabilities, it is unrealistic to expect Europe to contribute much beyond current commitments. The Europeans and Japanese at best can be expected to make significant financial contributions to future (typically US-led) military campaigns. In addition, the US is engaged in forging closer strategic ties with key regional states (e.g. Brazil, Indonesia, Turkey, South Africa and Nigeria). In principle, such states can prove instrumental in partnering with the US to cope with the complex challenges generated by rogue state and non-state actors, as well as the fallout from fragile and failed states in their respective regions.

Yet, the central take-away must be that most of today's complex strategic tasks demand a more cohesive combination of military and non-military assets. To conduct effective state building requires a more integrated effort in which the specialized skill sets of personnel from multiple governmental agencies and the private sector are coordinated. The key challenge, however, remains that so far "no one has solved the more serious problem of how to implement the second phase of nation-building – the transition to self-sustaining indigenous institutions" (Fukuyama, 2004).

Concluding remarks

Together with the 2007–2009 financial crisis and Great Recession, no other event has contributed so vigorously to the revival of US declinism as the 2003 invasion of Iraq. Many observers view the prolonged conflicts in Iraq and Afghanistan as precipitating the kind of imperial overstretch-cum-decline that Paul Kennedy famously described. Predictions abound that these draining campaigns will catalyze a steady contraction in the US global footprint. On its face, such a sobering outlook hardly seems farfetched, given the Iraq War's exorbitant cost in blood and treasure, and its debilitating effect on US stature. And restoring stability to Afghanistan, the "graveyard of empires," while coping with the challenges in neighboring Pakistan may prove a still more strenuous trial.

No doubt, new power centers and strategic challenges will complicate the exercise of hegemony well into the future. Nevertheless, on most accounts the scale and scope of US power today widely exceed those of the immediate post-Vietnam era, the last period during which the preponderance of US power was seriously questioned. The US, for example, continues to exert disproportionate influence over security in key regions while exercising broad stewardship of the global economy. Few would dispute that US leadership remains indispensable to an effective confrontation of major transnational threats. Militant non-state actors, such as al Qaeda, moreover are increasingly on the run, posing a serious but non-existential threat. Until or when China has realizable pretensions to challenge the US, the potential for counterbalancing coalitions should remain negligible. As subsequent chapters will demonstrate, the ongoing diffusion of power notwithstanding, its multi-dimensional power toolkit and many structural advantages continue to place the US qualitatively ahead of any plausible concert of rivals.

Notwithstanding some erosion of legitimacy attributable to "the war on terror" and the global financial crisis, the world community still views the US as the "go to" power for the resolution of conflict and the lynchpin of global capitalism. The US remains the single actor capable of exerting leadership around the provision of core public goods central to global prosperity and security. In sum, as blindsided and bungling as it may sometimes appear, the US arguably remains the leading bulwark against waves of global anarchy (Barnett, 2004; Ferguson, 2004).

Appendix 2.A: Measures of military overstretch

A series of indicators suggest that the US has faced a significant military overstretch challenge in recent years. A part of this challenge relates to capacity – manpower, equipment and supplies depleted in decade-long wars in Iraq and Afghanistan. Another concerns the scope of the operational duties with which soldiers have been charged, notably the (extra-military) rudiments of "state building." Indicators of overstretch include repeat deployments, shortened state-side recuperation and extended tours of duty. Excessive reliance on reserve duty troops, such as the National Guard, as well as the phased withdrawal of allied troops has amplified the stress on US forces. Accompanying these trends have been elevated levels of post-traumatic stress disorder (PTSD) and suicide rates. There is also some evidence that recruitment targets – both quantitative and qualitative – have been adversely impacted. Since these indicators tend to be volatile, the reader should view the following summary as only a broad qualitative impression of recent military overstretch.

Military overstretch: possible indicators

Multiple deployments	**From 2003 to 2008:**
	513,000 active duty soldiers deployed to Iraq
	197,000 deployed more than once
	53,000 deployed three or more times[a]
	• historically, third tour negatively impacts morale and retention[b]
	• tours extended to 15 months from standard 12 in 2007
Increase use of stop-loss program	• stop-loss is the involuntary extension of military service contract of retiring soldiers by six months
	• 2001–2008 roughly 120,000 troops have been affected by stop-loss;
	• scheduled to be phased out beginning in August 2009 and to end in 2011[d]
Excessive use of reserves/quality of non-commissioned officers (NCOs)	• automatic promotion of E-4–E-5 and E-5–E-6 because of shortages[c]
	• almost half of the 43% increase in stop-loss between 2007 and 2008 were NCOs
Mental health of troops	for NCOs:
	• first tour – 12% show PTSD symptoms
	• second tour – 18.5%
	• third and fourth – 27%[a]

upward trend of suicides in army:

US Armed Forces Suicides*

	Number of suicides	Percent in non-war deaths
2000	153	17.5
2001	153	16.0
2002	174	15.4
2003	190	16.2
2004	197	17.4
2005	182	15.7
2006	213	19.1
2007	211	20.5
2008	259	24.5
2009	302	26.0
2010	289	28.5

*Deaths not related to war/legal interventions, among individuals on active duty, US Armed Forces active and reserve components.

Note: "From 2005 to 2011, the proportion of deaths due to suicide increased sharply...as a result in 2010 and 2011, suicides accounted for more deaths of service members than transportation accidents..." (MSMR Vol. 19, No. 5, May 2012)

Source: "Deaths While on Active Duty in the U.S. Armed Forces, 1990–2011," MSMR Vol. 19, No. 5, May 2012; Defense Casualty Analysis System, https://www.dmdc.osd.mil

Recruitment marketing	• large financial incentive packages for new recruits • nationalization incentive for immigrants to join military[g]
Quality of new recruits	• 2007 – 79% of recruits have High School diplomas 2003 – 92%[h] • nearly 20% of recruits in 2006 needed a criminal waiver[i]
Quality and quantity of officers	• 58% of the West Point Cadets class of 2002 are no longer in active duty after their five-year commitment[j]; to compensate, more officers come from Officer Candidate School – rate tripled (400–1,500) since late 1990s[j] • law formerly required that only 70–80% of captains were promoted to colonel; law repealed by President Bush, -98% promoted[j]
Stretching of military suppliers	• National Guard has only 61% of its equipment[i]; equipment reset alone could cost $240 billion[i]
Use of private security firms	• mid-2007: 180,000 contractors in Iraq compared with 160,000 troops[j] • mid-2009: 132,000 contractors in Iraq, 68,000 in Afghanistan[k] • March-2011: 64,253 Department of Defense contractors in Iraq compared with 45,660 uniformed personnel in country • March-2011: 90,330 Department of Defense contractors in Afghanistan compared with approximately 99,800 uniformed personnel (Schwartz and Swain, 2011)

[a]Shanker, T. (2008) "Army Worried By Rising Stress of Return Tours to Iraq," *New York Times*, 6 April 2008, p. A1.

[b]O'Hanlon, M. and Kagan, F. (2008) *Increasing the Size and Power of the US Military*, The Brookings Institution.

[c]Krepinevich, A. (2009) "The Future of US Ground Forces," Testimony Before the US Senate Armed Services Committee, Airland Subcommittee, 26 March.

[d]Tyson, A. (2009) "Army to Phase Out 'Stop Loss' Practice", *The Washington Post*, 19 March.

[e]MSBC (2008) "Army Suicides Rose Last Year", 29 May, http://www.msnbc.msn.com/id/24874573/ (accessed online 22 July).

[f]Starr, B., and Mount, M. (2009) "Army Official: Suicides in January 'Terrifying' ", CNN.com, 5 February, http://www.cnn.com/2009/US/02/05/army.suicides/index.html (accessed 25 April 2012).

[g]Historically citizenship was a prerequisite for military service.

[h]New York Times Editorial (2008) "Fixing the Military", 18 May.

[i]Tilghman, A. (2007) "The Army's Other Crisis", *Washington Monthly*, December, http://www2.washingtonmonthly.com/features/2007/0712.tilghman.html (accessed 25 April 2012).

[j]Miller, C. (2007) "Contractors Outnumber Troops in Iraq", *Los Angeles Times*, 4 July.

[k]Simons, S. (2009) "War Zone Contractors Likely Here to Stay", *CNN*, 23 June, http://www.cnn.com/2009/WORLD/meast/06/19/simons.blackwater/ (accessed 25 April 2012).

Part III

Material Underpinnings of Global Power

3
Microeconomic Foundations: Innovation, Productivity and Competitiveness

How do US firms and workers stack up against their foreign counterparts? Is US prosperity under siege from ever cheaper imports and production off-shoring? Does the US retain its edge in innovation? Or, if no longer Japan, is China, India or Korea poised "to eat our lunch?" In recent decades, the accelerated pace of globalization and technological change has transformed the US workplace. Concern over how to cope has focused the political dialogue on enhancing international "competitiveness." But what does it mean for a country, as opposed to a particular firm or individual worker, to grow more or less competitive? And what are the implications for US hegemony?

The rest of this chapter is organized as follows. After critiquing the preoccupation with national "competitiveness" in the section "Competitiveness: An overview," the centrality of innovation to US economic performance is introduced in the section "US fundamentals: Innovation, entrepreneurialism and resiliency." The sections "The US and Europe: Competition at the frontier" and "The 'challenge' from the emerging economies" then examine US comparative performance vis-à-vis the advanced and emerging countries, respectively. The section "Remaining challenges" reviews core priorities for the future, beginning with the fallout from the recent financial crisis. Concluding comments follow in the section "Final thoughts."

Competitiveness: An overview

Debates over US "competitiveness" today represent a problem of public discourse. Although the concept seems more straightforward when applied to individual companies, its relevance to entire economies has never been obvious. While such discussion typically represents a wrong-headed "obsession" (Krugman, 1994), unscientific methodologies for aggregating minutiae of criteria into summary rank orderings of national competitiveness continue to be touted as objective measures of comparative economic performance.[1]

As a coherent economic concept, "competiveness" may be little more than a euphemism for productivity. Because it aggregates across many firms exhibiting wide variability in technical efficiency, national labor productivity is an inherently derivative category. But, unlike competitiveness, at least productivity mirrors a core economic reality – the pace of improvement in average living standards in the longer-term. If competitiveness connotes little material beyond productivity, what can it add about how to enhance national well-being? Rather than describing economics per se, the focus on competitiveness arguably is more a fig leaf for concerns with national power. In contrast to a focus on mutual economic gain through voluntary exchange, competitiveness tends to conjure up a universe that is zero-sum. While more than one society can simultaneously gain from trade, the same cannot be said about the power amassed by nation states, the measure of which is inherently relative.

Yet, such a strict Hobbesian/Smithian dichotomy seems a bit too tidy. After all, in addition to providing a basis for higher living standards, greater productivity growth also underpins the accumulation of national power. But does maximizing productivity growth require the ability to "outcompete" other economies for resources, markets and technologies?

No doubt state-led or highly managed economies tend to favor (often expensive) strategies to promote national champions or to "lock up" production resources globally. By subsidizing exports in order to keep state-owned enterprises afloat and to maintain employment, such countries can end up accumulating outsized foreign exchanges reserves. This buildup of financial claims on foreign residents represents a tax on current consumption (repressing access to foreign goods today) in return for acquisition of foreign goods in the future, albeit at undefined prices and at some indeterminate time. Yet, by lowering its external terms of trade such systematic export promotion actually represents a resource "give away" or gift to the importing country.

Presumably it is the augmentation of state (military) power by one's would-be strategic rivals that represents the real animating concern underlying the preoccupation with national competitiveness. Yet, were the concentration of state power the issue then the latter arguably could be more readily achieved by spending foreign exchange today to import more defense equipment or more generally to increase investment in the military. If competitiveness is ultimately about national power then the focus should still be on the underlying material base of that power – improving the efficiency of domestic resource allocation and maximizing labor productivity and economic growth.

To better appreciate the implications of a focus on national "competitiveness," it is helpful to distinguish two facets of globalization that are often conflated in the public discussion. First, trade deficits (surpluses), and their financing, hence changes in the stock of external debt, reflect mainly macroeconomic factors, notably the forces underlying the balance between aggregate production and spending and the net direction of cross-border capital flows. Leaving aside the shorter-term vicissitudes of the business cycle, if private spending proves insufficient to maintain full employment, in principle an appropriate mix of monetary and fiscal policies furnishes the requisite incremental stimulus to aggregate demand. But neither does full employment require a trade surplus, nor does a trade deficit per se imply higher unemployment.

Second, macroeconomic factors such as the determinants of a country's overall trade balance should be distinguished from microeconomic patterns, notably the commodity composition of imports and exports, the cross-border movement of people with particular skills, the off-shoring of specific products and services, and public tax-cum-subsidy policies targeting individual sectors. Microeconomic factors more generally encompass the relative efficiency of business organization, the quality of human capital and physical infrastructure, and the key institutions and factor markets that underpin the (static and dynamic) efficiency of societal resource allocation. In much public discussion these distinct macroeconomic and microeconomic factors are misleadingly lumped together, under the all-inclusive tent of "competitiveness," confusing the national policy debate

One sure fire, means for enhancing a country's international "competitiveness" – mirrored in the ability of its firms to compete for global market share – is to artificially depress the currency's relative value against other currencies. Provided domestic wage and price pressures are contained, the country's firms will enjoy a price advantage vis-à-vis foreign competitors. This country will tend to run larger trade surpluses because its exporters and import-competing producers are continuously positioned to under-price competitors without sacrificing profit margins. In addition to a chronically depressed currency exchange rate, which amounts to a uniform subsidy on exports and tax on imports, the trade surplus can be further expanded via more targeted subsidies to key production inputs, such as energy and capital.

China has become the poster-child for this strategy of development and some economists argue that its superior economic growth – like that of Japan, Korea and Taiwan before it – would have been inconceivable without such a policy-engineered export-led push (Rodrik, 2008). Yet, if enhancing competitiveness is to be equated with sustained and increasing prosperity, artificially prolonged export promotion (import suppression) via currency "manipulation" or more targeted policies can prove a fool's errand. Mercantilism *in extremis* can ensure a steady sacrifice of per capita income via the deterioration of a country's terms of trade. Like market-driven improvements in competitiveness, systematic state export promotion can no doubt harm individual workers and firms in import-competing sectors. But such foreign competitiveness-focused policies more generally redound to the benefit of the importing country as a whole.

Rather than adopting an overly defensive posture to cheap imports, a more sustainable basis for building a dynamic economy, including one that can support global power projection longer term, rests on erecting one's own sound regulatory, financial and other market institutions, incenting economic actors to invest, innovate and respond flexibly to market signals.[2]

The value of those signals in promoting efficient resource allocation presupposes that relative world market prices are generally aligned with domestic prices. Therefore, in the remainder of this chapter I assume that the "prices are right," and specifically that the real exchange rate[3] reflects the underlying fundamentals of the economy. Hereafter, I focus on the "set of factors, policies and institutions that determine the level of productivity of a country."[4] This brings us full circle: raising productivity growth will fuel higher living standards over the longer term. That one country may or may not dominate various national competitiveness tables in given years will prove less relevant to the longer-term foundation for prosperity (and power) than its consistent lead in average productivity.

The underlying determinants of productivity are numerous, and alternative factors will matter more at different stages of development. For example, sound macroeconomic policy, solid infrastructure, a healthy workforce and reasonably well-functioning core institutions are critical for all but in particular for countries at lower income levels. As countries develop, market efficiency, education and training, and the ability to exploit existing technologies become key factors underlying sustained growth. But the more closely a national economy approaches the global "technological frontier" the more its future economic growth will depend on its success at innovative activity – adapting cutting-edge technologies to higher value-added commercial applications.

US fundamentals: Innovation, entrepreneurialism and resiliency

Resilience in the hard sciences refers to the capacity of an organism or system to absorb shocks without losing the ability to function. The resilience of a body of water, for instance, is gauged by how quickly it returns to form in the face of an oil spill; the resilience of a forest by how it copes with a brushfire. To the extent that these systems survive such perturbations and remain qualitatively unchanged by them, they can be called resilient. If ever there were a social system to which this term could be readily applied, it would be the flexible and entrepreneurial US economy.

In the 1950s, experts pointed to Sputnik as testament to the allegedly superior innovativeness of Soviet central planning. In the 1970s it was Europe, roaring back from the ashes of World War II, which was poised to overtake its erstwhile benefactor. And in the 1980s, Japan loomed as the nation that would soon surpass the US. In the event, the more closely they approached

US per capita income levels, structural limitations in these economies tended to manifest.

De Tocqueville said that "the greatness of America lies not in being more enlightened than any other nation, but rather in her ability to repair her faults" (*The Economist*, July 4, 2009b, p. 30). From the vantage point of years spent abroad, most recently in China, *The Atlantic Monthly's* James Fallows comments:

> If we're worried, perhaps that's a good sign, since through American history worry has always preceded reform. What I've seen as I've looked at the rest of the world has generally made me more confident of America's future, rather than the reverse. What is obvious from outside the country is how exceptional it is in its powers of renewal: America is always in decline, and is always about to bounce back.
>
> (2010, p. 46)

Newsweek columnist Anna Quindlen (2010) adds: "There's no question that this is a moment in which the United States is poised for one future or another – the end of the American century or a new era of dominance based not on military might but on innovation." Looking beyond the exigencies of the recent economic crisis, the US seems relatively well suited to continue to adapt "Third Industrial Revolution" technology across the many segments of its manufacturing and services sectors, and remain a world leader in the sophistication of its companies and the quality of its business environment.

While much of the dynamism associated with the US economy reflects rapid job churning often via the replacement of older firms by new, more innovative ones, incumbent firms in contrast account for most economic advances in Europe (Nicoletti and Scarpetta, 2003). As one study bluntly puts it, "the United States eliminates its least productive companies; the EU does not" (Baumol et al., 2007, p. 210). Competition – particularly from the entry of new firms – emerges as an increasingly critical driver of innovation the closer a country approaches the world technological frontier. This helps to explain, for instance, why despite an absence of comparably strong competitive pressures, Europe and Japan were able to grow so rapidly after World War II but also why their growth slowed the closer they approached the knowledge frontier.

In discussing the entry of innovative start-ups, emphasis has often been placed on the flexibility of labor markets, facilitating rapid redeployment of people with specific skills to new projects demanding such skills. While this is indeed crucial (see below), the provision of credit to innovative, start-up firms may sometimes prove even more instrumental than overcoming labor market rigidities (Aghion et al., 2006). As one market participant puts it, the (more conservative) bank-dominated financial markets of Europe would have summarily dismissed a young Michael Dell seeking a start-up loan to produce personal computers, in contrast to the capital market-dominated US system – including venture capital and angel investors – that has been so much more receptive to ideas for commercializing new products or processes. US capital markets are deeper and broader than those of other advanced countries; and the variety of funding sources facilitates the emergence of new businesses. Continental Europe has long tried to mimic the US arms-length capital market model but the institutional barriers inherited from its traditionally bank-dominated systems remain difficult to surmount.

Equally characteristic of US capitalism has been a tradition of close collaboration among public, private and university actors. In concentrating talent and capital, technology hubs like Stanford University located in the heart of Silicon Valley facilitate collaborative innovation. The closer a country lies to the global technological frontier, the more important investment in higher education seems to become, while primary and secondary education tend to figure more prominently with the implementation of existing technologies (OECD, 2006).[5] And the US still boasts 17 or 18 out of the top 20 universities in most global rankings. In contrast to the relative isolation of European universities from local economies, the US university system has excelled in generating the ideas that lead to breakthrough technologies and widespread commercial applications.

Corporate giants like General Electric and DuPont collaborate with scientists and engineers at leading research universities. Private R&D funding has been generously supplemented by public sources, notably from the Department of Defense, the National Laboratories, the National Science Foundation (NSF) and the National Institute of Health. This uniquely dynamic collaboration among public, private and university researchers has been a key attraction luring scientists and researchers to the US from around the world. One example of public–private partnership is a three-year project joining Microsoft and the NSF to offer university and laboratory researchers free access to Microsoft's cloud computing service to store and analyze data (Markoff, 2010). As a deep pocket customer, the US military also funds the development of new technologies. For example, the Internet emerged from a Pentagon research project and satellites orbited to guide ships, troops and missiles are now used by automobile navigation systems. And civilian products such as iPods, iPhones and E-boxes have turned out to have important military applications (*The Economist*, December 12, 2009a, p. 16).

Recent research on innovation meanwhile has been reexamining standard measures of technological leadership (Bhidé, 2006). Traditionally, operating at the technological frontier presumed superiority in basic scientific research. The real crux, however, is the nature of the entire "innovation system," involving complex linkages throughout the economy, and not simply upstream ones like those between university research centers and commercial R&D laboratories. Significant innovation often involves creative applications of basic technology in downstream industries, and the widespread diffusion of such innovations more often assumes the form of continuous tinkering or modification of basic ideas incorporated into earlier product prototypes. For example, Microsoft's Windows operating system represented less a cutting-edge innovation than a "rapid-follower" application of existing technology. Its packaging as a system backed by superior customer support, adaptability, multiple applications and ongoing refinements made it the industry standard.

A principal stimulant to innovation is the American consumer, whose voracious appetite for new and improved products drives technological progress (Bhidé, 2006). The consumers' willingness to experiment with untested products and their ongoing dialogue with the manufacturer or service provider encourages ongoing product refinement. Without such continuous feedback, firms like Apple would be less able to enhance the functionality of successive generations of iPods, iPhones and iPads. The revolutionary impact of products and services, such as smart phones, e-books, digital music systems like iTunes, search engines and web social interaction services like Facebook and Twitter, typically becomes evident only over time, as firms discover more and more inventive applications for the original idea.

Another challenge for multinational corporations is to decide how to distribute segments of their increasingly global innovation systems – including R&D, product design, branding and distribution – between the home country and foreign subsidiaries. That US-based multinationals outsource certain research-intensive aspects of their product cycle to places like Bangalore remains consistent with retaining the highest value-added segments back home. Providing US-headquartered firms with a business environment that facilitates their operation at the cutting edge of technological change remains key to sustaining US dynamism.

The US and Europe: Competition at the frontier

The traditional, fundamental strengths of the US economy become more apparent when contrasted with that of other advanced economies. Besides what has already been suggested in the section "US fundamentals: Innovation, entrepreneurialism and resiliency," what seems to set the US apart?

Competing models of capitalism and comparative productivity

One incisive take on the dichotomy between the US, on the one side and much of Europe and Japan, on the other is offered in Baumol, Litan and Schramm's *Good Capitalism, Bad Capitalism, and the Economics of Growth and Prosperity*. They distinguish between two prevalent varieties of capitalism: entrepreneurial capitalism, "in which large numbers of the actors within the economy not only have an unceasing drive and incentive to innovate but also undertake and commercialize radical or breakthrough innovations" (Baumol et al., 2007, pp. 85–86), and big-firm capitalism, "where radical entrepreneurship [is] noticeably absent and where a combination of large enterprises, often 'championed' by their governments, and retail or 'mom and pop' shops dominate the economy" (Baumol et al., 2007, p. viii). While both forms can be found in the US and Europe, the more pronounced presence of the entrepreneurial tradition helps to explain why the US has in certain key ways leapfrogged other advanced economies. The US model's viability appears to lie significantly in the symbiotic relationship between entrepreneur and big firm. While "a small set of entrepreneurs may come up with the 'next big things,'... few if any of them would be brought to market unless [they] were refined to the point where they could be sold in the marketplace at prices such that large numbers... could buy them" (Baumol et al., 2007, p. ix). By contrast, in the predominately "big-firm" economies, entrepreneurs – "live at the margins and do not provide the economic fuel for the large firms in the way that is done... in the United States" (Baumol et al., 2007, p. 80).

This does not mean that leading pockets of innovation are limited to US firms. The UK provides a good example, yet in the words of a British entrepreneur, "In Britain we're great at the creative end [of new technology]. But in terms of converting this into serious amounts of revenues, it appears that people in the US are a lot better than us... " (Marsh, 2010). Promising, smaller technology companies in the UK and elsewhere thus often end up either moving to the US to be closer to its large market or being acquired by a US company.

Since average labor productivity – the production of goods and services per hour worked – provides the foundation for the standard of living over the longer term, inter-country productivity comparisons are especially germane in assessing comparative economic performance. Northwestern University economist Robert Gordon and colleagues have done leading work on comparative productivity growth (see e.g. Dew-Becker and Gordon, 2006). Among the main stylized facts are:

(1) From the 1950s until 1995, average labor productivity grew faster in much of Europe. Although significant catch-up to the US was expected once the conditions for rapid reconstruction were in place in war-torn Europe and Japan, the extent to which this convergence proceeded was still impressive.
(2) This convergence eventually reversed, depressing the ratio of EU-15 to US labor productivity from 93 per cent in 1995 to 82 per cent by 2003.
(3) This reversal in comparative productivity growth trends reflected both total factor productivity (TFP) growth[6] and capital deepening.[7]

In contrast to relative labor productivity, Europe never achieved a comparably high ratio of gross domestic product (GDP) per capita, the broadest

Table 3.1 European levels of income, productivity and labor intensity, relative to the US (%)

	1950	1973	1995	2007	2010[a]
Germany					
GDP per hour worked	35.4	72.6	99.5	94.1	89.4
GDP per capita	44.7	78.8	79.9	74.5	81.1
Hours worked per capita	122.6	105.1	80.4	79.2	NA
France					
GDP per hour worked	43.2	75.5	103.6	98.0	91.0
GDP per capita	55.4	78.9	76.2	73.1	73.3
Hours worked per capita	128.3	104.2	73.4	74.6	NA
UK					
GDP per hour worked	62.9	67.0	87.2	89.0	84.7
GDP per capita	74.1	73.5	72.8	77.1	79.2
Hours worked per capita	117.8	109.8	83.4	86.7	NA
Netherlands					
GDP per hour worked	63.9	95.1	108.3	99.3	100.2
GDP per capita	68.4	85.9	83.3	85.0	91.7
Hours worked per capita	107.1	90.3	76.9	85.6	NA
Sweden					
GDP per hour worked	58.4	81.9	84.7	87.7	86.0
GDP per capita	72.4	83.1	73.7	81.4	89.4
Hours worked per capita	124.0	101.4	87.1	92.8	NA
EU-15					
GDP per hour worked	42.7	70.4	95.1	88.0	81.7
GDP per capita	49.8	72.0	73.4	73.1	76.0
Hours worked per capita	115.6	101.3	77.3	83.0	NA

Source: [a]The Conference Board Total Economy Database (January 2011), and van Ark et al. (March 2009).

notion of average living standards. While its productivity was 81 per cent of US productivity in 2010, by that time GDP per capita in the EU-15 had reached only 76 per cent of US per capita GDP (see Table 3.1). The difference between relative labor productivity and relative GDP per capita levels can be explained by the differential in hours worked and in the employment rate of the working age population. Hours worked tend to be lower in Europe and traditionally higher levels of unemployment further limited Europe's potential to narrow the income gap (see Table 3.2).

US firms have demonstrated a particularly strong ability to produce and exploit information and communications technology, or ICT (see e.g. Mann, 2006). The productivity-enhancing impact of ICT investment has been felt most acutely in ICT-using sectors – for example, retail and wholesale trade.

Table 3.2 Labor productivity and average per capita income

| | Labor productivity per hour | | | Effect of | Labor productivity | Effect of | Average per capita income | | |
| | GDP/hour US$ | as % of US | Rank | working hours | per person as % of US | employment/ population ratio | GDP/Capita (US$) | As % Of US | Rank |
	(1)	(2)	(3)	(4)	(5)=(2)+(4)	(6)	(7)	(8)=(5)+(6)	(9)
US	62.1	100.0	3	0.0%	100.0	0.0%	48,087	100.0	3
France	59.7	96.0	6	−14.9%	81.1	−7.4%	35,451	73.7	19
Germany	55.5	89.3	7	−15.5%	73.8	7.9%	39,301	81.7	12
UK	49.7	80.0	13	−2.9%	77.1	2.3%	38,184	79.4	16
Spain	46.4	74.6	18	−0.6%	74.0	−9.1%	31,211	64.9	23
Italy	44.3	71.3	19	2.7%	74.0	−8.0%	31,766	67.9	20
Japan	42.6	68.6	20	0.8%	69.4	5.5%	35,999	74.9	20
Eu 15	50.7	81.7		−5.8%	75.9	−0.8%	36,105	75	18

Note: GDP levels are expressed in 2011 price levels ($), converted by purchasing power parities.
Source: The Conference Board Total Economy Database, January 2012; The Conference Board Total Economy Database, Summary Statistics 1996–2011; Table 9 http://www.conference-board.org/retrievefile.cfm?filename=SummaryTable_Jan20121.pdf&type=subsite (retrieved 11 April 2012).

For a variety of institutional reasons, Europe has proved comparatively ill equipped to imitate the US in its economy-wide application of ICT. That the US productivity lead mirrors not only the broad application of ICT *per se* but a process of organizational innovation and process restructuring is apparent, for example, at "big box" retail giants like Wal-Mart. Much expenditure on workplace reorganization, on-the-job skill upgrading and retraining, and corporate R&D is captured in the national income and payment accounts as current business expenses; yet, such "intangible capital" can be more accurately portrayed as supplementary investment driving much of the superior productivity growth effect.

Although comparative US productivity growth has been impressive on its face (see Table 3.3), adjusting for biases in cross-country productivity comparisons further amplifies the impression of superior US performance. Countries like the US which have tended to employ a greater share of the labor force, all else equal, also tend to exhibit lower levels of measured productivity growth because a greater share of (less-skilled and less-experienced) younger people are employed. Moreover, such countries with longer average working weeks should in principle also see lower productivity growth due to declining marginal productivity in the course of the work week.

In developing a "structural" hourly productivity measure for the US and European countries, which corrects for differences in the hours worked and unemployment rates between Europe and the US, estimates for European "structural" productivity turn out to be considerably less than measured productivity. Thus, lower hours worked and lower employment rates help, to some extent, to bias upward (measured) productivity growth in Europe. This may help to explain how a few European economies at times approximated or even exceeded measured US productivity levels: "The fact that the 'structural' hourly productivity levels are higher in the

Table 3.3 Labor productivity growth (GDP per hour, annual average, %)

	1996–2006	2006–2010	2010	2011 (estimates)
World	2.0	2.0	3.6	2.5
US	2.1	1.1	3.6	1.2
Japan	1.4	0.7	5.5	−0.3
France	1.1	0.3	1.3	1.0
Germany	0.9	0.5	3.2	1.7
Italy	0.3	−0.6	2.0	0.3
Spain	0.1	1.5	2.6	1.7
UK	1.9	0.2	1.1	−0.2

Source: The Conference Board Total Economy Database, Summary Statistics 1996–2011; Table 9 http://www.conference-board.org/retrievefile.cfm? filename=SummaryTable_Jan20121.pdf&type=subsite (retrieved 11 April 2012).

United States than elsewhere shows that the United States is indeed setting the 'technical frontier' in terms of productive efficiency and that other countries are lagging behind to varying degrees" (Cette and Bourkès, 2007, p. 4).

Even without making such structural adjustments, a leading compiler of cross-country productivity data concludes:

> Globally, the US productivity level is still the highest for the large economies in the world at four times the average level of the world economy (only Norway and Luxembourg have higher levels than the US). Euro Area productivity per worker falls about 25 per cent below the US level, and Japan's is about 30 per cent lower. In Latin America and Asia-Pacific the gap is almost 80 per cent; in China, it is 85 per cent and in India, 90 per cent.
>
> (The Conference Board, 2012)

That productivity growth had, unusually, picked up during the recent recession is mainly due to aggressive layoffs by US firms in response to the financial crisis. Moreover, US unit labor costs have fallen steadily in recent years as hourly worker compensation has persistently lagged behind hourly labor productivity. While measured productivity differentials between the US and its industrial peers appeared to narrow somewhat circa 2004, for the period 2006–2010 the US maintained a sizeable average annual productivity growth lead over its European counterparts (see again Table 3.3). While US productivity growth decelerated sharply in 2011, from an extraordinarily high 3.6 per cent pace in 2010, the US has maintained its cumulative lead relative to most advanced countries (Conference Board, 2012).

What explains the persistent productivity growth disparity between Europe and the US? One factor is surely innovation. According to the Prosperity Index published by the Legatum Institute, "the United States offers the most favorable environment for entrepreneurship and technological innovation in the world." Table 3.4 lists the top 20 countries in the category of entrepreneurship and innovation which captures country performance in starting new businesses and commercializing ideas in innovative new products. Following the US and the UK in 2009 are most of the remaining members of the G-10, the Scandinavian countries Denmark and Sweden, the East Asian newly industrialized countries South Korea, Hong Kong and Singapore, and a scattered assortment of other advanced countries. Notably, Japan, Germany and France are ranked considerably down the list at 7, 8 and 14, and in 2010 they drop further to 19, 15 and 20, respectively. The third and fourth largest economies in the European Monetary Union, Italy and Spain, are absent from the top 20 altogether.

Table 3.4 Innovation and entrepreneurship

2009a Countries		2010b Countries	
1	US	1	Denmark
2	UK	2	Sweden
3	Sweden	3	US
4	Canada	4	Finland
5	Netherlands	5	UK
6	Denmark	6	Norway
7	Japan	7	Ireland
8	Germany	8	Singapore
9	Finland	9	Iceland
10	Hong Kong	10	Canada
11	Singapore	11	Switzerland
12	Ireland	12	Netherlands
13	Switzerland	13	Australia
14	France	14	New Zealand
15	Australia	15	Germany
16	South Korea	16	Austria
17	Norway	17	Hong Kong
18	New Zealand	18	South Korea
19	Austria	19	Japan
20	Belgium	20	France

[a]Comparative Receptivity to New Enterprises and the Commercialization of Ideas.
[b]Comparative Entrepreneurial Environment, Innovation and Access to Opportunity.
Source: Legatum Institute Prosperity Index.

Underpinning US dynamism is also the greater flexibility of its hiring and firing practices. Labor market flexibility remains instrumental given the social challenge presented by rapid globalization and technological change. Although the associated insecurities attending this accelerated rapidity of change are more sharply experienced in the US, the longer-term rigidities in Western Europe exert a more durable impact on the standard of living (Blinder, 2006). The laggard performance of many continental European countries on labor market flexibility highlights the strong impediments to hiring and hence elevated unemployment rates, although the latter have receded somewhat in recent (pre-recession) years. While Germany in particular has implemented labor market reforms, most other European countries continue to favor "insiders" (those with permanent jobs) over "outsiders" (the unemployed or temporary workers), (*The Economist*, January 30, 2010, p. 16). A combination of more generous benefits systems, higher marginal tax rates, lower education expenditures per student and other labor market rigidities aggravate the overall picture (Trichet, 2006).

In addition, many EU countries suffer from relatively burdensome regulations and bureaucratic red-tape that impose high costs on business. Former EMU Governor Jean-Claude Trichet has commented that "a prerequisite for higher growth in the euro area is the unlocking of business potential by creating an entrepreneurial-friendly economic environment. This includes lowering costs imposed by public sector administrations for existing firms and business start-ups…" The start-up costs for a business in the Euro area can be as much as ten times as high as in the US. Japan, the world's third largest economy, likewise is hampered by "myriad rules, regulations, and restrictions that severely limit the scope for new entrants, innovation, and increased efficiency in many markets" (Trichet, 2006). The 2008 financial crisis notwithstanding, growth-enhancing elements of the US business model are broadly acknowledged as vital complements to existing varieties of national capitalism on the continent (Wolf, 2008). Barring a frontal assault on structural impediments in product and factor markets, Western European countries, on average, will likely continue to lag behind the US in average annual productivity growth for the foreseeable future (Schwartz and Saltmarsh, 2009).

In addition, as discussed in Chapter 2, longer-term demographic trends are another factor favoring the US vis-à-vis its industrial country counterparts. With more rapidly aging populations and high ratios of retirees to current workers, Europe and Japan face a stiffer demographic struggle. Meanwhile, American workers tend to clock longer hours. According to pre-recession 2007 data, the typical American had worked 1,800 hours per year, while the Germans and French amassed 1,430 and 1,536 hours, respectively (OECD, 2012). That translates into the equivalent of some seven to nine fewer weeks per year. Within Western Europe, only Italians worked comparable hours to Americans.

The point of comparing productivity and demographic trends among advanced countries is not to resurrect the zero-sum logic underlying notions of competing national economies. The point is rather to address assertions about U.S. decline, a multi-dimensional phenomenon discussed through the remainder of this book. Americans and, indeed, the rest of the world are ultimately better off the greater the level of productivity and the brisker the pace of labor force growth in Europe, Japan and anywhere else in the developed or developing world. A faster growth of production and incomes anywhere lowers the global cost of production and stimulates demand for the products produced everywhere else. Furthermore, ideas generated in one country help to generate new products and improve production processes elsewhere. In brief, a more dynamic and productive Europe and Japan is overridingly positive for the US, and vice versa.

In contrast, secular decline in Europe and Japan renders the task of sustaining US hegemony – through the alliance force multiplier – more challenging. Aside from important global contributions to peacekeeping, development aid and enlargement, the European Union no longer exhibits clear pretensions toward assuming the mantle of a global power. One critic puts it especially bluntly: "Unless it unites and manages to address its real problems, ten or twenty years from now Europe will seem the geopolitical equivalent of an old-age home: mostly harmless, quaint and perhaps even charming, but decidedly out of the flow of power and prestige" (Laqueur, 2010). Therefore, an expansion and deepening of US political and military alliances with other, dynamic states may prove an increasingly critical underpinning of US hegemony going forward.

The "challenge" from the emerging economies

Having explored the state of the US economy relative to that of some of its advanced country peers, how do US firms and workers compare with those in dynamic emerging countries? While such comparisons may seem premature, the emerging economies' potential to wrest away market share has increasingly fueled concern. Even if US influence has largely been about spreading market economics throughout the world, should the growing ability of emerging market producers to compete on the global stage be seen as a threat to US prosperity and hegemony?

The rise of China and the BRICs

As the global labor force tripled with the integration of China, India and the former Soviet Union into the world economy, significant developments ensued. The increase in the global supply of lower-skilled labor pressured import-competing workers around the world. Meanwhile, it encouraged greater corporate off-shoring to take advantage of lower labor costs and other inducements to foreign investment more directly. Also witnessed was a more gradual increase in the global supply of more highly skilled individuals. The off-shoring of certain higher value added jobs to emerging economies supported by increased investment in R&D and technical talent has led a few emerging countries to acquire higher end product capabilities more typically associated with the advanced countries. This trend has aroused concerns that China in particular and to a lesser extent India and certain other emerging countries may be positioned to compete head to head with the advanced countries in more sophisticated products and services. For example, economist Dani Rodrik notes: "China is an outlier in terms of the overall sophistication of its exports: its export bundle is that of a country with an income-per-capita level three times higher than China's" (2006).

At present however, China's main function within the global value chain remains as the principal location of final assembly: even though much of the measured value of Chinese final goods originates in the form of production inputs and intermediate products produced outside China, import data attribute the entire value of final goods purchased in the West to the Chinese mainland, aggravating political tension over a Chinese export juggernaut. The fact that in addition to labor-intensive, low value-added products China has become an increasingly important exporter of "high-technology products" has sounded further alarm bells. Detailed examination of such products, however, reveals a predominance of popular consumer electronics, such as DVD and CD players, display units and cellular telephones, many of which use parts and components from other countries and tend to be manufactured by foreign corporations operating in China.

While on average Chinese exports today reflect of the order of 50 per cent of value added in China, many sophisticated industries, such as computers, telecommunications equipment, and electrical equipment contain a more modest share of Chinese value added rarely exceeding 25 per cent (Koopman et al., 2008). Many high technology products requiring more highly skilled labor, are characterized by especially low shares of domestic content (around 15 per cent) compared with relatively low-skilled labor-intensive sectors, such as textiles, which can contain domestic content of around 75 per cent (Koopman et al., 2008).

Thus, while a growing share of Chinese exports has climbed up the value chain as compared with the preponderance of mass produced unskilled labor-intensive textiles and toys of decades past, these (higher-value added) products hardly employ the kind of cutting-edge technologies that would challenge advanced country technological prowess. For instance, China is now the world's largest producer of wind turbines and solar panels. Yet, the technology or knowledge creation part of the value chain in alternative energy used by the Chinese to produce such items tends to come from the US, Europe, Japan and Korea.

In an analysis of factors contributing to intensive-based growth, Antonio Fatas and Ilian Mihov remark that "growth in China will not be driven by the invention of new products and new management methods that push world innovation, but rather by learning and imitating what advanced economies have already invented" (Fatas and Mihov, 2009). Expanding one's purview to a broader class of emerging nations, the Legatum Institute's sub-index ranking of countries on innovation and entrepreneurship introduced in the previous section has the BRICs comprising "the middle swath of countries, showing that despite their economic ascendency, they still have a way to go to occupy global leadership as entrepreneurial societies" (Choi, 2009).

China requires more robust market-friendly institutions to facilitate a more conducive business environment for serious innovation (Fatas and Mihov, 2009). Among other things, such change presupposes reforms in China's financial institutions so that credit resources can better support the commercialization of new ideas. Equally required is a revolution in institutions of higher learning where rote learning still trumps creative thinking. This suggests in turn the eventual need for fundamental Chinese political reform. Meanwhile, despite its democratic institutions and niche strengths in certain services, India presently faces even more daunting prospects in progressing toward the world technological frontier.[8]

Nevertheless, in corroborating their claim of an erosion in US technological leadership, critics frequently cite some of the following trends:

(1) a declining share of science and engineering PhDs granted at US universities in favor of Europe, Japan and China (Freeman, 2005);
(2) a secular increase in the proportion of foreign-born students receiving advanced degrees in the sciences and engineering at US universities (Mann, 2006);
(3) decreasing dominance in the publication of scientific articles or the granting of patents (Prestowitz, 2006);
(4) increasing off-shoring beyond manufacturing to a growing share of services, including a segment only recently considered "non-tradable" (Blinder, 2006).

Does the weight of evidence suggest a veritable technological challenge from the BRICs and other emerging countries?

Chinese innovation

Increasingly, reports surface about the technological challenge posed by emerging markets, particularly China. A recent article puts this concern in perspective: "Hardly a week goes by without a headline pronouncing that China is about to overtake the US and other advanced economies in the innovation game. Patent filings are up, China is exporting high-tech goods, the West is doomed. Or so goes the story line. The reality is very different" (Gupta and Wang, 2011).

At 12.3 per cent, for example, China's share of the world's R&D in 2010 ranked second only to that of the US at 34 per cent. According to the World Intellectual Property Organization, Chinese investors filed 203,000 patent applications in 2008, behind only Japan (502,000) and the US (400,000):

> But more than 95 percent of the Chinese applications were filed domestically with the State Intellectual Property Office – and the vast majority confer "innovations" that make only tiny changes on existing designs. A better measure is to look at innovations that are recognized outside China – at patent filings or grants to China-origin inventions by the world's leading patent offices, the US, the EU and Japan. On this score, China is way behind.
>
> (Gupta and Wang)

According to OECD data, in 2008, China filed only 473 triadic patent applications versus 13,000–14,000 each from the US, the EU and Japan. Moreover, "half of the China-origin patents were granted to subsidiaries of foreign multinationals" (Gupta and Wang).

Gupta and Wang (2011) attribute this large gap between China's (R&D) inputs and innovation outputs to a relative lack of prior knowledge, the politicization of governmental funds allocated to R&D, the predominance of quantity over quality in China's research culture and the resort to local over international standards in rewarding research. They conclude: "Yes, China is making rapid strides in some areas such as telecommunications technology. However, on an across-the-board basis, it still has quite some distance to cover before becoming a global innovation power" (Gupta and Wang, 2011).

Those who view globalization as more of a threat to US prosperity tend to emphasize the more rapid pace of technological diffusion today. Some observers presume that this works to the distinct detriment of the most technologically advanced economies. What they underestimate is that the full absorption of advanced technologies presupposes significant intangible know-how and difficult-to-replicate assets, such as well-specified property rights and deeply embedded social trust:

> Economies and militaries ... today ... are composed of systems that link physical goods to networks, research clusters, and command centers. Developing economies may be able to purchase or steal certain aspects of these systems from abroad, but many lack the supporting infrastructure, or "absorptive capacity," necessary to integrate them into functioning wholes.
>
> (Beckley, 2011, p. 54)

Adam Segal among others stresses the lax intellectual property rights that encourage companies to reverse engineer already established technologies. While long disparaged for penalizing and diluting the advantages of Western businesses, such practices keep "Chinese companies lazy in terms of their own research and development" (2011, p. 62). Segal (2011, p. 63) sees the transition from "catch-up" to the innovative frontier as "incremental" and likely to last at least several decades. China in particular must continue to strengthen "trust, transparency, flexibility and creativity ... support new ideas, talent, new companies, and entrepreneurship". In sum, in contrast to China and most other developing or emerging economies, the US "is primed for technological absorption ... more like a sponge, steadily increasing its mass by soaking up ideas, technology, and people from the rest of the world" (Beckley, op. cit, p. 55).

Foreign students

The number of foreign students currently enrolled in US universities approaches 600,000, split roughly between undergraduate and graduate training up almost 13 per cent since 2006 (NSF, 2012; Table 2-7). During 2007–2010 the average share of science and engineering doctorates awarded to temporary visa holders was 37 per cent, up from 27 per cent in 1989 (Fiegner 2011; National Science Foundation, 2010b, 2012). Such figures represent a major vote of confidence in US higher education as well as a boon to the US economy as many of these students remain to work in the US. The stay rate, measuring the share of graduates with definite employment commitments who remain in the US after receiving a PhD, has been trending upward since the 1990s. Although peaking and moderating more recently, this stay rate remains especially high in the fields of engineering, physical science and the life sciences at around 80 per cent. Although PhD stay rates in the social sciences have declined by somewhat more in recent years they remain around 50 per cent[9] (see Figure 3.1; National Science Foundation, 2012).

The disproportionate flow of foreign students to US universities reflects the deep-seated advantages of the US research system in terms of the opportunities to grow one's skills as well as the financial returns to investment in education and training, particularly if one remains in the US. Knowledge spillovers related to interaction with the highest concentration of leading researchers and scientists (Easterly, 2002), the breadth of funding sources and close coordination between the public sector, private sector and universities all help to attract the best and brightest.

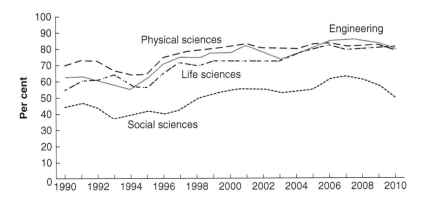

Figure 3.1 Stay rate of doctorate recipients with a temporary visa

Source: National Science Foundation, Division of Science Resources Statistics. 2012. *Doctorate Recipients from U.S. Universities: 2010*. Special Report NSF 12–305. Arlington, VA. Available at http://www.nsf.gov/statistics/sed/digest/2010

This phenomenon redounds not only to the advantage of those who choose to stay and work in the US. A 2007 Duke University/University of California Berkley study, for example, revealed that one-quarter of all engineering and technology firms founded in the US between 1995 and 2005 had at least one foreign-born founder; in Silicon Valley the number increases to 52 per cent of all firms. For instance, the co-founders of US titans eBay, Yahoo! and Google are all foreign-born (from France, Taiwan and Russia, respectively). Of venture capital-backed firms, in recent years as many as a quarter were started by immigrants, who otherwise at the time constituted some eight per cent of the US population (Anderson and Platzer, 2006).

Critically important to longer-term US prosperity is that the US continues to lure the best and brightest from abroad. Any shortfall in the training of US-born technical professionals can, in principle, be offset by the ongoing attraction of foreign students, provided they retain an ability to obtain an H1-B visa upon graduation (see discussion below). Even with growing numbers returning to their countries of origin, the connections forged and the improved understanding of American culture and business practice can only redound to the benefit of the US through future joint ventures and other, less tangible, returns. Meanwhile, a key to maintaining the higher skill level of the US labor force has been the attraction of immigrants, whose children are increasingly dominating the professions requiring advanced degrees.

In contrast, an oft-cited McKinsey Global Institute study concludes that China and India face a critical skills shortage and lack enough graduates to satisfy the business requirements of Fortune 500 companies (Farrell and Grant, 2005). Only an estimated one-quarter of India-trained engineers and one-tenth of those trained in China possess the communications, teamwork and applied skills to work in multinational companies. Many graduating engineers in India and China earn less demanding degrees; and many would qualify as little more than technicians in the US. Fareed Zakaria (2008, p. 189) mentions that "once you get beyond [India's elite academies] – which graduate under ten thousand students a year – the quality of higher education in China and India remains extremely poor, which is why so many students leave those countries to get trained abroad". Even if their graduates eventually obtain a level of higher education comparable to that offered in the US, numerous systemic barriers stand in the way of China or India mounting a serious technological challenge to America, at least in the near future.

Production off-shoring

To what extent has off-shoring impacted American workers? This contentious question is the subject of ongoing research.[10] On the whole, the adverse impact of off-shoring on select groups of workers to date seems to be more limited than much conventional wisdom holds. One pre-Great Recession study finds that "off-shoring may have accounted for 4–5 per cent of total large-scale layoffs in the United States" (Kirkegaard, 2007). Another estimates the number of jobs at risk for off-shoring to low wage, labor-abundant countries to be about 15–20 million, with many (40–50 per cent) of these in the manufacturing sector. This leaves fewer than 10 million non-manufacturing jobs that remain subject to off-shoring out of a 150 million-plus labor force (Jensen and Kletzer, 2008). Although Alan Blinder, the Princeton University economist who attracted major attention to the longer-term risk from services off-shoring, grants that off-shoring has thus far cost "a limited number of US jobs," he admonishes that these represent only the tip of the iceberg. He projects that as many as 40 million US jobs could be off-shored within the next two decades (Blinder, 2006). In contrast, UCLA economist Edward Leamer identifies "contestable" jobs that can be moved off-shore as "only the mundane codifiable tasks in the tradable sector for which there are global markets," adding that "you'd be surprised at how few of those remain in the United States" (Leamer, 2007, p. 101).

Complicating this picture is the increasing off-shoring of IT hardware to low-wage countries from which computers and peripherals are largely imported. In the first instance, this worsens the IT trade balance. But lower prices on computer equipment imports increase the return on IT investment in other US industries, as reflected in the higher US exports of IT-consuming (manufacturing and service) firms. This expanding globalization of IT, mirroring an increasingly advanced "unbundling of tasks," thus enhances US productivity more generally (Baldwin, 2006; Mann, 2006). For example, one study finds that a 10 per cent increase in Chinese imports to the US is associated with a 3.2 per cent increase in patent filing, a 3.6 per cent increase in IT spending and a 12 per cent increase in R&D by US firms (*The Economist*, October 15, 2011). More assembly jobs in China and more customer assistance jobs in India translate into more R&D jobs in the US and more jobs for the non-R&D workers in the same localities due to the job multiplier (Moretti, 2012). According to the work of Dartmouth economist Matthew Slaughter, every job outsourced generates nearly two, typically higher-skilled (e.g. engineering, marketing and design), jobs in the US (Moretti, p. 70).

The lead still enjoyed by many US exporters remains apparent in US balance of payments statistics. Although the overall trade deficit remains large for macroeconomic factors,[11] the US enjoys a substantial surplus in overall services trade, an increasingly important sub-component of the current account balance, and does particularly well with intellectual property exports and intensive ICT-using service exports in wholesale trade, finance and communications. The surplus on services can be expected to grow, especially if the trend US current account deficit adjusts downward in the future.

The foregoing discussion in this section is premised on taking the widening concern over the rising competitiveness of emerging market countries at face value. The idea was to place the more exaggerated claims on educational achievement and technological sophistication in perspective. It bears emphasis, however, that much concern with the challenge from emerging markets reflects a paradigm of "zero sum." Improvements in emerging market country skills and their successes at innovation and product quality only serve to enlarge world production possibilities, even pushing out the technology frontier for certain products or services. They thereby enlarge the knowledge base for advancing production and for expanding consumer variety in the advanced industrialized countries.

Remaining challenges

Since the mid-19th century the US's real GDP per capita growth has remained relatively constant, with significant deviations occurring infrequently as during the Great Depression and World War II (Fatas and Mihov, 2009, p. 3). Ed Leamer (2008) has commented that the extraordinarily steady growth rate of US GDP over many decades, notwithstanding shocks like wars, oil shocks and recessions, is the first fact that macroeconomists should strive to explain. Notwithstanding this impressively consistent trend, in the wake of the 2008 Great Recession there remains heightened uncertainty over whether the US economy can resume its historical growth path any time soon.

For several years now Mohammed El-Erian and Bill Gross of PIMCO, a leading investment firm, have asserted that the US economy is transitioning toward "a new normal," in which potential GDP growth will register at 2 per cent or lower over the next 10–20 years, well below its historical rate of closer to 3 per cent (El-Erian, 2009). They cite "DDR" as the main drivers – deleveraging, de-globalization and reregulation – with a public sector potentially overreaching in terms of regulation, combined with the decline in consumption growth to repair household balance sheets and a risk of greater protectionism. Moreover, by eroding skills and discouraging job searches, protracted unemployment can potentially increase the natural rate of unemployment (*The Economist*, 2009c). PIMCO has hardly been alone in forecasting a protracted economic slowdown. In 2010 Northwestern University productivity expert Robert Gordon predicted that non-farm labor productivity growth during 2007–2027 will range closer to the more sluggish rate experienced during 1987–1997 rather than more recent experience (Gordon 2010, Table 10). More recently, Gordon (2012) has waxed even more pessimistic on the sources of overall economic growth owing to such factors as a reversal in the earlier demographic dividend, stagnant educational achievement, the need to reduce the national debt overhang and a likely slowdown in the widespread application of cutting-edge ideas.

Other experts appear more sanguine on prospective US trend growth. For example, a leading producer of international productivity studies sees little reason why the US cannot "reinvigorate the innovation economy."

To ensure that applications of information technology and managerial innovations are allowed to fully work their way through the economy, the US needs to implement structural reforms "in public and regulated sectors" (such as education and health care) while "strengthening the skill base, infrastructure, and other underlying productivity enablers" (McKinsey Global Institute, 2011). Meanwhile, a potentially important factor involves recent breakthroughs in robotics, artificial intelligence, nanotechnology and additive manufacturing including 3D-printers. Such developments play to US strengths in innovation (Wadhwa, 2012). The Financial Times' John Gapper concludes a recent article touting the uncanny ability of US firms to rejuvenate when they appear to be lagging the competition: "The remarkable thing is how rapidly the US has managed to turn the technological tables in two of the most important global industries. For a few years, it looked lost in both telecommunications and energy, then it recovered and raced ahead. It hasn't lost its touch" (Gapper, 2012). Together with the shale gas revolution such technological achievements portend potential for "reshoring" and more medium- and high-end manufacturing jobs. MIT economist Enrico Moretti touts the special high-tech "clusters" or "hubs" of the US innovation sector and "creative class" as leading engines of job growth in advanced technology, manufacturing and local services (Moretti). The US also has untapped potential to increase labor force participation and enhance the quality of that labor force through strengthened vocational training, relaxation of quotas on skilled immigration (see below) and by encouraging greater competition in certain overly regulated sectors (McKinsey Global Institute).[12]

In sum, given the substantial headwinds facing the US and many other economies today, a "new normal" type of tepid recovery may well characterize the medium-term. Yet one sees little reason to reject out of hand more optimistic longer-term projections based on the enduring strengths of the US economic system and innovation complex. Once the economy adjusts to such current challenges, as household deleveraging, the depressed housing market and long-term unemployment, attention will refocus on how to better tap the country's enduring strong fundamentals. For example, the US should continue to boast deep and liquid (and hopefully better regulated) capital markets, a flexible labor force, an unrivaled university system with vital research linkages to private industry and government, and a population continually infused with the best and brightest from around the world. These are some of the underlying factors that can backstop longer-term prosperity in the future once the US progressively surmounts current obstacles.

Although the definitive case for a secular decline in US economic dynamism has yet to be made,[13] failure to make steady progress in confronting the key economic and social challenges of the day will increase such risk. I thus conclude this chapter with a brief review of some core impediments to the restoration of robust steady-state growth.

Employment and incomes

While ICT-driven productivity has been especially rewarding for those at the top of the income distribution – owners of capital, managers and those with advanced degrees – most workers have to date seen their real wages flat or falling (*The Economist*, November 19, 2011g, p. 84). Tyler Cowen describes many of today's innovations as "private goods" in that much of the gains from innovation are captured by a relatively small number. Companies like Google, Facebook and eBay may produce immense value but directly employ relatively few people, even if they generate higher multiplier effects in terms of the creation of adjacent (skilled as well as unskilled) jobs (Moretti, 2012). And some of the job openings at IT firms are reportedly difficult to fill due to "a fundamental skills mismatch... (with) the US labor market increasingly divided into a group that can keep up with technical work and a group that can't" (Cowen, 2011, pp. 50–51). In addition to technical progress, globalization has played some role in constraining median wage growth and employment prospects, exacerbating income inequality.[14]

A satisfactory overview of the complicated conceptual and data issues related to income inequality would require a separate book. It will have to suffice here to state a few generalities. First, although relative stagnation in the median wage and the coincident, secular increase in measured income inequality appear to be common features of many economies today, these trends seem pronounced in the US relative to other advanced countries.[15] One factor relatively unique to the US appears to be that wage and salary compensation have been significantly squeezed by the explosive growth in employer-based health care costs. Another factor impacting median real wages has been the excess cost growth of a US university education coupled with increasing returns to such education.

While there has been much discussion of the increasing share of profits in national income at the expense of wages, the latter may ultimately be less of a factor than the increasing dispersion within labor income in the direction of the highest 1 per cent or even the top one tenth (or one hundredth) of 1 per cent (Dew-Becker and Gordon, 2008). This disparate class of CEOs, superstar athletes, musicians and actors, leading legal and medical professionals and hedge fund managers are among the leading beneficiaries from globalization-cum-ICT revolution.

Second, the steady decline in manufacturing as a share of total employment represents a trend impacting many economies. A downside of strong productivity growth in the shorter-run has been an erosion of job opportunities, particularly in lower-valued added segments of manufacturing. The relatively "job-less" recovery may also reflect the lower labor intensity of many higher-wage paying advanced services firms. Nobel laureate Michael Spence has argued that much recent US employment creation has been in non-tradeables – notably health and government – as increasing jobs have been outsourced or lost to import competition. His proposed remedies are conventional: "improving education to meet the premium on highly educated workers, investing in infrastructure, and reforming the tax structure" (Spence, November/December, 2011). Yet, the implication that globalization is disproportionately to blame for the plight of the American worker remains contentious (Katz, 2011; Spence et al., 2011).

Finally, increasingly accepted on both the left and right of the political spectrum is a slowdown in certain measures of social mobility. An increasingly significant predictor of mobility is parental income. Meanwhile, escalating tuition costs threaten to price out increasing segments of the middle and lower classes from access to higher education. Greater mobility appears to characterize the middle of the income distribution, while separate data are unavailable for immigrants, a particularly successful sub-group of the diverse US population (DeParle, 2012).

However one weighs and interprets the factors impacting median wage growth, income inequality, employment and mobility, we will have to wait to see to what extent growing public discontent will force a comprehensive policy response. Grassroots campaigns and laser focus on these issues by the two major political parties remain at an early stage.

Primary and secondary education

Having underlined the unrivaled strength of the US university system, here I address the area of education in which the US has by many accounts long been "failing": K-12 education.[16] Despite higher average per-student spending than in other developed nations (OECD, 2006), American students have consistently underperformed on international standardized tests. For example, while US 4th graders have tested competitively against their international peers in reading, science and math, there is a marked deterioration by the time they reach the 8th grade, and by the 12th grade, American students have long tested substantially worse than their developed-country peers (Coulson, 2005).

More qualitative criticisms have also been leveled at the US educational system. Former US Senator Bill Bradley observes that as American students attend "pep rallies and driver's education," their counterparts in Europe and Asia are learning "a second foreign language and more science" (Bradley, 2008). Others note a marked "in-school hours" disparity between American and foreign students.[17] Behind these criticisms lies a fear that the under-educated American student of today will be the unproductive worker of tomorrow.

It should be emphasized that the disappointing K-12 statistics represent averages drawn from a larger, much more heterogeneous population than that of (say) Finland, which tops many comparative educational studies. The studies mix outstanding US schools whose students remain competitive with the best international students and mostly inner-city schools which account for a disproportionate share of the nation's dropouts. Council on

Foreign Relations so arguably "the real worry about the apparently poor math-science pre-college performance of US students may be more about what it portends for future income inequality than what it means for continued technical change" (Baumol et al., 2007). In other words, while the US K-12 education system is doing a poor job of educating all of its students, not all of its students are receiving a poor education. Few would dispute that income inequality in the US mirrors the disparity in educational outcomes in a world which increasingly rewards more advanced technical, analytical and computing skills. Nevertheless, certain other countries with significant inequities in income among different social strata perform on average significantly better on international standardized tests than do American students (West, 2011).

That structural change generally merits prioritization over additional funding seems to accord with consensus; but exactly what kind of reforms promise to make a difference to educational outcomes? Some argue that the key to reforming US schools lies in untethering them from local control by instituting national standards (Miller, 2009a, p. 207). Others argue in favor of targeting more funds to where they seem most needed – namely inner-city schools – where mobility and choice are more limited (Kotkin, 2008). While the social roots of US educational inequities are complicated, one factor is surely the disparity in inner city versus suburban funding:

> The scandal of American public school finance is that the suburbs... spend nearly twice as much per pupil as [inner city schools]. That is why the average teacher salary in these areas is much higher and that means that the best teachers routinely take to the schools where they earn much more, and much nicer working conditions and facilities and easier-to-teach kids. Until we make it possible and get rid of the old property tax system of school finance... we're not going to be able to get great teachers into poor areas and that's going to hold the country back over the long-term.
>
> (Miller, 2012)

Discussions about the shortcomings of US K-12 education and its centrality to (declining) US "competitiveness" are hardly new (see e.g. Huntington, 1988). It remains somewhat of a puzzle why average annual US productivity growth has outpaced so many of its peers despite lagging educational achievement. One explanation may lie in the role of other growth-inducing factors that effectively substitute for disappointing educational outcomes. According to one conjecture, "there is strong evidence that the cognitive skills of the population – rather than mere school attainment – are powerfully related to individual earnings, to the distribution of income, and to economic growth" (Hanushek and Wossman, 2007). That is, American culture and its educational system arguably promote a type of cognitive skill development poorly captured by standardized tests.

According to Diane Ravitch, Professor of Education at New York University, US schools "promote creativity and imagination when teachers have the time and resources to enable students to experiment, create, and question... Creative thinking grows from asking questions and exploring, not guessing the right answer" (Council on Foreign Relations, 2011b). According to Ravitch, the No Child Left Behind legislation of 2001 has increasingly "trussed and bounded" the nation's educational culture to rigid annual tests. Schools not meeting high national standards face "severe sanctions," with possible closure and mass teacher layoffs ensuing. These high stakes, while inducing higher test scores, might not be encouraging the creative abilities needed for innovation. They also overlook the interpersonal skills required for the jobs of the 21st century (Council on Foreign Relations, November 17, 2011, p. 10).

In their book entitled *The Race Between Education and Technology*, Claudia Goldin and Lawrence F. Katz (2008) conclude that while education outpaced technological change in the first half of the 20th century, technological progress has increasingly surpassed educational improvement since. High skill levels acquired earlier have supported technological progress with a lag, driving economic growth over a prolonged period. Yet, this longer-term dynamic can be expected to encounter diminishing returns in the absence of structural breakthroughs in educational strategies. The needs of inner-city schools represent a special case requiring a much broader societal approach.

Other critics have pointed to the ossified teacher union-backed contracts that prohibit comparative teacher performance as a factor in remuneration and advancement. Increasingly pilot projects and charter schools are working with teachers' unions to modify current ethics of performance and job protection. Non-governmental organizations, such as the Bill and Melinda Gates Foundation and Lumina, meanwhile are throwing significant financing behind systemic educational reforms (Council on Foreign Relations, November 17, 2011, p. 11). Measurable systemic-wide progress will take considerable time. By some estimates, it would take nearly 15–20 years to show significant results from attempts to fix failing US schools (Brill, Council on Foreign Relations, 2011).

Although the rights kinds of investments and reforms in education have potential to increase the quality of US human capital, it bears emphasis that the upgrading of skill sets around the world through formal education and on-the-job training portends higher living standards for citizens everywhere. That is, just like our discussion of national competitiveness more generally, differential educational outcomes are not a zero-sum game.[18]

Foreign students and immigration

Robust immigration has been, and remains, critical to the US economy. A task force report concludes that "more than half the recent growth in the US labor force has come from immigration and nearly all future growth will come either from immigrants or from current workers delaying retirement" (Council on Foreign Relations, 2009). While immigrants represent only an eighth of the US's population, nearly a quarter of all engineering and technology firms founded between 1995 and 2005 were done so by immigrants (*The Economist*, 2011, p. 74). In fact, 40 per cent of all Fortune 500 companies – including Intel, Apple, Google and eBay – were founded by immigrants or their children (Anderson, 2011). Therefore, not only is immigration good for those with "suitcases and dreams" but it is welfare-enhancing for the countries that welcome them.

Yet, US law renders it difficult for skilled workers to stay in the US due to restrictions on H1-B's, a temporary visa sponsored by US employers and granted to specialty workers for three years. Restrictions imposed following September 11th have made it more difficult to procure the visas required to work in the US. After reaching a high of 195,000 H1-Bs in 2003, the number granted has dropped to 65,000 per annum in recent years. This problem is further compounded by a lack of selectivity in the H1-B lottery-based allocation. Prior recipients have often been randomly selected from a much larger pool of petitions without a serious evaluation of credentials. Other nations, meanwhile, have begun to open their borders to individuals who otherwise might have chosen the US. The UK, for instance, automatically qualifies for work visas recent graduates from the world's top 50 business schools. Testifying before Congress, Bill Gates remarked: "it makes no sense to tell well-trained, highly skilled individuals – many of whom are educated at our top universities – that they are not welcome here" (Allison, 2007).

Certain critics of the H1-B program point to studies that claim that the US produces sufficient talent particularly in science and engineering to adequately staff domestic firms (Lowell and Salzman, 2007). Some such studies utilize a narrow definition of skills, thus underestimating the demand for skilled workers (NFAP, 2008a). Those who allege that H1-B holders are "stealing" US jobs, neglect to add that the annual number of H1-B visas represents a miniscule share of the US labor force (NFAP, 2009). In fact, technology companies that hire an H1-B worker on average show a gain of five additional jobs created; and that number jumps to 7.5 among smaller firms (NFAP, 2008b). The notion that companies hire foreign workers to the detriment of Americans simply because they are cheaper is not supported by the data. Hires of H1-B holders appear to rise and fall with the state of the labor market in the same manner as domestic hires (NFAP, 2008b).

The Kauffman Foundation presents the situation in stark terms: "More than one million skilled immigrant workers, including scientists, engineers, doctors and researchers and their families, are competing for [a limited number of] permanent US resident visas each year, creating a sizeable imbalance likely to fuel a 'reverse brain-drain' with skilled workers returning to their home country" (quoted in Pruitt and Philips, 2007). In addition to the scarcity of H1-Bs, US regulations requiring applicants to provide evidence of intention to return to their home country, coupled with improving career opportunities in many countries, are leading to foreign students returning home sooner (Kalra, 2009).

Meanwhile, as discussed above, the US remains the premier destination for international students. Many who studied in the US worked for a time in places like Silicon Valley or Boston's Route 28 start their own businesses upon returning home. Having studied and worked in the US, they often seek partnerships with US firms and with former colleagues. Training foreign students, whether or not they remain in the US after graduation, thus represents a leading manifestation of US prosperity and global influence.

The Kauffman Foundation found that 84 per cent of returning Indian entrepreneurs maintained at least monthly contact with American family, friends and colleagues. For entrepreneurs returning to China, this number was 81 per cent. Such cross-border connectivity spreads ideas concerning customers, markets, technical information and business funding (*The Economist*, November 19, 2011). This "brain circulation" provides a net benefit to both parties and can help ensure that US firms remain at the cutting edge (deVol et al., 2009). "People don't have to choose between two countries... their ceaseless circulation spreads ideas and expertise as the body's blood spread oxygen and glucose" (Newland, *The Economist*, November 19, 2011). In sum, a forward-looking policy is needed to ensure that the US remains open to talented foreign students and highly skilled foreign-born workers who do so much to enrich the US and global economy.

Corporate costs: Health care and taxes

At a time when unit labor costs have been otherwise well contained, the spiraling cost of health care constrains US corporate profitability. While currently 18 per cent of GDP, present trends show the share of the economy devoted to health care reaching 30 per cent by 2030 (Bernanke, 2008b). In contrast, other industrialized nations average around 10 per cent of GDP while insuring that all individuals are covered and without evidence of inferior health outcomes (Miller, 2009a, p. 78). While I defer discussion of government health care-related entitlements to a later chapter, a brief mention here of the effects of health care costs on the private sector seems appropriate.

The ubiquity of employer-provided health care is an accident of US history, having come about during the early 20th century notably because of corporate and union desires to fight the perceived threat of socialism (Miller, 2009a, pp. 62–78). Yet this system, under which 175 million Americans are covered today, accounts for a rapidly increasing percentage of employer costs (Johnson, 2010). Over the last decade the "average employer premiums have increased by 119 per cent while inflation increased by only 29 per cent and wage earnings increased by 34 per cent" (NCHC, 2011).

The present system constrains US companies in several ways. The inability of growing companies to match large corporations in the health care benefits they provide complicates the ability to attract talent. In addition, reluctance to forsake health insurance leads would-be entrepreneurs to forego leaving stable jobs to start their own companies (Baumol et al., 2007). "Employer-based systems... reduce the portability of health insurance between jobs, which reduces labor mobility and the efficiency of the labor market as well as creating a burden for those changing jobs" (Bernanke, 2008b).

Richard Wagoner (2005), former Chairman of General Motors (GM), brought this issue into focus at a 2006 conference: "the cost of healthcare in the US is making American business extremely uncompetitive versus our global counterpart". GM's earlier slide to unprofitability can be traced in part to the increasing cost of health care. The cost of providing health care added from $1,100 to $1,500 to the cost of each of the 4–5 million vehicles GM sold annually (Appleby and Carty, 2005). By 2008, GM was spending more on health care than on steel (Miller, 2009b, p. 78). In the long-run, restoring competitiveness in this regard means the US must move to "untether health care insurance from employment" (Baumol et al., 2007). While President Obama and Congressional Democrats promulgated comprehensive health care reform, they declined to move toward phasing out the current employer-based system. Until reforms rein in medical cost inflation, US companies will continue to suffer a decided disadvantage vis-à-vis their foreign counterparts.

In addition to the costs of health insurance, discussions of corporate competitiveness have long focused on taxes. In a background paper on corporate taxation and competitiveness, the US Treasury echoes the concerns of many business leaders and public officials, noting that "the current system for taxing businesses and multinational companies has developed in a patchwork fashion spanning decades, resulting in a web of tax rules that can harm the competitiveness of US companies" (US Department of Treasury, 2007).

It should be stressed that the burden of taxes on corporations is distributed in complex ways, often representing a form of double taxation. At the end of the day, the US's high corporate tax rate represents a tax on shareholders, employees or the consuming public (Miller, 2008). The country's statutory (federal plus state) corporate tax rate now stands as the highest in the industrialized world at 39 per cent. Even before Japan lowered its statutory rate, the US effective rate on one measure stood at 34.6 per cent, compared with Japan's 29.5 per cent (Chen and Mintz, 2011). While certain estimates of the US effective rate are somewhat lower, industrialized countries other than Japan tend to face effective corporate tax rates in the region of 20 per cent.[19]

Moreover, no other country taxes the foreign operations of its multinational companies. Taxing foreign subsidiaries controlled by large parent firms at high US tax rates threatens to encourage buy-outs by firms from the

UK to Brazil and India, which face lower rates. Aside from losing the "crown jewels" in this way, the US looks to sacrifice export market share as the foreign subsidiaries of these multinational corporations source much of their inputs from the US (Hufbauer, 2012a).

Companies that face high rates tend to locate legal means to shelter income. According to a study by the Government Accountability Office (2008) documenting the federal income tax for corporations from 1998 to 2005, almost two-thirds of all corporations in the US, both foreign and domestically owned, paid no income tax. This suggests that somewhat lower rates coupled with a phasing out of most tax expenditures might raise federal revenues.[20]

A study by the Tax Foundation captures a consensus view that "a nation will not attract new and expanded business and its attendant job creation if its corporate income tax is significantly higher than it is in comparable nations" (Attkins and Hodge, 2005). While one can dispute the absolute nature of this claim noting other advantages of the US business climate for firm expansion and job creation, it is not difficult to understand why a company with tight margins would opt to locate elsewhere to exploit less onerous rates (Moore and Grimm, 2008). For instance, John Chambers – CEO of Cisco Systems – highlights in a *Sixty Minutes* interview how Ireland's 12 per cent corporate tax rate persuaded more than 600 US companies to establish operations there, leading to approximately 100,000 new jobs (Fenton, 2011).

Moving forward, the attractiveness of the US as the location to do business will depend in part on whether the political will to lower effective corporate tax rates can be mustered. Still, corporate taxation represents only one facet of US tax reform. An overhaul of the tax code is ultimately required to reduce the deadweight loss from the current haphazard, inequitable and excessively complicated US tax structure. That issue can only be addressed in the context of the broader fiscal challenges facing the country (see chapter 8).

Financial market reform

The Great Recession has raised fresh doubts about the regulation-light, financial innovation-driven "Anglo-Saxon" model. Heretofore differentiated from other systems owing to its pro-market bias, in recent years US capitalism has arguably degenerated into a more pro-business arrangement involving unprecedented government "bailouts" of failed, albeit politically well-connected corporate interests. There is considerable risk that an incentive structure that once rewarded meritocracy, penalizing failure while facilitating restructuring, could degenerate into an ossified system characterized by stodgy "too big to fail" conglomerates taking excessive risks. An energized populist backlash against the abuses of Wall Street reveals a profound loss of trust in the system, with potentially devastating consequences for its erstwhile dynamism (Zingales, 2009).

The policy response to the recent crisis will not prevent future crises. Periodic breakdowns seem endemic to capitalism; indeed, by some accounts, significant financial crises occur every three or four years somewhere in the global economy. The severity of the recent recession, however, provides a wake-up call on the need for improved regulation of financial markets. And as other countries proceed with their own reform discussions, efforts to coordinate the most consequential changes internationally remain crucial to avoid "regulatory arbitrage."

Two and one-half years after the landmark Dodd-Frank bill was passed, regulators charged with composing the detailed rules of enforcement remained pressured by the financial sector and otherwise beleaguered by those who argue that the framework is too complicated or distortionary. Much remains to be done, notably on overcoming the moral hazard of "too big to fail" institutions, introducing more strenuous capital requirements and limits on leverage, and otherwise realigning the incentives affecting risk taking. Also needed are steps aimed at improving overall transparency and in particular at constraining the purchase of complex financial assets funded by short-term debt (Bailey et al., 2008).

The main functions of a robust financial system include ensuring a safe and efficient means of payment, attracting savings through a diversified menu of vehicles and directing these funds to the economy's most productive investments, and allocating financial risks according to the desire and ability to bear them. By creating a market for corporate control, the financial industry should facilitate the movement of capital from less to more efficient firms. Some of what has passed as financial innovation has performed these functions poorly. In contrast, certain other innovations have contributed importantly to the broader economy.[22]

While more must be done to avoid future situations where "profits are privatized and losses are socialized," a temptation to discourage most financial sector innovation can backfire. As Fed Chairman Bernanke (2008a) has stated, "regulators must consider what can be done to make the US financial system ... more stable, without compromising the dynamism and innovation that has been its hallmark". It seems sheer hyperbole to hear from some critics that the abuses committed with regard to instruments like credit default swaps or mortgage-backed securities proves that financial innovation writ large has been a complete and utter chimera.

Swaps, options and futures, for example, have facilitated the critical function of hedging risk, garnering businesses flexibility in the management of their debt structures and cash flows. These instruments furthermore render corporate debt and equity more attractive to sophisticated investors, while lowering the cost of capital. Venture capital, as well as junk bonds and mezzanine finance, has helped finance new ideas and products. Savers have benefited from the liberalization of deposit ceilings, the elimination of Regulation Q and other means of reducing financial repression. Credit card receivables, and auto and student loan-backed securities have generally facilitated a more efficient spreading of risk across investor classes. And despite the excesses that appeared in 2005–2008, home equity loans, reverse mortgages and even certain mortgage-backed securities arguably have provided a net long term benefit to households. Finally, there is the financial sector's facilitation of globalization, which has enlarged national and world GDP (Litan, 2010, pp. 40–41).

The challenge for regulatory reform, therefore, is to strike a reasonable balance between discouraging innovations that have proved detrimental to the economy-most collateralized debt obligations and structured investment vehicles, for example – while encouraging those innovations that have added value in terms of the major objectives the financial system is supposed to serve.

Final thoughts

Developments in the global economy today often seem to move at warp speed. This rapidity of change, in turn, requires continual investment, innovation and re-skilling. In such a fast-moving environment, general prosperity presupposes a proclivity toward flexibility, including a public willingness to live with dynamic resource reallocation in response to global competition and technological progress. Such changes are socially wrenching. And, as summarized in the section "Remaining challenges," the US must surmount core obstacles in rising to the test.

Nevertheless, the central take-away here is more optimistic. The systemic and institutional pillars underlying US productivity including an ability to continuously push out the technological frontier remain well entrenched. The US retains, in relative abundance, many of the essential prerequisites for maintaining a dynamic, flexible and resilient economy. As it copes with slower growth today, little evidence supports the fear that the US is in danger of squandering its formidable lead in innovation or that its superior labor productivity need be compromised in the longer term. The leading social challenge remains to spread the gains from productivity to a wider segment of the income distribution via more uniformly available quality education, skill acquisition and retraining, and hence a revitalized opportunity for social mobility.

Retaining objectivity amid the emotionally charged and largely misleading debate over national competitiveness requires dispensing with certain antiquated notions. Particularly outdated is the idea that robust growth requires an uncontested across-the-board advantage in basic technologies. Today, substantial two-way cross-border flows occur in cutting-edge, general use technologies or the products embodying them, which are then incorporated as intermediate product inputs into domestic industrial use. The key to improving living standards increasingly appears to be the downstream "absorptive capacity" to acquire and adapt innovations: "The political economy of growth policy has promoted excessive attention to antiquated measures of innovation as a determinant of technological change and productivity growth, to the neglect of attention to the role of conditions affecting access to knowledge of innovation and their adoption" (David, 2003).

A relatively neglected dimension of the innovation process lies in the role played by consumers. Mirroring innovation by corporate consumers of intermediate goods – to fully exploit new technologies firms using advanced inputs must adapt work processes and complementary inputs accordingly – the "venturesome and resourceful" final consumer assumes a comparably vital role. In contrast to the prevalent caricature of US profligacy (see Chapter 4), here the American consumer drives innovation. The American consumer's characteristic willingness to test run new products encourages ongoing product refinement. US-based firms devote a disproportionate share of investment dollars to practical application of ICT in pursuit of the American consumer's discriminating taste. And, after such a test, US firms are better positioned to deliver products that attract strong allegiance around the world.

Perhaps the most profound way in which traditional thinking obfuscates the gains from specialization and trade lies in the very construct of national competitiveness. From an economic perspective, the US (and the rest of the world) can only benefit from the most rapid possible growth in Europe, Japan, China, Brazil or elsewhere. The greater transnational mobility of capital and labor, coincident with the information and communications revolution, allows scientific breakthroughs anywhere to rapidly percolate across borders, stimulating follow-on ideas and commercial tinkering capitalizing on the latest inventions. The rest of the world gains when someone in the global economy produces at lower cost or adds to the variety of goods and services on offer.

Meanwhile, nothing has happened to alter the reality that more technologically sophisticated countries enjoy a comparative advantage in more highly skilled and knowledge-intensive tasks. For what it is worth, any notion that Chinese or other emerging market producers present a broad-scale challenge to US and, more generally, advanced Western firms operating at the technological frontier is premature at best. To accomplish that would require profound alterations in economy-wide systems of innovation, presupposing systemic reforms that lie well in the future.

To sum up, the US has demonstrated distinct advantages in the early phases of major technological waves owing to its openness, less heavy-handed regulation, freedom of entry and exit, liquid and deep capital markets, and labor market flexibility. And it would appear that we are still in the middle stages of a protracted technological revolution in which the US enjoys a substantial first mover advantage. This systemic superiority with applied innovation – the ability to translate basic science and discovery into more and more varied commercial products – will remain critical to maintaining a robust growth rate of total factor productivity over the next half century. The US can realistically be expected to outpace most advanced countries in average annual productivity growth for the foreseeable future, especially in the absence of bolder structural reform in much of Europe and Japan.

In addition to productivity, a necessary condition for longer-term economic growth remains a steady growth in the labor force. Here again, the US continues to wield relative advantages. In addition to higher fertility rates, the openness of American society, if maintained, should ensure a decidedly more rapid growth of its work force. The attraction of aspiring individuals from around the world will remain among the country's leading advantages. But the latter is premised on the ability of the US political system to surmount the current gridlock over immigration reform while waging a full-scale assault on its core educational challenge.

For the most part, globalization has worked for the US. The evidence is overwhelming that increased trade, capital, labor and technology flows over the longer term have accelerated the growth of productivity and living standards (Hufbauer and Grieco, 2005a, 2005b). That globalization, combined with technological change and shifts in product demand, has also increased economic insecurity, depressing wages and aggravating inequality, raises important social challenges. Nevertheless, a key test of its global leadership remains the ability of US leaders to credibly defend the net welfare gains from open markets and transnational mobility.

4
Macroeconomic Foundations: Global Imbalances and the Dollar

A leading historian once equated the US economy with the dinosaur (Ferguson, 2006). Like the diplodocus or brontosaurus, it roams the earth but must "consume almost incessantly to sustain its great heft." What caused the dinosaur's extinction? Presumably, a sudden meteor or global climate change provided "too little time to evolve and provided smaller and more dynamic life forms with an opportunity to take over." Analogously, excessive foreign indebtedness has rendered the US – a veritable *debtlodocus* – vulnerable to one or another shock and on the verge of surrendering its global status.

As former Treasury Secretary Lawrence Summers famously quipped, "there is something odd about the world's greatest power being the world's greatest debtor" (2004a). Underpinning such sentiment is invariably an analogy drawn with 19th/20th century Britain. Just as the UK's fall paralleled the loss of its net creditor status, with outsized external liabilities the US likewise courts closure to its global position today. Invoking evocative metaphors, like the "balance of financial terror" and "dependence on the kindness of strangers," prominent observers have tapped into public angst over reliance on fleeting foreign capital.

The Great Recession added grist to the mill, with many ascribing underlying causal blame to long-neglected global imbalances – the persistent deficits and surpluses in external trade and finance. Although an earlier "hard landing" hypothesis forecast a cataclysm arising from such imbalances, the crisis that materialized was other than the one predicted. Born in the very epicenter of global capitalism, the Great Recession nonetheless saw the dollar strengthen and Treasury yields decline, confounding the prognosticators.

Even as the world economy began to rebound, the "hard landing" paradigm enjoyed a revival (see e.g. Bergsten, 2009). Proponents cited renewed dollar weakness and foreign creditor clamor for alternative reserve assets as comeuppance for endemic overconsumption and "imperial overstretch." According to such critics, the expansionist bias of US macroeconomic policy, the fragility plaguing its financial system and an explosive national debt trajectory portend the more classic "hard landing" scenario catalyzing economic and geopolitical decline. With the events of 2008 helping to moderate global imbalances, predictions abounded that such progress would prove short-lived.

In Chapter 3 I argued that the longer-term, microeconomic foundations of US power remain robust. This chapter claims that the macroeconomic sinews of power, as reflected in US financial relations with the rest of the world, likewise remain sturdy. Variables that have sparked much angst in recent years – including household savings, trade deficits, external indebtedness and the dollar – together tell a more constructive story than is reflected in much popular commentary.

This chapter argues that external imbalances mirror endemic structural features of the global economy inadequately captured by caricatures of US profligacy. For the foreseeable future, US capital markets, product markets and the dollar will continue to comprise a global public good. Meanwhile, the US government, large firms and creditworthy households continue to benefit from abundant finance on attractive terms; and US "external indebtedness" has some way to go before approaching precarious levels. Little about its financial relations with the rest of the world today suggests the dangerous level of vulnerability often presumed. Continued excess demand for dollar-denominated assets, particularly "zero-risk" treasuries, if anything, reflects and reinforces US predominance (Levey and Brown, 2005a).

Finally, global imbalances were not a root cause of the Great Recession on a par with excess leverage, failed regulation and capital misallocation. A global excess demand for (ostensibly) safe US assets helped to facilitate the sub-prime crisis; but global imbalances per se, involving a net inflow of capital, proved incidental. A future hard landing that involves a precipitous drop in the external value of the dollar cannot be precluded. More likely, however, global imbalances will unwind gradually in response to slower-moving structural developments and mounting incentives for policy makers in core countries to adopt key reforms.

The remainder of this chapter is organized as follows. First, two broad perspectives are contrasted on the causes and effects of global imbalances. One argues that chronic overspending in the US requires foreign capital to finance its external payments deficit. The other views capital inflows as driving US trade deficits. Second, against the backdrop of concerns over US overstretch, I dissect the prominent "twin deficit" hypothesis linking fiscal and trade deficits. Third, core requirements of the global adjustment process are outlined, including an expanded role for domestic demand-led growth and currency appreciation in current account surplus countries. Foreign creditor willingness to maintain the current pace of lending versus the purported incentives – economic and political – for peremptory dollar "dumping" are evaluated. Finally, the chapter assesses the role of global imbalances in the Great Recession and its potential to trigger a future crisis.

The current account deficit and foreign "debt"

The variety of hypotheses advanced to explain persistent global imbalances in trade and finance is impressive; and the latter's causes and consequences continue to be the subject of lively debate. On one fact everyone agrees: the US has long been running large annual deficits on the current account of its balance of payments, the difference between what US residents spend and earn abroad. This external deficit rose gradually in the 1980s and early 1990s, later exploding from a moderate 1.7 per cent of US GDP in 1997 to around 6.5 per cent of GDP by the fourth quarter of 2005. In response to the dollar's broad-based depreciation during 2002–2007 but subsequently as a consequence of recession, the current account deficit has declined to the neighborhood of 3 per cent of GDP. Still, prominent voices forecast a reflation of imbalances once the economic recovery accelerates.

Persistent current account deficits, by definition, mean that the US government, households and corporations collectively have been importing more goods and services than they export; equivalently, the nation has been spending more than it produces. Filling the gap has been foreign capital. The latter involves an increase in (net) foreign financial claims that must be serviced through future interest and dividend payments to external creditors. Such claims represent a right to future purchases of US goods and services.

The US net international investment position (NIIP) – the difference between the foreign assets of US residents and the US assets of foreign residents; the result of that string of current-account deficits and associated foreign financing – in recent years stabilized in the (negative) 16–22 per cent of GDP range, albeit sharply up from (negative) 5.8 per cent of GDP as recently as 1995 (see Figure 4.1).[1] Having temporarily jumped to –$3.26 trillion in 2008 from –$1.79 trillion in 2007, the potentially explosive trajectory of the NIIP, popularly but misleadingly referred to as the country's "net foreign debt," reignited concern. The alarm proved short-lived as the NIIP shrank back in 2010 by some 5 per cent of GDP (from –22.6 to –16.9 per cent). However, 2011 saw the NIIP jump to $4 trillion or over 26 per cent of GDP.

Unpacking the NIIP into its major sub-components places US external financial relations into perspective. Notwithstanding a nearly uninterrupted string of current account deficits and associated "borrowing" from abroad over a generation, US foreign direct investment and other equity claims still exceed the cumulative stock of foreign resident equity claims on the US.[2] The overall imbalance in financial claims, therefore, mostly reflects debt claims – that is, net US borrowing from foreign residents.

Driving the fear of a "hard landing" has been a long anticipated precipitous decline in the willingness of non-US residents to hold increasing quantities of dollar-denominated paper. Such a slowdown in foreign resident desire to accumulate dollar assets would cause the dollar to tank, interest

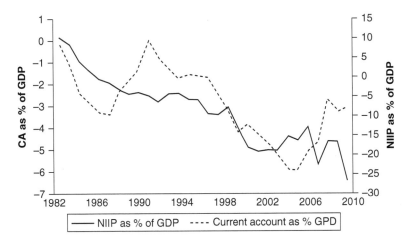

Figure 4.1 Current account and the NIIP as a percentage of GDP, 1982–2011
Source: Bureau of Economic Analysis; International Monetary Fund, World Economic Outlook Database, September 2011.

rates to skyrocket, US stock and bond markets to plunge and the economy to re-descend into recession or even depression.

To paraphrase Russian revolutionary Vladimir Lenin in a rather different context, the relevant question is "what is to be done?"[3] A first step surely is to understand the forces that precipitated this situation. The following macroeconomic truism provides a convenient starting point:

National savings – domestic investment = current account balance (CAB)

More precisely,

(Private savings + public savings) – investment = CAB

This identity holds for all countries at all times. It states that, ex post, national (private plus public) saving net of investment (purchases of plant, equipment, software and new home purchases)[4] must equal a country's current account balance annually.[5] Private saving includes household saving (the residual income with which individuals purchase financial assets after paying taxes and consuming goods and services) and corporate saving (retained earnings) plus depreciation allowances to finance the replacement of capital equipment. Public savings capture the consolidated (federal, state and local) government balance between revenues and expenditures; a budget deficit, therefore, connotes "dis-saving." Countries whose national saving exceeds domestic investment effectively export these surplus savings (capital) to countries with a residual demand for (foreign) saving. Therefore in the US today a surplus of domestic investment over national saving requires a net importation of foreign saving, the (financial) "capital account" counterpart of the current account deficit.[6]

While seemingly straightforward, the net saving/current account identity actually masks a rich cocktail of interactive economic forces and policy decisions, domestic and foreign. The goal, therefore, should be to penetrate beneath the proximate influences to get at the more fundamental, underlying drivers. Some additional clarity is suggested by the following related identity,

$$(\text{Saving} - \text{investment})_{\text{us}} = (\text{investment} - \text{saving})_{\text{row}}$$

where 'us' and 'row' connote the US and the rest of the world, respectively. The US saving/investment balance, or equivalently its current account, must by definition equal the investment/saving balance aggregated across all other countries. While certain countries may be running current account surpluses and others deficits of varying magnitudes, all countries excluding the US, on aggregate, must exhibit a current account surplus (net savings surplus) equal in magnitude to the corresponding current account deficit (net savings deficit) in the US.

Among the global economy's principal current account surplus countries are some of the world's largest economies – Japan, China and Germany.[8] Joining them are other East Asian economies and a more geographically dispersed group of energy exporters. That these two groups of current account surplus countries have accounted for the bulk of the current US trade (current account) deficit in recent years is clear from Table 4.1.

While the bilateral surpluses of China and Japan account for virtually half of the overall US trade deficit in 2011, China's large final goods exports actually incorporate large quantities of industrial materials, components and semi-finished products imported from China's neighbors. Supplementing such imports from Thailand and Indonesia (among others) are significant capital goods imports from Japan to China's enterprises, many of which are owned and operated by foreign multinationals. A significant share of annual US trade deficits thus reflects the exports of US (and other) foreign multinational subsidiaries in China. Therefore bilateral US trade deficits with particular Asian economies are understated, reflecting an intricate intra-Asian division of labor centered on China as manufacturing hub.

There has long been a secular increase in petroleum imports as a share of the trade deficit and US energy consumption. Such energy was imported from a variety of sources including OPEC and US neighbors Canada and Mexico. Today, however, imports as a share of US petroleum consumption have dropped to 40–45 per cent (down from roughly 60 per cent). Moreover by early 2012 the US became a net exporter of refined petroleum products

Table 4.1 US trade with top trading partners, 2011

Rank	Country	Percentage of total US trade deficit
	Total, all countries	100.0
	Total, top 15 countries	79.9
1	Canada	4.9
2	China	40.7
3	Mexico	9.0
4	Japan	8.6
5	Germany	6.8
6	UK	−0.7
7	Korea, South	1.8
8	Brazil	−1.6
9	France	1.7
10	Taiwan	2.1
11	Netherlands	−2.7
12	Saudi Arabia	4.6
13	India	2.0
14	Venezuela	4.3
15	Singapore	−1.7

Source: US Census Bureau, data as of February 2012.

and is poised to become a net exporter of liquefied natural gas owing to technological advances in the recovery of domestic shale gas. Such trends will progressively lessen the need to import hydrocarbons, particularly from outside the Northern hemisphere, lowering the energy component of the trade deficit in the future.

Yet, the US trade imbalance still presents its puzzles. In particular, large US trade deficits with emerging and developing economies confound conventional economic logic (Lucas, 1990). Historically, low- and middle-income developing economies have tended to run current account deficits. Given their modest capital stocks, hence high potential returns to incremental capital investment, poorer countries theoretically enjoy relatively strong growth potential; yet they face greater challenges in generating adequate domestic savings to fund the requisite investment. Therefore, according to traditional thinking, poorer countries should import the surplus savings of richer countries that already possess a sizeable capital stock. At least that is what economists once believed.

It thus seems paradoxical that the predominant importer of global savings has been the world's richest country. Such a pattern of "uphill" resource flows – from poorer to richer – strikes many as incongruous and even perverse. This paradox is in part explained by two factors. The first is that emerging market growth today may no longer be negatively correlated with current account balances (Kose et al., 2009). The second is that developed economies that still enjoy robust productivity growth – the US in particular – may continue to offer higher risk-adjusted returns on investment.

The global imbalances debate: An overview

The orthodox perspective

Consider two stylized, polar arguments concerning persistent global imbalances.[9] The more orthodox perspective can be summarized as follows. With households whose savings rate out of real disposable income collapsed from an average of 8 per cent during 1950–2000 to virtually zero in the early 2000's, coupled with a 5–6 per cent of GDP deterioration in the federal budget from the Clinton to Bush administrations (not to mention further recession-related deficit deterioration under Obama), the US has played the tipsy 800 pound gorilla staggering out of control. Debt-turbocharged over-consumption generates chronic trade imbalances. These trade deficits, in turn, require financing, effectively compelling foreign residents to provide the incremental resources to close the US saving–investment gap. In effect, the domestic structural imbalances and policy errors that generate the US current account deficit suck resources from abroad like some giant vacuum.

While greater expected real returns once may have attracted capital to the US – the latter half of the 1990s represented a period of exceptional dynamism – more recently, current account deficits have mirrored (unproductive) public and private consumption. Meanwhile, current account deficit financing has involved debt issuance to foreign central banks rather than foreign direct investment and portfolio equity inflows from profit-maximizing, private investors (Roubini, 2006a). Particularly worrisome is that the rapid accumulation of dollar assets in the coffers of foreign central banks will likely prove transient; few countries will seek to accumulate reserves at a comparable pace in the future (Feldstein, 2005). In fact, the share of US dollar assets in international portfolios has long since exceeded sustainable levels.

Saving little, Americans financed otherwise unaffordable imports by tapping into equity from an inflating housing stock or via ballooning credit card debt (Roach, 2006). Predictably, this asset-driven (or debt-based) consumption would ultimately unwind with the bursting of the real estate bubble. In short, Americans ran up consumer debt to precarious levels. Capital investment meanwhile was channeled to the non-traded sector (e.g. residential real estate and health care) rather than into tradables (exports and import-competing goods and services), where it could have generated the export capacity to comfortably service external debts. With import levels much higher than those of exports, the restoration of balance on the current account required an implausible jump in sustained export relative to import growth. Stabilizing the deficit would demand "discontinuous changes in growth rates, patterns of demand, or relative prices of different countries' output" (Summers, 2004b, p. 5).

In heralding the likelihood of a "hard landing," early proponents of this consumption binge story also lay major blame at the doorstep of expansionary macroeconomic policy (Roach, 2006; Setser and Roubini, 2005). Underpinning this argument was typically some variant of the "twin deficit" hypothesis: the effects of meager household savings (discussed above) are reinforced by chronic public dissaving. Not only are fiscal deficits and current account deficits highly correlated but a unidirectional causal relationship can be posited: a deteriorating fiscal posture largely explains the deteriorating trade position (see e.g. Bergsten, 2009). Although external factors contributed to imbalances, the real crux of the problem lies with Washington. The US stands at the precipice facing a stark choice: restore fiscal (and monetary) stability or risk prompting jittery foreign creditors to sever the country's tenuous financial lifeline.

While long integral to the over-consumption story, the deterioration in the medium-term fiscal trajectory has thrust public balances back to center stage. Foreign creditors predictably opine: how can this contradictory cocktail – of twin wars, tax cuts, monetary stimulus, and explosive entitlement spending – be unwound in the presence of such deep-seated political inertia? The impending hard landing – to be triggered by a strike on funding US deficits – promises pain all round. Hardly the behavior one expects from a (benign) hegemon!

A heterodox perspective

An opposing view on current account imbalances has been advanced over recent years. The US has lured significant foreign savings with the expectation of higher risk-adjusted returns. This characterization of US external deficits is concisely captured in an early statement by a former Federal Reserve Board vice chairman:

> First, higher productivity growth boosted perceived rates of return on US investments, thereby generating capital inflows that boosted the dollar. Second, these higher returns boosted equity prices, household wealth, and perceived long-run income, and so consumption rose and savings rates declined. Under this explanation, all of these factors helped to widen the current account deficit.
>
> (Ferguson, 2005, p. 5)

Others would add that the lower risk premium on US assets reflects a durable political stability, solid corporate governance, and the liquidity and depth of US capital markets.

Table 4.2   Official foreign exchange reserves: Asia and oil exporters

Billions of US dollars	2000	2007	2009	2011	June, 2012
Asia					
China	193	1,440	2,386	3,181	3,305
Japan	362	973	1,049	1,295	1,273
Korea, South	110	263	266	311	312
Hong Kong	106	147	245	285	295
India	44	267	259	296	290
Singapore	80	164	187	238	243
Oil exporters					
Russia	28	386	399	499	514
Algeria	14	104	149	186	n/a
Saudi Arabia	n/a	n/a	408	541	n/a
UAE	15	27	37	55	n/a

Source: International Monetary Fund, International Reserves and Foreign Currency Liquidity Database; The World Fact Book, reserves of foreign exchange and gold, CIA.

The marked resurgence in US productivity growth in the 1990s, meanwhile, was followed by a "global savings glut" or, alternatively, investment drought (Bernanke, 2005, 2007, 2011). Investment rates in emerging economies turned down relative to levels prior to the Asian financial crisis. In parallel, chastened policymakers, elected to build up large foreign exchange reserves to guard against future capital reversals (see Table 4.2). Supplementing this precautionary motive for the buildup of reserves have been export-led development strategies premised on managed exchange rates. That is, the increase in foreign exchange reserves can in part be explained by the purchase of insurance against future financial crises or as the by-product of a mercantilist development model.

As discussed in Chapter 1, a feature of financial globalization today is that emerging markets are net recipients of private capital flows.[10] Many of these flows reflect foreign direct investment in long-gestation projects as well as shorter-term portfolio inflows. Yet, much of this capital – supplemented by the receipts from trade surpluses – has been recycled to the developed economies (especially the US) via the investment of foreign reserves in lower-risk assets. In sum, given a shortage of viable domestic investment projects or their rudimentary financial system's limited capacity to allocate capital efficiently, emerging Asia parked its surplus savings largely in US treasuries.

Meanwhile, by furnishing a variety of low-risk securities including treasury bills, notes and bonds, and quasi-governmental agency paper (Fannie Mae and Freddie Mac) against its current account deficit and equity investment abroad, the US has demonstrated its comparative advantage as the world's banker or, if one prefers, "venture capitalist" (Gourinchas and Rey, 2005). From this perspective, robust net capital inflow seeking largely (but not exclusively) safe liquid assets requires an equally large US current account deficit. Such a win–win arrangement facilitated by financial globalization befits the leadership role of a public goods-providing hegemon.

To sum up, one can tell at least two alternative internally consistent stories about global imbalances. For the one, foreign thriftiness finances US profligacy. For the other, US capital markets provide ready outlets for surplus global savings. In one case, the current account drives capital flows; in the other, capital flows drive the current account. Moreover, these perspectives track closely the division between those who view global imbalances as inherently unstable, largely a US responsibility, and anticipate a hard landing, on the one hand, and those for whom imbalances reflect a relatively stable equilibrium and systemic co-dependency, on the other (see e.g. Xafa, 2007).

The twin deficits and household debt

The reader will recall that Paul Kennedy's "imperial overstretch" concerns state overextension owing to ever-expanding foreign entanglements. Meanwhile, as we will see in Chapter 8, the US fiscal deficit arguably represents *the* economic constraint on US global power today, even if domestic mandatory entitlement-rather than national security-related-spending represents the primary driver. Moreover, at the heart of the orthodox perspective on global imbalances is a notion of chronic overconsumption (under-saving) – a kind of macroeconomic overstretch (see e.g. Levey and Brown, 2005). Thus, to the extent that one demonstrates a high correlation and, better yet, a causal relationship running from fiscal deficits to current account deficits, one is well on the way to constructing a neo-declinist-cum-overstretch thesis.

In numerous accounts one confronts phrases like "dependence on the kindness of strangers" with the focus invariably on China's purchases of US public (or quasi-public) debt. That this provides a would-be rival with dangerous leverage represents a plausible concern (Setser, 2008). Alternatively, that the Chinese (among others) have little choice but to hold US assets and thus that the US may, counter-intuitively, enjoy the greater leverage has also been argued (Drezner, 2009). Otherwise, the twin deficits are viewed as crowding out productive investment. The state over-spends, leveraging the future by (unproductively) consuming foreign resources that must be serviced and paid back.

Proponents of the "twin deficit" hypothesis focus on the early 1980s and the first half decade of the 21st century, two periods during which fiscal and trade deficits moved broadly together. Yet, during other periods, such as the

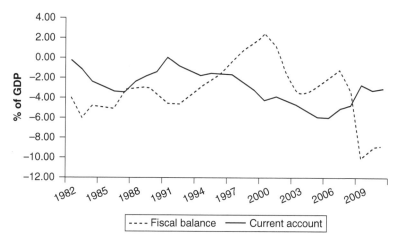

Figure 4.2   Current account and fiscal balance as a percentage of GDP, 1982–2011
Source: Congressional Budget Office, Bureau of Economic Analysis.

late 1980s, the 1990s and 2008–2010, the opposite proved the case – the current account improved (deteriorated) even as the budget moved increasingly into deficit (surplus). As recently as 2000, for instance, the US ran a current account deficit as large as 4 per cent of GDP while the budget was in surplus; and the current account deficit continued to deteriorate in 2005–2006 even as the fiscal balance improved further (see Figure 4.2). Associated with the fallout from the Great Recession, moreover, has been a declining current account (as a share of GDP) amid an exploding fiscal deficit. Econometric attempts to establish a robust causal link running from budget deficits to trade deficits in the US and elsewhere have generally proved disappointing.[11]

As discussed, conventional wisdom holds that the US runs current account deficits largely owing to deficit spending. But in the run-up to the financial crisis the finger was increasingly pointed at the decline in private savings. While certain observers have ascribed such behavior to a growing culture of profligacy, such moralizing seems misguided. Standard economic models hold that households tend to target a ratio of net worth to income in order to maintain a smoother life-time pace of consumption. Increasing current consumption in response to a perceived (permanent) increase in asset values accordingly represents predictable behavior. In the event, like populations in Spain, Ireland, Iceland, the UK and Australia, Americans took advantage of an ample credit supply and low borrowing rates as their nominal wealth climbed.

Presumptions of profligacy are beside the point. If an individual has overdrawn her credit card or can no longer pay her mortgage, adjustment is inevitable. In the event the increase in US debt-financed consumption ultimately proved costly. Having risen to $66 trillion by the end of 2007, household net worth subsequently fell by some $12 trillion in 2008, recovering to $60 trillion by end of 2011 (Federal Reserve, June 2012). The situation proved considerably worse for the median American family.[12] Although Americans ran up debt often to maintain living standards in response to slowing income growth, they overdid it and paid a price. Over longer periods US consumption has changed broadly in line with income.[13]

Moreover, the national income and product accounts tend to understate saving and investment. One reason is that these accounts exclude so-called "intangible investment," which is particularly important for the US.[14] Spending by businesses on new product development, workplace reorganization, worker training, branding and "knowledge-creating" activities in general, including some R&D, is treated not as investment – that is, activities to expand future consumption via stimulation of new ideas and technologies – but as intermediate costs of current production. Experts at the National Bureau of Economic Research and Federal Reserve earlier estimated that perhaps $1 trillion of "intangibles" per annum are missed in this way (Nakamura, 2001). Nobel laureate Edward Prescott and colleagues estimate that net intangible investment in the business sector climbed to over 8 per cent of GDP in the 1990s, before returning to its pre-early 1990s level of around 3 per cent in 2001 (McGrattan and Prescott, 2010). Over the period 1993–2000, they estimate that the difference in labor productivity growth due to the inclusion of intangible investment is as much as 0.8 per cent per annum.

Equally misleading may be the treatment of saving in the national income accounts.[15] For example, even though it raises life-long income prospects, investment in human capital, such as higher education, is not considered a form of saving (Cooper, 2005). Nor is the productivity-enhancing, on the job human capital accumulation, so-called "e-capital," that accompanies intangible investment. Thus both measured savings and investment in the US are probably understated, although the extent to which this is the case is open to debate.

In addition to the claim that Americans chronically under-save, some decry a dangerous shift in the deployment of foreign savings. External borrowing may have been warranted when resources were allocated to investment, but not once imported saving ostensibly went to finance consumption. One problem with this claim is that it is impossible to trace microeconomic patterns back to specific foreign funds. For example, central banks no doubt fund government consumption, but only because they must hold risk-free, liquid assets. But these purchases bid up bond prices, prompting private holders of government debt to sell and deploy their savings elsewhere. Furthermore, private capital still accounts for the bulk of foreign assets in the US, notwithstanding the more recent increase in officially held assets.

As the difference between savings and investment, an important point about the current account balance can also be made. First, the value added by foreign affiliates of US-based multinationals can exceed the scale of US exports by a factor of three or more (Chandler, 2009; Norloff, 2010, pp. 90–91). Rather than exporting from the US, these firms often find it more efficient to serve other markets from their foreign subsidiaries. Most of these firms are majority owned by American shareholders, accounting for investment income that helps American consumers and firms afford additional imports. Secondly, the globalization of production ensures that parts and services are partitioned to multinational branches all over the world. Much of what is recorded as US imports is provided by US multinationals, including intra-firm trade. Moreover, these imports create US jobs involving unloading, storage, transportation, marketing, advertising and accounting, to name a few. And, finally, the two-way flow of capital trumps by a wide margin the flow of goods and services into and out of the US.

One implication is that the balance of payment accounting that informs the global imbalance debate appears increasingly outmoded. Foreign exchange strategist Mark Chandler, for example, writes:

> The [balance of payments] is not necessarily a fair measure of the economic competitiveness of a particular country. It does not measure the economic prowess of the United States. It raises more questions than it answers. The BOP overweights the value of finished goods and under-weights the value of intellectual property. It doesn't reflect the way that multinational corporations operate, slicing, dicing, and distributing their operations around the world where it may make political and economic sense, for reasons that far outstrip comparative advantage as traditionally understood. And it causes people to make the wrong decisions that might actually hurt the US economy.
>
> (2009, p. 17)

Current account sustainability and adjustment: The special role of China

As discussed in the section "The current account deficit and foreign 'debt'," the US current account deficit cannot unwind without a rise in investment relative to savings in the rest of the world. US fiscal tightening or increases in personal savings can accomplish little without accompanying shifts in private saving and investment and/or complementary policy actions in Europe, Asia and elsewhere. As US spending for decades has been the principal locomotive for global economic growth (see e.g. International Economy symposium, 2007) it is unsurprising that the financial crisis-induced reduction in US domestic demand coincided with a global recession, despite significant macroeconomic stimulus elsewhere.

Heretofore, the relative (un)willingness among East Asian emerging markets plus industrialized Japan (as well as other large current account surplus economies, such as Germany) to countenance greater domestic demand growth limits the ability to reverse global imbalances. China takes center stage here as much of emerging Asia focuses on maintaining export competitiveness with its formidable neighbor. In addition to an outsized current account surplus of 11 and (almost) 10 per cent of GDP as recently as 2007 and 2008, respectively, China consistently attracts sizable foreign direct investment. The latter, combined with speculation over imminent currency revaluation and controls on capital outflow, explain the excess demand for renminbi (yuan) until fairly recently.[17] Until mid-2005, the Chinese maintained a rigid dollar peg. With China's persistent balance of payments surplus, maintaining the peg required regular currency intervention and accumulation of foreign exchange reserves. To date, Chinese authorities have proven only partially successful in sterilizing these foreign exchange inflows.

By July 2005 the Chinese appeared to yield to mounting international pressure for exchange rate adjustment. But their modest 2.1 per cent revaluation of the renminbi/dollar rate, combined with the adoption of a "managed floating" exchange regime based on a reference basket of currencies, had in the view of many observers failed to generate a change in the renminbi's real effective exchange rate sufficient to contribute meaningfully and sustainably to lower global imbalances. This is despite a cumulative 20 per cent yuan appreciation against the dollar up to September 2008, after which China reverted to a de facto dollar peg.[18] Much indignation has been directed at the meagerness of yuan appreciation (see e.g. Goldstein and Lardy), yet little convincing evidence has been offered as to how even a large yuan appreciation would reduce the US current account deficit significantly (see e.g. US Congressional Budget Office, July 2008). With the Chinese share of US exports and imports at around 13 per cent in 2011, a further 10 per cent revaluation would lower the nominal effective exchange rate by less than 2 per cent, exerting a negligible impact on the deficit. In the event, the yuan's pace of real appreciation – moderately faster nominal appreciation combined with higher Chinese inflation – has more recently been in the range of 10 per cent per annum. Consequently, the broad consensus is that the undervaluation of the renminbi has declined considerably in recent years.

One also needs to consider the large import content of Chinese exports. Only part of recorded exports represents Chinese value added – the value added to that already contained in the materials and intermediate products imported from neighboring countries that are then incorporated via final assembly into manufactured exports. By lowering import costs, a yuan revaluation would not be reflected in commensurately higher export prices. Moreover, even if currency appreciation were to slow China's export growth, some of the reduced Chinese share of US markets would be captured by still lower-cost competitors such as Vietnam (CBO, 2008). The implicit suggestion that Chinese revaluation would spark an automatic and equivalent revaluation in China's neighbors remains largely hypothetical (Cooper, 2005).

Furthermore, Chinese authorities exert less control over the exchange rate than is often assumed. While China can target the nominal exchange rate by accumulating the excess supply of dollars in the form of reserves, it cannot effectively control the real exchange rate – the relevant variable for resource allocation in the economy. While the relationship between the real effective exchange rate and the savings-investment balance remains poorly understood (Engel, 2009), one knows that changes in the exchange rate are associated with alterations in the trade balance only if the difference between national savings and investment is equivalently altered. Currency appreciation alone would generate lower inflation, leaving the real exchange rate unaltered. If this policy were allowed to culminate in deflation, economic growth would be depressed, as Japan's experience attests.

Although the quantitative contribution of international trade to China's growth is often overstated,[19] there is no disputing China's extraordinary reliance on investment. Meanwhile, the high savings rate reflects such factors as an underdeveloped social safety net and weak financial markets. Some attribute the surplus of domestic savings to China's one child policy: families of young Chinese men attract (scarcer) female partners through the lure of accumulated financial assets. Controlling for other factors, the level of savings appears to be higher in regions where the male/female disparity is greatest (Wei, 2010). Large national savings can also be attributed to the profits of non-dividend-paying enterprises. One certainly cannot blame low investment for the current account surplus as Chinese investment rates rank among the highest in the world.

At the time of writing, both the US current account deficit and China's current account surplus have declined to a more manageable range around 3 and 2 per cent of GDP, respectively.[20] Although whether these (lower) levels can be sustained is unknown, we know that China's exchange rate regime will fail to reduce global imbalances unless Chinese consumption rises. Increasing the national share of labor income and consumption has been a principal objective of the last few five-year plans. Since the savings–investment balance remains a matter of deep-seated structural change combined with stiff resistance by vested interests to the abandonment of export-led growth, one cannot be sure how successful such policy efforts will be in reducing external imbalances over time.

Exorbitant privilege

Former French Finance Minister Valéry Giscard d'Estaing coined the derisive term "exorbitant privilege" to decry chronic US balance of payments deficits in the 1960s (Eichengreen, 2011). This highlighted the US ability to consume in excess of what it produced, financing the difference at low cost in its own currency. Yet, such deficits were the vehicle for meeting the demand for dollars in the rest of the world during the Bretton Woods period, 1944–1973. Upon the collapse of the gold exchange standard, the dollar was de facto reconstituted as the global currency under the flexible exchange rate system introduced in 1973. Thereby the US retained its status as issuer of the international currency as the old periphery (Europe) under "Bretton Woods I" passed the baton to the new periphery (emerging Asia) of "Bretton Woods II."

While many currencies fluctuate freely against the dollar today, much of Asia, the Middle East, and parts of Latin America, remain on an effective dollar standard. According to Bretton Woods II proponents (Dooley et al., 2003), this arrangement remains stable, with East Asia in particular seemingly content to export more than it imports, adding to its financial claims on the US, and with the US obliging via an open goods market and ready supply of financial assets. As the world's principal reserve currency, the US retains the effective ability to print dollars and use them to purchase real goods and services from abroad – that is, to earn seigniorage. This neat trick will continue as long as the rest of the world is willing to hold additional dollar-denominated assets.

Yet, financial history casts doubt on the sustainability of a "net foreign debt" that climbs indefinitely as a share of GDP (Cooper, 2005; Edwards, 2005). For the NIIP/GDP ratio to stabilize presupposes a prior stabilization of the current account and, therefore, of the trade balance (trade and non-factor services), the main sub-component of the current account (see Table 4.3).[21] Comparing the NIIP to another stock variable like US national wealth arguably makes more sense than comparing it to an annual flow variable (GDP), and marketable US wealth may be some four times the level of GDP.[22] Nevertheless, an NIIP approaching (say) 80 per cent of GDP would likely be associated with a politically unfeasible share of US wealth held by foreigners (Mussa, 2006) and would likely trigger overwhelming protectionist pressure well before that point (Bergsten, 2006).

Stabilization of the trade deficit has long seemed urgent because a second sub-component of the current account – net investment income (current receipts of dividends and interest earned on the existing stock of US assets abroad minus comparable payments on US foreign liabilities) – has long

Table 4.3   US current account

	Billions of US dollars						
	1995	2000	2005	2008	2009	2010	2011
Current account	−113.6	−416.3	−745.8	−677.1	−381.9	−441.9	−465.9
Trade and non-factor services	−96.4	−376.7	−708.6	−698.3	−379.2	−494.7	−559.8
Investment income	20.9	19.2	68.6	147.1	119.7	183.8	227.0
Unilateral transfers	−38.1	−58.8	−105.7	−125.9	−122.5	−131.1	−133.1

Source: US Bureau of Economic Analysis (2012).

been expected to turn negative. If foreign residents hold claims on the US so much larger than the stock of claims held by US residents abroad, all other things equal one would expect a net flow of interest and dividends out of the country. That the US has remained a net international income recipient (despite a highly negative NIIP) remains the subject of much controversy. As Table 4.3 shows, net foreign investment income averaged $171 billion during 2009–2011.

This puzzle has given rise to a number of hypotheses. First, the positive investment income balance reflects certain properties of US external assets and liabilities, including:

(1) higher (measured) returns on US direct investment relative to comparable assets in the US;
(2) a greater relative share of (higher yielding albeit relatively riskier) equities and relatively smaller share of (lower yielding but less volatile) debt in US foreign assets.

First, factor (1) seems especially puzzling because one wonders why foreigner residents should consistently earn less on their equity investments in the US (see e.g. Curcuru et al., 2007). After adjusting for exchange rates and other risk factors, foreigners seem to earn lower returns in the US in every major investment category (Forbes, 2008). These differential returns are in turn amplified by a third factor: increasingly large gross inflows and gross outflows. Larger flows (in both directions) serve to leverage up even modest differentials in financial returns (see also Kroszner, 2008).

Second, the anomaly between the (negative) NIIP and (positive) net income receipts has fed speculation of unrecorded claims. Two Harvard economists thus advocated capitalizing net investment income to attain more realistic estimates of gross US foreign assets (Hausmann and Sturzenegger, 2005, 2006). They conjectured that discounting future cash flows would increase measured US foreign assets, reflecting the contribution of unmeasured "intangible capital," intellectual property incorporated in US service exports and foreign direct investment.[23] Economist William Cline likewise concluded "that the United States has remained a persistent 'economic' net creditor throughout the past three decades despite its transit into (measured) net debtor status 15 years ago" (Cline, 2005, p. 61). The upshot is that in a meaningful economic sense the US may have remained a net creditor as long as (actual) returns on US direct investment trumped payments on foreign debt (Cline, p. 54). In sum, at times the NIIP may exaggerate the US's real (external) burden.

Such conjectures remain contentious. And in any case one would expect the international investment income offset to a (negative) trade balance to disappear eventually. In the event, the trade balance would need to improve merely to offset increasingly large foreign debt service; otherwise the current account deficit could explode.[24]

The relevant issue is how soon the US approaches a binding external funding constraint. Catherine Mann (2009) argues that one should worry less about the US's "ability to pay" than foreigners' sustained "willingness to lend." The main concern is that external deficits will outpace foreign demand for the growing supply of US financial assets. Under an explosive fiscal scenario, an implausibly large share of incremental foreign wealth would have to be invested in US government assets (Mann, 2005, pp. 55–56).

If ongoing political paralysis causes the US to fail to slow the increase in its stock of debt, such fears could well be realized. Under less dire fiscal circumstances the US need for incremental foreign capital would not so obviously outpace foreign willingness to lend.[25] Indeed, the US may be pressured to run current account deficits as long as foreign wealth flows to the country as the leading global source of marketable assets. Such a scenario would be aggravated by another "risk off" episode, which would drive global capital toward "safe" assets. In contrast, if "home bias" were to reassert itself, countries with large financing requirements like the US would find it more difficult to attract funds at attractive rates (Broda and Piero, 2009). And if global confidence *were* to evaporate, "the pace of [dollar] depreciation [would] turn into a rout that jeopardizes the reserve currency status of the dollar ... " (Clarida, 2009).

According to the textbooks, the reversal of trade imbalances requires expenditure-reducing as well as expenditure-switching policies. The former refers to the need for the growth of domestic spending – consumption and investment – to fall relative to the growth of output, or, equivalently, for savings to rise relative to investment in deficit countries, mirrored by the opposite pattern in trade surplus countries. By rendering the country's exports less expensive, currency depreciation (expenditure-switching) can help to facilitate the desired reallocation in demand away from foreign to domestic goods.

One oft-cited early study (Obstfeld and Rogoff, 2004, 2005) foresaw a rapid dollar depreciation of as much as 30–35 per cent against a broad group of currencies to facilitate the needed current account adjustment. Another (Cline, 2005) anticipated a roughly comparable real effective depreciation against major currencies to restore a more sustainable trade (current account) balance. In the event, since February 2002 the dollar declined by some 25 per cent through 2011. This decline was particularly pronounced against the euro and considerably less so against the emerging Asian currencies. The sub-prime crisis as well as the Greek (EMU) sovereign debt crisis temporarily stalled this trend dollar decline owing to "flight to safety" effects.

As mentioned above, the measured NIIP during 2002–2007 deteriorated by **only a fraction of** cumulative US current account deficits. In addition to factors cited above concerning rates of return on US versus foreign assets, dollar depreciation also contributes. Dollar depreciation slows NIIP deterioration because US foreign assets increase in dollar terms while virtually 100 per cent dollar-denominated liabilities remain unaltered. Thus exchange rate adjustment can be prolonged as currency valuation effects "finance" part of the (gradually falling) current account deficit (Cavallo and Tille, 2006). Such effects have proved extremely powerful (Gourinchas and Rey, 2005), at least until 2008, when the dollar appreciated, and again once its depreciation resumed in 2009.

Yet, such forces can work in reverse as well. In both 2008 and 2011 the country's recorded net external liabilities increased sharply, well in excess of US current account deficits in these years. Such apparent deterioration in the underlying US external balance actually reflected greater global confidence in the US. Driving the deterioration in the NIIP was a surge in global demand for the perceived safest currency and asset, the USD and treasuries. In addition, NIIP deterioration reflected comparatively weaker conditions abroad, hence relatively poor performing US-held assets in places like Europe.[26] In sum, whether the country's measured net external liabilities improve or worsen year to year, flexibility in the USD's exchange rate, a stable US international (direct and portfolio) equity asset balance and persistently strong global demand for safe USD debt assets affords the US added degrees of freedom, helping it fulfill hegemonic functions while smoothing or transferring the real burden of macroeconomic adjustment.

Are the dollar's reserve currency days numbered?

The dollar's prominent role in global trade and finance represents a hallmark of US hegemony. It reflects the country's high labor productivity, relatively positive demographic outlook, the depth and liquidity of its financial markets, and its military and political clout. Moreover, by rendering the current account deficit more sustainable, the dollar's reserve currency status can for a time augment investment and consumption possibilities, indirectly consolidating domestic support behind the resource commitments necessary to maintain hegemony. That its dominance has been maintained even as the dollar's value against other currencies has declined and as the weight of the US within the global economy has diminished reflects the benefits of incumbency. It is simply more convenient to use the currency with which most international trade and finance is already conducted.

With the advent of the EMU, the basis for the dollar's unchallenged stature appeared to have ended. Before the flare-up of the euro sovereign debt crisis, for example, economists Menzie Chinn and Jeffrey Frankel (hereafter CF) (2008) predicted that the euro could replace the dollar as the dominant reserve currency as early as 2015. They hypothesized that reserve currency status depends on the size of the home economy (region), the depth and liquidity of financial markets, the currency denomination of existing official reserves and debt issuance in the global capital markets. CF also incorporate in their analysis the number of countries that peg to a particular currency and the extent to which one currency invoices global commodities or is used for foreign exchange intervention. Preventing an otherwise more rapid transition from the dominance of one reserve currency to another are "network externalities" – the inertia caused by the economies of scale and scope when so many other countries use a reserve currency. They analogize to the tepid pace at which the dollar replaced the pound sterling, despite the prior emergence of the US as the dominant economic power.

Several objections can be raised about such analysis. First, although the dollar's share of reported global reserves has receded, the decline has been gradual. The successful euro experiment would have predicted a certain rise in its global role after being introduced in 1999; yet, the dollar retains a roughly 60 per cent share of reported reserve assets compared with about 25 per cent for the euro.[27] Moreover, some of the decline in the dollar's share reflects valuation effects. That is, some "passive investment" in euros occurs as authorities accept a growing share of euros in total reserves simply from euro appreciation. In contrast, many central banks respond to dollar depreciation by buying more dollars so as to maintain a roughly constant share in their portfolios. Adjusting for valuation changes, the dollar may account for a some 4–5 per cent higher share in the composition of global foreign exchange reserves than is indicated by official IMF figures (Brown and de Kock, 2012).

Second, euro capital markets lack anything approaching the liquidity found in dollar markets. The euro sovereign debt market actually comprises 17 separate national segments, offering (increasingly) varying yields. Such segmentation lowers liquidity relative to that of the unified dollar market. For example, within the EMU the lowest risk sovereign asset is considered to be German government bonds. Yet the market for bunds is dominated by German banks and other longer-term holders who are seldom sellers, lowering the residual marketable supply. The euro-denominated corporate debt market likewise remains a fraction of the size of the comparable dollar market.

Third, although the EMU debt crisis may for a time constrain the progressive substitution of euros for dollars, CF are right that many economic variables – for example, the growing weight of the eurozone with the accession of more countries and the growing depth and liquidity of euro markets over time – predict a gradually expanding euro weight in global capital markets. The policy response to the current eurozone crisis that could catapult the euro to a greater role in global finance would be a true fiscal union, including the issuance of eurobonds that represent the "joint and several" guarantee of the member countries. But this would involve a seismic shift for which there does not yet appear to be sufficiently broad political support.

A final factor supporting the dollar's dominant role concerns politics (Posen, 2008).[28] CF allude to countries which tolerate exorbitant privilege in exchange for security benefits derived from the exercise of US power. Such non-economic motives arguably provide far more explanatory power than CF ascribe, as to why so many countries peg or manage their currencies against the dollar compared with relatively few non-contiguous countries that use the euro as their reference currency. It may also help to explain why non-US residents invest so much of their assets in the US despite relatively low notional returns. Europe today shows little inclination and possesses insufficient strategic assets to assume a global security role comparable to that of the US. The US would have to abuse this role through a successive string of foreign policy debacles, or engage in consistently disastrous economic policies, before its leading reserve currency status would be subjected to serious pressure.

Recent preoccupation with the renminbi's potential to rival the dollar appears even more premature. While Chinese economic growth has been extraordinary, and China enjoys net creditor status, the development challenges China faces over the next decades remain formidable.[29] Financial markets would have to evolve at an (implausibly) rapid pace, including a strengthening of the banking system, an expansion of domestic bond and equity markets, a progressive dismantling of capital controls and the achievement of full currency convertibility before the renminbi can assume a prominent companion role to the dollar and the euro. But one should certainly envision an expanding international role for the renminbi over time (Eichengreen, 2011).

Global imbalances, "safe" assets and financial crisis

Former Federal Reserve Chairman Alan Greenspan famously characterized the absence of higher longer-term interest rates in the US in response to monetary tightening as a "conundrum" (see e.g. Greenspan, 2003, 2005; see also Bernanke, 2005). In hindsight, a few explanations offered remain plausible. The first is declining "home bias" – that is, a fall in the (traditionally high) correlation between national saving and domestic investment rates around the world.[30] Before the recent recession at least, investors became increasingly less risk averse and hence more willing to invest abroad. Consequently, gross cross-holdings of foreign assets and liabilities increased markedly (Cavallo and Tille, 2006). The second is the confluence of a "global saving glut" (or, more accurately at times, investment drought) that coincided with robust US growth and heightened financial innovation. In effect, the US current account deficit and low rates mirrored a structural saving surplus elsewhere in the world economy. Such savings largely flowed to the country with the heretofore strongest growth dynamic, investment protection and array of financial assets (Balakrishnan and Tulin, 2006).

A complementary, persuasive argument has also been made (see e.g. Caballero, 2006, 2009) that helps to explain Greenspan's conundrum: emerging markets possess a demand for safe stores of value not offered by their underdeveloped financial markets. The resulting excess demand for treasuries, the global "riskless asset," drove up prices, lowering treasury yields in the early 2000s. Moreover, as the decade progressed, US capital markets responded entrepreneurially to the excess demand for treasuries and "search for yield" by holders of low risk assets whose returns were dragged down with treasuries.

The specific "solution" came via exotic financial structures, like collateralized debt obligations (CDOs). With the blessing of AAA ratings from the credit agencies, at least for the "upper tranches" of these CDOs, investors willingly held these opaque assets in return for somewhat higher yields. Basel II rules perversely incentivized investors including Western European banks, to favor mortgage-backed assets as they required lower capital charges than the original mortgages.

Had housing prices not collapsed, such financial intermediation may have succeeded in satisfying the excess global demand for "safe" assets without triggering a crisis. Securitization provided an inventive, albeit, in retrospect, hazardous, vehicle for maturity and risk transformation between foreign demand for liquid short-term public assets, on the one hand, and (decidedly less sound) longer-term, private residential mortgage debt, on the other. In reconciling global supply and demand for financial assets, the US banking and shadow banking system accommodated global demand, albeit via dangerous leverage and credit enhancement (Gros, 2009).

While foreign central banks were rarely exposed to sub-prime and derivative "toxic" assets, through their heavy purchases of treasury and agency paper, they furnished incremental liquidity to US financial markets, helping to drive down rates. In response, less risk-averse investors scrambled for higher risk-adjusted returns. This interpretation hardly absolves financial institutions, regulatory supervisors or the US Congress of irresponsible risk taking, excessive leverage, financial opaqueness and over-promotion of home ownership. In the event, the housing bubble burst with a vengeance, even as financial engineering exploited moral hazard to the hilt.

Does this mean that global imbalances played a major causal role in the crisis? Max Corden (2011) reminds us that trade imbalances represent a form of inter-temporal trade which under normal circumstances should generate mutual gains from trade. Given domestic saving that exceeds investment, surplus countries look to lend resources to deficit countries, in order to augment the former's consumption and investment possibilities in the future. In contrast, deficit countries with profitable investment projects gain by deploying foreign capital today. In principle, therefore, the associated net resource inflow to the US could have proved beneficial. That such potential gain went unrealized mirrored pervasive, perverse incentives at the heart of the financial, regulatory and legislative system, distorting economic signals and misallocating capital. In sum, while imbalances may have exerted a subordinate, indirect influence by, as the former chief economist of the Bank for International Settlements puts it, "the equivalent of allowing undergrowth to accumulate in a forest" (White, 2009), it would be akin to "looking a gift horse in the mouth" to blame an inflow of inexpensive foreign resources (that could have been put to productive use) for a crisis ultimately centered in the domestic financial system.

It has been argued that global imbalances "facilitated, if not overtly induced, the overleveraging and underpricing of risk" (Bergsten, 2009, p. 24). It seems as persuasive to argue that the causality was reversed: excess leverage and underpriced risk worked to induce capital inflow. That is, foreign investment in unsound US securities would not have been maintained were fewer high-risk US loans and derivatives originated in the first place. Moreover, such capital flows would likewise have been lower had regulators been more vigilant in restraining Wall Street from transforming long-term mortgage risk into short-term opaque securities (see Brender and Pisani, 2010; Munchau, 2009).

Furthermore, in ascribing major responsibility for the crisis to net capital flows, which even at their earlier peak amounted to less than 7 per cent of GDP, one is really raising more fundamental doubts about the US financial system's effectiveness in intermediating a much greater quantity of gross capital inflows and outflows, not to mention a still greater quantity of domestic savings (Dooley and Garber, 2009). If an under-satiated desire to lend to the US fundamentally reflected an imbalance in the global supply and demand for low-risk assets, the latter hardly required net capital inflows (global imbalances) per se.[31]

Thus, at its core, the Great Recession was born on Wall Street, in the halls of Congress, and in the regulatory institutions and credit rating agencies, not in emerging Asia, Middle Eastern oil exporters or other surplus countries.

Unconstrained credit provision to uncreditworthy borrowers and failed regulatory oversight over core financial practices sowed the seeds of crisis. At best, foreign capital inflow further lubricated the pistons that allowed a faulty engine to keep operating.

Looking forward, preoccupation with the prospects of a "sudden stop" in which US capital inflows precipitously slow and reverse conflates the experience of emerging markets with that of the richest developed economy. In some respects the lessons from emerging markets *are* germane. As with emerging market crises, in the Great Recession, capital inflow interacted with financial market distortions.[32] But to equate the US financial system and economy with that of the emerging markets seems a stretch even in these times.[33] One must thus concur with the assessment of a former IMF chief economist: "The United States does not have the economic and financial characteristics where a sudden massive run by foreign investors out of US based assets is a high probability event" (Mussa, 2006, p. 78).

In the future, a key to the reversal of current global trade and financial imbalances remains the ability of emerging economies to progress on financial market reform. With the maturation of financial sectors, households will find it easier to borrow to finance consumer durables, education and home ownership, demonstrating less need to accumulate large nest eggs (Eichengreen, 2006). As with most aspects of development, a meaningful revamping of the social safety net takes time. Such eventualities will also demand macroeconomic adjustment in the US, including the kind of household deleveraging currently under way as well as credible medium- and long-term fiscal consolidation. Barring shifts from export to domestic demand-based growth in the principal surplus countries however, US current account deficits may have to persist for an extended period (Cabellero et al., 2006).

For some, the prospects of re-enlarging global balances remain an especially ominous sign for future global economic stability. They implore key deficit and surplus countries to coordinate macroeconomic adjustment (under the auspices of the G-20 and the International Monetary Fund (Frieden et al., 2012). The obstacle however is an evident lack of confidence in the ability of the key players to overcome their collective action problem given strong vested interests and conflicting national objectives. Therefore, the persistence of (more moderate) US current account deficits might be realistically viewed as a transitional, structural necessity for the global economy – effectively a public good the US has long provided as importer and banker of last resort.[34]

Conclusion

The term "global imbalances" connotes an unstable disequilibrium in the world economy. Does this accurately describe what has been, at least until the Great Recession, an environment broadly supportive of global trade and economic growth?

During the bubble years, US households assumed excessive debt based on the belief that "housing prices never fall." In so doing, they responded to incentives provided by mortgage originators, credit rating agencies, the financial system and politicians. The US has since been in the throes of significant deleveraging. Historically, however, US household consumption has broadly mirrored income growth. Moreover, the downward bias of measured saving and investment suggests that attributing long-standing global imbalances to US "overconsumption" is unjustified.

US fiscal policy has likewise been blamed for global imbalances. Although evidence for the "twin deficit" view linking the federal budget and the current account is weak, medium-term fiscal consolidation in the US remains a crucial objective in its own right as discussed in chapter 8. Meanwhile, for US national saving to increase (and for its current account deficit to decline) a reduction in net saving and higher domestic demand growth in current account surplus countries is equally required. Yet, for many such countries this presupposes a profound economic and political transformation and is thus likely to be gradual and intermittent. As long as excess net demand for US financial assets persists, at least moderate US current account deficits can be expected to continue.

Meanwhile, claims that currency diversification by foreign central banks threatens the dollar's status seem shakily grounded. While no doubt compromised in the crisis, US financial markets remain unparalleled in depth and liquidity. The dollar's long touted vulnerability moreover presupposes reliable substitutes for holding wealth and providing other critical functions of international money. While it has acquired the attributes of a bona fide reserve currency, the crisis within the EMU will attenuate the euro's potential global role for some time. To the extent that Europe and Japan continue to encounter fiscal and financial fragility, the euro and yen are even less likely to offer a viable alternative to US treasuries and US dollar-denominated bank deposits. Moreover, the renminbi will not be in a position to assume a serious reserve currency role for the indefinite future. And neither the special drawing right nor gold remain realistic core reserve assets.

That hegemony is incompatible with "net debtor" status has become a veritable article of faith. All other things equal, it is true, the higher a country's external liabilities the greater the probability of default or currency crisis. Yet, for the US not everything else is equal. Owing to its leading reserve currency status and the economic, political and military fundamentals underlying it, the US enjoys greater, albeit not unlimited, degrees of freedom. Despite a string of current account deficits, it has been able to keep its stock of net external liabilities reasonably contained even as other countries have run up (negative) NIIP/GDP ratios two or three times that of the US (Bertraut el., 2008). Once one considers the specific composition of its liabilities and the nature of its structural interdependencies with other economies, the underlying picture appears still less ominous. Although the US will not enjoy its "exorbitant privilege" indefinitely, only naïve empiricism would equate debtor status per se to an erosion of global position:

> Despite the fact that even the enormous US economy is now more beholden to the whims of international financial markets, given its deep capital markets, powerful financial institutions, and enormous influence within the International Monetary Fund (IMF), globalized finance enhances the relative power of the US compared to virtually every other state in the world.
>
> (Kirschner, quoted in Brooks and Wohlforth, 2008)

If avoiding decline presupposes net creditor status, one is tempted to turn one's attention to the macroeconomic imbalances, financial fragility, reform inertia and demographics facing net creditors in Europe and Japan. As argued in Chapter 3, moreover, a key ingredient in sustaining global power involves remaining a pacesetter in technological innovation and productivity. Microeconomic dynamism, in other words, can loosen some otherwise binding macroeconomic constraints.

Part IV

Global Public Goods and the Re-ascent of China

5
Human Security: US Leadership on Counter-Proliferation

Among myriad transnational challenges, the threat of weapons of mass destruction (WMD) proliferation surely ranks among the more perilous. At a March 2012 summit in Seoul, President Obama laid out his longer-term vision for a nuclear free world, stating that "Nuclear terrorism is one of the most urgent and serious threats to global security" and "this is one of those challenges in our interconnected world that can only be met when we work as an international community." Seven years earlier, Senator Richard Lugar had conducted a survey assessing the chances of a nuclear attack somewhere in the world within the next ten years. Some 60 per cent of experts placed the risk between 10 and 50 per cent (Lugar, 2005). Indeed, "it's hard to find an analyst or commentator on nuclear proliferation who is not pessimistic about the future" (Potter and Mukhatzhanova, 2008).

Having reviewed the constituent dimensions of US power in Parts II and III, Part IV explores how such assets can be leveraged to provide global public goods. This chapter focuses on the campaign to combat nuclear proliferation.[1] What does Iran's pursuit of the bomb, in the face of intense international pressure, reveal about the limits of US power? Does North Korean intransigence over its nuclear weapons program support the case for waning US influence? Can the US and allies render negligible the prospects of al Qaeda or the Pakistani Taliban assuming effective control of nuclear weapons or fissile material?

The rest of the chapter is organized as follows. The section "Global public goods" reviews the basic logic of hegemonic stability theory. The latter remains the main inspiration for the idea that the predominant state in the system ensures the provision of vital public goods for the global community. Following a summary of US-led initiatives to date in the section "US leadership in nuclear counter-proliferation: An overview," we turn our focus to three ongoing threats to nuclear non-proliferation – those involving "rogue" regimes, "fragile" states and transnational terrorists. The section "Nuclear ambitions" examines efforts to combat nuclear proliferation in North Korea and Iran. The section "Nuclear terrorism and weak states" addresses the confluence of nuclear weapons and fissile materials with weak states and terrorist movements, focusing on Pakistan. Summary reflections on the implications for US power follow in the section "Conclusion."

Global public goods

International relations scholars have long debated the conditions necessary to ensure an adequate provision of "global public goods." The latter include everything from safeguarding critical sea lanes, through maintaining a reliable global monetary standard to securing the stable inter-state balance of power in strategically vital regions. Some argue that it takes the predominant state to ensure that core public goods are provided in sufficient quantity.[2] According to this view, less prominent actors lack the collective incentive to adequately furnish such vital stability- and wealth-enhancing services. Since public goods are, by definition, non-rivalrous and non-excludable, most nations can afford to "free ride."[3]

In practice, a hegemon need not conduct or finance all public goods provision. For instance, Japan, Saudi Arabia and other allies helped to underwrite the US military campaign during the 1991 Gulf War. Various navies partner with the US to patrol pirate-infested waters off the coast of Africa or in the narrow Strait of Malacca. World Trade Organization members agree to abide by and collectively enforce the principles of non-discriminatory trade. And supplementing the US dollar in its role as monetary numéraire are the euro and other less prominent reserve currencies. Numerous other examples of interstate cooperation can be cited. Yet, a widely held presumption remains that adequate delivery of core public goods more often requires a hegemon to prod and coordinate less prominent actors in collective action.[4]

Economic historian Charles Kindleberger applied this insight to the hegemon's charge to ensure the smooth functioning of a liberal world trading order.[5] In principle, a similar logic can be extended to any good, service or institution which provides broad-based benefits to the global citizenry. By virtue of its weight within the international system, the predominant state is able and willing to deploy its resources to maintain the existing global order. The legitimacy and other gains garnered by the leading state incentivizes it to help stabilize a world lacking more developed institutionalized governance. Such "benign" hegemony involves a commitment to lead in building institutions and in providing services benefiting the global community.[6]

US leadership in nuclear counter-proliferation: An overview

Possession of nuclear weapons today remains confined to a relatively small club of states. When the Non-Proliferation Treaty (NPT) was ratified in 1970, only five states – the permanent members of the United Nations (UN)

Security Council (including Russia, China, France, the UK and the US) – possessed nuclear weapons. Three non-NPT signatories – Israel, India and Pakistan – have crossed the nuclear threshold since NPT ratification.[7] For several decades this club of eight has remained fixed, notwithstanding President John F. Kennedy's forecast of a world filled with two or three times as many nuclear powers.

Agreements with South Africa, Libya and several Latin American nations dissuaded additional states from pursuing nuclear weapons programs. Following the collapse of the Soviet Union, programs to de-nuclearize the former Soviet republics of Ukraine, Kazakhstan and Belarus served to further stem the tide. Moreover, through successive bilateral agreements under the Strategic Arms Reduction Treaty (START), the US and Russia made steady progress toward a reduction of nuclear stockpiles. In 2012 the US and Russian presidents signed a new START, reducing nuclear arsenals by a third: "The United States and Russia have halted and reversed their nuclear arms race to a degree that would have astonished most of the framers of the NPT" (Lettow, 2010, p. 15).

As the leading nuclear state, the US has led the charge on counter-proliferation. It effectively maintains a nuclear umbrella for states facing nuclear weapons-aspiring neighbors: "The US nuclear arsenal is qualitatively different from all others. Uniquely, it is, in critical respects, an instrument of nonproliferation. In important cases, countries that could easily develop nuclear weapons have refrained because of explicit or implicit protection afforded by the United States" (Lettow, 2010, p. 16). Spurred by the conviction of four leading statesmen,[8] President Obama meanwhile has committed, under appropriate conditions, to shepherd a transition to a world altogether devoid of nuclear weapons.

Before this longer-term vision of a nuclear-free world can be realized, the imminent emergence of a nuclear Iran and the apparent full-fledged nuclear ascension of North Korea represent central challenges to the NPT-centered regime. By reducing the prospect of military measures against them, nuclear status can embolden such states. In response, a Saudi Arabia, Egypt, Turkey, Japan or South Korea could embark on its own nuclear weapons program, sparking regional arms races. Aside from increasing opportunities for a disastrous accident, an expansion in the number of nuclear weapons states would diminish the effectiveness of the US nuclear deterrent (Mandelbaum, 2005, p. 44). The prospect of weapons grade fissile material falling into the hands of extremist non-state actors in fragile states like Pakistan represents a still more ominous threat to global security.

Since the 1970s the US has led a series of initiatives to curb WMD proliferation. The first was the landmark NPT.[9] As the bedrock of the international nuclear non-proliferation regime, the NPT requires non-nuclear state parties to agree to refrain from acquiring or assisting in the development of such weapons, and for existing nuclear states to work towards steady disarmament. "The American government took an active part ... in coaxing and cajoling other countries to sign [the NPT]. Once it was in place, moreover, the United States assumed more responsibility than any other country with its terms" (Mandelbaum, 2005, p. 44).

Following NPT ratification, the US proposed the formation of a Nuclear Suppliers Group (NSG) in response to India's nuclear test of May 1974. The NSG established guidelines to impose "safeguards not only on the export of nuclear materials and equipment but also on the export of nuclear technology (e.g. engineering, design, and industrial information)" (Spector, 1996, Appendix F). Although not an NPT signatory, India, at the behest of the US, agreed not to share sensitive material and technology with other states. Starting with a small band of member countries, the NSG has since grown to include 46 nations committed to stopping the trafficking of nuclear materials and technology.

The dissolution of the Soviet Union in 1991 gave voice to concerns over "loose nukes." In response, Congress passed the Cooperative Threat Reduction (CTR) program, authorizing funds to help Russia and three other former Soviet republics housing nuclear weapons with three critical tasks: "to destroy nuclear weapons, chemical weapons, and other weapons; to transport, store, disable, and safeguard weapons in connection with their destruction; and to establish verifiable safeguards against the proliferation of such weapons" (Walker, 2006). The impetus behind CTR, better known as Nunn–Luger, has been to keep WMDs out of the hands of terrorists and aspiring nuclear regimes. As of 2010, Nunn–Lugar has been credited with dismantling 7,514 nuclear warheads, and destroying 768 intercontinental ballistic missiles and 32 nuclear submarines (Lugar, 2010). At minimal cost these initiatives have proved vital to the non-proliferation effort.[10]

In 2002 the So San, a joint Spanish and US force, interdicted a North Korean cargo ship suspected of weapons trafficking en route to Yemen. Packed alongside bags of concrete were Scud missiles and conventional warheads. However, the joint force lacked the legal authority to seize the cargo or prevent the ship from continuing to Yemen. (Under the Law of the Sea Treaty, ships cannot be stopped on the high seas except by a vessel bearing the same national flag). Spearheaded by the US in May 2003, the Proliferation Security Initiative (PSI) aims to interdict the transfer or transport of weapons of mass destruction, their delivery systems and related activities. Consequently by 2003 the BBC *China*, a German ship carrying nuclear parts used in centrifuge construction, was stopped en route, denying Libya equipment for its clandestine enrichment program (Boese, 2005). Interdiction since has been facilitated by enhanced intelligence sharing and by the strengthening of national and international legal frameworks to support PSI efforts (Coyle and Samson, 2009, p. 3).[11] South Korea's initial reluctance to participate threatened the PSI's viability vis-à-vis North Korea (O'Hanlon, 2009, p. 218). With US encouragement, South Korea joined the group in

May 2009, strengthening PSI's effectiveness in minimizing the trafficking of sensitive nuclear materials and technology across East Asia. Today, PSI boasts 94 members.

In sum, US initiatives like NSG and PSI, together with congressional programs like Nunn–Lugar, have galvanized international cooperation behind enhancing safeguards for nuclear materials and technology: "The United States took the lead in establishing and overseeing the work of each of these organizations; and a significant part of the technical and human assets of the American intelligence community was devoted to the surveillance of nuclear-weapons related activities around the world" (Mandelbaum, 2005, p. 47).

Nuclear ambitions

Iran

One of today's widely acknowledged security threats involves Iran's alleged aspirations to become a nuclear weapons state. This clerically-controlled regime underwrites terrorism in the region, publically embraces the destruction of Israel, and has pursued a nuclear policy of secrecy and concealment. The US has led international efforts to stanch Iran's pursuit of a nuclear weapons program.

The right to pursue civilian nuclear power is outlined in Article IV of the NPT, and the Iranian government has persistently proclaimed its sole interest in the use of nuclear-generated electric power. Article IV remains problematic because fissile material production constitutes a relatively modest technical advance from civilian energy usage. Former International Atomic Energy Agency (IAEA) Director General Mohamed ElBaradei has thus called the spread of enrichment and reprocessing capabilities the "Achilles' heel" of the nuclear non-proliferation regime. A group of 13 nations, including Iran, currently possess a uranium enrichment or plutonium reprocessing capability for potential weaponization (Dombey, 2007).

In 1957 the US and Iran signed a nuclear cooperation agreement. Ten years later a US firm, AMF, helped to build the Tehran Nuclear Research Center. In the early 1970s a subsidiary of Siemens began working on two nuclear reactors at the Bushehr power plant, while a French company initiated development of two reactors at Darkhovin. In the mid-1970s, Iran concluded nuclear fuel contracts with France and the US for a share in the Eurodif uranium enrichment plant. When Iran expressed an interest in establishing a domestic enrichment capability, the US and South Africa supplied it with enrichment technology and yellow cake.[12] US President Gerald Ford even considered approving the "reprocessing of US material in a multinational plant in Iran." At that time Iran's amicable relations with the West placed its nuclear program on a strong footing (Zarif, 2007).

With the 1979 Iranian Revolution and hostage crisis, the US ceased to supply fuel for the US-built research reactor. French, German and Chinese contractors working at Bushehr and Dakovin withdrew, leaving Iran with unfinished projects. US-led pressure effectively contained Iran's nuclear development.[13] In addition, the US suspended hundreds of millions of dollars of arms sales to Iran while bringing a sanctions case to the UN.[14] Although the UN failed to pass a sweeping sanctions resolution, the US persuaded Western European states and Japan to ban arms exports to Iran. This policy seemed to embolden Iran's pursuit of nuclear energy independence and alleged efforts to develop a nuclear weapons program.

During the 1990s the US imposed some of its toughest measures against Iran. Executive Orders 12957 and 12959 involved embargos on commercial transactions with the Islamic Republic. Congress later passed the Iran–Libya Sanctions Act, targeting US and non-US companies that invested more than $20 million in Iran's energy sector. Financial sanctions that target corporations knowingly or unknowingly linked to terrorism or proliferation activities represent relatively new initiatives. Stuart Levey (2008), former Under Secretary for Terrorism and Financial Intelligence, remarks: "While private companies traditionally seek to evade sanctions ... [they] ... are reluctant to be associated with specific Iranian programs once they are revealed to be linked to illicit activities, such as terrorism financing, money laundering or nuclear proliferation."

Since July 2006 the UN Security Council has passed a series of resolutions supporting sanctions in response to repeated Iranian defiance. Resolution 1696 demanded that Iran suspend uranium enrichment. After Iran refused, Resolution 1737 froze the assets of individuals and entities linked to Iran's nuclear and missile programs, demanding that Iran cooperate with the IAEA, the UN nuclear watchdog. Resolutions 1747 and 1803 expanded the list of sanctioned entities, with the latter placing a ban on the export of nuclear- and missile-related dual-use goods to Iran (UNSC, 2008). Resolution 1929 imposed a complete arms embargo; banned Iran from any activities related to ballistic missiles; authorized the inspection and seizure of shipments violating these restrictions; and extended the asset freeze to the Iranian Revolutionary Guard Corps and the Islamic Republic of Iran Shipping Lines.

Although China and Russia have resisted the most onerous US and European measures,[15] multilateral compliance with Iranian sanctions nonetheless advanced. For example, Russian President Dmitry Medvedev banned the delivery of S-300 missile air defense systems, a deal reportedly worth $800 million, as well as the shipment of tanks, armored vehicles, helicopters, ships and missiles (UPI, 2010). Moscow also barred entry to any individuals linked to Iran's nuclear program and placed a ban on Russian investment in numerous Iranian companies. Having long maintained warmer relations with Tehran, these measures represented a significant shift in Russia's stance.

Such developments foreshadowed a global community increasingly united around stepping up the pressure on Iran. The combination of unilateral and multilateral sanctions raised the costs of non-compliance. In particular, the Iranian oil industry has faced difficulties purchasing needed equipment, and Tehran has struggled to import sufficient refined petroleum to meet domestic demand (Warner, 2010). Fuel subsidies have been cut, prompting waves of public protest. Former President Rafsanjani told the council of experts, "we have never been faced with so many sanctions," urging the country's officials to, "take [them] seriously" (Erdbrink, 2010).

More recent sanctions on Iran's banking system have hindered the country's ability to receive payment for oil, its principal source of foreign exchange and government revenue. On June 28, 2012 the US started barring foreign banks doing oil-related business with the Central Bank of Iran from access to the US financial market. And as of July 1, members of the European Union have been prohibited from buying Iranian oil. Although the sanctions targeting the Central Bank were scheduled for implementation some six months after the US Congress passed the bill in December 2011, Iran's currency – the rial – depreciated by 10 per cent immediately following the announcement. Since 2010, the rial has depreciated by more than 60 per cent against the dollar, suggesting that multilateral sanctions had begun to bite (Xinhuanet, 2012). In early August 2012, Congress agreed on a new round of stiffer sanctions targeting Iran's energy, shipping insurance and financial sectors.

Sanctions expert Gary Hufbauer has described the recent sanctions regime imposed on Iran as among the most vigilant such efforts in the last century, given its emphasis on Iran's vital oil sector and on Iran's isolation from the global financial system (Hufbauer, 2012b and 2012c).[16] In addition to Europe's initiatives, Iranian enemy (and US ally) Saudi Arabia has increased its oil production to compensate for Iranian oil shipments being cut in half. In addition, India, Japan, Korea and China have all capped their purchases of Iranian oil. Exacerbating these actions has been the cut off of insurance for international tankers carrying Iranian oil. Meanwhile, the US has forced international banks to effectively cut their business ties with Iran lest they risk being closed out of the US financial system. (The US dollar's primacy in global transactions renders this decision reasonably straightforward). The US Treasury has also become more adept at identifying efforts to evade these restrictions; and most evasion has diverted Iranian business to less reputable (less safe) "second-tier" banks. It is even conceivable that sanctions can be tightened further via a more extensive ban on relations with Iran's central bank and even more provocatively, via cyber war directed not at nuclear centrifuges but rather at electronic transaction clearing in Iran's banking system.

Tehran has responded by threatening to shut down the strategic shipping channel, the Strait of Hormuz. Iranian Vice President Mohammed Reza

Rahimi vowed that "not a drop of oil will pass through the Strait" if more sanctions were imposed (Burleigh, 2012). To cope with the sanctions the Iranians have created new front companies, reflagged oil tankers and have attempted to open new financial channels. Such actions and threats remind one of the asymmetric tactics available to Iran, including efforts to disrupt traffic through the strait, or unleash terrorist proxies in neighboring states. In addition to generating spikes in global oil prices such tit-for-tat international and Iranian actions threaten to escalate into a military conflict.

That Iran has yet to achieve nuclear power status can, at least in part, be attributed to the success of earlier initiatives like NSG and PSI in attenuating the trafficking of WMD materials and technology across borders. Ongoing efforts to up the ante, targeting increasing numbers of banks, companies and individuals linked to Iran's clandestine programs have constrained financing. The ability to retard Iranian nuclear efforts is also epitomized by the Stuxnet computer malware, which in destroying centrifuges is estimated to have set back the Iranian program by some 18–24 months. An additional harsh deterrent has been contracts placed on Iranian nuclear scientists.

Such varied tools of dissuasion have no doubt raised the costs for Tehran while retarding its nuclear timetable. The logic is that diplomatic isolation and punitive sanctions could eventually persuade the Iranians (and other states intent on pursuing nuclear weapons programs) that the costs outweigh any tangible gains. The principal alternative to a mix of diplomacy, sanctions and show of force would be a (US and/or Israeli) air campaign. The latter could backfire however by setting back Iran's nuclear program by only a few years, meanwhile eroding multilateral support for stiffer sanctions (NYT Editorial, June 21, 2012). While tightened bilateral and international sanctions have no doubt hurt its economy, there is no assurance that they will ultimately restrain Iran's nuclear weapon ambitions. Nor is it clear that the resulting pain inflicted on Iran's population will increase effective pressure on the regime, as opposed to generating a "rally around the flag" effect. Although the global community may ultimately fail to foil Iran's nuclear weapons program, the calculation is that such sustained pressure on the regime can retard its pace of progress, buying time for tough diplomacy while delivering a warning signal to other nuclear weapon aspirants.

North Korea

Like Iran, most attention surrounding North Korea stems from its clandestine nuclear weapons program – one that has developed amid backdoor diplomacy, international condemnation and sanctions. Yet North Korea differs from Iran in that it has already crossed, perhaps irreversibly, the nuclear Rubicon. It is the only NPT signatory to subsequently renege and develop nuclear weapons. Achieving a Korean peninsula free of nukes thus requires rolling back an existing capacity – a prodigious task.

By 1992, North Korea had produced roughly 10 kilograms of plutonium at its Yonbyon research reactor – enough material for one to two nuclear bombs. The following year it signaled its intent to withdraw from the NPT, thus initiating a cat and mouse game with the US. In three months the US reached an accord with North Korea to freeze its nuclear program, under what became known as The Agreed Framework. Pyongyang shut down Yongbyon as well as its nearby plutonium separation plant and stored the fuel rods in canisters that the IAEA would monitor. A decade later it became clear that the country was pursuing a secret uranium enrichment program. The US suspended shipments of fuel oil previously made available under The Agreed Framework. North Korea, in turn, expelled IAEA inspectors, disabled IAEA equipment and announced its withdrawal from the NPT. Yongbyon was restarted, effectively marking the collapse of the US-brokered agreement.

In the wake of this breakdown arose the Six Party Talks. This multilateral approach brought together the US, China, North and South Korea, Russia and Japan to provide an arena outside of the UN or the NPT where diplomacy could address North Korea's decision to resume its nuclear weapons program. The multilateral talks also presented an opportunity to reconsider the provision of civilian nuclear energy to North Korea.[17]

On October 9, 2006, North Korea sent word to Moscow and Beijing that it would be conducting a nuclear test at its Punggye facility. Following on the heels of a ballistic missile test the previous July, this brazen act triggered international condemnation. The UN Security Council unanimously adopted Resolution 1718 (reinforcing Resolution 1695, which was a response to the July missile test), sanctioning trade and financial transactions related to conventional and non-conventional weapons as well as luxury goods favored by North Korea's elites. Resolution 1718 also encouraged states to inspect cargo entering and leaving North Korea, although China and South Korea opposed this measure.

The US Treasury's freezing of North Korean assets in a favored Macao-based bank appeared to secure Pyongyang's willingness to return to the multiparty talks. However, following shuttle diplomacy by US Secretary of State Condoleezza Rice in Beijing, Moscow, Seoul and Tokyo to discuss enforcement and follow up measures to Resolution 1718 on May 25, 2009, North Korea tested a small nuclear device, underscoring its resistance to external pressure. If anything, Resolution 1874 appeared to embolden Pyongyang, with its Foreign Ministry remarking: "it has become an absolutely impossible option for the DPRK [Democratic People's Republic of Korea] to even think about giving up its nuclear weapons" (KCNA, 2009). The Six Party Talks thus failed to prevent the rise of a nuclear North Korea, though the critical threshold seems to have been crossed with the prior collapse of The Agreed Framework.

In March 2010, North Korea attacked a South Korean military vessel, ROKS *Cheonan*, killing 46 sailors, and later bombarded Yoenpyeong Island.

In November 2010, revelations surfaced that Pyongyang had built a second nuclear production plant with analysts predicting that North Korea would conduct a third test in the near future. In December 2010 the USS *George Washington* conducted joint exercises with South Korea, reminding states in the region of US security assurances. In February 2012 the Obama Administration announced it was offering North Korea food aid after the country agreed to freeze its nuclear program. This offer was withdrawn however after North Korea unsuccessfully tested a long range missile two months later.

To appreciate failure to arrest Pyongyang's march toward nuclear weapons status requires an understanding of key regional players. No other country has greater interests concerning North Korea than neighboring China. From Beijing's perspective, an implosion of North Korea remains unacceptable: a failed state along its border and an ensuing flood of refugees, insatiable demands for aid and the prospect of uncontainable instability. In the mid-1990s the North Korean food crisis, stemming from a combination of flooding, heavy reliance on the former Soviet Union for assistance and internal mismanagement, led to mass starvation. Many Koreans fled to China only to be subsequently repatriated. Since 1995, Beijing has delivered close to 500,000 tons of food aid per year to prevent a second humanitarian disaster.

Hope of avoiding a crisis that could trigger the regime's downfall, keeps China from exerting its full leverage over the North Korean regime. Alternatively, any resolution that could culminate in Korean unification could bring US troops to China's frontier. Thus, "Beijing has done whatever it can to keep the Kim regime afloat..." (Moran, 2010). Fareed Zakaria offers an alternative hypothesis: China utilizes its relationship with North Korea to hedge against Japan and the US. China has learned that it can use North Korea, with its "unstable nuclear power" and harsh "anti-Japanese rhetoric," to keep Japan "off balance" (Zakaria quoted in Fish, 2010). A majority of Japanese perceives North Korea as a major military threat; with Beijing no longer Tokyo's chief concern, the former can arguably afford a few gambles.[18] Meanwhile, although seeking to stem the spread of nuclear weapons in its backyard, Moscow also looks to maintain its historical influence on the Korean peninsula. Unfortunately, "these objectives have often been conflicting and the pursuit of [each] has constrained Russia from pressing the North over the nuclear program" (Buszynski, 2009).

The US meanwhile adamantly opposes nuclear weapons acquisition by any of its East Asian allies. In return for eschewing such an option, Japan receives sweeping security assurances. Japan maintains a civilian nuclear power program that generates high-grade plutonium, a space launch capacity providing advanced ballistic missile capabilities and the technical expertise to reorient these activities into a sophisticated nuclear weapons development effort (Huntley, 2007, p. 465). Despite a far more advanced capability compared with Taiwan or South Korea, Japan has been even less inclined to consider joining the club of nuclear weapons states.[19] However, "a collapse in confidence in US security guarantees, especially vis-à-vis developments in Korea, might in the long run prove the crucial tipping point for going nuclear among key Japanese defense planners" (2007, p. 465).

Pyongyang has yet to be persuaded to dismantle its nuclear program, even in return for desperately needed economic concessions and desired security assurances. That the US and allies have been unable to exercise decisive pressure in part reflects the conflict of interests among regional players. In particular, China sees North Korea as a strategic asset, and Russia's pursuit of divergent objectives has also minimized the pressure on Pyongyang. Consequently, a poor and isolated North Korea continues to pose an intractable challenge to the international non-proliferation regime. In sum, at this juncture it is difficult to conclude that counter-proliferation efforts in North Korea have been anything other than a diplomatic failure.

Nuclear terrorism and weak states

> The proliferation of nuclear weapons poses the greatest threat to our national security. Nuclear weapons are unique in their capacity to inflict instant loss of life on a massive scale. For this reason, nuclear weapons hold special appeal to rogue states and terrorists.
>
> (National Security Strategy of the United States of America, 2006)

While regional nuclear arms races pose an ongoing threat to global security, the prospect of nuclear terrorism seems especially worrisome. In 2010, former Secretary of Defense Robert Gates wrote, "the prevention of nuclear terrorism and proliferation [are at] the top of the US policy agenda" (Department of Defense, 2010). President Obama echoed these concerns in noting that the most pressing dangers may revolve around the existence of unsecured nuclear material, the risk of a breakdown in the nuclear non-proliferation regime and the possibility of "a rogue state or nuclear scientist transferring the world's deadliest weapons to terrorists who won't think twice about killing themselves and hundreds of thousands in Tel Aviv or Moscow, in London or New York" (Meyer and Nicholas, 2008). Although more on the run today, that transnational networks like al Qaeda seem prepared to use nuclear weapons remains cause for vigilance (Montgomery, 2009, p. 31).

How exactly can a terrorist organization secure a nuclear bomb? Theoretically, there are four paths. First, terrorists can manufacture the fissile material needed to fuel a nuclear weapon (either by enriching uranium or by separating plutonium to weapons grade levels) and then use that material to construct a simple (by today's standards) nuclear device. Second, a terrorist group can seek out a state sponsor that already possesses nuclear weapons. Third, terrorists can steal a functioning nuclear weapon from one of the states possessing them. And, finally, a terrorist group can purchase fissile material and the technological know-how on the nuclear black market (the pathway pursued by Libya and North Korea, thanks to A.Q. Khan and his "nuclear Wal-Mart"),[20] or steal nuclear material from military or civilian facilities where it is less well guarded. Of the four, the last is often regarded as the only realistic scenario; a terrorist group with fissile material could construct a crude nuclear weapon (Montgomery, 2009, p. 10).

"It is virtually impossible" notes a member of the Security Studies Program at MIT, "for terrorists to create their own nuclear material, regardless of what material they use (uranium or plutonium)" (Talmadge, 2007, p. 24). Enriching uranium or separating plutonium to weapons grade levels requires a scientific know-how and technological capability beyond the sophistication of transnational terrorist groups. For former nuclear aspirants, enrichment typically proved the critical stumbling block. The likelihood of a terrorist group succeeding where nation-states have previously failed appears *de minimus*. As former Director of the Central Intelligence Agency Michael Hayden (2008) notes, "We are fortunate that those with the clearest intent to acquire and use weapons of mass destruction are also the least capable of developing them."

So-called rogue regimes are unlikely to transfer a nuclear weapon to an extremist non-state actor. For starters, all states are foremost concerned with their own survival. What ultimately deters them from supplying a terrorist with a nuclear device is attribution (the ability to determine a bomb's origin) and an understanding that doing so could invite a devastating response. The US employs the world's foremost experts in nuclear forensics to help to identify the origin of a deployed bomb. While not foolproof, attribution can serve as an effective deterrent strategy, reinforcing the imperative to tighten a state's grip on its nuclear stockpiles (Talmadge, 2007, p. 26).[21]

While the prospect of a third-party selling nuclear secrets to a state or extremist non-state group has arguably lessened with greater international vigilance, it cannot be discounted. During the 1980s and 1990s, Iran, Libya and North Korea purchased nuclear technology, centrifuge designs and know-how from Pakistan's A.Q. Khan and his nuclear black market. As nuclear proliferation expert Joseph Cirincione (2007) argues, states like North Korea are "not the most likely sources for terrorists since their stockpiles, if any, are small and exceedingly precious, and hence well-guarded." A more likely source is one of the more than 435 commercial nuclear facilities operating in 31 different countries (European Nuclear Society, 2012). Physical break-ins are not the only concern. Each year the IAEA receives reports of nearly 250 cases in which nuclear material simply goes missing (Bernstein, 2010). Lessening this risk has been a long-term concern (recall Nunn–Lugar). Despite work with nuclear states to improve safeguards, material leaks seemingly remain an unavoidable reality.

Pakistan

> Were one to map terrorism and weapons of mass destruction today, all
> roads would intersect in Pakistan.
>
> (Allison, quoted in Bernstein, 2010)

In the struggle to keep WMDs out of the hands of terrorists, weak states
can represent a serious risk. "Global terrorism seems to profit less from
failed states and more from weak ones, like Pakistan, where some aspect
of the regime is actively assisting the terrorists" (Mekhaus quoted in Zakaria,
2010a). In Pakistan, political instability and indications that members of
Pakistan's military, and intelligence communities directly or indirectly support extremist Islamist groups, raise fears that their "strategic assets" are
insufficiently secure. "If Pakistan were to lose control of even one nuclear
weapon that was ultimately used by terrorists," remarks Graham Allison,
"that would change the world. It would transform life in cities, shrink what
are now regarded as essential civil liberties, and alter conceptions of a viable
nuclear order" (Graham, 2010). Moderating Pakistan's internal threats, easing external pressures (particularly by reducing the potential for conflict
with neighboring, nuclear power India) and shoring up Pakistan's (irreso-
lute) support for US anti-terrorist efforts in the region are among the greatest
challenges facing Washington today.

Sandwiched between the Middle East, Central Asia and South Asia,
Pakistan's geographic location provides a window into its precarious position. To the west lies Shiite Iran and an embattled Afghanistan, and to the
south the Gulf of Oman and the Arabian Sea. While its ally China shares
a border in the northeast, India remains a greatly feared presence along
Pakistan's eastern front. As the sixth most populated country in the world
and home to more than 60 languages, Pakistan's intricate ethnic patchwork
reflects a confluence of influences. While there are Hindus, Christians and
Sikhs, the vast majority of Pakistan's population are Sunni-Muslim. Yet about
20 per cent of Pakistan's Muslims are Shia, among the largest such populations in the world. Stemming the recurrent outbursts of violence between
the Sunni majority and the Shiite minority is just one of the many challenges
facing this fragile state.

Islamist extremism has deep historical roots in Southwest Asia. The
Soviet invasion of Afghanistan in the 1980s and the ensuing insurgency
attracted Muslim fighters from many countries, including a young Osama
Bin Laden. After a decade of fighting, the Afghan mujahideen, with US support, succeeded in repelling the Soviet army. US officials publically supported
moderate Afghan mujahideen groups resisting Soviet expansionism. In the
event, arms from the US and Saudi Arabia were channeled via Pakistan's
intelligence agency, the Inter-Services Intelligence (ISI), to more extremist
groups, which eventually took power in the 1990s. In effect, the ISI became

the chief political and financial sponsor of the Afghan Taliban. "Without Islamabad's help...it is unlikely the Taliban would have come to power. And without a Taliban regime in Kabul, Afghanistan never would have become a safe haven for al-Qaeda." Pakistan "was more than a little responsible for September 11" (Carpenter, 2003).[22]

Since the early days of the US invasion of Afghanistan, Pakistan has proved to be, at best, a wavering ally. When the US had cornered Bin Laden in the Tora Bora Mountains, Pakistan denied American soldiers the right of hot pursuit. Credible reports emerged that elements of Pakistan's ISI helped to evacuate Taliban and al Qaeda personnel from Afghanistan (Carpenter, 2003). Today, Quetta, the capital city of the Baluchistan province, has become a Taliban oasis. "Old hands among the insurgents say it reminds them of 1980s Peshawar, where anti-Soviet mujahideen operated openly with the ISI's blessing and backing" (Moreau, 2011). A top Taliban commander, Mullah Momin Ahmed, summed it up as follows: "Pakistan is like your shoulder that supports your RPG [rocket-propelled grenade]. Without it you couldn't fight" (Moreau, 2007).

Pakistan's ties to violent extremism do not end with support for the Afghan Taliban. In its struggle with India over disputed Kashmir, Islamabad has consistently sponsored and supported radical jihadists with weapons, training and sanctuary (BBC, In Depth). Pakistan's assistance inspired more militant groups – such as Lashkar-e-Taiba, a pan-Islamist outfit with militants that are battle tested in fronts such as Bosnia, Tajikistan, Chechnya, Iraq and Afghanistan – to reinforce local Kashmiri insurgents. "These groups in turn attracted fighters drawn less by the cause of political self-determination for the Kashmiri Muslims than by bloodthirstiness, religious fervor, and greed" (Ganguly, 2006).[23]

Pakistan's geopolitical situation remains chaotic, upset by political struggles stemming from years of authoritarian rule as well as conflicts with its neighbors. Today the military is responsible for both security and foreign policy, reducing the current civilian government to a token role (Zakaria, 2010b). According to Pakistani journalist Ahmed Rashid, "Pakistan's counterterrorism policies continue to be run by the army, ostensibly without government objection" (2011).

Pakistan's military takes an uncompromisingly hostile approach to India, which has developed a close strategic partnership with the US. Pakistan's military seems unwavering in its stance on Kashmir, and continuously alarmed about India's encroachments in Afghanistan. Pakistan's military remains adamant that "an Afghanistan cleansed of the Taliban would be an Indian client state, thus sandwiching Pakistan between two hostile countries. The paranoia of Pakistan about India's supposed dark machinations should never be underestimated" observes novelist Salman Rushdie (2011).

Lashkar-e-Taiba appears willing to play its part in the struggle with India. Twice it has struck: first, in December of 2001 in New Delhi and, second, in November of 2008 in Mumbai, an attack that left 173 people dead. Both attacks elevated tensions between these two nuclear countries, once again bringing them to the brink of war. After the 2008 attack, Indian Prime Minister Singh asserted that the next major terrorist attack supported or sponsored by Pakistan would trigger a firm military response (Allison, 2010). Speaking before the Senate Committee of Foreign Relations, Michael Krepon of the Center for Strategic and International Studies opined, "The biggest challenge facing Pakistan's national security establishment is to recognize how continuing links to extremist groups mortgage Pakistan's future. Outfits like Lashkar-e-Taiba are the leading edge of Pakistan's national demise" (2011).

Consider, says nuclear expert Graham Allison (2010), that "over the past eight years, the Pakistani government has tripled its arsenal of nuclear weapons and nuclear weapons material." Pakistan is in the midst of building its fourth nuclear reactor and by 2021 could have as many as 200 nuclear weapons, making it the fastest growing nuclear weapons program in the world (Bast, 2011). As India increases the pace of its military spending Pakistan ostensibly seeks to balance India's conventional superiority with an increased nuclear capability.

Added to this ominous backdrop are anxieties surrounding the improved US–India relationship that mirror a steady deterioration in US–Pakistani relations over the assassination of Osama bin Laden and other recent incidents. The USA–India Peaceful Atomic Energy Cooperation Act, which conferred de facto recognition to India as a nuclear weapons state, "will allow India to now import nuclear technology for peaceful power production without having first to renounce its nuclear arsenal" (Carter, 2007). With greater access to nuclear technology and material, New Delhi can more easily expand its nuclear deterrent. India's plans, which include increasing its nuclear stockpile by 50 per cent in 2021, remain unacceptable to Pakistan. And in fanning perceptions of realpolitik-like favoritism the concessions granted to India's nuclear program remain problematic for the credibility of the NPT regime.

Meanwhile the Pakistani Taliban has become an effective insurgent force that threatens the viability of the state. "A massive growth in militancy has spilled over from the periphery into the heartland of the Punjabi and Sindhi interior," beyond the control of the Pakistani military (Vira and Cordesman, 2011). The civilian government remains a "fragile, fledgling, and splintered democracy" (Allison, 2010). Pakistan, it would seem, is nearing a tipping point.[24] Analysts concur that Pakistan represents a far more serious threat to global security than does its neighbor to the west. Council on Foreign Relations President Richard Haass (2010) proclaims: "Pakistan is much more important than Afghanistan given its nuclear arsenal, its much larger population, the many terrorists on its soil, and its history of wars with India."

In principle, the US possesses a variety of tools to help lend greater stability to Pakistan. First, since 2001 it has appropriated well over $20 billion in aid. While targeted mostly at the military, these dollars were intended to finance the campaign against the Taliban insurgency. Given a growing conviction that much of this aid has been squandered, an increasing share of US aid to Pakistan has been redirected to a needy local population, including some 60 per cent who live on less than $2 a day. In 2009, Congress passed the Enhanced Partnership with Pakistan Act (Kerry–Lugar–Berman) providing a 5-year $7.5 billion aid package of civilian targeted aid.[25] In the event, an offer of preferential access to the US market for the Pakistani textile sector would constitute a further strategic use of US economic power.

In addition to providing economic assistance to an impoverished population, this aid can be viewed as utilizing US cultural assets, including offering an educational alternative to radical Islamist indoctrination in the country's madrassas. One can only hope that such funds would help to moderate the virulent anti-Americanism that currently pervades Pakistan. Yet, it needs to be considered that the billions of dollars spent on development aid in Pakistan and Afghanistan over the last decade, much of it with the express goal of "combatting militant extremism," may have had "no demonstrable impact on the spread of Islamic militancy" (Blair et al., 2011).[26]

Diplomacy represents another US instrument for influencing Pakistan's trajectory. In concert with other regional actors, there is a growing case for strengthening US diplomatic efforts to help ameliorate the core India–Pakistan conflict. In lieu of a resolution to this long-standing struggle, the potential of escalating conflict between these two nuclear powers remains ever-present. A political solution to Kashmir would provide much needed stability to South Asia. While improved US relations with India can help, convening a forum of regional players akin to the Six Party Talks for North Korea would appear a logical use of US power.

Finally, there is the military option. American boots on the ground in Pakistan – ostensibly to destroy al Qaeda and related terrorist groups – seems currently out of the question. Pakistan's military leadership would regard such action as an unacceptable infringement of Pakistani sovereignty. Despite open condemnation by Pakistani officials, however, the US has succeeded (with clandestine Pakistani support) in taking out an increasing number of al Qaeda operatives in Pakistan through CIA drone attacks. The inevitable downside of this tactic, however, are civilian tragedies and a further inflamed Pakistani public.[27]

Shocked reaction to the killing of Osama bin Laden by US Navy SEALs portends future limits to the latitude Pakistan's military will extend to US forces.[28] Although the US maintains its cooperation with the military unit responsible for maintaining Pakistan's nuclear arsenal, and steps have been taken to enhance security controls, "many Americans continue to harbor concerns about the terrorist threat to Pakistan's nuclear scientists, technologies, and materials" (Lettow, 2010, p. 37).

While the deployment of the full array of US strategic assets can play a pivotal role, stability in South Asia rests ultimately on Pakistan's own leadership. If pragmatism can ever overcome the weight of historical animosities,

Pakistan's elites would focus unwaveringly on two, existential goals – a resolution of its conflict with India and an all-out assault on homegrown and regional terrorism.

Currently the military pursues a counter-insurgency strategy that attempts to "delineate[s] between groups actively hostile to Pakistani interests" and "those...that may have future strategic utility in reestablishing Pakistan's sphere of influence and helping contain its external enemies" (Vira and Cordesman, 2011). Meanwhile, Pakistan plays a parallel double game with the US, whose success against al Qaeda and allied groups requires Pakistani vigilance against terrorist sanctuaries in its northwestern provinces. Walking such a tight rope can end tragically, with a weak and nuclear Pakistan slipping further into the grips of radical Islamist insurgents. Herein lays perhaps the greatest (external) challenge to US hegemony.

Conclusion

With North Korea having crossed the nuclear Rubicon, will South Korea or Japan eventually follow suit? Will Iran's suspected nuclear weapons program threaten a pan-Mideast arms race engulfing Sunni states like Saudi Arabia, Egypt or Turkey? And what is the end game flowing from the confluence of nuclear weapons, weak states and Islamist extremism epitomized by Pakistan?

With such a perilous backdrop, one grades US leadership on nuclear proliferation against an imposing standard. On the whole, US-led efforts have met with significant success. From the vantage point of President John F. Kennedy's warning of an explosive nuclear arms race, the club of new nuclear entrants has been limited to three countries.[29] During this period, more states have been persuaded to dismantle their nuclear weapons programs.

Bolstered by the NSG, Nunn–Luger, PSI, and successive START agreements with Russia, the NPT-centered counter-proliferation regime has proved reasonably robust given the forces amassed against it over an extended period. US and allied efforts continue to be focused on preventing the acquisition of nuclear devices and fissile material by terrorists, providing an effective US nuclear umbrella in key regions, and experimenting with carrots and sticks to dissuade a capricious North Korea from progressing irreversibly down its current path. Meanwhile, there is the ever-increasing scope of bilateral and multilateral sanctions to deter Iran from pursuing a nuclear weapons program. Undergirding all of these initiatives is a longer-term vision of a nuclear-free world.

Despite valiant efforts to shore up the global public good of counter-proliferation, nuclear proliferation remains an ever-present danger. According to the opening lines of a Council on Foreign Relations report, the international non-proliferation regime "is under severe strain" (Lettow,

2010, p. 3). The report adds: "The North Korean and Iranian nuclear programs have exploited and underscored weaknesses in the regime that must be fixed if it is to serve its purpose. Those weaknesses are both structural – ambiguities and limitations in the current rules – and result from a failure to enforce the rules that exist" (Lettow, 2010, p. 3).

This raises a fundamental question: does the lingering risk of a nuclear arms race in Asia or the Middle East imply US (Western) impotence in the face of such a fundamental threat to global security? In fact, the history and future potential of counter-WMD proliferation efforts underscore both the depth and the limits of US power. That the predominant power whose leadership on this issue is universally acknowledged requires vigilant cooperation from other states and civil society institutions has never been in question. Without international coordination and consensus, the ability to decisively influence a state's decision-making calculus surrounding nuclear weapons is inevitably limited. Nevertheless, US leadership remains critical to shoring up the international counter-proliferation effort (Lettow, 2010, p. 19).

Following a half-century during which the USA with the backing of its allies has fortified the dam of counter-proliferation, it continues to work assiduously toward preventing the spread of nuclear weapons. No other state possesses anything approaching the array of power assets that the US can summon to backstop the NPT regime. Michael Mandelbaum captures this role succinctly:

> American political leadership, American surveillance techniques and intelligence-gathering organizations, and sometimes American military power have done more to keep these weapons from spreading than the efforts of any other country. The military forces that provide reassurance also aid the cause of nonproliferation . . .
>
> (2010, p. 56)

In sum, the US has played a unique role in containing WMD proliferation to date and it remains in the vanguard of this effort today. The argument advanced in this chapter, however, suggests that a decisive resolution – an end to proliferation and eventual elimination of all nuclear weapons – represents too exacting a standard for assessing US hegemony. Although ongoing uncertainty surrounding the spread of nuclear weapons may fail more demanding tests of leadership, a declining power would have lacked the will and means to accomplish as much has the US within this critical dimension of human security.

6
Global Public Goods and East Asia

Exemplifying a broad category of global public goods concerned with safeguarding human security, Chapter 5 focused on one such activity – the campaign to curb nuclear proliferation. The chapter concluded that although hardly devoid of setbacks and formidable ongoing challenges, US leadership in counter-proliferation had broadly succeeded in rendering a veritable tinderbox somewhat less explosive. Continuing with the broader theme of hegemonic stability, this chapter adopts a regional perspective on global public goods provision. Owing to its growing weight in the world economy, East Asia receives the spotlight here as a lead example of the more generalized regional impact of US power.

Two distinct US-furnished public goods are examined through this regional prism. First, there is the US championing of the rules-based, global trade and financial order and efforts to reconcile regional trading arrangements with global norms and institutions. The second public good relates to the pivotal US role in maintaining the balance of power within strategic regions of the world.

The rest of the chapter is organized as follows. The section "East Asia and the US" summarizes East Asia's historical strategic and economic relationship with the US. Two sections covering distinct public goods follow. The embedding of regional economic relations within the multilateral liberal trading order is analyzed in the section "Public goods pillar I: Multilateral trade." The section "Public goods pillar II: Regional balance of power" covers the maintenance of stable balance of power relations in the region. A brief conclusion follows in Part IV.

East Asia and the US

As discussed here, "East Asia" encompasses Northeast and Southeast Asia, incorporating China (including Hong Kong and Macau), Taiwan, Japan, South and North Korea, and the ten member countries of the Association of Southeast Asian Nations (ASEAN).[1] Located in the broader region are other important US allies, including the oceanic states of Australia and New Zealand further to the south. East Asia comprises almost one-third of the world's population and contributes around 25 per cent of world gross domestic product. This is remarkable given that many of these countries were agrarian-based, and relatively impoverished nations of the Global South a half century ago (World Bank, 1993).

Since the end of World War II, the US has maintained a strategic presence in the Asian Pacific, erecting a "hub-and-spoke" security order grounded in core bilateral relations. Thereby, "East Asian countries get protection, geopolitical predictability, and access to the American market and the United States gets front-line strategic partners, geopolitical presence in the region, and (in recent years) capital to finance its deficits" (Ikenberry, 2004).

Meanwhile, multinationals headquartered in the US, Japan and elsewhere have transformed their production process and cost structure by tapping into an evolving "globalization of production." Anchoring the manufacturing segment of this fast evolving global division of labor has been China. But China's ability to serve as the workshop for assembling consumer products destined for final sale, particularly in the US and Europe, requires a prior intricate flow of parts, semi-manufactures, intermediate products and advanced capital goods principally from neighboring Asian states.

Motivated by the dynamism of the region and in response to China's heightened assertiveness, strategic planners are heralding the US's recent "Asian Pivot." Secretary of State Hillary Clinton writes: "the future of politics will be decided in Asia, not Afghanistan or Iraq, and the United States will be right at the center of this action" (2011). And all dimensions of US global power will be brought to bear.[2]

Public goods pillar I: Multilateral trade

After World War II the US played an integral role in facilitating the expansion of global trade under the aegis of the General Agreement on Tariffs and Trade (GATT), succeeded by the World Trade Organization (WTO). Their cornerstone has been the principle of non-discrimination and reciprocal granting of most-favored nation (MFN) status. Although it has deviated from these principles at times, on the whole the US has "unambiguously favored free trade over protectionist interests" (Norloff, 2010, p. 72).

Economic theory holds that reasonably unfettered trading relations incentivize countries to specialize in goods and services in which they enjoy a comparative advantage.[3] Over time the resulting trading patterns ensure more efficient resource allocation and higher productivity growth (Irwin, 2002, p. 30). A genuinely open multilateral trading system thereby allows participating countries to utilize trade as an additional "technology" for augmenting national income. In addition, there is the liberal belief that an expansion of multilateral trade yields positive externalities by enhancing international cooperation and reducing the potential for conflict.[4]

US trade liberalization initiatives have not always been reciprocated. According to one trade expert, "US and European policy was generous to a fault to developing countries, permitting them to effectively 'free ride' on the trading system without undertaking substantive commitments to reduce barriers in their markets" (Schott, 2008, p. 1). Jeffrey Garten, former Under Secretary of Commerce for International Trade in the Clinton Administration, notes that "the US led every major round of global liberalization, providing the ideas and political muscle to bring negotiations to a conclusion and, most important, keeping American markets open in good economic times and bad so other economies could stay afloat" (1995, pp. 50–51). He adds that "no other country came close to exercising [the US] role" of freer trade promotion at least up to the Doha Round of trade talks.[5]

Relaxing its intellectual defense of multilateral trade by the 1990's, the US according to a leading trade expert had morphed into a "selfish hegemon" (Bhagwati, 1994, p. 284). This purported diminution in leadership might be attributed to a variety of factors, notably the cessation of the Cold War a period during which US trade concessions anchored the anticommunist alliance. Another contributor was the greater diplomatic effort on behalf of preferential trade arrangements notably the North American Free Trade Agreement (Free Trade of the Americas). Such efforts reflected strategic considerations but also growing US frustration over the diminishing global commitment to multilateralism (Garten, 2005, p. 60).

Although its basic principles require each country to treat all other member countries uniformly, as a concession to political reality the WTO (GATT) had granted exemption from MFN treatment for regional trade agreements. For example, NAFTA, and the European Customs Union are sanctioned forms of formal tariff discrimination. Intraregional trade has exploded in recent decades. Between 1948 and the WTO's creation in the late 1990s, 124 regional trade agreements were announced or signed. Within the last 15 years, on one account the world has seen 333 new notifications of regional agreements (Quinlan, 2011, p.99). Economists like Jagdish Bhagwati (1995) and Richard Baldwin (2008) argue that the "spaghetti bowl" produced by overlapping regional and bilateral trade pacts undermines the WTO's multilateral mission. In excluding non-members with a comparative advantage in certain product lines, trade diversion raises world prices and depresses product variety. A greater risk is that preferential trading arrangement proliferation degenerates into semi-autarkic regional blocs, increasing the chance of geopolitical conflict, as in the 1930s.

Since regional trade deals are inherently discriminatory, the challenge is effectively to "multilateralize" regionalism. This essentially means to organically embed regional economic arrangements within global trading and financial networks, notably via linkages with global supply chains. These elaborate production and trading networks link to any commercial concern globally where potential exists to add value. By integrating geographically dispersed companies into intricate global production systems, multinational companies can offset some of the efficiency losses otherwise arising from intra-regional trade overextension (Baldwin, 2008).

East Asian regionalism

In 2000, only three FTAs existed in East Asia; by 2010, 45 such agreements had emerged, with 84 more in the process of negotiation (Kawai and Wignaraja, 2010, p. 3). Moreover, a mushrooming web of bilateral pacts reinforced the appearance of a "spaghetti or noodle bowl syndrome" (see Figure 6.1) this proliferation of regional and bilateral trade agreements in East Asian trade prompts the question: does growing "regionalism" risk the formation of semi-autonomous regional blocs, retarding progress toward less-discriminatory multilateral trade?

Intensified regionalism in East Asia appears to have been driven by three main factors. First, in triggering a prolonged appreciation of the yen, the 1985 Plaza Accord incentivized multinationals to locate segments of their production process outside of Japan, precipitating a growing fragmentation of production and rationalization of global supply chains. This has "generated a web of intra-regional, intra-industry trade in parts, components,

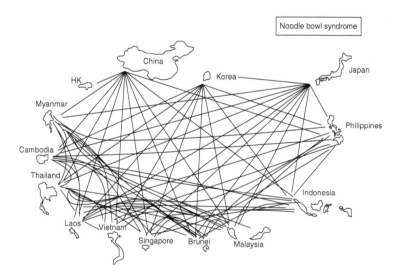

Figure 6.1 The East Asian "noodle bowl" syndrome

Note: the map shows FTAs signed or under negotiation in January 2006. East Asia is defined here as the 10 ASEANs, China, Japan and Korea.

Source: Baldwin (2008a, p. 4)

semi-finished products, and finished products within East Asia, contributing to a more efficient division of labor and deeper economic integration" (Kawai, 2004, p. 9).

Second, a perception grew that the multilateral trading system can no longer be relied upon to look after the interests of emerging economies. In parallel, preferential regional trade arrangements in Europe and North America seemed to grant them leverage in multilateral trade negotiations. Asian policymakers view regional integration as boosting competitiveness through scale economies, increasing bargaining power and raising their voice on global trade issues (Kawai and Wignaraja, 2010, p. 2).

Third, regional integration was spurred in response to disillusionment over Western responses to the 1997 financial crisis. For example, long-standing US allies, such as Thailand, were disappointed by its financial support relative to the funds offered Mexico a few years earlier. Viewed as dictating Western interests and applying inappropriate conditionality, the International Monetary Fund (IMF) also sacrificed prestige and legitimacy (Mahbubani, 2008, p. 104; Sheng, 2009). This experience encouraged policymakers to focus on regional-based insurance mechanisms to self-insulate from future economic shocks.

The 1997 Asian financial crisis also exposed the region's over-dependence on external savings, especially short-term debt flows. Such realization spurred the development of intra-regional bond markets and the accumulation of sizeable foreign exchange reserves. An early response came with the Chiang Mai Initiative established in May 2000 to provide a system of bilateral swap arrangements among the central banks of ASEAN, China, Hong Kong, Japan and South Korea. It also sought to monitor capital flows and increase financial policy dialogue and cooperation (Henning, 2009, p. 2).[6]

The Asian Bond Fund was created in June 2003 to help intermediate savings and promote longer-term regional investment. In August 2003 followed the Asian Bonds Market Initiative to establish primary and secondary regional bond markets. Finally, a more recent development has been China's decision to begin to use the yuan in cross-border transactions. While still at an early stage, the pace at which China's nascent attempts to launch the yuan as an international currency is proceeding has impressed informed observers (Eichengreen, 2011; Subramanian, 2011).[7]

Regionalism and hegemony

As noted above, some believe that regional trade and financial arrangements inexorably undermine the multilateral system. One might also argue that such arrangements subvert the position of a global hegemon whose *raison d'etre* consists in breaking down inter-regional impediments, consolidating a liberal, multilateral trading order. A global hegemon moreover may be threatened by would-be regional hegemons (hence, potential future global hegemonic challengers) in a position to exploit and leverage economic relations with its neighbors.

Yet, from an economic efficiency perspective, not all regional trading arrangements are alike. Former Peterson Institute of International Economics President Fred Bergsten (2007a, p. 5) has argued that intra-Asian FTAs have generally been "of relatively poor quality in terms of issue coverage and effective liberalization" compared with the "gold standard" variety of US-promoted FTAs that exhibit more "comprehensive coverage and extensive (even intrusive) reduction of impediments to trade and investment."

A US Congressional Research Service report opines that "the US market... is rapidly being displaced by China and intra-regional trade" (Nanto, 2008, p. 28). The decline in Western aggregate demand owing to the financial crisis and the rapid secular increase in per capita income in East Asia have further elevated the level of intra-Asian commerce (Jackson, 2012). Although buoyant regional growth has lifted US exports to the region, some estimate that US market share in key Asia-Pacific economies has shrunk by over 40 per cent over the last decade (Gerwin, 2012). Especially worrisome is the prospect for certain regional trading initiatives to exclude the US altogether. Thereby the would-be regional hegemon, China, could "assume the leadership mantle and work at cross purposes to American interests" (Nanto, 2008, p. 3).[8]

Fear over a drift toward increasing insularity in East Asia seems exaggerated, however. Regional trade arrangements to date have largely been market- rather than policy-driven (Pomfret, 2007). As mentioned, the recent increase in intra-regional trade reflects more rapid Asian relative to slower-growing Western demand. Otherwise, intra-regional trade appears, on the whole, to be organically embedded within an increasingly sophisticated global division of labor (Abonyi, 2008, p. 4).

This more constructive perspective on East Asian regionalism notwithstanding, the Obama Administration has taken precautions to hedge against China's potential to move regional trade in a less auspicious direction, to the detriment of the US and other extra-regional economies. In particular, the US has advanced the Trans-Pacific Partnership (TPP) initiative, a trade pact aimed at "supporting the wider liberalization process in Asia-Pacific Economic Cooperation (APEC) consistent with its goals of free and open trade and investment" (TPP Agreement, 2005).[9] Entrance negotiations express the "quiet hope" that TPP will serve as a starting point for an APEC-wide trading area (*The Economist*, 2011a). Thus, the eventual goal seems to be that a "TPP agreement with high standards can serve as a benchmark for future agreement – and grow to serve as a platform for broader regional interaction and eventually a free trade area of the (entire) Asia-Pacific" (Clinton, 2011, p. 14).

A series of negotiating rounds in 2012 was expected to result in a final agreement among the original nine TPP partner countries (USTR, 2011);

Mexico and Canada have recently joined and Japan has also declared potential interest (Harlan, 2011). Given the combined weight of US and Japanese trade, the TPP might entice other nations, such as Canada or South Korea, to join. That the TPP does not currently include China sends a signal that the US intends to "shape a high-standard, broad-based regional (trade) pact" with or without China's involvement (Kirk, 2009).[10]

Meanwhile, regional trade liberalization appears to be moving along two parallel tracks, a "Trans-Pacific track" and a "Pan-Asian track" involving ASEAN trade negotiations with mainly China, Japan and Korea. According to some these competing tracks are "already stimulating mutual progress," optimistically leading to an eventual, comprehensive free trade area in the Asia-Pacific (Petri and Plummer, 2012, p. 1).

While proponents of liberal global trade may regard still another region-centric trade pact as representing one further retreat from multilateralism, its proponents hope that arrangements like the TPP can become a stepping stone in the direction of a global Doha-type agreement. Moreover, such initiatives signal that "nations of the region need not succumb to the inevitability of a Pacific dominated by China" (Gordon, 2011). Others, including those broadly accepting of well-structured regional trade arrangements, are less impressed by the quality and motivation behind the TPP, regarding it as distinctly inferior to other initiatives like the Free Trade Area of the Asia Pacific (FTAAP).[11]

Looking forward, a two-pronged US approach seems likely. The first involves efforts to expand non-discriminatory trading links among a growing number of Asia-Pacific powers via the TPP or better yet, more comprehensive FTAAP. Such initiatives, according to proponents, can "embed Asia-only trade arrangements in a broader Asia construct to counter both the bilateral and systemic implications of Asian regionalism" (Bergsten, 2007, p. 5). The second more up-hill goal entails reviving WTO-level multilateral trade talks. The end goal of both endeavors is to promote, via alternative routes, the widest application of free and open trading relations globally. A parallel objective is to thwart Chinese ambitions to use intra-regional trade and financial arrangements as a means to diminish the US economic (and security) presence in the region. The TPP and ASEAN plus 3 (or + 6) alternatives, for example "are ever more widely seen as yet another facet of Sino-American rivalry." (The Economist, op. cit., 2012, p. 52).

Public good pillar II: Regional balance of power

A related public good that the US is uniquely positioned to offer is as a stabilizer of the intra-regional balance of power. Central to its exercise of global power has been the US effort to function effectively as a member of the region rather than as an extra-regional interloper. This is particularly important where one state is capable of dominating that region militarily and politically. An aspiring power can use the prospect of regional hegemony as a springboard for a more general challenge to the global status quo. This explains why the global hegemon, with support from other regional actors, would seek to curb such aspirations. Nowhere does this scenario ring more true today than in East Asia. Recent events have granted new impetus to concerns that Chinese ambitions could unsettle the strategic balance in the region. They have likewise lent renewed support to the US role as regional balancer.[12]

China's recent buildup notwithstanding, the US remains the overwhelming military power in the region. Roughly one-fifth of US military assets, comprising some 325,000 military and civilian personnel, are assigned to the US Pacific Command (USPACOM). The US Pacific Fleet includes five aircraft carriers and their accompanying strike groups. The Marine Corps Forces of the Pacific possesses about two-thirds of total US Marine Corps combat strength, with about 85,000 personnel (USPACOM, 2011).

While the "Asian Pivot" is the latest euphemism for stepped-up US involvement, the country's alliances with Korea, Thailand, and the Philippines and its general regional presence are long-standing. Some 28,500 and 40,000 American troops remain just outside of Seoul and in Japan, respectively, despite the cessation of combat operations over a half-century ago. In addition to the rapprochement with Vietnam in 1994, "US engagement with India, Indonesia, Japan, Mongolia, Australia and Singapore is deeper and broader today than it was at the end of the Cold War" (Mead, 2011).

Following the September 11th attacks, the US intensified its regional security presence. Indonesia, Malaysia and the Philippines, all of which confront indigenous terrorist groups, have received US development aid, technology and military training. In Indonesia, for example, the US has helped to create a 300-man elite counterterrorism force known as "Detachment 88." In a 2007 operation, US advisers helped the Philippine navy trap terrorist Abu Sayyaf on the island of Jolo (Kurlantzick, 2007a).

In addition to its military presence, the US can claim substantial "soft" power in East Asia. For example, USPACOM has participated in more than 20 disaster relief operations since 1996 (USPACOM, 2011). During the immediate aftermath of the 2004 tsunami, which devastated the coasts of Indonesia, Sri Lanka, India, Thailand and Myanmar, the US provided the lead on reconstruction. Some 12,000 relief personnel participated in the effort known as "Operation Unified Assistance," delivering 25 million pounds of relief supplies to victims throughout the affected area (US Department of Defense, 2006). While only 15 per cent of Indonesians held a favorable opinion of the US in 2003, one year after the tsunami relief effort that percentage had risen to 44 per cent. The unfavorable opinion of Indonesia's mostly Muslim population shrank from 48 to 13 per cent in that same time frame (Terror

Free Tomorrow, 2006). Such demonstrations of goodwill provide a welcome basis for sustained partnership in the region.

Protection of sea lanes

The US has long safeguarded international commercial traffic, particularly the sea-born flow of oil. The US navy protects the world's principal shipping lanes and chokepoints that would otherwise be prime targets for pirating, smuggling, terrorism or embargo. This public good of protected sea lanes is vital to East Asia, a region that is heavily reliant on oil and non-oil commodity imports. Dependency on oil imports has reached just under 60 per cent of East Asian consumption and is rising (Asian Development Bank, 2009, p. xiii).

Geopolitical strategist Robert Kaplan predicts that "the Indian Ocean area will be the true nexus of world power and conflict in the coming years," and thus an area where US power must focus its attention (2010b, preface). This region contains the world's principal oil shipping lanes and navigational chokepoints of world commerce. Some 40 per cent of seaborne crude oil passes through the Strait of Hormuz, while 40–50 per cent of the world's merchant fleet capacity travels via the Strait of Malacca (Kaplan, 2010b, p. 7).

Global energy demand is forecast to increase by 53 per cent by 2035, and nearly half of this new consumption will stem from China and India (Energy Information Administration, 2011). Most of China's oil enters the mainland via the Strait of Malacca patrolled by the US 7th Fleet. While China would like to see such dependence diminish, to accomplish this would require the attainment of a blue water navy. To maintain free sea lanes "requires aircraft carriers and the ability to move large numbers of troops or material by air or by sea to Africa or the Middle East, none of which China has yet" (Segal, 2011, p. 12).

The US lead role in safeguarding global energy and seaborne security includes a distinctly Asia-Pacific focus. US Secretary of State Hillary Clinton highlights the broader need for the US to "lock in a substantially increased investment" in the Asia-Pacific region on diplomatic, economic and strategic fronts:

> Just as Asia is critical to America's future, an engaged America is vital to Asia's future. The region is eager for our leadership and our business – perhaps more so than at any time in modern history. We are the only power with a network of strong alliances in the region, no territorial ambitions, and a long record of providing for the common good. Along with our allies, we have underwritten regional security for decades – patrolling Asia's sea lanes and preserving stability – and that in turn has helped create the conditions for growth.
>
> (2011, p. 3)

Maintaining a strong foothold in the dynamic East Asian theater remains central to the US's global strategy to facilitate interregional trade, global energy security and intraregional stability.

Rising concerns over China

For years Singaporean Prime Minister Lee Kuan warned of the "risk of increasing Chinese dominance over its Asian neighbors – and decreasing US relevance – should the US fail to engage economically and politically in the region." A 2011 Pentagon report corroborates this concern, predicting that China could be regionally dominant by 2020 (US Department of Defense, 2011).

After years of adopting a more conciliatory stance, recently more assertive Chinese actions have triggered increasing unease among its neighbors. Tensions between the world's second and third largest economies came to the forefront in 2010 when the Japanese Coast Guard seized and detained a Chinese fishing trawler near the disputed Senkaku (for Japan) and Diaoyu (for China) Islands. In retaliation, China temporarily cut off Japanese access to vital rare earth metals. A subsequent skirmish and surge in Chinese nationalism was triggered by the Japanese government purchase of certain Senkaku islands from their private Japanese owner. This incident over "tiny outcrops and shoals" albeit ones located near energy-rich sea beds prompted a cover story in the Economist titled "Could Asia really go to war over these?" (Economist, 2012).

In addition, Vietnam, Indonesia, Malaysia, the Philippines, Taiwan and Brunei all have long-standing maritime-boundary disputes with China in the East or South China Seas. Given its lack of territorial interests in East Asia, East Asian countries generally view the US as a regional security guarantor and essential hedge against Chinese belligerence or expansionism (Sutter, 2006, 2008).

The US appears committed to furnishing this regional security balancing role. During a July 2010 Asian security forum in Hanoi, US Secretary of State Clinton stated that the US has a "national interest in freedom of navigation, open access to Asia's maritime commons, and respect for international law in the South China Sea" (Clinton, 2010). A few days later, Chinese Foreign Minister Yang Jiechi accused the US of "internationalizing" bilateral matters and harboring imperialistic designs (*The Economist*, 2010b).

China's leaders increasingly appear to be advancing a Monroe Doctrine-like position with respect to the South China Sea. Yet, no one in the region wants to be forced to choose between allegiance to the US or China if they can avoid it: "US policymakers will have to walk a fine line, therefore: providing enough reassurance to convince Asian partners that balancing will work, but leaving enough doubts so that Washington doesn't end up doing all the heavy lifting itself" (Walt, 2011). Meanwhile the US must avoid falling into a "structurally adversarial relationship" with China. As Zbigniew Brzezinski puts it the US, which remains officially neutral on the region's territorial claims, needs "to respect China's special historic and geopolitical role in maintaining stability on the Far Eastern mainland" (2012, p. 101). President Obama has attempted to defuse Chinese concerns over a containment strategy:

> We've sent a clear signal that we are a Pacific power and we will continue to be a Pacific power, but we have done this all in the context of a belief that a peacefully rising China is good for everybody... The only thing we've insisted on, as a principle in that region is, everybody's got to play by the same set of rules, and everybody's got to abide by a set of international norms. And that's not unique to China. That's true for all of us.
>
> (quoted in Zakaria, 2012)

The overarching strategic goal is not to "quarantine" China but, rather, to discourage its leadership from pursuing a form of regional domination. This involves a difficult balancing act. Concern has been expressed over an excessively "muscular approach" towards China, rather than one of "balancing, hedging and insurance" (*The Economist*, 2011c). Hugh White (2011), a former Australian defense official and professor at the Australian National University, for example, decries a potentially "escalating strategic rivalry between the world's two strongest states... threatening the future peace and stability of Asia".

Neighboring powers

As large contiguous South Asian and Eurasian powers, India and Russia cannot be excluded from the broader geopolitical context impacting East Asia. India has emerged economically over the past decade, gaining status as one of the four BRIC nations in the early 2000s. The uptick in its productivity growth following the 1991 reforms (Bosworth and Collins, 2008), combined with long-run projections that have it dominating demographically by the end of the century,[13] mean that India will be a major force to reckon with in East Asia.

India is taking important strides in East Asian regional leadership efforts. Its "Look East" policy represents a push to further integrate India with East Asia. Started under Prime Minister Rao in 1991 and gaining greater prominence under Prime Minister Manmohan Singh, "Look East" has both economic and strategic motivations. Establishing alliances with East Asian partners offers India greater economic-cum-strategic options. For states anxious to transcend the strict confines of the China–US bilateral relationship, India can serve as an alternative balancing power. Major economic initiatives include FTAs with Myanmar, Singapore, Thailand and Sri Lanka, while negotiations are ongoing with South Korea and Japan. To help balance

China's advances within the context of ASEAN + 3, Japan, Singapore and Indonesia have encouraged Indian participation in ASEAN + 6 (Dean, 2007). India is also considering joining APEC.

Despite an increase in bilateral economic relations, the residue from historical conflict between India and China lingers. Unresolved territorial disputes, competition over resources and the relative trajectories of these two powers portend ongoing potential for conflict. As a counterbalance to Chinese power, the strategic importance of the recently strengthened US alliance with India is difficult to overstate. In the words of one observer: "India's desire to dominate the Indian Ocean unnerves the People's Republic because of the ocean's importance in transporting Middle East oil. China has consequently built port facilities in the surrounding area – the so-called 'string of pearls' – which New Delhi believes are precursors to military bases" (De Santis, 2012, p. 215).

That neighboring, Russia remains the world's largest exporter of oil and natural gas and among the largest exporters of other primary products, ensures a heavy regional reliance on Russian resources. Since the launch of the Eastern Siberia-Pacific Ocean (ESPO) oil pipeline in 2009, Russia and China have made plans to pump crude oil from Siberia to the Kozmino oil export terminal on China's Pacific shore (CIA, 2011b). Before its construction, all overland transport of crude to East Asia was conducted via an inefficient rail-based system. Accordingly, most East Asian nations relied instead on energy supplies from the Middle East. Upon the ESPO's completion, expected in 2014–2015, Mideast oil could encounter increasing competition from this source (Chazan, 2010).

Unifying Russia and China at present is resistance to a perceived Western assault on national sovereignty as in the freedom of nation-states from internal interference under the banner of the "right to protect." Also uniting them is resentment of US "exorbitant privilege" (see Chapter 4) and some greater conviction that, after the (US-centered) financial crisis, Russia's and China's respective versions of state capitalism represent more the wave of the future.

Despite such apparent commonality and other building blocks for a Chinese–Russian alliance, historical enmities and lingering mutual suspicion render this relationship an unstable strategic counter-weight to US hegemony. Russian policymakers have long been wary that the Chinese will encroach into sparsely populated, energy- and mineral rich East Siberia. Meanwhile, some leading strategic thinkers envision a (still somewhat distant) future where a more democratic Russia becomes a more likely candidate for an expanded Western alliance. In the event, a Western strategic arrangement incorporating Russia would form a solid bulwark against Chinese designs at power aggrandizement. Alternatively, it could afford improved prospects for "accommodate[ing] China's rising global status" (Brzezinski, 2012, p. 97).

Concluding remarks

The world is witnessing an unmistakable shift in economic and political gravity towards Asia. Still, the geopolitical, economic and social trials facing the region's great powers – China, India and Russia – remain formidable. China's particular challenges and potential are sufficiently momentous for the future constellation of global power to merit a separate follow-on chapter. India and Russia likewise face major development, transitional and demographic trials.

Meanwhile, impediments to a durable alliance between any grouping of these states reduce the potential for a broad challenge to US influence. Its profound economic, diplomatic and military engagement with East Asia affords the US substantial leverage in balancing conflicting interests within the region. In the absence of a new global agreement any time soon, progress on the TPP (or FTAAP) arguably provides a more pragmatic means of advancing the multilateral trade agenda in the medium-term. In the meantime, the globalization of production – the intricate global supply chains that exploit any opportunities for enhancing production efficiencies – militates against any drift in the direction of greater regional autarky.

The demonstration of US power provides a hedge for smaller regional states in relation to China's transformative re-ascent. The US presence restrains Beijing's maneuverability in deploying its military assets. While the influence of an extra-regional power has been a source of some frustration, Beijing to date has adopted a broadly pragmatic posture. This realpolitik reflects in part US restraints on the region's other great power and China's historical rival, Japan.

For its part the US can do more "to incorporate India and Japan into a greater regional power-sharing role" (De Santis, 2012, p. 215). In the final analysis, it may be reasonable to conjecture that "America's approach to Asia offers Asians as well as Americans the best available chance to create a Pacific Century worthy of the name" (Mead, 2011).

7
China's Challenge

"The direction that China and US-China relations take will define the strategic future of the world for years to come. No relationship matters more – for better or for worse – in resolving the enduring challenges of our time." So begins a thoughtful overview of China's economic and political evolution (Bergsten et al., 2006, p. 1). If it looms so large within the 21st century power equation, how can a study of global power justify devoting merely one chapter to China's rise? That no other (non-US) actor has merited a separate chapter seems an unsatisfactory explanation. In fact, China's impact is evident in each theme and chapter of this book.

China's reemergence[1] to the ranks of the great powers is a leading feature of today's international political economy. Less certain is whether this country will eventually share the stage with the US at the apex of world power, persistently lag the US or instead outpace it in overall influence. Compared with previous historical power transitions – for example, the peaceful transfer from British to US primacy versus an earlier, more militant German challenge to the UK – is cooperation or conflict more likely to dominate the US-Chinese relationship going forward? Strict "realists" view conflict between rising and incumbent powers as more or less inevitable, even if ideological divisions recede over time. In contrast, "liberals" stress the potential for cooperation as economic interdependence and common concerns over the environment, terrorism and nuclear proliferation intensify. "Constructivists" ask whether the erosion of US legitimacy will afford China greater space to influence the norms underpinning global governance. Whichever perspective one adopts, no one doubts that prospects for US hegemony are inextricably linked to China's trajectory.

This chapter considers the implications of China's re-ascent for US global power. The remainder of the chapter is organized as follows. In the section "China's re-ascent and global challenge," I recap the book's themes as they pertain to the nature of China's challenge to the international system. The sections "The size of China's economy and prospects for future growth" and "China's development challenges," respectively, explore the Chinese economy's constituent sources of economic growth and the obstacles that may confront it in the future. The section "China's resource appetite and the military" focuses on China's preponderant impact on global commodity markets and the implications for China's military posture. In the section "Is Chinese Capitalism Exportable?", I consider whether the Chinese "model" of authoritarian state capitalism provides an attractive alternative to that of the less fettered US, or more social democratic variants of Western capitalism. The chapter concludes with an overall assessment of the Chinese challenge to US hegemony.

China's re-ascent and global challenge

China represents an unprecedented development story for a population of well over a billion people. Having recorded average annual economic growth rates approaching 10 per cent over three decades, hundreds of millions of Chinese have been lifted out of abject poverty.[2] Chinese reformers have lent stability to a society wracked by social upheavals in the Great Leap Forward and Cultural Revolution. While retaining its single-party monopoly and prohibiting fundamental criticism of the party or state, China's leadership has grown more responsive to social grievances, extended certain personal and economic freedoms, and granted greater latitude to a nascent civil society.

Among the main drivers of China's blistering growth has been its progressive integration into the global economy. This overriding factor has accelerated China's "catch up" advantage as a developing economy that can import cutting-edge technology and managerial acumen. Meanwhile, increasing numbers of young Chinese study abroad, building the skill sets integral to a market economy while gaining exposure to Western norms. Having emerged as the world's assembly workshop at the center of today's global supply chains, China delivers a torrential supply of final manufactured products onto world markets. Its ferocious growth has buoyed global commodity markets, enriching (pressuring) net commodity exporters (importers). China has long been the leading emerging market recipient of foreign direct investment, while its leading enterprises are increasingly prominent investors abroad.

Harboring a deep-seated mistrust of markets, the Chinese have sought to "lock down" physical energy, metal and food supplies throughout the developing and developed world. Chinese companies have signed long-term agreements to develop energy fields and mines while building ports and other transport infrastructure throughout Latin America, Africa, developing Asia and elsewhere. In return, claims have been accumulated on the future output of these foreign concerns. China has meanwhile amassed staggering external financial claims through a relentless buildup of foreign exchange reserves.

Having eliminated the most glaring inefficiencies inherited from its experiment with central planning, China's ability to sustain robust growth well into the future presumes an ability on the part of China's new generation of leaders to manage the transition to a second generation of reforms. New and strengthened market-supporting institutions will be needed to confront the profound challenges still awaiting this large, dynamic country. Notwithstanding its extraordinary turnaround from decades of economic stagnation and social dislocation, linearly extrapolating China's most impressive record over another generation would appear risky. Historical example reveals a tendency for growth in middle income countries to slow; and as a large, developing and transitioning country, China faces formidable challenges in the decades ahead.

Until relatively recently its foreign policy has mostly been oriented toward assuaging the fears of its neighbors over Chinese designs at power aggrandizement and encroachment. Meanwhile, the leadership has adopted a policy of benign neglect toward social and political conditions in countries with which Chinese enterprises conduct business.[3] Accordingly, in contrast to global condemnation of the 1989 crackdown in Tiananmen Square, in recent years one has heard frequent reference to Chinese "soft power." For some developing countries the so-called "Beijing Consensus" appears to offer a more palatable model of state-controlled markets against the more discredited, less fettered "Anglo-Saxon" alternative.

In sum, China has emerged as a pivotal actor on the global stage. Although reluctant to prematurely embrace the mantle of "responsible stakeholder," by sheer dint of its size, dynamism and resource needs, China exerts a disproportionate impact on the world economy and global politics. It looms as the sole country with potential to credibly challenge the US's global power position. Is this what a January 2011 *Wall Street Journal*/NBC News poll portends when 38 per cent of Americans named China as the most likely leading nation in 20 years compared with 35 per cent citing the USA?

Along with India and other emerging economies, China represents an extraordinary success story of US-led globalization. Accordingly, at the beginning of this book I raised the following issue: Having engulfed much of the formerly semi-autarkic world, would the juggernaut of US-inspired globalization ultimately redound to the detriment of the West? Were the advanced countries vulnerable to overwhelming competition from (still) largely state-directed economies that march to different rules of the game? Would endemic state management of the economy and an entrenched mercantilism allow a burgeoning China to exploit the gift of globalization at the expense of its main progenitor?

The perspective one takes on these questions can be informed, alternatively, by the marketplace logic of an Adam Smith or the power-augmenting argumentation of a Thomas Hobbes. From a Smithian perspective the world has benefitted immeasurably from China's integration. As a poorer country China's comparative advantage has lain principally in lower value added, labor-intensive production. In contrast, most advanced country firms specialize in higher-value segments of manufacturing and advanced services, representing the comparative advantage of a post-industrial, knowledge-based economy. China no doubt employs a (costly) web of cross-subsidization that can entail low- and occasionally negative value-added production[4]; but the associated reduction in prices represents a boon for global consumers. In general, the absorption of some 3 billion additional workers into the global economy via the integration of China, India and the former Soviet Union has generated substantial gains from trade that are shared between these economies and the rest of the world.

In contrast, zero-sum Hobbesian logic focuses on the systematic (systemic) taxation of Chinese households,[5] by dint of which resources are channeled to powerful vested interests, notably state-owned enterprises and the military. Discriminatory policies such as "indigenous innovation" and illegal activities such as enterprise theft or computer hacking advantage Chinese firms, diverting employment and income from workers abroad. The monopoly power wielded by Chinese rare earth metal producers or the aggressive "locking up" of global energy and metal supplies naturally arouses consternation over Chinese Communist Party designs. Such policies are principally pursued to augment state military assets, a goal to which no strategic rival can remain indifferent. In prioritizing state power over the welfare of its citizens, the character of China's integration undermines the global "rules of the game." Such beggar-thy-neighbor, market-distorting practices imperil the world.

This struggle between Smithian and Hobbesian mindsets has also played out along the macroeconomic dimension of "Chimerica" or global imbalances. The continuous accumulation of US IOUs in exchange for Chinese manufactures has led the Chinese to call for a diminished global reliance on the dollar. Meanwhile, US officials implore the Chinese to increase domestic consumption and allow greater currency flexibility. Beneath the grandstanding and saber rattling lies the fundamental political economy question: who holds the greater power card – the net creditor (China) or the net debtor (US)?[6]

Where does the argument outlined in this book come out on this controversy? The short answer is that we lean in the direction of Smith regarding the mainly auspicious (global) welfare implications of Chinese economic integration. Yet, as Hobbesians would suggest, it also makes sense to hedge against a China that resists playing by global rules. As with any significant structural change, this process has caused dislocation, particularly for lower- and semi-skilled workers. There is scant evidence, however, that China's commodity composition of trade is grossly out of line with its underlying comparative advantage (Branstetter and Lardy, 2006). And even where its enterprises advance to higher value-added product lines, such progress serves to expand the variety of products and services globally available. Moreover, China's success in graduating more educated and skilled personnel enlarges global technological possibilities.

For the most part World Trade Organization conventions adequately insulate import-competing firms against egregious "unfair trade practices."[7] More also needs to be done to encourage greater vigilance in China over the protection of intellectual property rights and enforcement against accounting fraud. Yes, even Hobbesian logic suggests that the US can best prepare for a Chinese strategic challenge by focusing on internal improvement. The overriding preoccupation of a hegemon actively seeking to maintain its position would presumably be on perfecting its infrastructure and domestic business climate to support robust innovation, productivity growth and higher value added employment creation.[8] Eschewing an overly defensive posture against wily foreign (state or private) competitors, a hegemon's leading firms would prioritize upgrading production processes and commercializing new and better products and services, exploiting technological achievements wherever in the world they happen to materialize. Such a national income-maximizing agenda would seem to represent the most effective hedge against the strategic designs of any would-be "peer competitor."

We have meanwhile argued in Chapter 4 that cumulative current account deficits in the US have yet to amount to a dangerous stock of external liabilities. Owing to the dollar's leading reserve currency status, the depth and liquidity of its capital markets and today's low policy rates, the government and large corporations can borrow exceedingly cheaply. While the public and household sectors face a protracted period of deleveraging in response to the financial crisis, the eurozone sovereign debt crisis and Japan's ongoing struggles with deflation have cemented the safe-haven dominance of dollar-denominated assets for the foreseeable future. Meanwhile, in amassing external financial claims of uncertain future value, the Chinese have forsaken, or at least postponed, substantial gains. Furthermore, China's widely acknowledged need to transition to domestic consumption-led growth appears at least as challenging as demand rebalancing in the US (see below).

The size of China's economy and prospects for future growth

In an earlier, widely referenced study, global bank Goldman Sachs forecast that China will overtake the US as the world's largest economy by 2027 (Goldman Sachs, 2007; see Figure 7.1). More bullish forecasters have since brought forward the date when China will reach parity with the size of the US economy.[9] For example, PricewaterhouseCoopers (PwC) predicts that China's share of world Gross Domestic Product (GDP) (at purchasing power parity) may surpass that of the US as early as 2020 (PricewaterhouseCoopers, 2010). According to PwC forecasts, by 2050 the Chinese economy will have

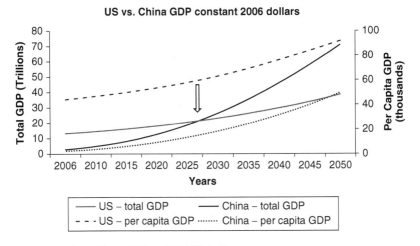

Figure 7.1 US vs. China GDP in 2006 US dollars
Source: Goldman Sachs (2007).

Table 7.1 Alternative US/China GDP projections

Goldman Sachs (2007)

	2006	2010	2020	2030	2040	2050
US (MER: 2006 US dollars)	13,245	14,535	17,978	22,817	29,823	38,514
China (MER: 2006 US dollars)	2,682	4,667	12,630	25,610	45,022	70,710

Source: Goldman Sachs

Carnegie Endowment (Albert Keidel, 2008)

	2005	2010	2020	2030	2040	2050
US (MER: 2005 US dollars)	12,000	14,000	18,000	24,000	33,000	44,000
China (MER: 2005 US dollars)	2,000	4,000	10,000	22,000	45,000	82,000
China (PPP: 2005 US dollars)	5,000	8,000	18,000	35,000	63,000	104,000

Source: Albert Keidel, Carnegie Endowment of International Peace

PricewaterhouseCoopers (country indices with US = 100), 2008

	2007	2050
US	100	100
China (MER)	23	129
China (PPP)	51	129

Source: PricewaterhouseCoopers et al., 2008.

grown to 130 per cent of the US economy (PricewaterhouseCoopers et al., 2008; see Table 7.1). The IMF meanwhile has advanced the cross-over date to 2016. Among others who have played this guessing game, there is even one observer who claims that China's GDP surpassed that of the USA in

2010 (Subramanian, 2011). Although many others forecast that China will become the largest economy sometime during the next 15 years, pinpointing the year depends on several strong assumptions. Inter-country comparisons are especially hazardous between advanced and developing economies, on the one hand, and, on the other, between fully fledged market and transition economies that still rely on administered pricing.

A more tangible factor impacting inter-country comparisons concerns the choice of exchange rate for converting yuan-denominated GDP into US dollar equivalent units. The choice between evaluating economic output at market exchange rates (MER) or at so-called purchasing power parity exchange rates (PPP) has significant consequences for assessing the relative size of the Chinese economy. MER-based comparisons tend to understate the relative size of lower income economies. In contrast, by comparing the average price levels of a common basket of goods between two countries, PPP-based comparisons better reflect actual purchasing power. Since poorer countries tend to exhibit lower wages and prices, particularly for non-traded goods, in correcting for this factor, PPP-based estimates arguably provide a more accurate measure in certain contexts, such as assessing the relative standard of living. In contrast, if one's main focus is the foreign exchange cost of acquiring particular goods and technologies from abroad, the market exchange rate seems the more appropriate measure (Cooper, 2005).

One can appreciate the impact of this difference by comparing PwC's MER figures where Chinese GDP is 23 per cent of the US compared to 51 per cent based on PPP in 2007 (Table 7.1). Alternatively, if one compares the PPP- and MER-based measures provided by China expert, Albert Keidel, Chinese GDP would surpass the US in 2020 as compared to well beyond 2030, respectively. Although PPP and MER measures tend to converge over longer periods, there is disagreement over when this will happen for China – 2050 according to PwC but 2100 according to the Carnegie Endowment.[10]

Yet, comparing the per capita GDP lines in Figure 7.1 shows that even by mid-century the standard of living of the average Chinese should remain markedly lower than that of the average American. While aggregate output comparisons provide a certain window into relative power, a comparison involving per capita GDP (or per capita net worth) underscores the power dynamics that reflect a healthier and more productive labor force, richer capital stock and more efficient economic system.

China's economic growth

In explaining longer-term economic growth, economists often rely on so-called "aggregate production function" analysis or growth accounting. In this framework, economic growth is estimated as a function of the growth of factor inputs – mainly labor (hours worked) and capital (investment in equipment and structures) – and the efficiency and technological sophistication with which such factors are combined to yield economic value. The latter element, total factor productivity (TFP), is estimated as a residual or the fraction of measured economic growth statistically unexplained by the combined growth rates of labor and capital.

Such exercises have been applied to China's economy. Their key merit lies in their insight into whether China's pattern of growth has been largely "extensive" (attributable to rapid accumulation of human and physical capital) or rather "intensive" (involving greater economic efficiencies). The latter involves either the movement of resources from low-productivity agriculture to more productive manufacturing or structural reform-induced technological change in industry or services. As Soviet and even East Asian experience amply shows,[11] countries can grow rapidly over extended periods owing to massive capital accumulation and greater labor force participation. Yet, barring institutional reforms, such growth patterns eventually encounter diminishing returns. In the Soviet case, thanks to extraordinary rates of investment and "over" full employment, but also an ability to exploit such low lying fruit as moving underemployed peasant farmers out of agriculture into manufacturing, early economic growth proved rapid. Eventually, however, the growth rates achieved through successive increases in (labor and capital) "inputs" declined, and were not offset by commensurate improvements in allocative efficiency (TFP).

In production function (growth accounting) studies China's growth has been attributed significantly to both increases in capital and labor, on the one hand, and a rapid annual growth of TFP on the other (see e.g. Bosworth and Collins, 2008; Brandt and Zhu, 2010). Brandt and Zhu argue, for example, that while the movement out of agriculture to other economic branches moderately impacted China's growth, the transfer of labor and other resources from the state to the non-state sector (combined with rapid TFP growth in the non-state, non-agricultural sector) has more significantly impacted the growth equation.

It is well known that China has relied upon an extraordinary rate of investment. The latter raises doubts about the sustainability of this growth model since capital accumulation at the pace of some 40–50 per cent of GDP – far exceeding that of any other large country – increases the prospects for costly capital misallocation, excess capacity and deflationary pressures. Nouriel Roubini (2011) puts it nicely:

> The problem, of course, is that no country can be productive enough to reinvest 50% of GDP in new capital stock without eventually facing immense overcapacity and a staggering non-performing loan problem. China is rife with overinvestment in physical capital, infrastructure, and property. To a visitor, this is evident in sleek but empty airports and bullet trains (which will reduce the need for the 45 planned airports), highways to nowhere, thousands of colossal new central and provincial government buildings, ghost towns, and brand-new aluminum smelters kept

closed to prevent global prices from plunging. Commercial and high-end residential investment has been excessive, automobile capacity has outstripped even the recent surge in sales, and overcapacity in steel, cement, and other manufacturing sectors is increasing further. In the short-run the investment boom will fuel inflation, owing to the highly resource- intensive character of growth. But overcapacity will lead inevitably to serious deflationary pressures, starting with the manufacturing and real- estate sectors. Eventually, most likely after 2013, China will suffer a hard landing. All historical episodes of excessive investment – including East Asia in the 1990's – have ended with a financial crisis and/or a long period of slow growth. To avoid this fate, China needs to save less, reduce fixed investment, cut net exports as a share of GDP, and boost the share of consumption. The problem is that the reasons the Chinese save so much and consume so little are structural. It will take two decades of reforms to change the incentive to overinvest.

China's extraordinary pace of investment reflects systemic incentives generating feverishly rapid development and urbanization, reminiscent of the earlier Soviet experiment. A web of subsidies lowers the effective cost to state-owned enterprises of capital, energy and other resources. Financing this arrangement is systematic taxation of Chinese households through negative real interest rates on savings and repressed wages, helping to explain why consumption represents a meager 35–40 per cent of national income.[12]

In addition, China's unfavorable demographic outlook will progressively exert a constraining effect on extensive economic growth in the future. While average annual US population growth will remain positive (from 0.96 per cent in 2005–2010 to a projected 0.36 per cent in 2045–2050), population growth in China is forecast to turn sharply downward – from a positive 0.63 per cent in 2005–2010 to a negative 0.33 per cent in 2045–2050 (UN Population Division, 2010). While US fertility is predicted to remain stable around the replacement rate of 2.1 children per woman over the next 40 years, China's fertility rate had already fallen below replacement level by 1992, settling around 1.5 since 2001. As a result, China will have more than 440 million people over 60 years of age in 2050 – an increase from 10 per cent in 2000 to roughly 30 per cent of the population (UN Population Division, 2010). By 2100 the ratio of China's population to that of the US is forecast to decline to 2:1, in comparison with a ratio of 4.3:1 in 2010.

This demographic trend, which reflects the country's one-child policy, comes with two major effects. First, it will retard labor force growth as the average age of the population increases. Secondly, funding even a rudimentary safety net for an ageing population will prove fiscally burdensome. Working age Chinese will be confronted with the so-called 4-2-1 problem, as one working age person supports two parents and four grandparents. The upshot is that population aging burdens a relatively shrinking work force, thus reducing funds for competing priorities.[13]

In sum, the underlying sources of China's growth have been multifaceted: high savings and investment, transformative changes in economic structure and ownership, an amalgam of market-oriented reforms and an opening of the economy to global trade and investment. The test for its future trajectory will be an ability to reproduce the core prerequisites to strong trend growth, once the convergence process associated with underdevelopment is complete. Few countries, including those with less momentous social and political challenges than those facing China, have proved able to match the record of sustained TFP growth achieved by the US and a few other advanced countries. This helps explain the general pattern, involving few historical exceptions, that middle income countries tend to slow markedly once they surpass an estimated threshold of $16,000 in per capita income (Eichengreen et al., 2011).[14]

China's development challenges

As China begins its once-in-a-decade leadership transition at the end of 2012, its overriding objectives are to maintain internal political stability and to stanch centrifugal regional tendencies by ensuring broad-based development, while responding pro-actively to public discontent over core social shortcomings. Significant poverty reduction alongside pockets of prosperity seems to have contained the impulse behind more pervasive demands for change and greater political participation from below. The growth of the middle class and the spread of information technologies can be expected to increase demands for political liberalization. In the event, any marked slowing of growth, declining employment prospects and an inability to make inroads on other social priorities can progressively erode the legitimacy of China's authoritarian regime.

The relative optimism (pessimism) with which various commentators approach China's potential to challenge US global power rests on the extent to which they linearly extrapolate past successes, versus how much they discount economic, social and political challenges certain to test China's leadership over the coming decades. Historical experience suggests that China can maintain relatively rapid growth, assuming pragmatic policy foresight prevails. This will require increasing devolution of economic authority to private enterprise (or state-owned enterprises facing harder budget constraints), and greater reliance on market prices and market-supportive institutions. Eventually it will almost certainly require some political liberalization, if not wholesale removal of the Communist Party monopoly of power. Since a proper accounting of its core development challenges would require a separate book-length study, here I provide only a brief, impressionistic overview of potential obstacles to sustained development in China.

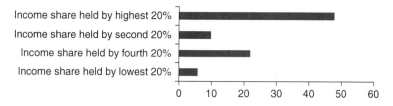

Figure 7.2   China's income distribution
Source: World Bank, World Development Indicators (2010).

Income and regional inequality

A potentially serious aggravation of political pressures could result from a continuation of China's current trends toward greater social inequality. Growing inequality remains particularly problematic to the extent that the ethos of solidarity and egalitarianism still provides a vestige of ideological support behind the Communist Party. Together with disaffection over corruption and pollution (see below), bitterness over inequality has sparked social unrest (Lum, 2006). As can be seen from Figure 7.2, almost 50 per cent of national income is received by the top quintile of the population, with the top 10 per cent of earners receiving almost a third of national income. Already a half decade ago China's Gini coefficient had climbed from 0.25 – roughly the equivalent of egalitarian Norway today – to 0.41, placing it 54th among 134 countries in overall inequality (Dollar, 2007, p. 21). By some estimates, China's current Gini coefficient approximates 0.5, among the world's highest (Whyte, 2012, p. 234). According to a provocative study by Wang Xiaolu, of the China Reform Foundation, inequality can be still higher due to factors such as the underreporting of income to evade taxes. He suggests that in contrast to an official figure of 9, the top 10 percent of urban incomes could be 23 times that of the poorest 10 percent of urban residents. (Economist, 2012b).

Many factors account for this apparently steep upward drift in income inequality. One is the predictably differential impact of globalization on rural versus urban workers and across groups with varying levels of skills and education. Another is the hukou system of household registration which discriminates against rural migrants. And residual state control over the economy promotes cronyism (differential access to resources and opportunity) that further exacerbates inequality (Economist, 2012b).

Structural inequality is apparent not only across the income distribution but also across geographical regions. For example, per capita GDP in the western provinces of Xinjiang, Tibet, Qinghai, Gansu and Ningxia is reportedly just one-third that of the east coast provinces of Jiangsu, Shanghai and Zhejiang. Differential access to quality education and disparities in infrastructure are just some of the factors that may underlie these differences.

Whatever their specific causes, such inter-regional inequalities could impose an increasing political challenge for Beijing in the future.

The environment

While creating jobs and raising living standards, rapid industrialization has come at a cost. Although China's landmass is comparable to that of the US, China's environment is in much worse shape. For example, only 20 per cent of cultivatable land remains unscathed by soil impoverishment, and 35 per cent of Chinese land is severely degraded (UN FAO, 2012).

Water shortages impact at least 60 per cent of China's 660 cities, with 110 facing extreme shortages; and close to 90 per cent of Chinese cities encounter water pollution. Water problems lower the productive capacity of industry and agriculture alike, resulting in less tax revenue and billions in foregone economic activity (for example, pollution of the Yellow River costs the Chinese economy between $1.4 billion and $1.9 billion annually). Two-thirds of the rural population is without piped water, contributing to life-threatening diarrheal diseases and cancer of the digestive system (The World Bank, PRC 2007).

One can distinguish between three major impacts of China's pollution problem. First, it imposes significant direct and indirect health costs, while depressing labor productivity. Second, China has to divert significant resources toward abating the impact of environmental degradation. Despite investments in better air quality, for example, China's officials concede that air pollution is expected to worsen considerably over the next two decades (Bloomberg News, 2010).

Finally, pollution spurs social unrest. For example, deforestation and grassland overgrazing are converting vast stretches into desert, forcing rural migrants into cities, where they are unwelcome. Water shortages lead to battles over access to limited supplies. For example, around a thousand villagers fought in 2000 for two days against the police over access to irrigation in Shandong Province. In October 2004 in Sichuan Province, 90,000 peasants fought with police over losing their homes for little compensation to make way for a hydroelectric dam. Demonstrations against environmental damage have grown in size, frequency and sophistication (Keidel, 2005).

Why has a succession of environmental protection regulations failed to decrease pollution commensurately? One explanation is that local officials lack the incentive to implement such directives. If the overriding state goal is economic growth, officials are less incented to focus on negative externalities. Fines remain too low for enterprises to invest in new pollution-abating technologies. In general, environmental protection is typically considered an extra burden not worth assuming (Economy, 2007).

In addition, compared with a relatively diversified USA, China is overly dependent on coal (Figure 7.3). Cheap but dirty coal accounts for more than

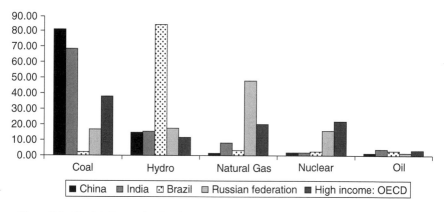

Figure 7.3 Electricity production by sources
Source: World Bank, World Development Indicators.

80 per cent of total power, almost twice the worldwide average. And the centrality of coal to the Chinese economy is increasing. In the early 1980s it was used for roughly 55 per cent of total energy production or about 164 billion kWh. By 2007 coal was used to generate 2,656 billion kWh – more than 16 times as much. Although China invests heavily in wind and solar power-by 2020 it hopes to generate a fifth of its energy needs from renewable sources (Borger and Watts, 2009)-coal-powered electricity will remain the backbone of China's economic growth for the foreseeable future. Rapid urbanization and the absence of a national (or even extensive regional) electricity grid (Cooper, 2004), combined with the dominance of coal, have been major contributors to the country's pollution challenge (Fan, 2005).

Corruption and social protest

China ranks 75 out of 182 in the Transparency International's 2011 Corruption Perception Index. Much of this corruption involves economic offences, such as bribery, fraud, theft, smuggling and unauthorized trading in foreign exchange (Wedeman, 2004). The pervasive pattern of corruption hampers capital accumulation, including via embezzlement or the stripping of state-owned assets. It rewards unproductive, illegal behavior at the expense of entrepreneurial activity. And it undermines the implementation of core development goals (He, 2000). Besides its negative effects on the economy and society, corruption left unchecked ultimately poses a threat to the Communist Party's legitimacy. In addition to debates over the pace of market reform and the role of the state, the pervasiveness of corruption has aggravated fissures within the ranks of the party.

The social dislocation attending China's economic and political transition has been marked by a notable increase in so-called "mass group incidents."

While strikes and other protests were once concentrated in the key cities and directed at the central government, protests today are more dispersed and focused on local officials and enterprise managers (Walder, 2009). With the major exception of Tiananmen over two decades ago, social disaffection has yet to pose a direct challenge to Beijing: "The mass protest incidents that have become ever more common in recent years are mainly a response to abuses of power and other procedural justice issues, rather than being fueled by feelings of distributive injustice and anger at the rich" (Whyte, 2012, p. 234).

The Communist Party has developed survival strategies, including co-opting opposition leaders, appealing to nationalism and slowly expanding individual freedoms (for example, by opening up the Internet to non-political content). Perhaps most importantly, the party arrived at an efficient solution for dealing with rural discontent: the central government publicly sympathizes with the protestors while castigating local officials, many of whom are imprisoned following perfunctory trials. In so doing, the party avoids becoming a principal target of public ire (Shirk, 2007, p. 66). Yet, the overriding strategy for containing discontent still appears to be the drive to maintain a superior rate of economic growth and the associated (albeit slower) growth of household incomes.

Debt

China tends to fare reasonably well in many inter-country comparisons over macroeconomic stability. Its net creditor status reflects a consistent balance of payments surplus. Its enterprise and household sectors run among the highest savings rates in the world, and it reports relatively modest central government debt. Having engaged in successive bouts of recapitalization, its banking system has defied periodic forecasts of impending collapse. The underlying macroeconomic backdrop may prove less propitious, however. As the previous quotation from Nouriel Roubini attests, no country can run investment-GDP ratios approaching 50 per cent without courting capital misallocation and associated social losses on a significant scale. Non-performing loans impose losses on the banking system, eventually showing up on the consolidated government balance sheet.

A more recently acknowledged threat has been that posed by an explosion of loans to regional governments, particularly during the two-year stimulus program in response to the global financial crisis. Moody's estimates that the share of these loans that could prove delinquent may approach 50–75 per cent (Vaughan and Back, 2011). Meanwhile, Beijing directs local governments to spend liberally on affordable housing initiatives among other social welfare- and growth-supporting programs. If local governments fail to service them, these loan obligations will need to be transferred to the central budget. Even official Chinese estimates place local debt at some half of annual GDP by the end of 2010 (Shih, 2011). Given inadequate transparency, public debt data need to be treated cautiously. According to one estimate, adding contingent liabilities to explicitly recognized public debt could have raised China's consolidated public debt to as high as 150 percent of GDP by end-2010 (Rabinovitch and Anderlini, 2011).

China's resource appetite and the military

Among the leading concerns China's development fosters is its impact on global resource supplies. To name a few examples, the country dominates world markets in aluminum, iron ore, nickel and steel. Although its aggregate energy demand lags behind that of the US, the growth rate of Chinese (plus other large emerging country) energy requirements is expected to ensure a secular increase in real petroleum prices in particular.[15]

China's resource appetite once propelled expansion to the Asian heartland, leading to the incorporation of Tibet and Xinjiang. Although Uighurs account for less than 1 per cent of China's population, they make up 45 per cent of Xinjiang's. Together with the Tibetan minority, they stand in contrast to China's majority Han population, which is heavily concentrated in the lowlands. This ethnic-cum-geographical pattern instills a permanent source of tension, as the government seeks to maintain control over these tablelands, which are rich in oil, natural gas, copper and iron ore, and views the prospect of greater autonomy with trepidation (Kaplan, 2010).

Over the last decade, Chinese enterprises have gone on a global shopping spree. China Petroleum & Chemical Corporation (Sinpoec), for example, now develops oil fields in Iraq and Canada and is involved in off-shore explorations in Africa. China National Petroleum Corporation has purchased concessions in a wide range of locations including Azerbaijan, Canada, Indonesia, Iraq, Iran, Kazakhstan, Sudan and Venezuela, and China National Offshore Oil Corporation is exploring in Indonesia, having earlier failed to acquire California-based oil company Unocal (Cooper, 2005). In 2009 the state-backed aluminum company Chinalco tried to acquire the Anglo-Australian mining giant Rio Tinto.

Reportedly China's state-supported companies pay well above market rates to secure long-term supply contracts or privileged access to strategic materials located abroad (Bremmer, 2009a, p. 45). Attracting recent notoriety has been CNOOC's offer to buy into Canada's Nexen Inc. at a 60 percent equity premium. This deal appears motivated to gain access to advanced Western drilling technology, even at a seemingly exorbitant cost. One observer characterizes this general Chinese strategy (here in specific relation to electric cars) so: "China's buying spree could be the making of an economic jugger-naut. It could also be stocking the world's greatest technological junkyard" (Sternberg, 2012).

Highly dependent on sea-based supply routes for its energy supply, it looks to decrease this dependence by building secure overland pipelines from Russia or other states, such as Kazakhstan and Pakistan. Notwithstanding such investment in supply diversification, China remains reliant for most of its energy demand on the Persian Gulf. As such it is forced to depend on the US navy to secure safe passage from the Persian Gulf and Africa through the Strait of Malacca. Understandable wariness over such dependence explains Beijing's strategy to eventually establish a blue water navy, and more imme-diately to invest in additional ports and pipelines that can diversify China's commodity sources and transit routes.

China has been increasing its military budget, albeit from a low base and roughly in line with the growth of its GDP, at a double digit annual pace since 1989, excluding 2010. Aside from modernizing all military branches, it has built an aircraft carrier and stealth fighter, and it is expanding its submarine capability. China has improved its anti-ship missile capacity, it has advanced its anti-satellite program, including jamming devices, and it is investing heavily in cyberwarfare.

While comparing military expenditures is fraught with challenges and cer-tainly not tantamount to measuring capabilities, such exercises nonetheless provide a rough order of magnitude concerning relative strengths and poten-tial. In their estimates the Stockholm International Peace Research Institute includes personnel (expenditures on current civil and military personnel, retirement pensions and social services), operations and maintenance, pro-curement, R&D, construction and military aid. It should be noted that China's costs per soldier are substantially lower. The US, in contract, main-tains a well-trained but expensive professional army. Even if China's military expenditures were to significantly exceed what is officially reported, they are dwarfed by that of the US (see Figure 7.4) without even considering the US's huge legacy advantage.[16] Although second in defense spending glob-ally, fears that China poses even a medium-term threat to conventional US military supremacy seem farfetched.

Yet, the relative sizes and overall capabilities of the US and Chinese mil-itaries are less the issue at present. China's military effort today is focused on its immediate region (see Figure 7.5). The Pentagon's major concern is China's investment in an "anti-access" or "area denial" capability. This asymmetric strategy features anti-ship missiles, taking down US computer networks and satellites, and forcing US aircraft carriers farther afield from the immediate outskirts of Chinese territorial waters. The motivation is first China's persistent designs on Taiwan. A second factor is the ability to patrol more freely near regional islands of disputed ownership containing valuable resources in the East and South China Sea.

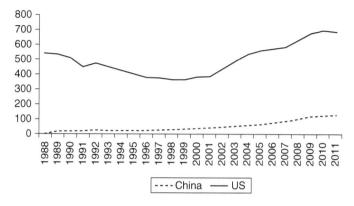

Figure 7.4 Military expenditure in constant 2010 US dollars (billions)

Source: Information from the Stockholm International Peace Research Institute (SIPRI), http://milexdata.sipri.org/

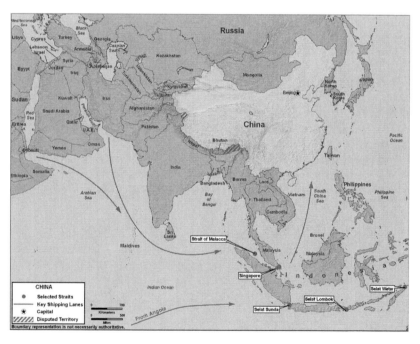

Figure 7.5 China's neighborhood

Source: US Department of Defense (2009).

Is China's Capitalism Exportable?

The collapse of the Soviet Union in 1991 marked the denouement of a protracted competition between two world systems. The US-Soviet struggle represented in part a clash of ideologies. In the aftermath of the Cold War, little illusion remained that classical communism represented a bona fide alternative to Western capitalism. China's leadership remains well aware that the economy's outperformance had much to do with avoiding certain pitfalls of Soviet central planning. While embracing international trade and investment and adopting core economic reforms, the leadership is careful to defend certain hallmarks of the traditional system: namely single-party rule and the danger of unfettered individual rights. China's variant of authoritarian capitalism may appeal to certain developing states, particularly those wary of Western-style democracy and threats to national sovereignty – notably the "right to protect." As such it is reasonable to ask: does China offer a viable alternative to the liberal Western model?

It has long and widely been presumed that a sustainable capitalism presupposes political as well as economic liberalization. Since the advent of its reforms, China has made great strides with economic reform while making only grudging concessions to democratization. The advantages should not be underestimated: while freeing up ownership and allowing greater scope for market-based decision-making, Beijing retains control over the "commanding heights." It is constrained neither by the need for democratic consensus nor as significantly by human rights issues. Decisions can be made and implemented more expeditiously, as US observers, disgruntled over crumbling infrastructure and other manifestations of political paralysis, have duly noted. China has managed to maintain broad social stability for a 1.4 billion population, even as the leadership pursues highly disruptive development initiatives. For example, when building the Three Gorges Dam, China relocated more than 1.2 million people without triggering protests anywhere comparable to that of the Tiananmen Square demonstrations in 1989 (Shirk, 2007, p. 66).

Another example of state pragmatism and central control involves the global financial crisis: Beijing promptly responded with a $586 billion economic stimulus package, geared towards investments in infrastructure projects and programs to increase domestic consumption in rural areas. Additionally, the government ordered banks to expand loans to local governments and businesses (Morrison, 2009). Intent on avoiding the Asian financial crisis, the leadership held to its cautious policy on yuan appreciation and (limited) capital account liberalization, notwithstanding mounting Western pressure. Meanwhile, the Chinese state was able to exploit the crisis propagandistically, blaming it on a venal Western capitalist mentality and slipshod regulation. The episode reassured the leadership that strategic control over the commanding heights remains the pragmatic route to growth and stability (Bremmer, 2009b).

China's authoritarian state capitalism also entails disadvantages. For example, as cited earlier in a system whose incentive structure prioritizes economic growth over other objectives, local authorities have little reason to aggressively pursue ancillary directives on crucial objectives like environmental protection. That the system is geared towards regional economic output expansion helps to explain why Beijing's well-intentioned exhortations on supplementary goals have largely failed to penetrate the veil of regional and local bureaucracy. Meanwhile, pervasive corruption impedes efficient resource allocation and reinforces public distrust.

The lack of more expansive personal and political freedom also takes its toll. Human rights are subordinated to the state-defined national interest, political participation outside the Communist Party is disallowed and media outlets are censored. Such social and political realities in turn influence the economic model: although China invests heavily in R&D and education, its economy lacks many of the inherent innovative capabilities integral to intensive-based growth.[16]

The upshot is that Chinese state-led capitalism appears more attractive as a model for countries at a lower level of development, especially for governments already disinclined toward democratization. An authoritarian government facilitates more expedient decision-making concerning industrialization, infrastructure and development writ large. At some point, however, increasing wealth seems insufficient to offset the desire for political participation and expanded liberties. A lingering question is whether the transition from extensive to intensive growth can be successfully completed if the required second generation of economic reforms collides with the political requirements of authoritarian control.

China's hegemonic challenge

China is situated within a tough neighborhood: a revanchist Russia to the north, historical rival India to the west, traditional enemies Japan and South Korea and an unpredictable North Korea to the east, ancient antagonist Vietnam to the south, and with US allies and bases dispersed throughout the region. Such menacing surroundings must preoccupy a considerable part of China's strategic thinking. Before it is in any position to project global power, it will first have to consolidate its position in a region comprising competing national interests, political ideologies, ethnicities and historical animosities. Its basic power dilemma rests on the natural tendency of its neighbors to react defensively to any perceived increase in Chinese assertiveness or belligerence. While smaller states recognize China's critical role as economic locomotive, they remain equally wary of encroaching Chinese power. Hence, they continue to regard the US as a regional security guarantor and the US military presence as a hedge against Chinese expansionism.

China's leadership is well aware that its growing clout engenders anxiety. Accordingly, at least until recently, China had moderated its actions vis-à-vis long-standing territorial claims. While disputes in the East and South China Seas remain unresolved, until recently China has resisted moving aggressively on what it considers its rightful property. China scored additional diplomatic points by refraining from currency devaluation and offering financial assistance during the Asian Financial Crisis. It has meanwhile forged important economic ties through such initiatives as ASEAN + 3 and the Asian Regional Forum.

Some view China's heretofore restrained foreign policy as temporary and tactical. Allusions are made to the country's imperial past or parallels are drawn with previous Japanese or German aggression. Neorealists tend to argue that a more assertive China is inevitable, owing to its rising power and expanding security imperatives. China may seek to exploit opportunities for expanded geopolitical reach precisely to counter perceived threats from other powers. Such moves may relate to unresolved territorial claims, increasing dependence on foreign energy sources, or fear of rearmament, notably in Japan. Having been hegemonic in Asia for millennia, China arguably seeks to restore this status, if for no other reason than to enhance its own security, surrounded as it has been by historically hostile neighbors.

In the public relation wars, the Chinese authorities underscore the shortcomings of a US-dominated global order. For example, they decry a reckless macroeconomic policy epitomized by chronic fiscal and trade deficits and a monetary policy that weakens the external value of the dollar. They heap criticism on the US for running a reckless regulation-light financial system. In contrast to US values-based conditionality, they assert that the developing world can rely on a less demanding, longer-term commitment from Chinese investment. And Chinese leaders deride US offers to arbitrate territorial disputes as thinly disguised influence peddling or, worse, "imperial" interference. To paraphrase, China's official state narrative is that the US is no longer a dependable steward of the global order.

In relation to US interests, the extent to which China has been cooperative is open to debate. As discussed in the last chapter, China has played a complex diplomatic card in North Korea. It has muted its criticism of the Iraq War while taking economic advantage of US intervention in Afghanistan. It has firmed its export controls on weapons of mass destruction technology transfer while broadly cooperating on intelligence sharing related to counterterrorism. In contrast, its compliance with US and European sanctions on Iran has been reluctant and inconsistent. Alongside Russia, more recently China has frustrated United Nations Security Council condemnation of Syrian President Bashar al-Assad.

Other irritants in US–Chinese relations include alleged state-sponsored hacker attacks on computer networks, weak safeguards of intellectual property and ongoing currency disputes. While arousing understandable concerns among import-competing firms and workers, various manifestations of Chinese mercantilism tend to entail a resource loss for China itself. These include the myriad of subsidies that often engender capital misallocation, foreign direct investments involving above-market cost locking up of commodity supplies and the low return on holding (excessive) foreign exchange reserves.

Any pretension to challenge US global hegemony presupposes China's hegemony within its immediate region. As a stepping stone toward regional hegemony, China's medium-term objective, according to some observers, is to work to nullify or seriously dilute the credibility of US presence in the region. Motivating the Chinese in no small part is their prior "century of humiliation," following the intervention of foreign powers. They argue moreover that growing US resource constraints and the absence of a credible commitment to a bolstered presence in the region could encourage US allies to peel off one by one, opting to bandwagon with China (Friedberg, 2011). As we have already noted, however, China's immediate neighborhood is hardly receptive to Chinese regional dominance. One thing seems certain: The intensity of Chinese nationalism notwithstanding, it is in no way clear that China's leadership envisions a Chinese 21st century. In the event, China's path to position itself eventually for a credible strategic challenge to US hegemony seems steep indeed.

Concluding remarks

Hegemony presupposes predominance among multiple dimensions of power. In no single dimension does China currently rival the US or possess the potential to do so within the foreseeable future. First, in the main, China remains a poor country wrestling with core developmental challenges. Second, aspirations toward global power projection capability presuppose an ability to first navigate and grow one's power base regionally. In contrast to the hegemony the US achieved in the Western Hemisphere during the 19th century, China faces a neighborhood with formidable states wary of China's re-ascendancy. As the preponderant power both external and internal to the region, the US engages, largely successfully, in a tight-wire act to discourage any Chinese expansionist impulses. Meanwhile, the US works to encourage a regional integration compatible with multilateral norms, while keeping unobstructed the major sea lanes and strategic chokepoints vital to East Asian commerce.

Although its mode of conducting business and other facets of its "soft power" may be attractive in certain quarters, China offers no unifying vision for global civil society, global governance or the global economy. Aside from broadsides against US "hegemonic imperialism," China provides no compelling ideological or political alternative that would galvanize the support of an otherwise disparate bloc of nations. China's trajectory relies heavily on the existing global economic system. It has benefited too much from the liberal world order's rules of the game to substitute a distinct, systemic alternative (Ikenberry, 2011). Meanwhile, China has yet to assume meaningful leadership alongside the US and others in the provision of core public goods integral to safeguarding global security and prosperity.

By dint of its overwhelming population and ongoing convergence potential, the size of the Chinese economy will surpass that of the US sooner or later. Its recent military buildup can be rationalized in a variety of ways, not least owing to its rapid economic growth and by an understandable desire to lower dependence on US security services. Yet, China possesses few serious alliances with which to pose a credible, counterbalancing threat. In contrast, backing the US is a formidable array of traditional allies and more recently enhanced strategic relationships spanning most regions of the world.

Given the ongoing evolution in facets of Chinese power, the parameters underlying US–China relations are sure to evolve in unanticipated directions. The admonitions of liberal internationalists who tend to view economic interdependence as an antidote to future rivalry must therefore be weighed against neorealist concerns that the reality of convergence is more likely to increase the scope for conflict. Just as economic integration historically has failed to prevent earlier conflagrations, US–China synergies and common interests do not obviate a hedging strategy vis-à-vis a potentially more aggressive China in the future. Yet, a tit-for-tat neo-mercantilist posture would surely prove self-defeating. The more viable longer-term strategy would appear to be consolidation of the core preconditions for US dynamism and a reaffirmation of central non-material assets integral to the exercise of US hegemony.

Part V

Domestic Constraints on US Power

8
The Deficit

Introduction

Recent decades have witnessed a profound evolution in the global strategic landscape. Nevertheless, this book has argued that the core external challenges confronting the US qua hegemon remain broadly manageable. The rise of competing power centers and proliferation of transnational threats notwithstanding, the US remains a dominant economic player, an overriding military force and disproportionately weighty in global politics, technology, and culture. On balance, its corporations and workers can harness globalization and technological change to deliver robust growth in the longer term. While reforms in finance, health and education are needed to cope with structural headwinds, including unemployment and inequality, the country's enduring strengths remain impressive.

Part IV isolates a more pressing risk to US hegemony – the ability to operate within two domestic constraints. The first concerns the deteriorating medium- and longer-term fiscal outlook. The second involves the limits of contemporary US politics in coping with the pressures of globalization and the demands of hegemony. The former is the subject of the present chapter; the latter is examined in Chapter 9.

Already featuring prominently in the global imbalances debate is the US federal budget deficit. I showed in Chapter 4 how the (external) current account and (internal) fiscal imbalances – the so-called "twin deficits" – have been, at best, tenuously linked historically, punctuated by periods during which they have moved inversely.

One particular preoccupation is US federal debt held abroad particularly by China. Foreign holdings are currently just under half of government debt held by the public. Moreover, of total government debt held by the public, about 10 per cent is held by China.[1] The rest is distributed broadly across a myriad of foreign private and official holders, including Japan, Taiwan and the UK (see US Treasury Department 2011).

While much is made of this by some, the increase in the share of foreign-held US debt is a predictable result of globalization (Johnson and Kwak, 2012, p. 145). While US residents will have to service this debt, sending real resources out of the country, this only reverses the net supplement to US resources when the funds were borrowed. And although rates will increase in the future, on any realistic accounting today's historically low US government yields have represented an extraordinary bargain for US residents.

That so many investors continue to favor US government debt is unsurprising as treasuries offer superior liquidity to that of competing financial assets. Furthermore, it remains unlikely that even modest credit downgrades will dissuade investors facing increasingly fewer safe investment alternatives from purchasing US debt in the future. In the event, investor reaction to rating agency Standard and Poor's (S&P's) downgrade during the summer of 2011 should have significantly dispelled such fears.[2]

This chapter argues that the country's unsustainable fiscal trajectory rather than any over-dependency on foreign financing represents the central concern for US global power. The restoration of longer-term fiscal balance involves, first and foremost, the imperative to confront explosive health care inflation, reflected in ballooning unfunded liabilities in the country's major health entitlement programs – Medicare and Medicaid – over the longer term.[3] Meanwhile, requiring some attention is the escalating trajectory of US public debt, reflecting projected annual federal budget deficits averaging as much as $1 trillion over the next decade (see Figure 8.1).[4] Such historically unprecedented federal deficit levels come on top of state and local financial pressures and a prior large buildup in household debt. While the aggregate US corporate balance sheet appears comparatively healthy, the household sector will undergo a protracted deleveraging for years. The crux is that fiscal normalization – alongside household deleveraging – is integral to restoring the robust long-term growth that underpins US hegemony. To what extent does fiscal stabilization also require a meaningful retrenchment in the far-flung commitments marking US global power projection today? Which defense expenditures will need to be scaled back (Mandelbaum, 2010)?

The rest of this chapter is organized as follows. The section "Fiscal policy under Clinton and Bush II" draws the relevant conclusions for future fiscal policy of spending and revenue decisions made under the Clinton and George W. Bush presidencies. In the section "Obama's budgets: The short- and medium-term outlooks," I review the budgetary record and outlook under President Obama. The section "Long-term/entitlements" outlines what it will take to ensure longer-term fiscal solvency, against which the role of defense expenditure is assessed in the section "Defense spending." The section "Politics and reform" considers the political backdrop to fiscal reform, followed by summary remarks on the relevance of fiscal policy for US hegemony in the section "Conclusion."

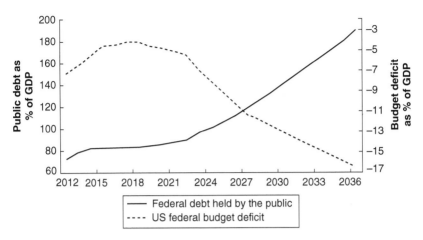

Figure 8.1 US federal budget deficit and debt held by the public
Source: CBO (2012) "Summary Data for Extended Alternative Fiscal Scenario," CBO's 2012 Long-Term Budget Outlook (June, 2012) (for the years beyond 2022); An Update to the Budget and Economic Outlook: Fiscal Years 2012–2022 (August, 2012) (for the years 2012–2022).

Fiscal policy under Clinton and Bush II

Among other things, the Administration of George W. Bush was noted for its fiscal profligacy, a trait at odds with the Republican Party's traditional advocacy of smaller government.[5] In the inter-party squabbles, Bush's reckless spending and revenue policies remain a favorite trope of Democrats who contrast them with the fiscal conservatism exercised under Clinton. Out of this partisan discussion the following conclusions stand up to scrutiny. First, heeding the advice of Treasury Secretary Robert Rubin, Clinton subordinated his ambitious domestic agenda to fiscal probity and was duly rewarded by the bond market with lower yields.[6] While the restoration of fiscal balance during the Clinton Administration represented a significant accomplishment, one cannot attribute all fiscal improvement during the 1990s to policy choices. For example, the budgetary surplus during 1997–2001 reflected, in part, a surge in economy-wide productivity growth, the transient effects of the bubble economy – including outsized capital gains revenue, and taxable option and bonus payments – unexpectedly (and temporary) low health care cost inflation and sharp reductions in military expenditure (the so-called Cold War dividend). Furthermore, demographics buoyed the fiscal balance with the baby boomers in their peak earning years and with mass retirements more than a decade away. Accordingly, payroll tax receipts were elevated with benefit payouts correspondingly low (Johnson and Kwak, 2012, p. 86). In sum, total federal revenues exceeded 19 percent of GDP for five successive years, an historical first.

Second, the recession that occurred at the beginning of the Bush Administration – aggravated, in turn, by September 11 and corporate governance scandals – justified timely and temporary tax cuts to bolster aggregate demand. Third, September 11 signaled a need for increased spending on homeland security and renewed outlays for defense. The subsequent wars in Afghanistan and Iraq drove defense expenditure higher. Nevertheless, the federal deficit was held below two percent of GDP in 2006 and 2007. Subsequently, Hurricane Katrina and the sub-prime debt fallout would raise necessary federal expenditure further.

Far less defensible was the Bush Administration's extension of the 2001 and 2003 tax cuts,[7] combined with a failure to contain discretionary and entitlement spending growth. Particularly egregious was the passage of a prescription drug benefit, the largest expansion in entitlement spending since Medicare; but even in the absence of this additional mandate, significant overall expenditure restraint was required. Having accounted for the revenue losses attributable to the 2001 recession, legislative action significantly explains the deterioration in the budget outlook during much of the Bush Administration. Framing his presidency, Bush's term concluded with a second recession beginning in 2008, triggered by the sub-prime debt crisis. This deep economic downturn cratered revenues, presenting incoming President Obama with a rapidly deteriorating budgetary outlook.

While basic fiscal prudence presupposes balancing the budget over the business cycle except where the spending involves genuinely productive infrastructural investment, the Bush II Administration's taxation and expenditure policy generated a structural budget deficit out of an overall budget surplus of 2.4 percent of GDP in 2000. The persistence of red ink driven by (intentionally) permanent tax reductions set against unconstrained spending eventually exerts a pernicious effect on confidence, risking a "self-reinforcing negative cycle among the underlying fiscal deficit, financial markets, and the real economy" (Rubin et al., 2004).[8] Structural deficits imply a lowering of national savings available to the private sector, hence less potential to expand productive capacity, unless additional resources can be garnered through an increased pace of household or corporate savings or through incremental foreign borrowing.

Obama's budgets: The short- and medium-term outlooks

Having inherited an economy in deep recession and financial chaos, the Obama Administration took timely measures to break the momentum of the crisis. But the president's plans also brought significant consequences for the short- and medium-term budget outlook. In January 2009 the non-partisan Congressional Budget Office (CBO) had estimated that the 2008 baseline budget deficit of 3.2 per cent of Gross Domestic Product (GDP) would increase to 8.3 per cent in 2009. Only two months later the

CBO increased its baseline to 11.9 per cent of GDP. This increase in the CBO baseline deficit in such a short time reflected the passage of the stimulus bill but also profound uncertainties over the depth and duration of the financial crisis. In particular, the outlook for revenues had deteriorated beyond earlier expectations; and the rapid climb in the unemployment rate triggered additional automatic stabilizer-related and discretionary stimulus spending. In the event, the US ended up running record post-war deficits of 1.3–1.4 trillion dollars per annum during 2009–2011 (CBO, 2011a).

Although prominent economists such as Stanford's John Taylor and Harvard's Robert Barro question the general efficacy of discretionary fiscal stimulus, others such as Harvard's Martin Feldstein, attribute the disappointing multiplier effect of the 2009 American Recovery and Reinvestment Act to poor design. Still, most mainstream economists accept that fiscal – along with monetary – stimulus remains essential during a deep economic downturn; and Alan Blinder and Mark Zandi (2010) may be broadly representative of academic and market economists who believe that the economy's trajectory would have been much worse in the absence of the Obama (and Bernanke) stimulus program.[9] The rationale for a Keynesian-type response is that additional public spending and tax cuts help replace the loss of demand from the retreat of private investment and consumer spending.[10]

But fiscal probity demands that the increase in spending be well targeted and temporary. To avoid the persistence of structural deficits that underlie unsustainable public debt trajectories, accelerated expenditures and tax cuts should be reversed when the economy is on track to sustained recovery. In this sense, Obama's intention to permanently extend the Bush-era income tax cuts for families earning less than $250,000 (and for the first $250,000 earned by all US families) is momentous. Together with inflation indexation for the Alternative Minimum Tax, the CBO has estimated that extending the Bush income tax cuts for ninety-eight percent of Americans would result in a 1.3 per cent increase in the annual federal deficit over the next decade (CBO, 2009b).

By 2011 the CBO's alternative fiscal scenario (see Figure 8.2),[11] had primary (non-interest related) spending at 1.1 per cent points higher as a share of the economy in 2021 compared with CBO's baseline forecast (CBO, 2011b, p. 3). Outlays for net interest expenditure were projected to increase from 1.4 per cent of GDP in 2011 to 4.1 per cent in 2021 (CBO, 2011c, p. 8). This would represent a startling change over ten years, reflecting the degree to which future federal spending would be needed to service past borrowing. According to the CBO's latest revision to its alternative outlook published in August 2012, public debt held by the public is projected to increase to 90 per cent of GDP in 2022, from 72 per cent in 2012 (CBO, 2012, p. 22).[12] According to CBO director, Doug Elmendorf, to stabilize the debt to GDP ratio one would need some combination of expenditure reductions and tax increases of $750 billion a year by 2022 (Wessel, 2012, pp. 158–159).

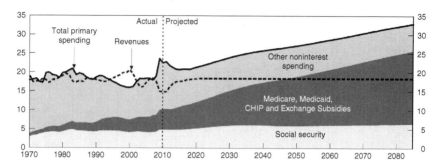

Figure 8.2   Primary spending and revenues, under CBO's alternative fiscal scenario (% GDP)

Notes: Primary spending refers to all spending other than interest payments on federal debt. CHIP = Children's Health Insurance Program.

Source: CBO (2011) Long-Term Budget Outlook, June.

What seems reasonably clear is that the deterioration in the medium-term fiscal outlook can be attributed largely to two factors. The first concerns the massive revenue loss and extra (automatic and discretionary) spending related to the Great Recession. The second concerns the permanence of the Bush-era tax cuts. Together these two factors account overwhelmingly for the rapid rise in the public debt to GDP ratio (Johnson and Kwak, 2012). In addition, as 2012 draws to a close the US economy faces a reduction in net government stimulus (fiscal drag) on economic activity even before the impending arrival of the "fiscal cliff" on January 2, 2013. For the medium-term in its latest (alternative) forecast the CBO foresees federal outlays as a share of GDP rising by slightly over 1 percentage point from 2012 to 2022 (CBO, 2012).

Fiscal drift: major considerations

Economists Carmen Reinhart and Ken Rogoff have shown that countries exceeding a public debt to GDP threshold of 90 per cent statistically tend to suffer a reduction of 1 percentage point in average annual growth. While the USA may enjoy greater degrees of freedom than other countries, it cannot defy economic gravity indefinitely (Reinhart and Rogoff, 2010). To stabilize the debt to GDP ratio will require real fiscal measures on the expenditure and/or revenue sides of the budget. Such measures would help to slow the current debt trajectory by improving the primary balance (the fiscal balance net of interest payments) while slowing the rise of interest payments on the debt.[13] In lieu of such (politically contentious) measures, the increasing supply of government paper on the market (to finance higher and higher budget deficits) eventually will drive up interest rates, curtailing private investment and hence future growth. Thereby, chronically elevated deficits threaten to propel the public debt to GDP ratio further upward in a destabilizing spiral.

During the recent recession and tepid recovery, rates all along the Treasury yield curve have fallen to historically low levels. As epitomized by a ten-year Treasury yield around 1.7 per cent at the time of this writing, longer-term rates fell to historically depressed levels during 2011–2012 despite the ominous fiscal outlook.[14] While the Federal Reserve's slashing of its target federal funds rate to 0–0.25 per cent affected mainly shorter-term government rates, the broader fall in rates along the government's yield curve can be attributed to a number of factors. First, the financial crisis precipitated a global "flight to quality." In the spring of 2010 and again in the first half of 2011, the bond crisis in Europe's periphery elevated foreign demand for treasuries. A re-flaring of this crisis increased the demand for treasuries again during 2012.[15] Second, the Federal Reserve's policy of "quantitative easing" helped to moderate rates and expected future rates. Finally, bank and household deleveraging have depressed the supply and demand for credit in the private sector.

Although rates remain depressed at present, their temporary rise in the first half of 2009 – the yield on the ten-year Treasury note at one point climbed 150 basis points – provides a cautionary sign for the future.[16] The rise in rates in 2009 can be attributed to three possible factors. First, following (tentative) signs of economic recovery, investors reacquired an appetite for risk, exchanging treasuries for riskier, higher-return investments and thus reversing the earlier flight to quality. Second, the increase in the marketable supply of treasuries associated with ballooning deficits temporarily outpaced incremental demand, depressing the price of treasury notes and bonds, and in turn elevating their yields.[17] The third and most ominous prospect is that the rise in rates arguably augured in part growing market concerns over the severity of medium-term US public funding needs.

Early 2009 also witnessed a noticeable uptick in the credit default swap (CDS) market spread for treasuries. A CDS is a financial instrument that provides insurance against the prospect of default. An increase in the CDS spread indicates an increased demand for protection, implying a higher perceived likelihood of default. In the event, CDS spreads on US debt increased from 8 basis points in June 2008 to almost 100 basis points in February 2009 (IMF, 2009, p. 30).[18] Although spreads have since settled back down, CDS spreads should continue to be monitored for signs that the market is pricing in a greater risk of default on what has historically been perceived as a "riskless" asset. While both the cash bond and CDS markets currently suggest relative complacency over the ability of US politicians to adopt credible fiscal measures, markets can also "turn on a dime."

After the "Volcker shock" in the early 1980s it had become virtually unthinkable that the Fed would resort to inflation as a debt management tool; yet monetization may be perceived as an increasingly unavoidable option should large deficit spending continue. In the event, during the crisis the Fed performed certain "quasi-fiscal" actions.[19] Furthermore, during the last few years the Fed has been leveraging its balance sheet by purchasing a wide assortment of assets in an effort to re-stimulate credit.[20] Yet, the Fed's policies also amount to a form of "financial repression" – a classic strategy that relies on the artificial depression of rates as a means of containing fiscal deficits but at significant cost to private savers.[21]

Any perception that prolonged monetization of the debt will prove necessary can lower global confidence in US monetary policy. Expansionary monetary policy in recent years has already helped to weaken the dollar against foreign currencies, posing a downside for non-dollar based investors.[22] Despite the dollar's trend decline since early 2002, however, there seems little sign that global capital flows reflect any serious concern over the US fiscal outlook. Instead, foreign capital inflow has significantly helped to depress Treasury yields. However, were budget deficits to remain elevated with public debt mounting faster than economic growth, investors would eventually demand higher Treasury yields to compensate for the higher credit and inflationary risk.[23] By driving up debt faster, the increase in borrowing rates can eventually spark a collapse in confidence, sending the debt to GDP ratio spiraling upward in a vicious cycle.

Beginning in early 2009, one leading creditor leveled open criticism at the declining value of its dollar-denominated foreign exchange reserves and the lower perceived creditworthiness of the US government. Central Bank of China Governor Zhou Xiaochuan's suggestion that the dollar be gradually replaced as the global reserve currency by an extra-sovereign "currency" like the special drawing right was no doubt politically or tactically motivated.[24] But it also reflected genuine reservations about the US fiscal trajectory and the danger of structural dependence on a single fiat currency.

Recent events have hardly been propitious for fiscal consolidation. One bellwether event was the eleventh-hour raising of the debt ceiling in August 2011. The political grandstanding and partisan jockeying surrounding what historically has been an essentially automatic action – the need to raise the ceiling is dictated by earlier congressional action on spending authorization – helped to trigger a downgrade decision by S&P. Having failed to endorse something like the Bowles-Simpson Commission's deficit-reducing recommendations,[25] President Obama authorized a bipartisan "super committee" to agree concrete proposals for reducing the ten-year deficit.

The super committee's subsequent failure to reach an accord means that, barring congressional agreement during 2012 on how to achieve deficit reduction, an automatic sequestration procedure of $1.2 trillion is scheduled for January 2013, forcing equivalent reductions in defense and non-defense spending.[26] Although President Obama has pledged to veto any interference with the sequestration endgame, one would not be shocked by congressional attempts to subvert the process, including renewed skirmishing over the next scheduled lifting of the debt ceiling.

With the decision to extend the payroll tax reduction and long-term unemployment benefits through 2012, as well as to employ the annual "doc fix" on physician reimbursement under Medicare, meaningful debt reduction would remain virtually impossible until after the presidential election in November 2012. In the meantime, the country could face an extraordinary "fiscal cliff" beginning on January 1, 2013, when some 4 per cent of GDP in stimulus measures could be removed (for fiscal year 2013) if certain offsetting decisions are not taken. This would occur against the backdrop of already sharply slowing spending at the state and local levels. The appropriate solution would appear evident: the announcement of a clear and credible road-map for medium-term fiscal consolidation combined with a recommitment to short-term (monetary and/or fiscal) stimulus.

Long-term/entitlements

As serious as it may seem, the need to contain the medium-term fiscal deficit pales against the overriding need to ameliorate the explosive long-term growth in the principal US entitlement programs. The biggest challenge comes from massive unfunded liabilities related to financing the retirement and health care costs of an aging population.[27] Expenditures for Social Security, Medicare and Medicaid account for some 44 per cent of total federal spending today; and such mandatory spending is on an explosive trajectory, threatening to progressively crowd out discretionary (defense and non-defense) spending.

In this context the concept of a "fiscal gap" is useful. It can be defined as "the size of the immediate and permanent increase in taxes and/or reductions in non-interest expenditures that would be required to set the present value of all future primary surpluses equal to the current value of the national debt" (Auerbach and Gale, 2011, p. 9). As defined above, primary surpluses represent total revenues minus non-interest expenditures. Taking account of the time value of money and the future timing of projected revenues and expenditures, gives one a measure of the longer-term fiscal challenge expressed in (discounted) present value terms.

Taking the 75-year period through 2085 into account, Alan Auerbach and William G. Gale estimate the fiscal gap to be more than $67 trillion (Auerbach and Gale, 2012, table 3). This means that an immediate and permanent increase in revenues, decrease in (non-interest) expenditures, or a combination of the two amounting to 7.1 per cent of GDP would close the 75-year deficit, stabilizing the debt to GDP ratio at current levels (see Table 8.1). While delaying the time of adjustment inevitably increases the gap, one does not need to eliminate the fiscal gap in its entirety in order to stabilize debt to GDP at a reasonable level.[28] Confining average annual deficits to a range of 2–3 per cent, for example, would accomplish the task of stabilizing the debt trajectory in a less disruptive manner. Yet, there is still

Table 8.1 US (present value) fiscal gap[29] through 2085 (US dollars, trillions)

	Through 2085
CBO baseline	38,385
% of GDP	4.07
A&G extended baseline	67,626
% of GDP	7.16

Source: Auerbach and Gale (2012) "The Federal Budget Outlook: No News Is Bad News," April 10, 2012, table 3.

no denying that the latter presupposes a prodigious fiscal effort and public sacrifice, particularly given the growing burden of the entitlement programs.

The principal challenge for the social security system lies mainly in population ageing and longevity. The average age of retirement has failed to keep pace with rising life expectancy, while the ratio of working age individuals (aged 20–64) to would-be retirees (65 and older) is expected to shrink from around 5 to nearly 3 by 2030. However, compared with social security, where the 75-year actuarial gap can be closed through less than 1 per cent of GDP in fiscal measures,[30] a genuine crisis looms over Medicare and Medicaid barring decisive preemptive action.

The major long-term challenge remains the so-called "excess cost growth" of health care spending. Excess cost growth refers to (age- and sex-adjusted) per capita growth of health care costs that exceeds per capita GDP growth. Population ageing represents an additional critical factor. For example, by 2035 and 2080, respectively, excess cost growth will be responsible for an estimated 52 and 71 per cent of the projected growth in federal health care spending with aging accounting for the residual 48 and 29 per cent (CBO, 2011b, p. 10). In other words, that more and more people will be utilizing Medicare and Medicaid as the population ages, even as payroll revenue growth slows, is worrisome. But the aging factor becomes progressively dominated by escalating health care costs per beneficiary in later decades.

In 2011 some 48 million people were covered by Medicare, including 40 million aged 65 and older, and 8 million disabled Americans. Benefits amounted to $549 billion, and assets held in special issue US Treasury securities were $325 billion. While costs began growing faster than income in 2005, the hospital insurance (HI) trust fund began running a cash flow deficit in 2008, and it is now projected to be exhausted of funds by 2024 (see Table 8.2).[31] The potential crisis is not only, or mainly, a fiscal issue. The single most significant contribution to rising fiscal expenditures involves excess health care costs in the wider economy. The national economy spent around $2.7 trillion on health care in 2011 – nearly 17.4 per cent of economic output. National health expenditures are expected to grow to almost $4.6

Table 8.2 Trust fund outlooks

	Year of expected deficit	Year of expected fund exhaustion
Social Security (OASDI)	2011	2033
Medicare-HI (Part A)[32]	2008	2024

Source: Social Security Trustees Report (2012), p. 3, April; CMS Medicare Trustees Report (2012), April, p. 6.

trillion by 2019, or roughly 20 per cent of GDP (CMS, 2011b, table 1). Projections for this period have nominal excess health care costs growing annually by 1.7 per cent faster than nominal GDP (CBO, 2011b).[33]

Several years ago, Brookings Institution fiscal expert Henry Aaron argued that, through concerted cost saving measures, the US could, in principle, converge over a decade or longer to the Europeans' health care expenditure share of GDP.[34] This presupposes, at a minimum, that the US shaves percentage points off its health care spending to GDP ratio relative to the current trajectory. Optimistically this would amount to stabilizing health care spending at a quarter rather than a third of GDP (Aaron et al., 2005).

Note that this (still enormous) share of economic activity devoted to health will provide important benefits to the population, including marked improvements in life-extending technology, for which it may be reasonable for a richer society to strive. Still, it is widely accepted that increasing the quality of health care services can be delivered at lower per capita cost through appropriate reforms.[35] Yet, the devil lies in the details: the politics of entrenched special interests within the health care complex constitute a major constraint (see below). At present the rapid inflation of health care services combined with Americans' revealed preference for the latest medical technology, particularly in the last years of life, implies an explosive fiscal burden.

Already a decade ago historian Niall Ferguson and economist Lawrence Kotlikoff (2003) recast Paul Kennedy's overstretch argument in terms of such fiscal pressures.[36] They conjectured that an ageing American electorate wedded to a mass consumption lifestyle will refuse to sacrifice to sustain the costs of US "empire." In principle, this dire outlook could be offset by certain mitigating factors (Boskin, 2004).[37] Nevertheless, in *The Coming Generational Storm*, Kotlikoff (2001) persuasively shows that accounting for plausible offsetting factors, such as an extended retirement age, cannot circumvent an inescapably painful choice between much higher future taxes and a marked reduction in promised benefits for future retirees.[38] Neither faster economic growth nor higher taxes, alone or in combination, represent feasible options for handling this explosive growth in healthcare-related entitlements. With the projected increase in entitlement spending, closing the fiscal gap through the revenue side alone would entail an untenable 50 per cent or greater increase in the country's tax burden. A majority of voting Americans is likely to postpone retirement, save more and eventually acquiesce to program changes in the social security and Medicare systems to avoid such an otherwise required outsized increase in the federal tax burden.

The US does not stand alone in its entitlements challenge. Other industrial countries face increasingly onerous burdens as well. But while the larger long-term threat to the US involves excess health cost growth, the dominant risk for other nations lies more with demographics per se. While this is well known for Europe and Japan, it is less widely recognized that China – with its increasing longevity and low birth rate – is ageing rapidly. It will have the demographic structure of the advanced industrial countries, albeit at a much lower level of average income (United Nations, 2010).

Many other emerging market countries are expected to experience of the order of a tripling of the elderly relative to working-age population. Still, one saving grace of being an emerging market is the opportunity to design social welfare schemes that are more feasible in the longer run. The advanced countries no longer enjoy that luxury. Yet, as argued earlier in this book all else being equal, a superior pace of long-run labor productivity growth should favor the US over most European countries in financing its welfare state.

Defense spending

When discussing the US fiscal outlook, the outsized level of annual defense appropriations is difficult to ignore. Having attributed the leading US fiscal challenge to health care costs, the burden of defense spending can be placed in proper context. Line item accounting for US defense expenditures can be a frustrating endeavor. It is therefore little wonder that former Comptroller of the Currency and Head of the Government Accounting Office David Walker was wont to declare that performing a proper audit of the Pentagon remained futile.[39] That being said, confining one's scrutiny to the Pentagon's top line budget, in 2011 the US government allocated $549 billion towards its baseline defense outlays (see Table 8.3). Adding operations in Iraq and Afghanistan, the 2011 defense budget increased to $708.2 billion, representing 52 per cent of discretionary spending and 20 per cent of total outlays.

Notwithstanding the agreement to locate $487 billion in defense savings over the next decade,[40] the political economy of US military appropriation may ultimately require a somewhat greater defense expenditure commitment, at least over a transitional period,[41] than that assumed by the Office of Management and Budget (OMB) or projected by CBO on the basis of current law (CBO, 2012 August). Included presumably would be a medium-term investment to replace equipment that has depreciated at an exceptional rate

Table 8.3 Cost of national security and defense, 2011 (US dollars, billions)

	2011
Baseline defense	549.1
Overseas operations	159.1
Department of Defense	
(DoD) subtotal	**708.2**
Homeland security	43.9
Veteran's affairs	57.0
DOE nuclear arsenal[42]	11.2
DOD mandatory outlays	5.7
State Department involvement[43]	51.4
Interest[44]	42.6
Total	**920.0**
% of GDP	6.1%

Sources: OMB (2011) "The Budget for the Fiscal Year 2012," Table S-11, pp. 64, 119 and 199–200, February; CBO (2011) "An Analysis of the President's Budgetary Proposals for Fiscal Year 2012," Table 1-5, p. 14, March.

through war use (so-called "resets") and incremental spending required to reduce "military overstretch."[45] The latter refers to the unsustainable redeployment of American troops (see discussion in Chapter 2). The circle may well be squared, at least initially, by a significant and sustained scaling back in overseas commitments. (Indeed, the pattern has been significant real reductions in US defense spending following the conclusion of major conflicts). Alternatively, contingent on future global developments, the pace of US economic recovery, and the extent of the country's residual "war weariness," the elimination of military overstretch could ultimately be achieved through a subsequent ramping up in the recruitment of army and marine personnel or (equally expensive) transition to a more capital-intensive (procurement-heavy) military.

In *The Three Trillion Dollar War*, Joseph Stiglitz and Linda Bilmes estimate the present value of total budgetary outlays for the Iraq War through 2017 at $2.7 trillion. Adding Afghanistan raises this estimate to $3.5 trillion.[46] Stiglitz and Bilmes include the interest costs of financing the war and an estimate of the life-time health care costs related to American casualties. Their projections may appear somewhat elevated in light of the conclusion of the Iraq war and current plans to conclude the war in Afghanistan in 2014. Nevertheless, these provide a reasonable order of magnitude or benchmark against which to compare the fiscal burden of the entitlement programs.

One can perform the following back of the envelope calculation, for example. Note that the Stiglitz and Bilmes estimates assume that operations in

Iraq and Afghanistan continue for a half decade longer. Although current plans are to wind down the war in Afghanistan in 2014,[47] whoever is elected president will face significant political pressure to respond to evolving conditions on the ground in Afghanistan and Pakistan. Let us assume in line with Stiglitz and Bilmes' assumptions that the prior pace of war related cash outlays for the combined wars is roughly maintained and spread evenly over the next five-year period. This would amount to roughly $650 billion of additional nominal spending or $130 billion per year during 2012–2017. (On the basis of Stiglitz and Bilmes-type accrual accounting, the eventual cost would be somewhat greater). If 2011 OMB projections of 3.3 per cent of GDP in baseline defense spending ten years out are realistic, even a war-inclusive outlay would not exceed 4 per cent of GDP. Hence, already in ten years – before mandatory program expenditure becomes even more explosive – the three major entitlement programs could account for more than three times the level of defense spending.[48]

That mandatory spending will increasingly dwarf military spending will not exempt the Pentagon from contributing to overall deficit reduction (it should be recalled that US defense spending is not much less than the sum of all other national defense spending). In fact, the potential savings from lower defense spending could be considerable especially if one considers estimates of the all-in defense budget, including wars, Veteran's Affairs, military retirement funds, Homeland Security, State Department activity, and interest owed on prior defense-related deficit spending. Adding such factors to the baseline Department of Defense appropriation for FY2011 generates a figure of $920 billion (while adding the cost of operations in Iraq and Afghanistan elevates the total to over $1 trillion; see Table 8.3).[49]

That said, political elites appear to be heeding the warnings of Admiral Mike Mullen (2011), Chairman of the Joint Chiefs of Staff, who has echoed the concerns of others in calling the nation's debt "the biggest threat to our national security". This threat has been summarized elsewhere as follows: "It is not reckless American activity in the world that jeopardizes American solvency but American profligacy at home that threatens American power and security" (Altman and Haass, 2010). If gaining greater control over the main driver of long-term expenditures – entitlements and, more specifically, health-related entitlements – proves elusive, by how much can defense spending be realistically curtailed beyond eliminating "fraud, waste and abuse" before materially compromising US hard power?[50] Even were greater efficiencies in defense spending to be achieved, there seems ample basis to expect that the scope for US power projection will need to be scaled back; the US military will simply lack the resources to do all that it does today (Mandelbaum, 2010). And military capability and a great deal more would be further compromised were the country to fail to invest requisite public resources in the physical and human capital that sustains overall economic growth.

Politics and reform

While the imperative to reduce the excess cost of health care seems inescapable, the means to achieve this end remain contentious. Although President Obama's initiatives on comparative cost efficiency research and expanded IT medical record keeping eventually may yield significant cost containment, profound and far ranging structural changes across the economy's medical complex will prove indispensable to restore long-term sustainability in the Medicare and Medicaid programs. For example, measures like treating some share of employer-provided health insurance as taxable income could provide significant savings. More generally, the challenge of reform lies in altering incentives for health care consumers and all key players involved in delivering health services, including doctors, hospitals and pharmaceutical and private insurance companies. Transitioning from a "fee for service" approach to health care delivery to one based on "fee for value" seems indispensable. For perspective, at present, "per capita, the US has five times more CT scans than Germany and five times as many coronary bypasses as France" (Peterson, 2009). America needs to do much better on disease prevention, integrating and coordinating best practice, and narrowing the enormous gap in medical costs across different regions and cities, among countless other cost-saving initiatives.[51]

As the denouement over the lifting of the debt ceiling in August 2011 approached, Democrats and Republicans appeared to concur in principle over taking significant fiscal measures over the next 10–12 years as a down payment on the longer-term deficit (Obama, 2011; Ryan, 2010). Yet, the two sides remain deadlocked over the specific mix of expenditure and revenue measures to be taken. Under pressure from the Tea Party wing of the party, Republicans adopted a no incremental tax pledge while Democrats favor heightened taxation on wealthier Americans as part of the mix.

Although the strict exclusion of additional revenue measures would be tantamount to gutting much of the non-defense discretionary budget, an eventual compromise will likely favor greater expenditure reduction over increases in income and/or payroll (social insurance) taxes.[52] Moderate Democrats, for example, accept that expenditure control must trump additional revenue measures as part of the longer-term fiscal mix to avoid approaching the politically unpalatable drift to a continental Western European (and, even more so, Scandinavian) scale of government. Still, there is no "free lunch"; and the US has yet to achieve broad consensus on the scope of governmental services it is willing to finance.

Economic theory provides little guidance on the appropriate level of government expenditure. While one side of the US political debate advocates bringing revenues back to their long-term historical average (just north of 18 per cent of GDP), the other side argues that even with significant expenditure measures this would be draconian, given the aging of the population.

The key requirement is that sufficient revenue be raised to cover authorized expenditure and that this revenue be collected in the least distortive manner. If revenues are to be increased efficiently, comprehensive tax reform is essential. Such an approach would enlarge the tax base via income tax simplification, including the removal of many tax loopholes, potentially permitting lower marginal tax rates.[53] Beyond that, certain European countries have demonstrated that reasonably efficient tax measures can be designed to raise additional revenue without sacrificing growth (see e.g. Lindert, 2003). Various sensible reforms, particularly ones that shift the taxation burden away from savings and investment, relying more on broad-based consumption taxation, have long been suggested.[54]

A scenario in which non-defense discretionary spending bears the full brunt of fiscal adjustment would impact that part of the budget dealing with education, R&D, infrastructure and other critical functions of government. Within this constraint it is difficult to see how a significant real reduction in defense spending can be politically avoided. Equally difficult to envision is a decision to render permanent the 2001 and 2003 Bush tax cuts (on the middle class as well as wealthier Americans).

While politically challenging, as an integral part of tax reform the US would cap many of the incentive-distorting annual tax expenditures – subsidies embedded in the tax code totally some $1.1 trillion – including everything from the employer health care tax exemption to mortgage interest rate deductions, deductions for state and local taxes and a host of subsidies to energy, agriculture and other politically powerful industries. After feasible tax expenditure reduction the (controversial) introduction of a moderate value added tax (or alternative consumption-based tax) ultimately might prove necessary to finance a necessary level of federal expenditures moderately higher say, 1.5–3 (per cent of GDP) than the long-term historical average of 21 per cent of GDP.[55] All of this presumes essential progress in addressing unfunded liabilities in the major entitlement programs.[56]

Whether the US political system is capable of breaking the current deadlock over fiscal adjustment, staving off a crisis-induced sell-off of the dollar and treasuries, remains an open question. In particular, powerful interests have so far thwarted most prospects for introducing incentives within the health care system that can appreciably slow cost growth. Any feasible reform requires compromise by all the key parties – including lobbies for hospitals, healthcare providers, insurance companies, the pharmaceuticals industry and consumers. That many of these groups have engaged the reform process more seriously than during the last big health care push during the Clinton Administration instills some hope. Although there arguably are promising cost-saving measures embedded in the president's 2010 Patient Protection and Affordable Care Act,[57] much more legislative effort will be needed to achieve tangible measures that bend the health care cost curve. Meanwhile, the overriding dynamic of excess cost growth will continue until tangible cost-reducing policies are implemented.

Given current congressional gridlock, meaningful fiscal measures would amount to a veritable sea change. While the required fiscal adjustment would fall well shy of the burden endured during World War II when defense spending reached 38 per cent of GDP, it would nonetheless require extraordinary leadership and public sacrifice.[58] Alternatively, the catalyst can be a full-blown fiscal crisis, punctuated by successive credit ratings downgrades, a much-elevated price for US Treasury borrowing and even the loss of the country's hard-won reserve currency status. The sooner fiscal measures are taken, the lower in magnitude such measures ultimately need to be.

Conclusion

The US public debt has been rising rapidly and remains on a worrisome long-term trajectory. This suggests that the US government risks losing, at some indefinable point in the future, the kind of low-rate access to global capital markets it now enjoys. In the midst of a crisis, making rational economic decisions on fiscal correction will prove much more difficult. Given the long lead times involved, it makes sense to avoid further delay in planning changes that can take place gradually over time, beginning once the economy attains more momentum in recovering from the recent recession.

One can credibly argue that the US's debt burden remains qualitatively no worse, if not better, than that facing many other advanced nations.[59] This seems self-evident from the fiscal pressures impacting the European Monetary Union today. Meanwhile, the US enjoys significant advantages over other states, notably in its relative dynamism and unsullied debt service history. Yet, exercising hegemony also requires resources well beyond those needed by states with more modest geopolitical roles.

Hegemony no doubt represents a societal-wide and not merely governmental phenomenon. US individuals, corporations and myriad other non-state actors transact with and transfer money, services and technical assistance to the rest of the world. Still, the security footprint financed out of the federal budget remains central to US global influence. A full accounting of these security-related expenditures underscores the degree to which the federal budget represents a window through which to assess constraints on US power projection going forward. A budgetary crisis is also a power projection crisis. And the adverse impact of a fiscal crisis on the domestic economy would further limit the scope of additional contributions to global prosperity and security emanating from civil society.

Failure to respond decisively to a future crisis or major conflagration owing to binding fiscal constraints would reinforce perceptions of US overstretch and decline. Such perceptions could embolden rivals while discouraging rising states from bandwagoning with the US. Remaining hegemonic presumes that one can address one's core domestic challenge. Failure to do so reflects poorly on US democracy and dilutes the credibility of US power.

A striking feature of the global system today is the rapid uptick in growth among key emerging markets against the relative stagnation experienced in the more developed world. It is also reflected in the contrast between the current and prospective fiscal burdens facing these respective groups of countries. In the key dimensions of growth and fiscal-cum-financial stability, the balance of power indeed appears to be shifting from the advanced to the emerging countries.

Slowly rebounding from a profound financial crisis while facing a looming fiscal challenge, where does the US fit within this broad secular trend? To date there has been little serious public debate on the underlying tradeoffs between the entitlements, future tax burdens, defense-cum-homeland security requirements and the costs of "nation rebuilding" at home. Left unattended, the yawning fiscal gap will impede economic growth and aggravate social polarization. It may ultimately take the threat of a capital market-induced fiscal crisis to propel the political system into bolder action.

While no Greece, the US will share certain characteristics with that embattled country in the absence of serious change. Continuous delay in legislating medium- and long-term fiscal consolidation will only increase the correction that will ultimately prove necessary. With meaningful fiscal adjustment alongside a renewed commitment to address other medium-term social challenges, the country's resources and underlying capabilities remain sufficiently strong to grow median living standards, comfortably service its debts and maintain its projection of global power. In addition to the issue of public support behind US hegemony, discussed in the following chapter, the fiscal outlook represents the leading constraint on US prosperity and global influence today.

9
Politics

On August 2, 2011 the world looked on in disbelief as a Kafkaesque specta-cle played out in the halls of Congress. To many, a radical fringe appeared to have hijacked the political process, holding the country hostage. The drama over raising the debt ceiling placed the government on the brink, risking its unblemished history of on-time and in-full debt service. Skepti-cism deepened over the prospects that a divided government could conduct the nation's business with requisite deliberation and compromise.[1]

Although creditworthiness typically refers to a state's ability to service its obligations, global capital markets were awakened to the perverse prospect that the US could risk default as a means of achieving eventual deficit reduc-tion. While hardly the first episode of gridlock witnessed in US politics, pundits decried the escalation of partisanship and polarization. Although Congressional representatives stepped back from the abyss at the 11th hour, the damage had been done. Fresh doubts were triggered over the US's credibility in anchoring the international debt and monetary system.[2] To some, this showdown between the two major parties reinforced a broader foreboding of national decline (Kohut, 2011).

Does this widely embraced account of the August 2011 debt ceiling episode capture the full story? Consider for a moment an alternative syn-opsis. What appeared little more than a cynical ploy by Tea Party-inspired zealots brought into sharp relief the ideological clash that divides the nation. A deep financial crisis had succeeded in finally galvanizing the polity to con-front head-on the most fundamental of public policy questions – the future role and scope of government. Would this crisis force as well a referendum on the US's future global role?

This book has argued that external developments ultimately pose a lesser challenge to the US's global position. While a parade of regional and transnational threats competes for diplomatic attention, the US remains sit-uated at the apex of a global system that, for all its remaining problems, has grown more democratic and less violent. Meanwhile, the US presides at the center of a world community that increasingly embraces markets and

207

the rule of law (Zakaria, 2008). US policymakers hardly "dictate" events or "impose" solutions globally, but nor did they ever do so to the extent ascribed to them (Kagan, 2012; Nye, 2011). The point is that the largest trials confronting US hegemony appear home grown. The first of these, the US's longer-term fiscal trajectory, was featured in Chapter 8. There it was argued that the unsustainable US public debt trajectory remains eminently arrestable. Political decisions about the deficit will largely determine the sustainability of US hegemony. The purpose of the current chapter is to outline a second potentially binding domestic constraint on sustainable hegemony – public opinion on resource priorities, globalization and the US's prospective role in the world.

Against the backdrop of the 2012 election season, can one determine whether the American public retains its underlying support for US hegemony? Without the requisite backing of the people how could the US maintain its forward deployment of military assets, sustain its traditionally pivotal role in global affairs and successfully shepherd a liberal global economy? While volatile, polling and other indicators generally suggest a majority of Americans supports a robust US engagement in the world, albeit sometimes with greater or lesser enthusiasm. Also indicated however is a clear public reluctance to embrace the role of global policeman or to engage in protracted and inconclusive exercises in state (nation) building in far-flung lands. A war-weary nation facing intense economic pressures has seen the public mood shift toward greater preoccupation with domestic priorities. Yet, the political pendulum has yet to swing to the point of fundamentally re-questioning the US's vanguard role in world affairs.[3]

In addition, this book has argued that a hegemonic liberal order presupposes US leadership in the maintenance of open and competitive markets. That is, a critical lynchpin of US global power involves a robust defense of globalization. While the goal to maintain relatively unfettered trade in goods and services, broadly unrestricted capital mobility and significant scope for immigration-cum-guest workers – continues to elicit broad tacit support, cyclical and secular stresses impacting American workers have inevitably moderated enthusiasm for such policies.

Meanwhile, American society is immersed in a fundamental debate about the role and scope of government. The latter relates for example to whether government will be granted the wherewithal to robustly defend globalization and technological change. If so, will the most vulnerable be afforded an adequate safety net; and will a greater swath of Americans be granted the opportunity to remain gainfully employed and raise their living standards? And in this era of more binding resource constraints, can the federal government and US civil society maintain their commitment to the country's pivotal role in global affairs?

The rest of the chapter is organized as follows. The section "Electoral politics and hegemony" summarizes public opinion and its crystallization in the 2012 presidential debates on the nature of US global engagement and economic security today. The section "Globalization and the 2012 election" focuses more definitively on Americans' attitudes towards "openness," including specific perceptions on international trade, capital flows and immigration. The section "Political constraints on US fiscal actions" examines the political preconditions for meeting current national challenges related to the federal budget. Concluding remarks on the future role of public opinion follow in the section "Conclusion."

Electoral politics and hegemony

Postwar reconstruction and the "Blue Social Model"

For the last half-century, Democratic and Republican parties have embraced a relatively narrow consensus on the US's global role. Excluding minority opinion on the extremities of left and right,[4] the post-World War II US policy consensus has favored "free but fair" participation in the global economy and a vanguard role to advance global prosperity and security. In the aftermath of that war, growing wealth at home amid devastation abroad allowed the US to meet these commitments generously.

After World War II, the country's leaders worked to reshape the international order on the basis of alliances, partnerships, and multilateral institutions designed to open markets and bind democracies in collective security. US leaders sought to construct a global environment conducive to long-term growth and security in contraposition to the Soviet bloc. This order was "built on two pillars: the American market and the American security umbrella" (Ikenberry, 2011, p. 168).

Rather than a hierarchical "patron-client" order, the international community centered on the transatlantic relationship would be largely based on the principles of consensus and reciprocity. The US would lead in the creation of the United Nations (UN), General Agreement on Tariffs and Trade (GATT) and the Bretton Woods institutions. The rebuilding of Japan and Germany followed by aid to Turkey and Greece were delivered via the Truman Doctrine, the Marshall Plan and the Dodge Line in Japan. With the UN Charter, the Universal Declaration of Human Rights and the Atlantic Charter, the US worked to imbue the international order with progressive ideals regarding human security. In the words of one authority, "no world power had ever sought to build such an order in the past...Three features in particular gave it a liberal character: public goods provisions, rule-based cooperation, and voice opportunities and diffuse reciprocity. This is not empire – it is an American-led open-democratic political order" (Ikenberry, 2011, pp. 160–161).

As the allies sought greater security amid Soviet encroachment, the international system became progressively more US-centered. The pendulum shifted from the UN Security Council to the US-led North Atlantic Treaty

Organization (NATO); and the world economy moved from the Bretton Woods system to one centered on a gold de-anchored US dollar and US commodity and financial markets. In sum, the US would serve as the functional-operational leader of the global system.

With certain caveats, the American public endorsed this liberal hegemonic order. This did not always ensure majoritarian public support for foreign actions, the collapse in backing for the Vietnam War being a notable example. But outside of a small segment of the populace that consistently embraced a neo-isolationist politics, many Americans have, at least tacitly, equated a forwardly deployed military, in concert with a rules-based liberal international order, with the promotion of US national security interests.

Paralleling this bipartisan consensus on liberal hegemony, macroeconomic policy was conducted to target full employment and low inflation. The post war dominance of US multinationals helped to ensure, for a time, broad job security, rising incomes, and robust health and pension benefits for American workers. Although US producers dominated the world economy, the country's leaders suspected that the safety net eventually would require strengthening to cope with the increase in foreign competition that was facilitated in no small part by US financial assistance (Ikenberry, 2011, pp. 174–176). In the event, a viable balance between openness-cum-integration and social protection was achieved, through what one observer has coined the "Blue Social Model" (BSM) (Mead, 2010).

An expanded New Deal launched under President Johnson ushered in major new spending commitments in Medicare and Medicaid; and preceding the deregulation wave initiated under the Carter and Reagan administrations, a complex of regulations governed core industrial sectors. Central to this social bargain were controls on transnational movements of capital, at least for several decades after World War II. Facing only a modicum of international competition, US industry could afford to be complacent. A seemingly stable social fabric was built on accord between Big Business, Big Labor and Big Government.

In today's more competitive global economy, the BSM's premise of guaranteed increases in living standards for most workers appears moribund. This raises fundamental questions. Will economic insecurity cause Americans to turn inward, demonstrating a reluctance to accept the consequences of the ever-intensifying pressures associated with "the rise of the rest"? Will mounting fiscal pressures lead Americans to grow less willing to shoulder as broad an array of global responsibilities as in the past? Or will the US re-chart its economic compass, investing more vigorously in its own human and physical capital while avoiding a broad-scale retreat from its foreign commitments? Recent polling and electoral debates provide certain clues to prevailing sentiment regarding these overarching questions for public policy.

Hegemony and the 2012 election

At the time of writing the 2012 presidential election season is in full swing and its final outcome will precede the publication of this book. Through the smoke of electioneering rhetoric, one can locate the contours of competing positions on the leading question of this book – the future of US hegemony. Economics typically trumps foreign policy in presidential contests, but given the current fragility of the US recovery it is even more the case that economic issues – mainly, jobs and incomes, and the role of government in supporting them – would be salient in the 2012 election. Nevertheless, to date the candidates[5] have also clarified where they stand philosophically and pragmatically on the future of US power.

Although some on the right have accused President Obama of "apologizing" for the US exercising global power contenders for the Republic nomination were forced to moderate their traditional calling card – accusing the Democratic Party of defeatism and weakness on defense. This tactical shift reflects a spate of foreign policy successes and bipartisan-supported actions under the Obama Administration, including the killing of Osama bin Laden, the toppling of Muammar Qaddafi, stepped-up drone strikes in Pakistan and elsewhere, and offensive cyber warfare and heightened sanctions against Iran. This relatively unassailable record at least from the vantage point of military assertiveness, combined with a waning public appetite for an even more muscular stance involving additional boots on the ground, has left the Republican establishment more hesitant to focus their attacks on foreign policy issues.[6]

A range of views nonetheless differentiated the Republican candidates on foreign policy and defense during the electoral contest. Rick Santorum supported unhesitant projection of US military might to defend human rights, criticizing Obama's Libyan policy as "leading from behind." While Mitt Romney has been less declarative on the imperative of intervening on behalf of human rights, he has advocated undiminished defense spending and has been particularly focused on maintaining the war against radical jihadism. Although none of the candidates, save possibly Ron Paul, could be considered "isolationist," some endorsed at least a tactical turn toward a less activist military posture abroad (Traub, 2011).[7]

While President Obama has generally injected a more conciliatory tone into US foreign policy – recall, for example, his 2009 Cairo speech offering a "new [more cooperative] beginning" between the US and the Muslim world and earlier efforts to diplomatically engage Iran – his endorsement of the surge in Afghanistan, his neo-realist Nobel Peace Prize acceptance speech and even his reluctant participation in the Libyan conflict hardly suggest a repudiation of classic global power projection. Having followed through on his pre-electoral commitment to wind down the war in Iraq, the conflict in Afghanistan continues even after he authorized a drawdown of the surge he originally authorized. Meanwhile, Obama's marked increase in Predator strikes on al Qaeda and affiliated groups lodged in Pakistani and other sanctuaries, and recent revelations about reliance on cyberattacks (the "Olympic Games"), suggest a willingness to aggressively deploy high technology assets (Sanger, 2012).

Obama's emphasis on the escalating costs of war and the need to focus greater attention at home nonetheless suggests a strategy of retreat, according to the president's detractors. Yet, his ostensible reorientation of strategic policy may reflect more of a tactical difference with principal Republican opponents. In particular, Obama's approach can be interpreted as broadly consistent with our discussion of military overstretch in Chapter 2. Confronting military overstretch involves realigning the military's resources and the commitments with which the civilian leadership has charged it. The latter involves either a relatively straightforward commitment of incremental resource allocation to the military – for example, to alleviate the need for chronic repeat deployments or to facilitate equipment reset following prolonged campaigns in Afghanistan and Iraq – a scaling back of foreign military commitments or some combination, on the margin. Such moderate corrections to the upward trend in defense commitments as the president appears to countenance are not of a scale that would make a material difference to overall fiscal solvency.[8]

Meanwhile, Obama's invocation of a new "Sputnik moment" and a commitment to "winning the future" appears to reflect a strategy to reignite US economic dynamism, a goal to which Mitt Romney would hardly object, although he would criticize Obama's specific approach to doing so. This objective has been framed not as a substitute but rather as a more durable basis for sustainable power projection. Meanwhile, although there is every indication that the military will be asked to share in the country's broader fiscal retrenchment, today's strategic debate suggests no call for qualitative retreat from traditional global obligations.[9] Indeed, the lack of greater distance between the policies of Obama and his major Republican rivals has been duly noted with chagrin by the leftwing of the Democratic base.

Alliances and multilateral cooperation

Hegemony has never been equatable with unilateralism. Its central position in the global power hierarchy notwithstanding, US hegemony presupposes international cooperation and reliance on strategic alliances and partnerships. Whether promoting freer trade through the World Trade Organization (WTO), galvanizing cooperative action through NATO or resolving international disputes through organs of the UN, most on both sides of the political aisle would concede that US power is generally enhanced. Nevertheless, the American public has approached these intergovernmental organizations and agreements with varying degrees of acceptance and skepticism. A prime example is the public's nuanced opinion of the UN. Although forging international consensus through the various offices of the UN remains a key component of the broader US foreign policy agenda, to the American public and political elite, UN crisis resolution has proven less than consistently effective. The majority of Americans believes that the UN has done "a poor job in trying to solve problems it has had to face."[10] A majority nonetheless supports central UN involvement in solving international problems, notably as a means of burden sharing and comparative effectiveness for certain objectives[11]:

> Majorities favor giving the United Nations the authority to go into countries to investigate violations of human rights (72 percent); creating an international marshals service that could arrest leaders responsible for genocide (73 percent); having a standing UN peacekeeping force selected, trained, and commanded by the United Nations (64 percent); and [...] having a UN agency control access to all nuclear fuel in the world to ensure that none is used for weapons production (64 percent). An overall majority of Americans (55 percent) also favors giving the United Nations the power to regulate the international arms trade.
> (Chicago Council on Global Affairs, 2010, p. 22)

Americans welcome multilateralism as a source of international legitimacy for US actions as well as a means to avoid national overstretch. For these reasons, a majority of Americans rejects the role of "world's policeman," "with 79 per cent believing the United States is playing this role more than it should be" (Chicago Council on Global Affairs, 2010). With the possible exception of Ron Paul,[12] the 2012 presidential candidates have endorsed this preference for collaboration. For example, while affirming that "the objective of the United States of America is strength, not popularity (Romney, 2010, p. 99)," Mitt Romney (2011) talks of the US's strength being "amplified when it is combined with the strength of other nations."[13]

Does the public repudiation of "world's policeman" reflect a waning desire to assume global leadership? Even after the September 2008 events on Wall Street and subsequent economic fallout, polls show that a large majority of the American public expects the US to work at the forefront to "prevent the spread of nuclear weapons" and want it to take the lead in "combating international terrorism" (Chicago Council on Global Affairs, 2010). For most disputes, Americans view military action as a last resort,[14] preferring a concerted reliance on diplomacy including direct talks with recalcitrant states like Iran and North Korea.[15] Where diplomatic initiatives fail, Americans tend to back the imposition of more coercive measures but preferably ones that fall shy of military force. For instance, regarding the threat of Iran acquiring nuclear weapons, a plurality favors maintaining pressure via economic sanctions to discourage plans for nuclear armament (Chicago Council on Global Affairs, 2010).[16] Although they understand that overwhelming military superiority represents a key asset and occasionally required US power resource,[17] Americans historically have displayed a distinct caution concerning resort to military power.[18]

Globalization and the 2012 election

As argued above, the American public broadly supported post-war priorities associated with expanded integration in the global economy and strong strategic engagement abroad, provided that the latter was supplemented by meaningful social welfare protections. The post-war BSM aimed to increase federal entitlements, work benefits and job security for a stable and thriving middle class. The "losers" in globalization would in principle find their situations ameliorated via various redresses and safeguards.

As Mead argues, the BSM has become increasingly unviable in today's more dynamic global economy. As he puts it, fierce global competition has eroded the market share of "lazy, sclerotic American firms – like the Big Three automakers." Meanwhile, a combination of high skill-biased technological change and the global "rise of the rest" have increased pressure on those with lesser education and skill levels. Abandoning the BSM means that governments will have to shed "bureaucratic habits of thought" in order to become more responsive to change (Mead, 2010).

While many Americans seem to have accepted, intellectually, that heightened globalization together with rapid technological change facilitates a secular rise in average living standards, the growing gap between winners and losers from the system is increasingly contentious. The financial crisis may have brought public anxieties to the surface but the underlying causes have been festering for decades. If Americans are unwilling to pay the higher taxes necessary to maintain the BSM today, are they willing to accept the growing insecurity and inequality generated by its absence?

The Occupy Wall Street movement (OWS) looked to be one response to such inequalities, employment insecurity and diminished social mobility. According to Joseph Stiglitz (2011), "(the) protestors are asking for very little: a chance to use their skills, the right to decent work at decent pay, and a fairer economy and . . . a market economy that delivers on what it is supposed to." Although their positions are evolving, compared for instance with the 1999 Seattle WTO protests, OWS sentiment and, to some degree, that of the Tea Party on the right reflect less a rejection of economic openness. The OWS movement appears most exercised by the perceived reemergence of a US plutocracy with disproportionate access to the political process:

> The sense of injustice . . . is not just about the unfairness of a small part of society living in unimaginable wealth while so much of the rest of society lives in economic desperation . . . It's about the degradation of politics

that turns wealth into power through campaign financing, lobbying, and the revolving door of business and government... Washington responds to rich constituencies rather than to the median voter, much less to the poor.

(Sachs, 2011)

One theme that arose during the Republican and later presidential debates was whether the federal government should strive to influence the inter-sectoral flow of investment. The difference between Romney and Obama appeared most evident in their discussion of government policy toward the energy sector. Both embraced energy independence as a primary public policy goal and the need to promote all sources of domestic energy. Yet, President Obama stressed the impact of governmental regulation on reducing gasoline consumption, the removal of subsidies to the oil and gas industry and governmental encouragement of renewable energy sources of the future. Romney, in contrast, derided the (wasteful) subsidies extended by the Obama Administration to the solar and wind power sectors and the regulations restricting a fuller exploration of oil and gas on federal lands.

During the course of the long election campaign both parties, but especially President Obama and Republican candidate Rick Santorum, proposed to use industrial policy to favor manufacturing over services. Obama's 2012 State of the Union address, for example, was littered with references to an "economy built to last," a phrase once employed by General Motors and one intended to link the secular decline of manufacturing employment with the rise in income inequality. During the president's address, he put it simply: "If you're an American manufacturer, you should get a bigger tax cut. If you're a high-tech manufacturer, we should double the tax deduction you get for making products here... you should get help financing a new plant, equipment, or training for new workers" (State of the Union, 2012).

In part, this (largely) bipartisan bias in favor of manufacturing reflects the (highly questionable) notion that former levels of manufacturing employment can be restored, and that services are intrinsically less valuable or employment-generating. While public fury over reckless practices perpetrated in the capital markets seems perfectly justified, the broadside against the financial sector for destroying jobs or producing "phony profits" rather than "real things" masks the continued comparative advantage the US possesses in financial markets as well as other high-end engineering, legal, business and high-tech services.

Furthermore, although the US share of global manufacturing output today remains essentially unchanged, the secular decline in manufacturing employment over recent decades can be attributed largely to high productivity growth reflecting "labor-saving" technological change. While signs abound that, aided by declines in relative unit labor costs and the US dollar's secular (real effective) depreciation, US manufacturing may be poised for some rebound, including greater incidence of "re-shoring," manufacturing per se can no more be the foundation for a major recovery in US employment than agriculture was over a century ago.[19]

Moreover, the notion that American workers should be able to "win" or "outcompete" in every product or service category provided there is a "level playing field" recalls a concept of international exchange as zero sum, conflating unfeasible "absolute advantage" with a more theoretically sound "comparative advantage" – relative cost superiority in the production of particular types of goods and services, including within high-end manufacturing. Obama puts the notion of full-spectrum dominance simply: "Our workers are the most productive on Earth, and if the playing field is level, I promise you, America will always win" (State of the Union, 2012). While innocuous as mere political sloganeering, such rhetoric can be harmful if implemented through neo-mercantilist policy.[20] In the event, there is already a large body of international law to arbitrate charges of unfair trade. To center one's national economic strategy on combating unfair trade, particularly with one large and dynamic country with which the US happens to benefit substantially through bi-directional trade and investment, appears exceedingly defensive and, as already argued, ultimately self-defeating for the world's leading power.

Another undefended proposition is the implication that outsourcing is a principal explanation for the US's unemployment crisis. Here the differences between Obama and Romney were sharply drawn, with the President arguing that the US tax structure discriminated against domestic relative to foreign investment by US multinationals. The details behind this claim should no doubt receive close scrutiny in the context of a comprehensive tax reform. More generally, if remaining competitive requires US firms to lower their costs by relocating lower-skilled segments of their production process, is it ultimately welfare-enhancing for the country as a whole to prevent this? In this respect, the contradiction seemed glairing when the President, on the one hand, celebrated the innovativeness of a Steve Jobs and on the other, railed against firms that outsource their simpler labor-intensive tasks as is the case with all of Apple's products. Meanwhile, it behooves us to remember that American consumers and workers also benefit from substantial corporate insourcing.

Meanwhile, the presidential debate arguably trivialized the complicated issue of inequality by offering simple palliatives, such as the Buffet Rule.[21] A more intellectually satisfying approach would be to ask whether it makes greater economic sense to tax every source of income the same at the margin. If so, wealthier individuals who earn their income disproportionately in the form of capital gains (or more egregiously hedge funds which exploit rules on "carried interest") would be taxed at much higher average rates.

In the event, it needs to be asked whether taxing capital income more punitively would contribute to a more dynamic, employment-generating and fair economy.[22]

Public policy probably cannot do much in the short run about inequality, even if more properly recast as disappointing income growth for lower quintile groups and the median household. As discussed in chapter 3, meaningfully improving educational outcomes will require deep institutional reform including measures inimical to strongly entrenched interests. A progressive shorter-term solution arguably would be to marry comprehensive tax reform with enhanced investment in job retraining and wage subsidies to provide dislocated workers with greater wherewithal to contend with rapid change. The upshot is that the contrast between "fairness" and redistribution, on the one hand, and opportunity and "rewarding success," on the other, around which the Obama–Romney battle-lines formed early in the election season, offers an exceedingly rigid dichotomy for the challenge of reinvigorating US dynamism, employment creation and social mobility.

Americans and globalization

Concerns over job security and income inequality-cum-mobility notwithstanding, most Americans seem to accept that "open trade around the world," "encouraging foreign investment" and "continuing high levels of immigration" remain pivotal to US economic success. Although reasonably robust support for such components of globalization survives, anxiety over global competition pervades American attitudes, especially against the backdrop of the weak economic recovery.[23]

While the majority of Americans appears to accept that globalization is "mostly good" overall,[24] the number that believes otherwise has been growing steadily.[25] Although one can marshal evidence that technological change represents the greater threat to job security, Americans remain understandably worried about off-shoring, imports and immigration. Roughly half of those polled argue that globalization exerts a net negative impact on the US economy when other countries fail to play by the rules. Americans largely believe that US companies are too often left competing on an uneven playing field when (say) foreign subsidies or laxer consumer-safety and child-labor standards favor foreign competitors in the developing world (Chicago Council on Global Affairs, 2010).[26]

Evolving public opinion has largely mirrored the deterioration in domestic economic conditions. While in 2002, as the economy was emerging from a comparatively mild downturn, 80 per cent of the population voiced approval for international trade, by 2007 the Pew Global Attitudes Project had chronicled a 21 per cent drop-off in support (down to 59 per cent; Pew Research, 2007). These numbers have dropped even further since the financial crisis of 2008. A 2010 NBC/WSJ poll found that 47 per cent of Americans felt free trade has "hurt," compared with 23 per cent believing it has "helped" (NBC

News/WSJ, 2010). Between 1996 and 2008, the number of Americans favoring trade restrictions, ostensibly to level the playing field, increased.[27] The public's support for free trade agreements (FTAs), such as the North American Trade Agreement, also appears to have declined.[28] Even though Americans think that globalization is mainly good for them qua consumers,[29] there remains a palpable fear of job loss and depressed incomes, and a corresponding muted emphasis on the more dispersed benefits from low-priced imports.

Capital flows: A focus on China

Globalization-related concerns extend to transnational capital movements. In particular, anxiety over the injurious effects of globalization manifest prominently in views on off-shoring. This process of contracting out to foreign firms or subsidiaries of US companies, thereby reducing the short-run demand for American workers, is understandably viewed with consternation. Such sentiment moreover is not confined to lower levels of the income distribution. Some 61 per cent of Americans with a post-graduate educational level, and/or Americans earning more than $75,000 a year, believe that off-shoring involves a net welfare loss for the country (Chicago Council on Global Affairs, 2010).

Public concern is also apparent over inward-bound capital flows. While most Americans recognize the positive contribution of foreign direct investment on employment, they can grow preoccupied with transactions that allegedly pose national security threats. It remains unclear to what extent incidents such as the Dubai Ports imbroglio and the China National Offshore Oil Corporation's thwarted efforts to buy a controlling stake in Unocal reflect a more general, heightened concern about foreign capital inflows.[30]

The allegations that surfaced around these cases hark back to the late 1980s, when it came to light that a Japanese company was going to purchase a controlling stake in the firm that owned Rockefeller Center. Just as the public perceived Japan as a peer rival during the 1980s, many Americans view China as today's major economic threat. Asked whether or not companies from certain countries should be allowed to hold a controlling interest in US companies, Americans were overwhelmingly opposed, with disapproval most pronounced with respect to China (71 per cent opposed) and India (66 per cent opposed), and somewhat less with respect to the European Union (55 per cent opposed; Chicago Council on Global Affairs, 2008). While there remains a latent skepticism about foreign investment more generally, this tends to be aggravated if the countries of origin are considered would-be strategic rivals.

Moreover, foreign financing of US federal budget deficits remains a major preoccupation. In both the public's perception and the 2012 political contest the issue with the federal debt is not just "how much?" and "how fast" but "who owns it?" Mitt Romney made the most of this issue when he said that he would judge all federal expenditures by whether they were worth borrowing from China. According to Pew Research polling from 2010, 59 per cent identify China as the owner of "the most US debt" (Pew: Public Knowledge, 2010). As of October 2012 China is the largest foreign holder of US Treasuries at \$1.15 trillion, followed closely by Japan with \$1.12 trillion. While China and Japan together account for roughly 42 percent of the total US debt held abroad, China by itself accounts for little more than 10 percent of total US debt held by the public. In any case, as argued in chapter 4 fears of China peremptorily selling off its treasuries for economic or political reasons appear exaggerated. Nevertheless, many remain wary that the Chinese may deploy their US security holdings as a financial weapon (Zakaria, 2011).[31] Presidential candidate Michele Bachmann, for example, during a CNN national security debate, mirrored the view of many Americans when she characterized paying interest to China as "sending our power: our money will be used to grow China's military at the expense of the United States military" (CNN, 2011).

Many Americans seem convinced that competition from China in particular poses an overriding threat.[32] A growing percentage views China as being at the forefront of the global economy[33] today. A plurality sees China as the leading economic power in 20 years,[34] notwithstanding the large economic lead the US enjoys, particularly in per capita income and technological advancement. Still, most Americans who fret over China attribute its rapid ascension to "unfair trading practices,"[35] mirroring an earlier (but long since jettisoned) preoccupation with Japan (Chicago Council on Global Affairs, 2008, pp. 5–6).

Both Republicans and Democrats have jumped on the China blame game wagon. For example, following years of threats, the Senate passed a bill that would label China a "currency manipulator." The Obama Administration meanwhile has studiously avoided branding China's "heavy intervention in currency markets" as "manipulation," even though President Obama, Hillary Clinton and Timothy Geithner have all attacked Chinese intervention on behalf of an undervalued exchange rate for the renminbi in the past (Jaffe, 2011). At a presidential debate on October 11, Mitt Romney declared: "On day one, I will issue an executive order identifying China as a currency manipulator... If you're not willing to stand up to China, you'll get run over by China. And that's what's happened for 20 years."

That this view was not universally held among presidential contenders is evident, for example, from what John Huntsman, former Republican presidential candidate and former Ambassador to China, had to say: "China is not a threat to the US, if the US economy can grow again. It would be bad policy to label the Chinese currency as undervalued." Once in office and after the looser rhetoric displayed in his first presidential campaign, President Obama has been more circumspect: "I absolutely believe that China's peaceful rise is good for the world, and it's good for America... We just want to make sure that that rise occurs in a way that reinforces international norms and international rules, and enhances security and peace" (Condon, 2011). While the issue of currency manipulation is only one among many perceived unfair trade practices, China's exchange rate policy has served as a lightning rod for public sentiment.[36]

Immigration

Buffeted by hyperbolic political rhetoric, Americans offer a broad range of responses when questioned about immigration's impact on jobs, the economy, national security and culture. Although polling fails to adequately capture much of the nuance in American public opinion on this emotional subject, it remains striking that a majority of Americans remains supportive of legal immigration, even if many remain troubled by perceptions of ever-mounting illegal immigration.[37]

Asked in a March 2006 Pew poll which was the more serious problem, 60 per cent selected illegal immigration, as opposed to only 4 per cent who selected immigration more generally (Kusnet et al., 2006). Americans remain relatively amenable to immigration at a level far greater than that of their peers,[38] so long as it occurs legally, auguring well for the ongoing openness of American society. In a 2011 Gallup poll, 59 per cent believed immigration contributed significant social benefits, while only 37 per cent found immigration to be problematic overall (Jones, 2011). However, a 2010 study conducted by the Chicago Council on Global Affairs revealed that three-quarters of Americans viewed immigration as detrimental to job security.[39]

Americans have increasingly voiced the opinion that illegal immigrants represent a significant social drain – by way of taking jobs and absorbing social services – rather than as an asset by virtue of their willingness to perform arduous work and lend desirable skills to the US economy (Pew Research, 2006). In addition to a fear of job losses, in some circles immigration has even spurred alarm over an erosion of "American" culture.[40] Conservative commentator Patrick Buchanan has been a major proponent of this perspective. His 2011 book *Suicide of a Superpower* argues that Judeo-Christian values are being eroded, diversity has eclipsed social unity, and immigration has compromised ethnic cohesion (Buchanan, 2011). Though reflecting a distinctly minority viewpoint, according to one poll of those desiring tighter restrictions on illegal immigration, 70 per cent believe that their way of life needs to be protected (Chicago Council on Global Affairs, 2010, pp. 21–26).

Vying for the crucial Latino vote, both parties have toned down rhetoric related to deportation of undocumented workers and their families. Obama has touted immigration reform focusing on a streamlined visa process and encouraging American-educated foreign-born individuals to stay in the country and utilize their skills (*Wall Street Journal*, 2011). With Congress having failed to pass Obama's Dream Act, which would have granted legal status to young immigrants, by recent executive order the President has introduced a program which grants deportation deferrals for two years and work permits to certain illegal immigrants who arrived in the US as children.[41]

Republicans have meanwhile voiced support for continued legal immigration coupled with a "modernized" visa system.[42] Mitt Romney, for example, suggests that the US expands legal immigration for foreign students by "stapling a green card to her diploma" to encourage those with advanced degrees and critically important skills to stay and work in the US (2010, pp. 123–124). Not only are Republican politicians amenable to more high-skilled immigration, but many support enhanced immigration of all skill levels. Sounding tough on border security, Newt Gingrich supported a guest worker plan, elements of the Development, Relief, and Education for Alien Minors (DREAM) Act and an approach to "incorporating" the 11 million undocumented immigrants currently living in the US (Moffett, 2011).

The Obama Administration has framed illegal immigration primarily as a public safety issue, deporting record numbers of illegal immigrants with misdemeanor and felony convictions, and prioritizing these deportations above illegal immigrants living in the country peacefully (Bennett and Dinan, 2011). The Republican consensus has been broader sweeping and focused on fears of immigrant induced job losses. The 2012 Republican presidential primaries exhibited a growing concern for controlling the flow of illegal immigrants, especially from Mexico, with proposals for building a border fence, putting "boots on the ground," denying amnesty and turning off "the magnet" of social services, education and jobs that attract immigrants into the country.[43]

To sum up, while factors such as the stalled multilateral trade agenda, opposition to offshoring or further tightening of US immigration controls may be straws in the wind or glimmers of mounting concern, they need not pose a meaningful current challenge to broad US support for globalization. In contrast, if today's employment challenge were to be framed in a manner that places the onus of blame on non-Americans, then one building block of the liberal hegemonic order – the commitment to openness – would be called into question. Such an eventuality could take the form of significantly increased resort to administered protection, broader restrictions or disincentives to capital flows, and sharply lowered quotas for (legal) immigrants. Yet, such tendencies do not seem obviously apparent, today's difficult economic backdrop notwithstanding.

Political constraints on US fiscal actions

The US today finds itself at the dawn of a critical public discussion over the future role of government. The Tea Party champions smaller government, while OWS promotes a more equitable distribution of economic gains, and a political system less beholden to lobbying on behalf of powerful, corporate interests. These movements have emerged amidst an increasingly diverse and aging population and a more sharply drawn political-cum-philosophical divide. The unfolding fiscal battleground potentially pitches young against old; immigrants against resident workers; and the middle class against the more affluent. Meanwhile, Americans' revealed preference for larger government in the form of major entitlements has wavered little (Newport and Saad, 2011).[44]

Traditional ideological leanings meanwhile continue to differentiate the two major political parties. Democrats argue that the binding constraint on current hiring is lagging private demand; and that governmental stimulus or at least the postponement of greater "austerity"– paid for by longer-term deficit reduction – is needed to bolster aggregate demand and investors' "animal spirits" in the shorter run. President Obama and many Democratic members in Congress also favor tighter regulation, a stronger social safety net and redistributive policies to help reverse the longer-term trend toward higher income inequality and economic insecurity. They seek solutions to the country's fiscal challenge that do not rely disproportionately on expenditure cuts, particularly for those impacting the most vulnerable. They argue that overall spending must rise well above the historical 20 per cent of Gross Domestic Product (GDP), owing to postponed investments and population aging. The Democrats look to shift the taxation burden to higher income individuals, on the margin.[45] Such policy preferences have done well in polls, but whether they can find legislative success will depend on the outcome of the 2012 presidential and congressional elections.[46]

The overwhelming weight of Republican criticism of President Obama concerns the proliferation of regulatory burdens on the private sector.[47] The Republican mantra is that the pall of governmental regulation aggravates investment uncertainty, slowing employment creation. In addition to alleged governmental overreach in the areas of financial reform, health care and initiatives on energy-cum-climate change, opprobrium is heaped on the size of government via the upward trajectory of government spending and the threat of marginal tax rate increases, especially on wealthier individuals. In the Republican view, smaller government entailing lower taxes and reduced spending, alongside a scaling back of regulation, is the key to bolstering business confidence and returning to robust economic growth.[48]

While Republicans claim to desire a smaller government, the US federal government has grown as a share of the economy under both Republican and Democratic administrations. Fiscal conservatives in both parties thus worry that unarrested growth in spending will sooner rather than later trigger the long-anticipated hard landing. Beneath the polarized rhetoric, however, one sees some glimmer of a gradually expanding bipartisan realization that the long-term growth of entitlements needs to be curtailed and that longer-term deficit reduction will succeed only through an eventual political compromise involving both revenue increases and spending cuts, including on defense.

Defense spending

A plurality of Americans believes that overall defense spending is excessive.[49] In fact, as a purely political matter in the current fiscal climate, it would be unfeasible to exempt the Pentagon from meaningful cuts in the growth of discretionary spending. Given the notorious waste in the Pentagon budget and shifts in geopolitical realities,[50] the country can well afford a moderate, phased reduction in the growth rate of defense spending relative to the current baseline – something the public seems to understand and support.

Yet, there seems no appetite on the part of the main presidential candidates or Congress to "gut" defense as a contribution to overall deficit reduction. Some estimates, particularly from Defense Secretary Leon Panetta, have warned that anything more than the $450 billion in defense "cuts" over ten years, agreed by Congress in August 2011, could take the US military "to the edge" and "truly devastate our national security" (Alexander, 2011). Thus far, President Obama has concurred, limiting defense reductions relative to the baseline agreed to in the bipartisan debt ceiling deal (Taylor, 2011).[51] However, the congressional super committee's failure to agree on $1.2 trillion in deficit reduction measures could trigger an additional $500 billion in indiscriminate defense cuts.[52]

Republican leaders John McCain and Mitt Romney, among other party stalwarts, continue to advocate maintaining current or even increasing real defense spending (Mataconis, 2011). In *No Apology,* Romney warns that "if we do not pay enough in dollars (on defense), we may be forced to pay the price in blood" (2010, p. 87). Focusing on perceived threats from China, Russia, Iran and global terrorism, Romney calls for accelerated investment in a modernized nuclear arsenal, larger navy, army and marine increases of 100,000 soldiers, and defense against space and cyberspace threats (2010, pp. 88–96). Promising to set a defense spending floor at 4 per cent of GDP, Romney's answer to ensuring US power is to maintain its commanding lead in overall military power (*The Economist*, October 15, 2011).

A clear majority of Americans believes that the imperative of maintaining a strong economy today trumps a preoccupation with military spending as the basis for sustaining national security and global power projection.[53] In addition to President Obama, several Republican candidates in the 2012 race appear to agree. While strong defense spending has historically been a central plank of the conservative agenda,[54] presidential candidates Ron Paul, Michelle Bachmann and Jon Huntsman all accept that, to achieve fiscal consolidation, defense cuts would be required. But then again, none of these candidates succeeded in defeating the victorious Republican nominee, Mitt Romney.

Conclusion

However great the external challenges confronting the US, they pale in comparison to that most internal of challenges – maintaining the support of the American people. Owing to the aftershocks of the 2008 financial crisis, two decade-long wars, the rapid ascension of China and, not least, a gridlocked political system, some have succumbed to a gnawing sense that the US's best days are behind her. Nearly three out of four Americans feel the country is moving in the wrong direction.[55] Concerned over dwindling finances and job prospects, the majority of Americans, at least as of August 2011, expected a still bleaker economic future.[56] Trust in government has fallen to an historic low.[57] Increasing numbers feel the political system is rigged in favor of elite interests. More and more Americans fear the system may no longer be up to the task of resolving core social challenges. It thus may be no exaggeration to suggest that certain core US institutions risk a fundamental loss of legitimacy.

Despite this downbeat mood, Americans historically have retained an inherent optimism, a passion for remaining on top and a belief in their collective ability to surmount core obstacles. The faith in American resilience underlying much political rhetoric, whether involving a "Sputnik moment," "winning the future" or "American exceptionalism," still fires the public imagination. While few would be familiar with the term, most Americans support (or can be persuaded to support) US hegemony. This observation rests on the following considerations.

First and foremost, Americans seek a secure and prosperous future, and they accept that the country must make certain structural adjustments to achieve this goal. They appreciate that the country must reform and invest in neglected dimensions of physical and human capital. They understand the enduring contribution of an entrepreneurial culture of innovation, even if this offers economic displacement and uncertainty as part of the bargain. Measured inequality is ultimately less important to most Americans compared with a sense that opportunity exists for rising incomes along the income distribution.

Second, the American people support an activist role abroad. They embrace having the leading military but no longer want to serve as the world's policeman. Tired of war, the public mood has shifted toward domestic priorities; but if history is any guide, upon achieving greater economic relief the pendulum will swing back. The key distinction is one between a temporary drawback from the current scale of foreign engagement, versus an enduring drift toward neo-isolationism. Although the latter as always may capture the mood of a solid minority, it remains outside of the feasible political choice set for the vast majority.

As emerging countries like China and India gain greater prominence, Americans want the US to retain its status as technological trailblazer and most productive economy. With a few key caveats, maintaining openness – the relatively free movement of international capital, labor and goods – is generally accepted as a necessary means to this end. Preventing concerns over unfair trading practices from snowballing into generalized protectionism remains a watchword for policymakers as long as the domestic economy flounders. American politicians must also become more adept at explaining that an objective assessment of corporate off-shoring must incorporate the gains in jobs and technology from insourcing. And although it is especially difficult to do amid an anemic economic recovery, Americans need to be disabused of the invidious lump-of-labor fallacy that views an economy as capable of producing only a fixed number of jobs over which immigrants and resident workers must fiercely compete.

Americans do divide over the role and size of government. Significant variation exists on where to strike the balance between on the one hand, strengthening the social safety net and redistributing income, and on the other, expanding opportunities for more Americans to attain the skills required to benefit from economic growth. While polls indicate a general aversion to over-taxation, equally evident is opposition to a serious scaling back of entitlements. A majority appears to support some increase in the taxation burden on wealthier Americans, a proposal adamantly resisted within Republican ranks.

In an international context, however, the divide between the two main political parties can be exaggerated. While they part significantly over spending and regulation, neither party seeks a scope for governmental intervention akin to most of Europe. Both parties and most Americans meanwhile understand that the nation must find more durable solutions to debt, health care and jobs. While paying lip-service to neo-mercantilist sentiment, most of the political and corporate elite, supports efficient (private and public) investment in physical and human capital to enhance national "competitiveness."

On the issue of America's global role, except for a neo-isolationist minority, both parties support robust US leadership, dividing only over tactical differences that mirror the competing perspectives of neorealism and liberal internationalism. Both the center-right and center-left are united, at least in principle, on the overriding imperative of arresting any movement toward national decline. President Obama thus speaks to the hopes and aspirations of most Americans when he says: "Anyone who tells you that America is in decline or that our influence has waned doesn't know what they're talking about" (State of the Union Message, January 2012). In contrast, when the President's detractors accuse him of policies that will precipitate the country's decline, such claims trigger immediate disavowal.

If political polarization were to inhibit problem solving to the point where Americans abandon faith in its representatives, the legitimacy of US democracy would be called into question. Yet, the current gridlock and perceived voter disenchantment is not unprecedented.[58] Recall, for instance, the turbulence attending the heydays of Barry Goldwater, George McGovern and Newt Gingrich's rein as Speaker of the House to mention only more recent examples. In times of apparent intractability, the US political system has eventually forged compromise. One might therefore be excused for remaining guardedly optimistic that with the election season behind us, meaningful progress on the country's leading challenges will resume. In sum, ample precedence exists to expect the system to eventually deliver compromises that suffice to maintain the basic contours of US dynamism and US hegemony.

Part VI

10
Conclusion: Maintaining Hegemony

For the foreseeable future the US looks likely to remain the one and only truly global power. In extrapolating recent setbacks into a forecast of generalized, systemic decay, today's case for decline ultimately fails to persuade. Within the global power hierarchy ascendant actors still find themselves situated well below the top rung singularly occupied by the US. Reinforcing this perception is the dustbin of successively invalidated "declinist" hypotheses (Kagan, 2012).

The US's unique structural position within the global system reflects its superior capacity across multiple dimensions of influence and a singular ability to project power globally. In addition to the instruments wielded by the state, its global footprint features a profound economic and cultural-cum-ideological impact exerted by civil society. US-headquartered transnational actors range from corporate stalwarts like Google and Apple to major service and advocacy non-governmental organizations and from top-ranked universities to flush, internationally focused philanthropies. Even the disproportionate remittances accounted for by US-based expatriate workers underscore the transcendent impact of the world's largest economy and multicultural society. The pervasive penetration of American values, business and popular culture, and cutting-edge technologies, not to mention English as the global lingua franca for politics and commerce helps to render the composite US "product" *sui generis*.

Epitomizing US power has been its vanguard role in the erection and defense of multilateral institutions and as a leading provider of global public goods.[1] That actions to buttress global stability and prosperity have been consistent with safeguarding US national interests has been critical to cementing broad-based American public and international support. Presumptions concerning the transient nature of hegemonic power, arising from pockets of resistance and the burden of exercising power globally, have generally not been borne out by US experience[2]; nor have most claims of strategic overextension. Moreover, the pressures attending globalization

229

have proved less inimical to US economic and geopolitical influence than often predicted.

While particular actions are condemned, concerted contra-US balancing seems nowhere apparent. Other states pursue alternative variants of capitalism or work to redistribute the rights and benefits within prevailing institutions. Some repudiate US- (Western-) championed norms, such as "the right to protect." But no other actor has advanced a genuinely alternative structure of global governance. Whether the exercise of US power has, according to one or another normative criterion, consistently enhanced global welfare is a more complex question, and one that this book has studiously avoided addressing.

Declinism

Over the decades "declinism" has arrived in periodic waves. While defying the skeptics with bouts of resiliency and renewal, a conjuncture of US missteps, and the upward trajectory of other actors renders US decline today sufficiently plausible to reopen the case.

In responding to the psychological blow of September 11th, the US has sacrificed blood, treasure and legitimacy in two wars spanning a decade, yielding modest tangible gains. Its political clout in the greater Middle East has waned even as this perennially volatile area continues to divert attention from other strategically vital regions. The epicenter of the 2008 financial crisis, the US suffered a loss of credibility as purported model of economic rationality and market efficiency. In the Tea Party and Occupy Wall Street, the fallout from the financial crisis has sparked a grassroots revolt against mounting debt, crony capitalism and income inequality. The imperative to reverse an ominous longer-term fiscal trajectory has been met with chronic congressional gridlock. Core elements of its infrastructure suffer from disrepair and neglect.

Armed with such a formidable list of impediments, purveyors of a declinist perspective would appear to have a strong case. If by "decline" one has in mind a relative loss in geopolitical, economic, military and/or cultural clout, some erosion in composite US power over the last two decades has undoubtedly occurred. Yet, a global hegemon worthy of the name cannot be so easily toppled owing to cyclical downturns or episodic policy errors, even momentous ones. Such factors can prove to be at best accelerants of more fundamental trends.

More than any other single factor – Afghanistan/Iraq, al Qaeda, the sub-prime financial crisis or domestic political gridlock – any decisive narrowing of the US power gap arguably must reflect the secular impact of (US-championed) globalization. In conjunction with improving national policies, economic integration together with the modern revolution in technology and communication accounts most profoundly for the acceleration of growth and the mitigation of poverty in the world's two most populous countries, among others. Yet, economic convergence today mirrors that experienced during an earlier era when the US helped to facilitate the postwar reconstruction of Europe and Japan. One could equally have argued – as some have – that the US encountered significant decline for a generation after World War II as the income gap between the US and war-ravaged nations progressively diminished.

The core question is not whether US influence remains unshaken after a decade marked by war, financial crisis and political stalemate during which time others around the world have made steady strides. At issue is whether the US-inspired liberal world order has proved so successful as to have created the conditions for uprooting its preeminent position. Owing to the broad forces of globalization, does the country's qualitative power projection capability look to fall below some definitive threshold heretofore differentiating hegemony from a lesser status of "first among equals"?

The "rise of the rest" captures the acceleration of economic growth in the emerging market world – a phenomenon, it bears repeating, that can largely be attributed to US-driven globalization. Although superior economic growth must be maintained to succeed in demonstrably narrowing the standard of living gap with the more advanced economies, the sustained progress achieved in a group of emerging economies to date already highlights the more marked relative decline of a core sub-segment of the "West," namely Japan and much of Western Europe. In terms of long-term trajectories, hampering these nations are adverse demographics, long-postponed structural reforms, and a challenge to regional integration arising from the debt, trade and banking fissures within the European Monetary Union. The demographic pressures relate to a combination of slowing fertility, population aging and often impediments to the social integration especially of Muslim immigrants. Insularly focused on domestic economic and political stability, moreover, Europe and Japan exhibit little will to commit the requisite resources to meaningfully project power beyond their immediate regions.

In contrast, while the longer-term outlook for real per capita growth has arguably deteriorated relative to more dynamic periods (see e.g. Gordon, 2012), the US is still positioned to outperform other advanced countries owing to relatively healthier demographic and productivity trajectories. Other US advantages include a battle-tested fiscal federalism and a history of (inter-regional) labor mobility, as compared with the more fundamental impediments to an optimal currency area in Europe. Therefore, at question is not whether the dynamism of the emerging markets threatens to eclipse the West. The former are already making steady progress toward this goal. The issue is whether more rapid convergence in the East and Global South remains compatible with US hegemony even as the geopolitical and economic weight of much of the remaining developed world diminishes.

This drives to the heart of a theme featured throughout this book. We have argued that the array and depth of US power assets today remain historically unparalleled. Yet, the US and its allies also face a daunting, perhaps unprecedented, array of challenges. First and foremost is the re-ascendancy of China. Although the US encountered what appeared to be a formidable systemic rival in the former Soviet Union, today one better appreciates that the USSR was a uni-dimensional power with feet of clay. The same cannot be said of China, whose size and dynamism makes it a would-be rival of a wholly different cloth.

Aside from its longer-term military potential and geopolitical aspirations, China epitomizes the more immediate challenge from globalization. While enlarging opportunity throughout the world, the increase in competition and the increasingly complex fragmentation of production occasioned by global integration imposes extraordinary pressures on workers in the developed and developing countries alike. The latter has likewise facilitated the ascent of second- and third-tier powers, with distinct agendas and growing ambitions. Also facilitated by globalization is the rather different challenge posed by religiously motivated non-state actors engaged in global terrorism; their potential acquisition of fissile materials or other weapons of mass destruction represents an ever-present threat. Amplifying such risks is the ever-present prospect of a nuclear arms race that threatens to engulf key strategic regions. Myriad conflicts around the world but particularly in the Middle East and Southwest Asia illustrate the extent to which localized conflicts can at any point mutate into global conflagrations. Adding to such developments is a growing list of transnational challenges arising from fragile and failing states, the solutions for which necessitate enhanced regional and international cooperation and leadership.

Mitigating such economic and eventual geopolitical challenges is the possibility of a more cooperative and mutually beneficial relationship with China in particular. Such potential is rooted in the latter's progressive stake in the global economy, the absence of any distinctly anti-capitalist, ideological posture, and its shared interest in resisting terrorism and opposing other risks to regional and global instability.

Buttressing the US's strategic position further is a group of older and newer allies, including an expansive list of (Western, Central and Eastern) European nations, Japan and a host of other East Asian nations hedging against an overly assertive China, Turkey, India, and other second- or third-tier powers around the world that extend at least tacit support to the US. It seems unlikely that China or for that matter any other would-be rival can field as formidable an array of allied force multipliers. And without minimizing the challenge they continue to pose, extremist actors such as al Qaeda appear increasingly on the run. Meanwhile, while remaining ongoing risks nuclear aspirant states seem increasingly isolated within the global community.

Dimensions of global power

Essential preconditions for the maintenance of US predominance seem straightforward. First, the US must continue to demonstrate an ongoing ability to leverage its composite, power potential into disproportionate influence on the direction and stability of the global economy and global governance more generally. The requirement is not that the US always gets its way; it never has. Rather, with due regard to competing interests and perspectives, the US would prevail more often and decisively in promoting its core preferences for updating the global institutional architecture. The latter would involve a superior record of success in promoting the core norms of a liberal global order. Second, the US must avoid falling prey to counter-balancing by an aspiring, system-altering hegemon in concert with a sufficient phalanx of allies. In the event, the only apparent would-be systemic rival would be China, and such a concerted challenge seems at best a distant prospect.

In no other facet of power is the US universally acknowledged as more dominant than in its military superiority. In addition to its unrivalled war fighting capability, the US military remains the central actor in the provision of critical public goods, including the safeguarding of shipping lanes and maintaining the intra-regional balance of power in key strategic areas.

Although the scope and scale of US military predominance was documented earlier, several points bear reemphasis here. First, having devoted a sizeable share of national resources toward consolidating its military lead over decades, the US enjoys a huge legacy advantage. While this hardly means it can cease investing in new capabilities, the scope of investment that would have to be taken by a group of other states to markedly bridge the military gap with the US remains formidable. Second, this US lead provides ample scope for alleviating military overstretch while contributing to longer-term fiscal consolidation.

One counter point to consider is whether US military superiority has lost some deterrence value. Recognizing that they could not survive on a conventional battle field against US forces, its enemies invest in asymmetric capabilities. Counterinsurgencies utilizing sophisticated guerilla tactics have challenged US forces. Furthermore, cyber war could conceivably be a game changer, given the profound economic and military dependence on complex, computing systems and networks. Meanwhile, the proliferation of nuclear weapons and other weapons of mass destruction can alter the military power equation dramatically. In upgrading its defensive and offensive capabilities and as the vanguard of international counter-proliferation efforts, the US defense and diplomatic establishment has had to exhibit unceasing adaptability.

Overall, the net assessment has to be that the full gamut of US military assets, including the varied and sophisticated skill set of its troops, its technological sophistication and its full-spectrum ability to project power globally, represents an unequalled asset.

One of the virtues of globalization has been an enriching intermixing of cultures. This has brought, for example, India's Bollywood or the music scene of West Africa international notoriety. In comparative terms, however, few would contest the pervasive impact of American culture. Aside from the international exposure of its music, film, literature, sports and fashion, the influence of particular, US-championed ideals merits reemphasis here. One such ideal concerns a respect for tolerance and diversity. The US stands as a shining example of how people of different ancestries can unite around a concept of nationhood that transcends sectarian allegiance to religion or ethnicity. In progressively dismantling the pernicious legacy of slavery, American society today overridingly repudiates advancement based on color or creed. The belief in equality of opportunity, meritocracy and social mobility provides a powerful example for nations transitioning from very different economic and political systems, even if the unsatisfactory realization of these ideals has recently engendered greater concern in the US itself.

In addition, while susceptible to certain charges of hypocrisy, the US has more often than not been a leading voice in defense of human rights. Its reluctant alliances with certain dictatorships mirror a complex foreign policy agenda buffeted by a struggle between liberal humanitarian values and more realist impulses. Certain notable lapses notwithstanding, the US has generally championed a liberal notion of personal liberty, while defending core economic and political freedoms.

Finally, arguably more than any other nation the US has promoted the global returns to "openness." Through its dominant voice in international institutions, it has advocated expansively free scope for transnational movements of goods, capital, people and ideas. While this has not precluded leveraging its power to defend or favor particular interests, no other country has as consistently led the world in expanding the scope of global commerce and mobility.

Pockets of anti-Americanism as do persist have failed to overwhelm the global transition toward greater reliance on markets and expanding support for democracy, trends with which the US is inextricably associated. More authoritarian versions of contemporary state capitalism have no doubt evolved at a time when the reputation of Anglo-American capitalism has been significantly tarnished. Nevertheless, US-championed liberalism has yet to meet a more viable global alternative for economic and political governance.

In terms of political influence today, the situation is more nuanced. The US retains a leading voice in most international fora. For example it continues to wield singular veto power in leading international financial institutions and is among five veto-wielding permanent Security Council members in the United Nations (UN). When confronted by consistent opposition from Russia and/or China, its leadership within the North Atlantic Treaty Organization and its broader set of alliances and partnerships provide alternative vehicles for confronting geopolitical challenges. In acceding to more representative, albeit less proven, multilateral institutions such as the G-20, the US has demonstrated adaptability in acknowledging the growing geopolitical weight of key emerging states.

As with its share of global output, expecting the US to retain the same degree of political clout that it wielded in the aftermath of World War II or the Cold War seems unrealistic. With the success of globalization and the collapse of communism has come a diffusion of power and desire among rising states to chart their own futures. The increase in the number of significant (economic and geopolitical) players today complicates international diplomacy. The extent to which their respective priorities deviate from the core principles of the US liberal order varies.

In the final analysis it seems difficult to abandon the perception that US objectives and actions continue to command disproportionate global attention. The US retains, uniquely, strategic stakes and allies in every region. And an "ability to organize very diverse coalitions is one of America's core strengths" (Brookings Institution, 2012). That few foreign statesmen allow anti-Americanism on their "street" to undermine relatively amicable relations with the US, testifies to the latter's ongoing political stature. In making consequential decisions, actors around the world more readily internalize anticipated US reactions than virtually any other state for most purposes. While absolute US political predominance may have waned, whether one's focus is a solution to regional issues such as the Israeli-Palestinian conflict and the standoff over resources in the South China Sea, or transnational issues like nuclear proliferation, successfully confronting any significant challenge seems inconceivable without a prominent US role.

Perhaps the weightiest aspect of inter-country power comparisons involves the multi-faceted dimension of economics. One immediate issue concerns the relative size of economies. For example, as I have noted earlier with a population as much as four times that of the US, coupled with the likelihood of a more rapid, sustained average annual economic growth rate, Chinese GDP will eventually surpass that of the US. What are the implications of this development for relative power?

No doubt the size of an economy exerts an important impact on the balance of power. It is difficult, for example, to conceive of a state the size of Chile or Sweden exerting pervasive global influence.[3] Other things being equal, a larger national economy (and population) allows for more resources with which to project power. If GDP were decisive however then serious discussion of US hegemony would be difficult to sustain. In the event, there are equally if not more influential facets of economic power to consider.

One such element involves per capita income. A large, rich country by definition possesses an outsized capital stock; and a wealthy, dynamic country tends to operate at the technological frontier across multiple sectors. While heightened cross-border spillovers complicate one's assessment of the return to investment, a hegemon is likely to be among the leading generators of cutting-edge scientific ideas and one with the ability to apply these ideas commercially in the form of novel products and production processes.

For a poorer country to even attempt to rival a richer one technologically would entail a crippling tax burden. This seems especially true given a legacy effect involving many years of greater prosperity, technological lead and investment in a spectrum of assets afforded the richer state. Resorting to reverse engineering, copying or theft is no substitute for the evolutionary perfection of sophisticated institutions that underpin endemic entrepreneurial, innovative activity. A rich country with sustained, robust productivity growth will more likely be the beneficiary of advanced institutions including leading universities, flexible labor markets, robust regulatory systems, and capital markets with unusual depth and liquidity. The opportunities afforded by such an economic and social system would in turn disproportionately attract capital and talent from around the world.

Largely as a legacy or network effect, but more sustainably as the result of remaining at the technological frontier with among the highest national levels of productivity, the most sophisticated capital markets and the soundest system of property rights, not to mention military predominance, an economic hegemon is uniquely positioned to furnish the world's reserve currency. To achieve leading reserve currency status it would not be necessary to monopolize the principal international functions of money – medium of exchange, store of value and unit of account – but its currency would tend to dominate all others. With an ability to furnish global liquidity particularly in a crisis, its central bank would be the closest thing to a world central bank. In sum, rather than an independent source of hegemonic influence, reserve currency status is best viewed as an endogenous result of possessing the most important economic (and certain non-economic) attributes of a leading power.

Finally, a poorer population would be less likely to accept state largess in the form of foreign assistance. More to the point, by definition it would possess fewer resources with which to transfer advanced technology and technical assistance. According to some accounts, China's growing foreign economic involvement appears to subvert this argument. Yet, China's (unrequited) transfers, as opposed to the foreign direct investment of its SOEs, public infrastructure-for-commodity swaps, and other profit-motivated or national security-driven transactions can be expected to face greater domestic scrutiny as an increasingly middle class society demands more say over national resource allocation.

The preceding paragraphs serve to underscore the core, attributes of economic hegemony the US enjoys today. There is no denying that the US economy faces major headwinds. Yet, in acknowledging such trials, one wants to avoid missing the forest for the trees. As the discussion in this book has systematically demonstrated, the longer-term microeconomic and macroeconomic pillars of US power remain formidable. In sum, while overall size remains one element of economic power, the latter's impact is dwarfed by the myriad institutions underpinning systemic innovation capacity, entrepreneurialism and superior productivity.

Where the various dimensions of global power just reviewed – economic, military, political and cultural – coalesce is in the provision of core global public goods. Already cited has been the contribution of reserve currency status to global monetary stability. More generally, one can conjecture that in the absence of US leadership, other powers would coalesce to furnish the core services that underpin global security and prosperity. Possible, yes, but hardly assured. The historical record of international cooperation leaves much to be desired, at least as concerns the maintenance of core global functions. What one does know is that the US has taken the lead in circumventing collective action problems and that its leadership reflects the deployment of multiple facets of US power.

Sustaining hegemony

Having referred to credibility and legitimacy in global affairs, this book has argued that whether the US remains hegemonic ultimately is not mainly a function of external factors. While global forces inevitably impact its relative power, the binding constraints on the sustainability of US hegemony are domestic in origin. What are the core conditions at home that will determine whether the US can retain its current global position?

First, the US must avoid losing its technological, innovative and entrepreneurial edge. Above all else, maintaining its characteristic dynamism requires the US to adapt flexibly and smartly to the pressures of global market forces, and foreign state efforts to subvert market forces. No doubt a stronger societal commitment can upgrade the quality of K-12 education and expand opportunities for higher education and vocational training. Investment in physical infrastructure has also lagged, yet is something that can be more easily rectified through the requisite investments, as compared with the more complex educational challenge.

In addition, prudent regulation of financial institutions to reduce the incidence of future crises will remain a public policy priority. The goal must be to bolster systemic safeguards against excessive leverage and "too big to fail" institutions. While a more streamlined financial sector will prove necessary to enhance efficient resource allocation, systemic reform must avoid extinguishing the incentives that have made US capital markets, the recent crisis notwithstanding, a fundamental strength of the economy.

The pressures from globalization represent a significant source of potential discontent and political mobilization. Especially unskilled and semi-skilled workers have suffered employment and income losses owing to heightened international competition, even if the impact of technology is often the more consequential force for change. Sufficient historical experimentation demonstrates that trying to insulate such individuals through a ready resort to protectionism, impediments to technical progress or elaborate industrial policies would arrest US dynamism, impoverishing society at large. The objective must surely be to maintain broad societal support for globalization (and technological change) by a better targeting of the social safety net. In addition, a renewed social commitment is needed to expand opportunities for upgrading the education, skills and training afforded those Americans increasingly left behind by rapid change.

An equally urgent public response to the dual pressures from globalization and demography involves a far-sighted immigration policy. While vigilant defense against illegal immigration remains a perquisite of sovereignty everywhere, the attention afforded this requirement must be balanced against the need to attract aspiring immigrants to continually infuse American society with vitality and skills in support of economic growth and an aging population. The ability to attract the most talented and ambitious individuals from around the world has been among the most critical sources of the US's success historically, as well as its credibility as global pacesetter. Their special contribution is evident in the professional outperformance of immigrants and that of their children. In the event, it is widely accepted that post-September 11th, policy has discouraged entry to exemplary individuals whose prospects for employment outside of the US have meanwhile mushroomed. A failure to reverse this development would undermine a key edifice of US hegemony.

To summarize, notwithstanding these and other medium-term challenges, many of the core fundamentals underpinning longer-term prosperity remain in place. Maintaining its global power position requires first and foremost that US policymakers in concert with civil society reinforce the institutions that underlie robust growth. The overriding imperative is thus for US firms and workers to harness the advantages rather than resist the signals from global competition. The challenge and opportunity posed by globalization can be adroitly managed, provided the US makes the requisite forward-looking investments in its people and institutions.

Potentially binding domestic constraints on US hegemony

The fiscal deficit

Among the leading constraints on US global power is the country's current fiscal trajectory. The US's longer-term debt outlook is ominous but reversible. While fiscal consolidation requires sacrifice from many quarters, the overriding contribution must come from the broader economy – in particular, in arresting the unsustainable escalation of medical costs. In the absence of steady progress in reversing this economy-wide trend, healthcare-related entitlements will progressively crowd out other fiscal priorities or eventually drive US federal and state debt to levels that can precipitate a full-blown financial crisis.

Although secondary to the burden of (mainly health care and ageing related) entitlements per se, a concerted approach is required to ensure a sustainable balance between public resources and global commitments. This will involve durable solutions to "military overstretch," including efforts to elicit greater burden sharing among the US's allies. Can feasible enlargement of active duty troops and reserves alleviate the strain or should foreign commitments be scaled back and re-prioritized? Can the currently deployed mix of hard and soft US assets be realigned so as to respond more effectively to the varied array of strategic challenges, including countering nuclear proliferation, maintaining the defense of liberal multilateral trade and coping with the re-ascent of China?

That a fiscally driven financial calamity has yet to occur may testify to similar pressures elsewhere, notably in Europe and Japan, and the central position the US occupies within the global monetary and financial system. Barring a timely end to the country's current political stalemate, however, vulnerability to a market-driven assault on the dollar and US bond markets can only mushroom.

Given current ideological polarization over the burden of fiscal adjustment and the future scope of government, it may well take the threat of a market-driven crisis to galvanize fundamental solutions to the medical cost and tax reform dilemmas. If that is what it will take to slow the buildup of public (and private) debt, a central edifice of US hegemony could be undermined. While recent inaction can be disillusioning, one is left with the hope that Alexis de Tocqueville was prescient in remarking that "the greatness of America lies not in being more enlightened than any other nation, but rather in her ability to repair her faults."

American public opinion

In addition to the country's rising debt burden, a second potential constraint on US power would be mounting opposition to globalization. While American public opinion remains nuanced and fluid, most polling fails to indicate any decisive political momentum in favor of significantly heightened protectionism, or for that matter political or military disengagement. Americans have traditionally accepted mounting economic integration, provided that the latter translates to a steady rise in living standards for most and adequate social welfare protection for those who fall behind. Although recent financial pressures have served to moderate support for still greater transnational mobility of goods, labor and capital, one does not detect from polling, electoral campaigns or grassroots movements any inexorable drift toward a broader rejection of the liberal economic order.

Renewed attention to an "uneven playing field" periodically triggers increased consideration of a more defensive posture toward economic openness. While such sentiment has resurfaced in the 2012 presidential debates, the greater focus on fairness writ large relates more generally to the secular stagnation in median worker compensation and the heightened insecurity attending the Great Recession. Moreover, rather than heaping opprobrium on China and other foreign competitors, the ire of the American people appears centered more on a perception of undeserved wealth associated with crony capitalism. What one does not detect is that Americans view the rise of the rest as the principal cause of their problems.

Although more inwardly focused after a decade of war punctuated by economic crisis, Americans still look for their government and myriad civil society organizations to remain centrally engaged in global affairs. Favoring greater cooperation to solve global problems, Americans nevertheless continue to view the US as a leading bastion of global stability. They prefer the deployment of non-kinetic instruments of power and endorse military options only as a last resort. Although the domestic political climate demands that the Pentagon plays its part in deficit reduction, Americans still seem to favor maintaining an overwhelmingly powerful military.

Although few would be familiar with the concept of hegemony, the majority of Americans appears to support its essential underpinnings. To endorse a hegemonic posture for the US, Americans need not embrace the role of world's policeman, something they decidedly do not. But they must, and do in fact, provide at least tacit approval for a disproportionate and pivotal economic, military, political and cultural influence on global affairs.

False idols

One can add to the list of internal constraints on US hegemony the confused state of US public discourse. I have argued that certain ill-defined ideas have exerted a deleterious impact on the public policy debate. Among the leading constructs that have escaped critical scrutiny are notions of (national) competitiveness, energy independence, "net creditor" status, the inherent superiority of manufacturing over services and "imperial overstretch." This book has systematically questioned the assumptions and logic underlying these concepts. To put it succinctly here, such notions have been misleadingly proffered as intellectual pillars in support of staving off national decline. It would be ironic therefore if their uncritical acceptance serves to misdiagnose the real challenges confronting US power, thereby undermining efforts to sustain it.

In summing up this wide-ranging exploration of the underpinnings and future prospects for US power, the following can be concluded. The international system has altered profoundly since the Cold War, the conclusion of which marked the purported arrival of a "unilateral moment." Contrary to much contemporary opinion, the parallel "rise of the rest" has yet to prove a game changer for the US as distinct from the West writ large. Relatively, external pressures have proved manageable while internal developments remain the more reliable bellwethers of the US's future trajectory. Reassessing the sinews of US power leads one to reject the latest case for decline. While its specific contours will no doubt evolve, US hegemony looks like it is here to stay.

Notes

Delusions of Decline: US Global Power in a Turbulent Era

1. It is thus a misconception that the US presence in the Middle East is primarily premised on securing oil specifically for American industry and automobile owners. See, for example, Stokes and Raphael (2010).
2. A logical alternative to an open and rule-based liberal order is one with "illiberal geopolitical blocs, exclusive regional spheres, and closed imperial systems" (Ikenberry, 2010).
3. While a robust case for free trade cannot always be made, a general presumption in favor of multilateral trade and investment seems justified. While generating losers as well as winners, the broad historical record suggests that relatively unimpeded trade in goods and services tends to promote greater prosperity for most people over the longer-term. Most market failures warrant policy interventions in the form of targeted, domestic tax-cum-subsidies or regulations, as opposed to blunter trade instruments that tend to introduce undesirable distortions to resource allocation (Bhagwati, 1989).
4. The US political system's promotion of home ownership and the still mounting losses plaguing Fannie Mae and Freddie Mac come to mind.
5. Public goods can also threaten certain powers concerned over the predominant state's outsized strategic leverage. China's dependence on the US for the safeguarding of oil shipments is a case in point.
6. More generally, a hegemonic power grounded in the principles of openness and the desirability of spreading the gains from globalization would encourage a proliferation of value-added transfers from all states as a contribution to greater global stability.
7. While ideology inevitably informs this author's broad defense of market principles, the broad historical record arguably supports this bias. For a good discussion of the role of ideology in economics see Backhouse (2010).

1 US Power: Past and Prologue

1. A more in-depth analysis of national decline and its relationship to overstretch is provided in Chapter 2.
2. In the event, the US has usually topped most competitiveness rankings. More recently, however, it has fallen behind certain smaller states, such as Finland, Denmark and Singapore. For an in-depth discussion, see chapter 3.
3. These arguments build on Phillips' earlier reflections on imperial overstretch. The latter incorporate political factors such as an alleged disproportionate influence of evangelical Christiandom on US foreign policy (Phillips, 2006).
4. See Chapter 3 for a more extensive discussion.
5. One can also include in the camp of US decline rejectionists German journalist Josef Joffe (2006, 2009).

6. By this Friedman means the reluctance of European states to delegate increasingly greater powers to the supra-sovereign entities of the EU and the EMU, as well as instability related to Russia's ongoing geopolitical aspirations.

7. The hierarchical structure of global power within which the US uniquely occupies the top rung is persuasively defended in Buzan (2004).

8. In contrast, Joseph Quinlan is representative of those who view the financial crisis as a watershed, marking an unambiguous onset of US decline (Quinlan, 2011).

9. This combination of enduring economic strengths coupled with major political system inadequacies is shared by others, like James Fallow (2010).

10. In showcasing East Asia's successful adoption of "Western pillars," such as freer markets, Kishore Mahbubani (2008) serves as a useful accompaniment to Zakaria.

11. Zakaria inspired a range of reactions as, for example, assembled in Clark and Hoque (2011). This publication's contributors notably disagree over whether Zakaria represents more the optimist or the pessimist on US power.

12. Also see *China's Rise* (Bergsten, 2008) and *China Shakes the World* (Kynge, 2006).

13. For contrasting assessments on China's re-ascension, see the essays by Subramanian (2011b) and Babones (2011).

14. Ezra Vogel (1979) is perhaps the best known of earlier commentary heralding the inexorable overtaking of the US by a Japanese economic juggernaut.

15. Among those who believe that "empire" accurately captures the exercise of US power, see, for example, Ferguson (2004b), Krauthammer (2002), Odom and Dajarric (2004), Lal (2004), Johnson (2004), Chomsky (2004) and Bacevich (2002).

16. Functioning as an outside balancer involves limiting one's military intervention in strategic regions to instances when the balance of power appears to be tipping in favor of a rising and potentially belligerent state.

17. See Robert Kaplan (2005). Also, Christopher Layne portrays the forward deployment of US military forces "primarily as a means of preserving unipolarity." Chalmers Johnson (2004) views the expansion of US bases as the epitome of modern (post-colonial) imperialism.

18. Nichols (2005) shows how a greater willingness to intervene in "failed" states on a preventive basis while invoking the United Nations principle of the "responsibility to protect" has emerged as an operational, international norm.

19. While facilitating greater national and global prosperity, such arrangements typically advantage hegemon-headquartered corporations that are well positioned to exploit their technological lead through FDI, mergers and acquisitions, and the expansion of corporate global reach more generally. In addition, providing the reserve currency offers somewhat greater prospects for national overspending financed by cheap credit and supplemented by the receipt of seigniorage revenue (see Chapter 4).

20. This concentration of industrialized country-bound capital flows in the US can be expected to strengthen as long as the EMU debt crisis lingers.

21. For a critical overview of the earlier US declinist literature, see, for example, Cox (2001).

22. The phrase "unipolar moment" as employed by staunch believers in US global power captures the singularly dominant US strategic position with the end of the Cold War. For an insightful analysis of unipolarity, see Buzan (2004). On US unipolarity more specifically, see Brooks and Wohlforth (2008).

23. Charles Kupchan provided some of the earliest arguments for why US predominance would wane and give rise to competing power centers or "multipolarity"

(2002a, 2002b). For an elaboration of this idea with greater application to non-state actors, see Haas (2008).

24. Niall Ferguson (2004b) raises the prospect of a world governed neither by global hegemony nor by a rebalancing of state power but instead by "an absence of power."

25. For a well-argued call, from a liberal perspective, on how to restore US legitimacy, see Beinart (2006).

26. An common colloquialism is that rising powers are positioned to "eat our lunch." See, for example, Fehr et al. (2005).

2 Dimensions of US Power, Decline and Overstretch

1. While Kennedy's assessment of US power has fluctuated over time, an unwavering defense of US primacy can be found in Brooks and Wohlforth (2008).

2. This distinction between latent and realized power remains an important feature of the literature on national and global power. See, for example, the RAND studies (Tellis et al., 2000; Treverton and Jones, 2005). A similar distinction is made in older studies on US power (e.g. Nye, 1990).

3. The US accounts for a full 43 per cent of total world defense expenditure, more than the next 10 countries combined. Some 85–90 per cent of this expenditure supports military activity abroad rather than homeland security (Haas, 2005, p. 8).

4. A more inclusive measure of defense outlays including off-Pentagon budget items, however, can be several hundred billion dollars higher than the defense budget appropriations alone (see Chapter 8).

5. Yet, large weaknesses in peace keeping and nation building were also showcased.

6. The civilian death toll reported varies depending on the source. Washington claims that the vast majority of those killed are militants, whereas locals claim that victims are disproportionately civilian (Bergen and Tiedemann, 2011).

7. One person's notion of a public good may be another's idea of imperialist expansionism. For the latter view, see Burbach and Tarbell (2004) and Chomsky (2003).

8. The US has engaged in a concerted four-year offensive program of cyberwar against Iran's nuclear program known as "Olympic Games" (Sanger, 2012).

9. The CIA has for many years farmed out the right to torture on its behalf to other states at secret interrogation centers, beginning in the 1950s and continuing in the 1960s under the Phoenix program in Vietnam (Weiner, 2007, p. 481).

10. This case is made by Peter Beinart (2006) in *The Good Fight*. Among others, Beinart argues that failure to better meet the needs of its own population has eroded US credibility.

11. Russia's relatively high ranking as an immigrant country is arguably overstated by the dissolution of the Soviet Union and the impact on ethnic Russians residing in other former Republics of the USSR. Economics broadly conceived to incorporate human and physical capital resources, technology and the myriad of societal and institutional factors that contribute to what economists call "total factor productivity" has long been considered central to the exercise of national power. See, for example, Tellis et al. (2000) and Treverton and Jones (2005).

12. For a detailed discussion, see chapters 3 and 4.

13. The relationship between the military and the broader economy works in the opposite direction as well. For example, under the auspices of the Defense Advanced Research Projects Administration (US Department of Defense), early

advances were made with the Internet, and the military has pioneered other technologies, including those it later spins off to the broader economy.

14. In 2006, a full year before the onset of the Great Recession, Americans spent some \$9.7 trillion. In contrast, China and India, which represent 40 per cent of the world's population, managed to consume less than one-sixth of this amount.
15. See discussion in Chapter 4.
16. For a broader discussion, see Chapter 4.
17. One clear example was President Nixon's unilateral decision to close the gold window, effectively ending the Bretton Woods system, in 1971.
18. See, for example, various contributions by Layne (1993, 2006a, 2006b, 2006c) for references to hard and soft balancing.
19. Phillips (2008). On the role of the American-Israeli Political Action Committee (AIPAC), see Mearsheimer and Walt (2007).
20. For example, if winning the next election is the single factor motivating politicians, arguably the political system is rigged against considering longer-term consequences in contrast to matters of short-term, political expediency.
21. Missing from Kennedy's conceptualization of relative national power was also any serious reference to a broader national identity – "the political, cultural and historical factors that motivate [countries] to accumulate and use power" (Nau, 2001, p. 582). Such factors often drive technological change and economic growth. They also lend legitimacy to governments and sustain the kind of public support that militates against national decline.
22. For an example where overstretch drives decline, see Layne (2012c).
23. Inter-country output comparisons using purchasing power parity exchange rates tend to favor the relative standing of poorer countries, compared with official exchange rates. While the Goldman Sachs forecasts use constant 2006 prices (valued at official exchange rates), they build in an assumption of real exchange rate appreciation, augmenting the forecasted growth rates of emerging market countries. For a more detailed discussion in the context of China, see Chapter 7.
24. According to UN projections, the US working age population will comprise 54 and 61 per cent in 2025 and 2050, respectively, of the total population of the "West" (including the US, Canada, Western Europe and Japan).
25. Adjusted for the economic cycle.
26. While the US remains the world's largest net importer of crude oil, it has recently become a net exporter of petroleum products – gasoline, diesel, jet fuel and other refined fuels (Pleven and Gold, 2011).
27. Low natural gas prices in the US alter this picture somewhat. See discussion below.
28. For example, Brookings expert Michael O'Hanlon (2009) speculates that a substantial commitment of manpower could be required to deal with a breakdown in authority in the Korean peninsula, Pakistan and/or populous countries such as Indonesia, Nigeria or the Congo, as well as in a showdown with China over Taiwan.

3 Microeconomic Foundations: Innovation, Productivity and Competitiveness

1. For example, in its annual Global Competitiveness Report, the World Economic Forum ranks national competitiveness.
2. This prescription assumes that "market" prices broadly reflect relative scarcity. In the case of market failure, targeted government intervention in principle, can play an important role in realigning social and private costs and benefits.

3. The real exchange rate is the relative value of a currency, adjusted for differential inflation in the country and its trading partners.

4. This is in fact the basic definition of competitiveness applied in the annual country rankings by the World Economic Forum. See Lopez-Claros (2006; WEF, 2009, p. 3).

5. As of 2006 the US invested 2.6 per cent of its GDP in higher education, compared with 1.2 per cent in Europe and 1.1 per cent in Japan (Zakaria, 2008, p. 191).

6. TFP is estimated as a residual in an exercise known as growth accounting, after accounting for the direct, separate contribution to economic growth from increases in each employed factor of production (e.g. labor and capital). The presumption is that dynamic, advanced economies rely disproportionately on the overall efficiency with which resources are employed (TFP) or "intensive" growth, in contrast to undue reliance on the employment of more "inputs" (worker hours and capital investment), or "extensive" growth.

7. Capital deepening is measured by an increase in the capital/labor ratio weighted by the share of capital in national income.

8. Arvand Panagariya identifies the paucity of large scale manufacturing as a primary factor behind India's lagging position relative to China. The causes include educational inadequacies, restrictions limiting the size of firms engaged in large scale manufacturing, as well as "draconian labor laws ... costly power, and poor transport infrastructure" (Panagariya, 2008).

9. "The number of S&E doctorate recipients with temporary visas decreased 7.4 per cent from 2009 to 2010 ... the second consecutive year of decline after several years of growth. Despite the recent downturn, the number of S&E doctorates awarded to temporary visa holders grew 8.4 per cent from 2005 to 2010. The number of S&E doctorates awarded to U.S. citizens and permanent residents increased by 1.4 per cent from 2009 to 2010 and by 24.5 per cent over the 5-year period. The proportion of S&E doctorates awarded to temporary visa holders declined from 37.3 per cent in 2005 to 34.1 per cent in 2010. Temporary visa holders constitute a much smaller share of the doctorate recipients in non-S&E fields, earning 15.6 per cent of the non-S&E doctorates awarded in 2010" (Fiegener, 2011).

10. For a summary of studies on the impact on US workers of trade and off-shoring see Subramanian (2011b).

11. See discussion in Chapter 4.

12. Several years ago leading authority Dale Jorgenson projected US productivity growth at 2.0–2.5 per cent between 2006 and 2016, well above the rates of the country's industrialized competitors (Jorgenson and Vu, 2008), and certain other economists, such as Berkeley professor Brad DeLong, have maintained that potential GDP growth will continue to hover around 3 per cent, given the still to be untapped innovation in the ICT and biotechnology sectors for example (DeLong, 2010).

13. For an alternative perspective, see Phelps and Tilman (2010).

14. See, for example, Michael Spence (2011) and the exchange between Spence, on the one hand, and Katz and Lawrence, on the other (2011, November/December).

15. Complications include definitions of household versus taxpayer units, pre- versus post-taxes, and transfers and wages versus non-wage compensation.

16. Although US higher education is universally recognized as second to none, it bears mention that many other countries have been investing heavily in higher education in recent decades. Also noteworthy is the stagnation in the

share of American students graduating from high school and completing college degrees.

17. Former Senator Bradley contrasts the American student, in school 180 days a year for 6.5 hours a day, with the Chinese student, in school up to 220 days a year and for 9.5 hours a day.

18. West (2011) makes a similar point concerning the relationship between education, international competitiveness and national productivity growth.

19. It is unclear whether such estimates of the effective corporate tax rate incorporate all the loopholes that benefit parts of the business sector through the vehicle of "tax expenditures" discussed in Chapter 8.

20. Hufbauer also estimates that the US statutory rate can be reduced to 25 per cent or somewhat less without lowering overall corporate tax revenue.

21. A short recent list of innovations that have expanded access, enlarged convenience or enhanced economy-wide productivity would include the rise of venture capital, the introduction of credit and debit cards, indexed mutual and exchange traded funds, inflation-protection treasury securities, some (but not all!) asset-backed securitization and certain derivatives like options and futures markets, including interest, currency and (properly used) credit default swaps. For a more complete list and extended discussion on the pros and cons of financial innovation, see Robert E. Litan (2010).

4 Macroeconomic Foundations: Global Imbalances and the Dollar

1. The NIIP remained consistently positive from the end of World War I through 1989.

2. This explains why equating the NIIP with "net foreign debt" is misleading. Not all financial claims on the USA involve (official and corporate) debt obligations. The NIIP also includes substantial equity claims.

3. *What is to be Done?* is the title of Vladimir Lenin's famous political tract on the Bolshevik Party's strategy in early 20th century Russia.

4. Residential home purchases are included in domestic investment, as is stockpiling of inventories for future sale.

5. This identity is a basic result of national income accounting. It is also straightforward to show that it is identical to the statement that the current account surplus equals the difference between national output (income) and domestic expenditure ("absorption") (see e.g. Mankiw, 2010, Chapter 5).

6. The current account and capital (financial) accounts are the two main subcomponents of the balance of payments.

7. The (external) inter-temporal budget constraint shows that a "net debtor" country (one with a negative NIIP) must run sufficiently large (discounted) trade surpluses in the future to finance its stock of net external liabilities.

8. Although the eurozone has a roughly balanced current account, the largest EMU country, Germany, runs a consistently large surplus.

9. There are numerous variations in opinion concerning the causes of external imbalances. Here I focus on two stylized positions in order to bring out core disagreements.

10. The financial crisis precipitated a sharp reduction in net private capital flows to emerging markets. These flows have since rebounded.

11. This seems unsurprising because private savings and investment rarely move in lockstep. For a sample of econometric attempts to establish causality running from fiscal to current account deficits, see Gruber and Kamin (2005), Laxton et al. (2005), Corsetti and Muller (2005), Erceg et al. (2005) and Chinn and Ito (2008).

12. According to the Federal Reserve's Survey of Consumer Finances, a triennial survey of American families, U.S. families' median net worth fell by 38.8 per cent from 2007 to 2010. These levels are now near to where they were in a 1992 survey.

13. Real investment in 2006 was up by 90 per cent from its 1994 level, while consumer spending rose by only 53 per cent. When consumer goods prices rise as the prices of capital goods fall (Doms, 2005), current dollar value comparisons mask changes in the real quantities for consumption and investment. Moreover, since investment is more volatile, comparing the investment/GDP ratio in a given year to the peak of the previous boom will show consumption growing at the expense of investment. A comparison that relates similar points in the business cycle provides a more accurate picture.

14. While seemingly arcane, public discussion of "intangibles" was featured on the cover of *Business Week*. See Mandel (2006a and 2006b) for a rebuttal of arguments made by intangible investment skeptics.

15. For an excellent overview of the literature on the US savings puzzle, see Guidolin and Jeunesse (2007).

16. For example, some claim that savings should also include purchases of durable goods such as houses, appliances, and cars, which provide services over many years.

17. The pace of yuan appreciation accelerated during 2007–2008 but came to a halt in 2009 in response to the financial crisis. The appreciation of the yuan subsequently resumed in June 2010. Since July 2005, the yuan has appreciated a cumulative 30 per cent against China's trading partners.

18. A change in the REER is a trade-weighted currency depreciation or appreciation against the currencies of a country's trading partners, adjusted for inflation in the home and foreign economies. Hence, a real depreciation (appreciation) represents an improvement (worsening) in "competitiveness."

19. Trade sometimes subtracts from China's measured growth even when the volume of exports is large, as when import growth exceeds export growth.

20. At the time of writing the latest monthly Chinese trade figures show a sharp decline to a 1 per cent year-on-year increase in exports.

21. Technically, sustainability requires that the stock of net external liabilities (NIIP) do not exceed the present value of current and future US external primary surpluses. The latter is the trade balance plus net current transfer payments. A simpler rule of thumb is that the economy's growth exceeds the rate of interest paid on foreign liabilities.

22. Even at its lowest historical level, at minus $4 trillion the NIIP represents only 5–6 per cent of household net worth.

23. For a critique of the dark matter hypothesis, see Gross (2006). For alternative explanations of the current account/NIIP discrepancy, see Lane and Milesi-Ferretti (2008) and Kroszner (2008).

24. For perspective, consensus projections of net income payments for the foreseeable future tend not to exceed 1 per cent (see Mann, 2009, p. 43). Higher projections presume a more severe, fiscal scenario (Cline, 2009).

25. A number of commentators (see e.g. Bertaut et al., 2008; Higgins and Klitgaard, 2005; Swiston, 2005) argue that the world might still be "underweight" US assets.
26. Moreover, this 25 per cent share is still less than the total reserves denominated in the currencies that were abandoned in creating the euro (such as the French franc and the German deutschmark).
27. Roughly one-third of the $1.5 trillion deterioration in the NIIP in 2011 reflects the current account deficit, with the rest attributable to valuation changes, mostly in the prices of US and foreign assets, respectively, and to a more moderate extent due to USD appreciation.
28. One can raise more technical reservations about the CF analysis as well (e.g. see Posen, 2008). The rest of this discussion is largely based on Posen.
29. This issue is discussed at length in Chapter 7.
30. The strong historical correlation between national savings and domestic investment rates is known as the Feldstein–Horioka paradox. Feldstein later noted the marked decline in this traditional relationship (Feldstein, 2005).
31. Bernanke (2011) notes that eurozone banks added to gross global demand for US financial products, including collateralized debt obligations (CDOs).
32. Ben Bernanke concedes this point in a recent address and accompanying paper (Bernanke, 2011).
33. Moreover, the US enjoys the advantage of floating exchange rates – a dimension of flexibility denied many emerging market countries (as well as members of the European Monetary System). In addition, many emerging market crises can be traced to "balance sheet" effects involving currency mismatches, a feature uncharacteristic of the US economy. Currency mismatches refer to countries with in foreign currency liabilities and with assets denominated in domestic currency. A depreciation of the local currency can involve large losses given such a mismatch.

5 Human Security: US Leadership on Counter-Proliferation

1. Leadership in counter-proliferation here exemplifies the response to a myriad of threats to human security, including programs to eradicate poverty, to stanch genocide and to ameliorate the exploitation of women.
2. For an analysis of collective action problems, see Olson (1971) and Kindleberger (1974).
3. Non-excludability concerns the inability to prevent non-contributors from consuming the good. The non-rivalrous property allows one access to its services without diminishing the access of others. Where access can be confined to a less than universal membership, as in limited security alliances or trade agreements, it is more precise to speak of "club" goods and services.
4. The intention here is not to defend hegemonic stability theory. It is rather to exploit its useful insight that hegemonic leadership can be critical to meeting certain global challenges. For leading critiques, see, for example, Keohane (1984), Keohane and Nye (2000), Snidal (1985) and Gilpin (1982). More recent discussions of the theory's merits and controversies can be seen in Norloff (2010) and Ikenberry (2011).
5. The latter includes, among other functions, the furnishing of adequate liquidity to finance global transactions and upholding the principles of free, non-discriminatory trade (Kindleberger, 1974, 1976).

6. The term "benign" is normative only in a loose sense. The thrust of this book has been to explore what "is," not what "should" be. While certain states may strongly oppose particular US actions, US imposition of a generally welfare-reducing global order presumably would provoke widespread resistance. That the sustainability of hegemony presumes a strong degree of international assent helps to explain why legitimacy remains a critical component of US power.

7. Israel, India and Pakistan have always eschewed the NPT. Iran signed the treaty but was caught cheating. North Korea signed the treaty, tested in violation and has since withdrawn. All these cases test the long-term viability of the treaty.

8. The four statesmen lending their intellectual support and credibility to this goal are Henry Kissinger, Sam Nunn, William Perry and George Shultz (see Shultz et al., 2010, 2011).

9. "The international nuclear nonproliferation regime comprises the Nuclear Nonproliferation Treaty; the International Atomic Energy Agency safeguards system; export control arrangements, such as the Nuclear Suppliers Group; UN Security Council resolutions; multilateral and bilateral initiatives, including the Proliferation Security Initiative (PSI); and bilateral nuclear cooperation agreements between supplier and purchaser states. It is supported by a broad range of alliances and security assurances. The NPT is the cornerstone of the regime" (Lettow, 2010, p. 6).

10. Some would argue, however, that ongoing congressional funding of Nunn-Luger remains grudging and inadequate to the task at hand.

11. In addition to PSI, other multilateral groups have been involved in counter-proliferation efforts, including the Organization for Security and Co-operation in Europe, the G-8, the G-20, and the US–ASEAN (the Association of Southeast Asian Nations) dialogue.

12. Yellow cake (U_3O_8) is uranium ore that has been mined and milled. It is used in the first stage of the uranium fuel cycle. It is then converted into uranium hexafluoride (UF_6), which is enriched before being made into nuclear fuel (USNRC, 2011).

13. The exception was the Soviet Union, which continued to supply Tehran with nuclear technology and material (Department of State, 2003).

14. This approach suffered from glaring inconsistencies, as revealed by the exchange of arms for hostages under "Iran-Contra."

15. China has recently reduced its purchase of Iranian crude, but largely over pricing disputes with Iran (Bradsher and Krauss, 2012).

16. Under the terms of The Agreed Framework (1994), two light water reactors were supposed to be built in exchange for shutting down the facility at Yongbyon, a project that stalled repeatedly.

17. For instance, China has adopted a more aggressive stance on contested islands in the East and South China Seas. For a discussion, see Chapter 6.

18. As the only nation to have experienced the destruction of a nuclear bomb, there is obviously major reluctance to enter the nuclear club. Furthermore, the recent tsunami and civilian nuclear disaster should reinforce Japan's disinclination to pursue a nuclear weapons program.

19. For further discussion, see Langewiesche (2005).

20. During the Cold War it was believed that Mutually Assured Destruction minimized the threat of nuclear escalation between the US and the Soviet Union. Despite many close calls (e.g. the Cuban Missile Crisis), both understood the

stakes. As rational actors, they exercised restraint to avoid a potential nuclear exchange.

21. For a detailed account of the relationship between al Qaeda, Afghanistan and Pakistan, see Pillar (2011).
22. This does not detract from the fact that Pakistan is itself the victim of an internal insurgency that has killed or injured some 35,000 Pakistanis since 2004.
23. It should be noted that concerns about an existential threat to Pakistan have been voiced often in the past.
24. It can be noted that this shift in aid policy inflamed Islamabad, which viewed such conditionality as an affront to Pakistani sovereignty.
25. According to this study's findings, while not negating the importance of development assistance more generally, "arguments tying support for militancy to individuals' socioeconomic status – and the policy recommendations that often flow from this assumption – require substantial revision."
26. Such drone attacks may also be contestable at the level of international law.
27. The lower and middle ranks of the Pakistani military are reportedly less inclined than the higher brass to countenance ongoing US involvement in Pakistan.
28. This excludes North Korea, which currently lacks full deployment capability.

6 Global Public Goods and East Asia

1. Members of ASEAN include Indonesia, Malaysia, the Philippines, Singapore, Thailand (founding members), Brunei, Burma (Myanmar), Cambodia, Laos and Vietnam (ASEAN, 2009).
2. According to Clinton, this Asian pivot will proceed in six key ways: (i) strengthening US security alliances; (ii) developing "working relationships" with emerging powers (including China); (iii) engaging regional multilateral institutions; (iv) expanding trade and investment; (v) forging a military presence; and (vi) advancing democratic values.
3. The principle of comparative advantage outlines the conditions for production (and export) specialization on the basis of relative costs. Thus, "even if a developing country lacks an absolute advantage in any field, it will always have a comparative advantage in the production of some goods," and therefore "there is no country whose economic circumstances prevent it from engaging in mutually beneficial trade with other countries" (Irwin, 2002, p. 28).
4. Thomas Friedman's Golden Arches Theory and Dell Theory of Conflict Prevention (2000, 2005) popularized the notion that heightened economic interdependence discourages conflict. For a more skeptical view of the relationship between economic cooperation and strategic rivalry, see Friedberg (2011). For a good summary of the debate, see also Rachman (2011).
5. A willingness and ability to conclude the WTO Doha round would reinvigorate multilateralism. By addressing the BRICs' concerns over agricultural subsidies in the US and the European Union among other outstanding issues such a bridging of the "North-South divide" would advance the multilateral cause.
6. As of 2009 the number of swap arrangements had grown to 16, though this is constantly shifting due to ongoing renegotiation (Henning, 2009, p. 2). As of mid-2009 the Chiang Mai Initiative had raised a pool of funds valued at $120 billion, with China and Japan each contributing $38 billion, together making up nearly two-thirds of the funding (Rathus, 2009).
7. For an in-depth discussion, see chapters 4 and 7 of this book.

8. The alleged desire to curb US economic influence may not always be limited to China. Already in 1997, for example, staunch US ally Japan had tabled a proposal for an Asian Monetary Fund and proposed a 16-country East Asian Free Trade area, which would have excluded the US. US authorities staunchly opposed this initiative, fearing it could sap the authority of the IMF and by extension the US (Bergsten, 2007, p.2). China also opposed the Asian Monetary Fund proposal, which was eventually reformulated into the less ambitious Chiang Mai Initiative.

9. The architecture of East Asian trade and finance has been anchored by the Asia-Pacific Economic Cooperation (APEC) founded in 1989. APEC has 21 members, including China, and the U.S. APEC seeks to coordinate and spur investment, trade, and economic development and growth in the Asia-Pacific region, and has until recently been the US' preferred economic framework for regional relations. It was feared however that APEC would eventually be superseded by some form of China-led regionalism (De Santis 2005, p. 31). For example, the East Asia Summit launched in 2005 has a membership that includes the ten countries of ASEAN plus China, Korea, Japan, Australia, New Zealand and India (but excluding the US).

10. Strict limitations on the participation of state-owned enterprises are a major constraint on China's inclusion in the TPP. Other onerous provisions could also dissuade other countries from signing up (Economist, 2012). Other observers have a more cynical view of the TPP process: "All the trade-enhancing hype aside, the primary reason for the TPP and the anticipated FTAAP appears to be geopolitical: to resist a regional balance of power that has increasingly shifted to China" (de Santis, 2012, p. 210).

11. For example, trade expert David Richardson views the TPP as a rather cynical US effort to use its leverage over smaller trading partners to exact unjustified concessions (author's private conversation, May 2012).

12. An increasing number of international relations scholars advocate a transition away from a balancing role requiring an ongoing regional presence to that of an "over-the horizon" off-shore balancing posture. See, for example, Walt (2005) for a cogent analysis of off-shore balancing.

13. According to United Nations projections, by 2050, India and China's populations will be 1.3 billion and 1.7 billion, respectively. By 2100 the forecasted differential is even more striking as India leads with 1.6 billion people compared with China's 941 million (United Nations, 2012).

7   China's Challenge

1. The word "reemergence" is used advisedly because the Middle Kingdom dominated Asia and was the world's leading economy for a millennium before 1500, when Europe began its ascent. At one point China accounted for roughly one third of global output.

2. According to World Bank figures, the percentage of China's population under the poverty line ($1.25 per day in PPP dollars) decreased from almost 85 per cent in 1981 to less than 14 per cent in 2008, while life expectancy at birth has increased from 65 to 73 years (World Bank Development Indicators).

3. While some see US willingness to lead receding, China has routinely declined significant involvement on many issues – the eurozone crisis, global climate change, the Arab Spring and rebalancing the global economy (Bremmer and Gordon, 2011).

4. Negative value-added production implies real economic losses since the value of production inputs exceed the value of output, at realistic market prices.

5. This consumption tax can take a variety of forms, including the paucity of financial instruments and financial repression involving highly negative real interest rates for savers. See also endnote 12.

6. For competing perspectives on the power implications of net debtor and net creditor status, the reader can review the arguments in Chapter 4, and revisit Setser (2008) and Drezner (2009).

7. Allowable "administered protection" under World Trade Organization (WTO) rules is actually often unjustified on normative economic grounds. Yet, China's agreement to abide (over a transition period) by "nonmarket" anti-dumping treatment of its exports has led to some particularly egregious duties on Chinese imports to the US and Europe (Brown and Haas-Wilson, 1990).

8. This presupposes, among many other things, ongoing improvements in education and training.

9. Having once projected 2041 as the cross-over date for Chinese and US GDP, following their well-publicized 2007 prediction (a crossover date of 2027) Goldman Sachs economists have subsequently advanced the date forward.

10. According to the Balassa–Samuelson effect, periods of rapid economic growth in developing countries tend to be accompanied by real currency appreciation. While this appreciation raises real incomes further, it also means that MER and PPP measures converge.

11. See, for example, Krugman (1994).

12. The best source on the implications of China's high rate of savings is Michael Pettis. He sees China's meager consumption rates as originating from a development model that taxes consumption in hidden ways. First, wage growth has not risen as fast as growth in productivity. This translates into higher enterprise profits at the expense of household income, and thus lower household consumption. Second, an undervalued exchange rate acts as an implicit consumption tax by raising import costs. Finally, the Chinese state banking system sets low interest rates to promote growth and investment. By artificially depressing deposit rates, the banks can lower their lending rates to SOEs. Given restrictions on capital flows coupled with the immaturity of China's financial markets, households are afforded few opportunities to move savings out of the banks. These factors all act to subsidize investment while lowering the potential income that can support greater consumption (Pettis, 2011b).

13. Another important effect is a growing gender gap. About 20–30 million Chinese men will be unable to find partners due to the country's decades-long sex imbalance (BBC, 2010).

14. Specifically, Eichengreen et al. (2011) estimate that at a threshold (PPP) income level of \$16,740, average growth rates drop on average from 5.6 per cent up to this level to 2.1 per cent beyond this level.

15. Moderating the secular real increase in world oil prices may be recent unconventional (shale) oil discoveries adding to global supply. Still, recovering such oil involves high marginal costs of production.

16. In the past 15 years, China has ostensibly never invested more than 2.1 per cent of GDP in defense in contrast to a minimum for the US of 3 per cent (Stockholm International Peace Research Institute, 2010).

17. See the broader discussion in Chapter 3.

8 The Deficit

1. This does not include China's holdings of US government sponsored (GSE) debt which is more difficult to estimate.
2. In response to the one-notch S&P downgrade, global investors accelerated their purchases of treasury bonds, driving down their yields.
3. The challenge with social security remains more manageable (see discussion below).
4. The average annual trillion dollar figure refers to the CBO's "alternative fiscal scenario"; the CBO's baseline projections are roughly a third of this figure (CBO, 2012).
5. Sizeable deficits were run up during Ronald Reagan's presidency.
6. Furthermore, Clinton's task would have been larger had it not been for President H. W. Bush's difficult decision to strike a budget deal in 1990 which required raising taxes. (See Bruce Bartlett quoted in Wessel, 2012, p. 55).
7. While not everyone agrees, the majority of economists would argue that the Bush tax cuts disproportionately favored higher-income households.
8. A school of macroeconomists influenced by Milton Friedman argues that the focus of attention should be on the level of public spending rather than the deficit per se. According to this view, governmental spending effectively taxes private incomes through either current taxes or later taxes to finance current deficits.
9. Economists John Taylor and Robert Barro, among others, criticize the econometric models used by Keynesians inside and outside of the Obama Administration. Hence they question the veracity of estimates on the stimulus effect of recent government stimulus programs. See, for example, Barro (2009).
10. Although beyond the scope of this book, debate continues among macroeconomists over the relative efficacy of fiscal versus monetary policy under the current conditions facing the US economy.
11. I refer here to the alternative scenario, rather than the CBO's baseline scenario. The latter assumes a continuation of current law and, consequently, is considerably less realistic than the former. The former assumes among other factors an extension of the Bush tax cuts, and adjustments to the alternative minimum tax and Medicare doctor fees.
12. It bears mention that the projected debt/GDP ratio inside the ten year window (CBO, Jan 2012) was reduced by some 7 percentage points owing to $1 trillion in upfront spending reductions specified by the Budget Control Act in August 2011. Following the debt ceiling debate in August 2011, the Budget Control Act adopted expenditure reduction measures, the budgetary impact of which was only partially reduced by the economy failing to grow as fast as projected in 2011.
13. The fiscal cliff refers to the across-the-board spending cuts that are scheduled to be automatically enacted at the start of 2013 unless Congress takes action. Bushera income-tax cuts will expire for tens of millions of Americans, and billions of dollars of spending cuts will go into effect because Congress couldn't reach a deal last year to reduce the deficit by at least $1.2 trillion.
14. The fiscal dilemma is captured in the expression $\Delta(D/Y)_t = [(r-g)/(1+g)]^*$ $[D/Y]_{t-1} - pb$ where D is nominal debt stock, Y is nominal GDP, r is the nominal interest rate, g is the nominal growth rate of GDP, pb is the primary fiscal balance as a share of GDP and Δ indicates a change over the previous year. "t" is an index for the current year so that $t-1$ indicates the previous year. The debt ratio stabilizes when $pb = (D/Y)(r-g)/(1+g)$.

15. At one point ten-year treasuries actually dropped to 1.4 per cent, mirroring a similar decline in yields experienced in the UK and in certain northern states of the EMU.
16. In addition to treasuries, demand for German bunds, UK gilts and other perceived "safe" government assets has also been driven higher during the European debt crisis.
17. At the time of writing, the current account deficit, hence the requirement for US external financing, has moderated significantly (as discussed in Chapter 4). Meanwhile, foreign demand for a perceived safe store of value has remained robust.
18. The inverse movement of bond prices and yields is an arithmetical certainty.
19. This means that it cost as much as $100,000 to purchase $10,000,000 worth of protection against the prospect that the US Treasury would default on any of its obligations.
20. One example is the Term Asset Back Loan Facility (TALF). This and other facilities created during the crisis have been criticized as unwarranted credit policy (as opposed to legitimate monetary policy) wherein the Federal Reserve issued loans to troubled companies who pledged non-government securities as collateral (Buiter, 2009).
21. When the Fed decided to end quantitative easing (QE2) at the end of June 2011, the size of its balance sheet was trillions of dollars greater than that of the pre-crisis period. The Fed's total assets on August 1, 2007 were approximately $847 billion. As of July 6, 2011, they were $2.874 trillion (Fed, 2011).
22. In the post-war period when the debt to GDP ratio had surpassed 100 per cent, "the liquidation of debt via negative real interest rates amounted on average to 3 and 4 per cent of GDP a year" in the US and UK (Reinhart and Sbrancia, 2011, p. 16).
23. The dollar's nominal effective exchange rate has been broadly flat year to date in 2012.
24. Reflating offers little solution today as (roughly) a third of marketable Treasury debt rolls over each year at rates that reflect changing expectations of future inflation and thus risk premia. Moreover, the critical drivers of the longer-term deficit are generally indexed to inflation.
25. Blaming US macroeconomic policy for endangering the external value of the dollar is also a deft way of deflecting US criticism leveled at the Chinese for "manipulating" the yuan–dollar exchange rate.
26. The National Commission on Fiscal Responsibility, colloquially known as Bowles–Simpson, was just one of several commissions issuing broadly similar recommendations. For example, the Gang of Six, the Rivlin and Dominicie Plan, and others offered reductions in tax expenditures, a scaling back of Medicare growth rates and entitlement reform more generally. In contrast, under Congressman (and Republican Vice-presidential candidate) Paul Ryan's plan (April 2012), Medicare would be converted to a voucher-like "premium support system." New enrollees after 2022 would receive government subsidized healthcare vouchers to purchase private insurance. These would increase with general inflation each year. Medicaid would be converted to block grants allocated to states. Many components of the Patient Protection and Affordable Care Act would be repealed. Presidential candidate Mitt Romney endorsed the Ryan plan.

27. As part of this sequestration agreement, certain mandatory spending (particularly for low income entitlements, such as Medicaid, and also for social security) is exempted and reductions in Medicare spending are capped at 2 per cent.

28. As stated in the text, the fiscal gap is defined as "the size of the immediate and permanent increase in taxes and/or reductions in non-interest expenditures that would be required to set the present value of all future primary surpluses equal to the current value of the national debt" (Gale and Auerbach, 2009, p. 9).

29. Spending decisions are dictated either by discretionary spending authority, which is appropriated annually by Congress, or mandatory spending authority, which is authorized by law and administered via trust funds.

30. As numerous think tanks and deficit commissions have stressed, the key objective of fiscal normalization is first to stabilize the debt to GDP ratio – through some combination of revenue and expenditure measures – as soon as possible and then to gradually lower it to a safer steady-state level. While gross US federal debt (debt held by the public plus inter-governmental obligations, such as IOUs held by the major trust funds) has now exceeded 100 per cent of GDP, debt held by the public is on a trajectory to reach near 90 per cent in 2022, according to the CBO's (2012 August) alternative fiscal scenario. Many advocate targeting a lower debt to GDP ratio in the medium term of around 60 per cent (see e.g. National Research Council, 2010). Johnson and Kwak (2012) propose a target of 50 per cent to be reached by 2030.

31. Medicare is made up of four parts labeled A through D. Part A is known has hospital insurance (HI), parts B and D are supplementary medical insurance (SMI) and part C is Medicare Advantage, provided through private companies. Although the trustees admit that it is an unrealistic assumption for the future, SMI is self-financing by law, so technically there are no unfunded liabilities in the future.

32. Robert Pozen, among others, has offered plausible scenarios, mainly involving indexing of social security payments to prices rather than (generally more rapidly increasing) wages for richer households (Pozen, 2005).

33. See CMS (2011a, p. 27).

34. Medicare and Medicaid, respectively, per beneficiary grew by 2.4 and 2.0 per cent faster on average than per capita GDP during 1975–2007 (CBO, 2011b, p. 42). By 2085, CBO projects that Medicare's excess cost growth will have fallen to 1.0 per cent (CBO, 2011b, p. 43).

35. This assumes that health care expenditure growth slows to a pace below that of economic growth for an extended period.

36. International health care and cost comparisons, and large quality-adjusted health cost differentials across cities in the US among other factors, underscore the potential to restrain health care cost inflation.

37. Kennedy's original focus was that foreign entanglements overwhelm the domestic economy, eroding the material basis for maintaining the same level of external commitments.

38. For example, Ferguson and Kotlikoff forecast health care cost increases that outpace GDP growth (involving a continuation of current policies and laws) at the historical rate over an exceedingly long period, and they assume large real benefit increases in social security. Furthermore, the US tax code exhibits pronounced income tax bracket creep, suggesting that current revenue to GDP will increase even in the absence of further future tax rate increases.

39. This is similar to the "good future" conclusions of the Medicare Trustees, CBO, and Auerbach and Gale.

40. Wheeler claims that since 20 per cent of the budget goes to defense, 20 per cent of the interest paid on the national debt should be attributed to defense. The interest estimates in the table thus represent 20 per cent of the CBO's interest estimates.

41. In the event that the current sequestration provision is realized, the Pentagon's budget will be reduced relative to the current baseline by an additional $487 billion over ten years.

42. In addition, there are large line items within the federal budget applying to departments such as State, Energy and Veteran's Affairs that should properly be added to the Pentagon's base line, plus supplementary budgets to obtain a more comprehensive measure of total defense expenditure.

43. The Department of Energy credits spending toward defense as costs found in its National Nuclear Security Administration.

44. Wheeler argues that military and economic aid to Iraq and Afghanistan, gifts and loans to Israel, Egypt and others, United Nations peacekeeping costs and other State Department involvement in such areas should be considered defense spending. These figures were taken from Department of State and Other International Programs' spending.

45. Resets are included as a separate expenditure item in the Stiglitz and Bilmes study (see below).

46. For example, a study by Brown University's Watson Institute for International Studies estimates the cost of war to be between $3.7 trillion and $4.4 trillion (see www.costofwar.org).

47. All US combat troops have left Iraq.

48. This comparison fails of course to capture the enormous human cost (and opportunity costs) of these wars.

49. Many of these expenditures are on-budget as non-defense discretionary spending (see CBO, 2011b, Table 5-1, p. 60).

50. For a discussion of how proposed Pentagon savings can be achieved and potential consequences, see transcripts of the Brookings Institution conference on defense spending at www.brookings.edu/articles/2011/0124_defense_budget_kagan.aspx (Kagan, 2011).

51. In the event, some success on the health care cost-saving front in recent years has been claimed by informed observers. See, for example, the comments of former OMB head, Peter Orszag on Fareed Zakaria's television program, GPS.

52. In any case, the effective marginal tax rate on labor and capital is expected to climb over the next few decades (CBO, 2011b, Table 6-3, p. 71).

53. For a useful compilation of possible reductions in tax expenditures and spending on mandatory programs and how much they each can contribute to fiscal adjustment, see Johnson and Kwak (2012, Table 7-1).

54. See, for example, earlier proposals in Rivlin and Sawhill (2004) and Gale and Steuerle (2005).

55. Returning federal expenditures to their long-term historical average seems unrealistic to many, given the aging of the population and the retirement of the baby boomers, on the one hand, and the growing interest burden on the existing stock of debt, on the other. Raising federal revenues gradually to somewhere closer to 21–23 per cent of GDP (coincident with major reform of entitlements) may still prove necessary.

56. For a variety of feasible fiscal adjustment scenarios, see National Research Council (2010, Chapter 9). See also Johnson and Kwak (2012).

57. For an optimistic view of these savings, see, for example, Orszag (2011). For a more skeptical view, see Tanner (2011).
58. There is no economic or political basis today for the sharp decline in the debt to GDP ratio experienced after World War II when this ratio dropped from 122 to 75 per cent over five years (see US Government Debt, 2011).
59. See International Monetary Fund (2011).

9   Politics

1. For example, see David Brooks (2011) and Clive Crook (2011).
2. PIMCO co-CEO Mohammed El-Erian employs similar language in an interview on Bloomberg Surveillance, July 12, 2011.
3. Policy sentiment has varied during periods of post-conflict. For example, in 1964 only 18 per cent of Americans felt "we should mind our own business" in world affairs, which later jumped to 41 per cent (post-Vietnam) in 1976. In 2002 only 30 per cent felt we should "mind our own business," which has now jumped to a 40-year high of 49 per cent in 2009 (Pew Research Center, 2009).
4. This in no way is meant to disparage the outer boundaries of the political spectrum, notably the neo-isolationist and pro-protectionist positions taken by libertarian-leading or economic nationalist voices on the right or left. The point is that such perspectives have generally not carried the day on questions of US power projection in the post-war period.
5. While the candidacies of Bachmann, Cain, Huntsman, Pawlenty and Perry proved unsuccessful, ultimately their views serve in our examination of the variance of opinion on US hegemony.
6. As of the date of this writing three weeks before the election the Republican attack on President Obama's handling of the terrorist attack that led to the deaths of four US diplomats in Benghazi, Libya is intensifying.
7. For example, former candidate John Huntsman favors reducing the US military footprint through closing foreign bases and avoiding the deployment of troops for open-ended state building ventures. Instead, Huntsman's mantra has been "nation building at home." Meanwhile, former candidate Michelle Bachman, who otherwise backs a muscular foreign policy, characterizes Obama's commitment of US military assets to Libya as incompatible with core US national security interests. While endorsing a strong military posture overall, former candidate Rick Perry voiced a traditional reluctance to unilaterally deploy American troops abroad for causes that do not directly affect US national interests or that of its principal allies. Newt Gingrich's defense and foreign policy posture has been more difficult to pin down (see e.g. Fisher, 2012).
8. Had Obama's approach represented a strategic reallocation of resources away from defense to domestic objectives, the president's "Asia pivot" strategy and other defense-cum-foreign policy priorities would arguably prove less feasible.
9. By "traditional" I do not have in mind recent, protracted campaigns of state building in Iraq and Afghanistan.
10. Gallup: "Do you think the United Nations is doing a good job or a poor job in trying to solve international problems it has had to face?" 2003–2011. Sixty-two per cent feel the UN has done "a poor job" while 31 per cent believe the UN has done "a good job" (Gallup, 2011).
11. Some 64 per cent of Americans want the UN to have the leading or major role in solving international problems (Saad, 2009).

12. Ron Paul has consistently opposed the UN – for example, proposing to "evict the organization from its New York headquarters." His adamant non-interventionist approach to foreign affairs and consistent advocacy of avoiding "entangling alliances" makes him a non-supporter of US hegemony (Rockwell, 2007).

13. While supporting "go(ing) it alone when necessary," former presidential candidate Rick Perry warned against "excessive unilateralism."

14. BBC/Harris Interactive Polling, 2011: "There is widespread support for military intervention under the following circumstances: to prevent terrorist attacks on the US (79 per cent), to prevent nuclear weapons from falling into the hands of terrorists (78 per cent), if a strong and friendly ally is attacked (74 per cent), to prevent a country that is hostile to the United States from building nuclear weapons (71 per cent), if a dictator is killing large numbers of their own people (66 per cent) and to overthrow a dictator who is very hostile to the US (55 per cent)" (Harris Interactive, 2011).

15. Some 62 per cent of Americans favor diplomatic engagement with North Korea and Iran (Chicago Council on Global Affairs, 2010). Whether these talks should ensue before preconditions are met is not captured in the poll.

16. Mirroring public sentiment, sanctions against Iran have generally met resounding support from Congress.

17. According to Gallup polling, Americans believe the US's number one strength to be the American people, followed by military superiority and then technology/innovation (Saad, 2010).

18. Although public support for high levels of defense spending has been reasonably steady, Americans have been cautious on actually deploying military power (Chicago Council on Global Affairs, 2010, p. 55).

19. This does not fully account for the fact that classifying activities into manufacturing rather than services is often arbitrary.

20. Obama in his own words has "brought trade cases against China at nearly twice the rate as the last [Bush] administration." He also requested a special Trade Enforcement Unit charged with "investigating unfair trade practices in countries like China" (State of the Union, 2012).

21. Mitt Romney's effective federal tax rate was 13.9 per cent in 2010, and it was criticized by many as unfairly low for such a wealthy individual (Confessore and Kocieniewski, 2012). In line with the "Buffet Rule," President Obama has proposed that families earning more than 1 million dollars pay a minimum 30 per cent average tax rate.

22. What often gets overlooked is the issue of double taxation; capital gains and dividends are previously taxed when they are earned as normal income.

23. Some 74 per cent of Americans believe that the US is on the "wrong track." This percentage was approximately 30 per cent for much of the latter 1990s, and down to 20 per cent in 2002 (NBC News/Wall Street Journal Poll, 2011).

24. Some 56 per cent replied "mostly good." This is down 8 points from a high of 64 per cent in 2004 (Chicago Council on Global Affairs, 2010).

25. Some 50 per cent of Americans felt globalization was "mostly bad" in 2010 compared with 31 per cent in 2004 (Chicago Council on Global Affairs, 2010).

26. A 2008 NBC/Wall Street Journal poll found that 58 per cent of Americans believed free trade was bad because it "subjected American companies to unfair competition and cheap labor." This number was up from 48 per cent in 1997 (NBC News/Wall Street Journal Poll, 2008).

27. Support for trade restrictions increased from 55 to 68 per cent.
28. A 2010 NBC News/Wall Street Journal poll found that 53 per cent of Americans view trade agreements similar to NAFTA as hurting the US, a 21 point increase from 1999 (NBC News/Wall Street Journal Poll, 2010).
29. Some 59 per cent believe it's good "for consumers like you, an 8 per cent increase since 2008" (Chicago Council on Global Affairs, 2010).
30. Just 17 per cent favored the Dubai Ports Deal, in February 2006, while 64 per cent believed the deal should have been barred from continuing (Rassmussen Reports, 2006). The validity of these results have come under suspicion for several reasons: (i) Rasmussen conducts its polls entirely by automation (that is, with pre-recorded/computer voices and pre-programmed questions, thus potentially skewing results); (ii) this poll was taken during the height of the controversy, which leaves one wondering to what degree the alarm was unnaturally high as a result of media coverage; and (iii) Rasmussen asked respondents if they thought the ports in question were currently owned by a US firm – only 39 per cent were able to give the correct answer: that, no, they were not currently owned by a US firm but by a foreign firm (Blumenthal, 2006).
31. Recent US arms sales to Taiwan induced Chinese senior officers from the Chinese National Defense University and Academy of Military Sciences to call for selling off US debt securities as a means of "oblique and stealthy feints" of warfare (Gertz, 2010).
32. Some 50 per cent of Americans see China's growth as "equally positive and negative," 38 per cent believe it to be mostly negative and only 8 per cent find it positive (Chicago Council on Global Affairs, 2010, p. 30).
33. Some 40 per cent of Americans see China as the current economic leader compared with 10 per cent in 2000 (Saad, 2008).
34. 2011 Gallup polling shows 47 per cent of Americans believe China will be the leading power in 20 years compared with 35 per cent selecting the US. This number has nearly quadrupled between 2000 and 2009 (Saad, 2011).
35. Some 63 per cent of Americans believe China practices "unfair" trade (Chicago Council on Global Affairs, 2010, p. 29). In a related poll, almost two-thirds of Americans (62 per cent) believe that China practices "unfair trade." However, only 40 per cent of Americans wish "to get tougher" with Chinese trade compared with 53 per cent wishing for a stronger relationship with China (Pew Research Center Publications, 2011).
36. For a criticism of China's mercantilist trade policies, see Hubbard and Navarro (2010).
37. Another dimension of opinion on immigration is ambivalence. Many Americans have little or no opinion either way.
38. See *The Economist* (2007b).
39. These polling figures do not distinguish between legal and illegal immigration.
40. A 2007 Pew Poll showed that 10 per cent feel immigration "hurts the way of life and culture" (Pew Research, 2007).
41. A description of the conditions for President Obama's initiative are described in a June 15, 2012 Department of Homeland Security official news release (US Department of Homeland Security, 2012).
42. During the October 18, 2011 Republican primary debate in Nevada, Mitt Romney was greeted with crowd applause when he said, "it's important for us as Republicans on this stage to say something which hasn't been said. And that is I think every single person here loves legal immigration. We respect people who come

here legally. And the reason we're so animated about stopping illegal immigration is there are 4.5 million people who want to come here who are in line legally, we want that to happen in an orderly and legal process" (CNN Transcripts, 2011).

43. This despite a marked slowdown in the face of immigration from Mexico owing to fewer job openings in the US and improving opportunities in Mexico.

44. 2011 Gallup polling shows Americans currently oppose social security cuts (64 per cent) and Medicare cuts (61 per cent). Cuts to other areas of government spending were also unpopular: education faced the strongest opposition (67 per cent) while foreign aid and funding for the arts were least opposed (37 and 52 per cent, respectively; Newport and Saad, 2011).

45. Both president Obama and Senate Democrats have floated ideas to increase the marginal tax rate on wealthier Americans. Obama has called for the expiration of the Bush tax cuts for those families making more than $250,000.

46. A CBS News/New York Times poll found that 56 per cent supported raising taxes on incomes above $250,000 (Dulton, 2011).

47. At the October 11 Republic Debate, Mitt Romney said, "To all of the Obama regulations we say no. It costs jobs." Rick Perry said, "Regulations are strangling the American entrepreneurship out there," and Rick Santorum said, "Repeal every regulation the Obama administration put in place."

48. Americans broadly support both tax increases and spending cuts in order to reduce the debt – 69 per cent (Gallup July 7–10, 2011) and 67 per cent (Quinnipiac University July 5–11, 2011). And while a majority of Republicans signed Grover Norquist's "Taxpayer Protection Pledge," revenue increases through tax "loophole elimination" were supported by John Boehner, Pat Toomey and Tom Coburn, among others (Krauthammer, 2011).

49. Some 39 per cent of Americans say current defense spending is "too much" (Newport, 2011).

50. For example, there are growing voices that question whether the US really needs eleven aircraft carriers and a myriad of other (more Cold War-related) military assets in a world marked by cyberwar and counterinsurgency.

51. Much of these cuts will come from downsizing commitments in Afghanistan and leaving only a vestigial troop presence in Iraq by the end of 2011.

52. Although Panetta has warned that cutbacks of this magnitude will "tear a seam in the nation's defenses...lead(ing) to a hollow force incapable of sustaining the missions it is assigned," Obama has promised to veto any effort to scuttle the automatic sequester unless an equivalent deficit reduction of $1.2 trillion passes Congress (Allen, 2011).

53. Americans feel a strong economy is more important to power/influence than a strong military (72 to 23 per cent; Chicago Council on Global Affairs, 2010: Maintaining a Strong Global Military Posture).

54. This, of course, is not meant to assert that members of the Democratic Party have been "weak" on defense.

55. Some 73 per cent feel the US is headed in the wrong direction compared with 22 per cent in the right direction (NBC News/Wall Street Journal Poll, 2011).

56. A 47 per cent plurality of the public believes "the worst is yet to come," according to an August 2011 Ipsos/Reuters poll (Ipsos/Reuters, 2011).

57. Gallup polling from September, 2011 shows a 30-year low for satisfaction about how the nation is being governed at 19 per cent, with 81 per cent showing dissatisfaction. Some 57 per cent of Americans show "little or no confidence" in the federal government to handle domestic problems (Saad, 2011).

58. For example, while the congressional approval rating reached an all-time low of 9 per cent in a CBS News/NY Times poll on October 25 (CBS News/NYT Polls, 2011), in 1992, congressional approval was as low as 18 per cent and yet the political system continued to function (Saad, "Congress' Approval Rating," 2011). While President Obama has also seen his approval rating slip to a low of 38 per cent in October 2011 down from a high of 69 per cent in January 2009 (Gallup, Presidential Approval Ratings, 2011), Nixon, W. Bush, Carter and Reagan are just some of the presidents who have had lower ratings and still managed to effectively fulfill executive duties. Protests against the government during the Civil Rights Movement and the Vietnam War were substantially greater than those being seen by either the Tea Party or OWS. Thus it is difficult to assert conclusively that there is now an unprecedented crisis of confidence in the US political system.

10   Conclusion: Maintaining Hegemony

1. This observation has not eliminated the perception that US actions have sometimes been heavy-handed or destructive.
2. Such presumptions have mainly emerged from the hegemonic stability tradition.
3. Perhaps a few select leading energy producers, such as Saudi Arabia, would comprise a limited exception here.

Bibliography

Aaron, H., et al. (2005) *Can We Say No? The Challenge of Rationing Health Care.* Washington, DC: The Brookings Institution.

Abonyi, G. (2008) "Knitting Together Asia: East Asian Economic Integration and Its Implications", *Asia Policy Briefs*, Syracuse, NY: The Maxwell School, http://exed.maxwell.syr.edu/exed/sites/policy/files/gabonyi-knitting-together-asia-sb.pdf (accessed 3 November 2009).

Abonyi, G. and Van Slyke, D. (2009) "Governing on the Edges: Globalization of Production and the Challenge to Public Administration in the Twenty-First Century", *Public Administration Review*, Special Issue, December, 537.

Abrams, E., et al. (2011) "Iran's Nuclear Program", *Council on Foreign Relations*, 9 November, Transcript.

Aghion, P., Blundell, R., Griffith, R., Howitt, P. and Prantl, S. (2006) "The Effects of Entry on Incumbent Innovation and Productivity", http://www.economics.harvard.edu/faculty/aghion/files/Effects_of_Entry.pdf (accessed 12 March 2011).

Agnew, J. (2005) *Hegemony: The New Shape of Global Power.* Philadelphia, PA: Temple University Press.

Alexander, D. (2011) "Budget Cuts Take US Military 'To the Edge: Panetta'", *Reuters*, 13 October, http://www.reuters.com/article/2011/10/13/us-usa-defense-budget-idUSTRE79C50Q20111013 (accessed 12 November 2011).

Allen, J. (2011a) "Stop Automatic Defense Cuts, Panetta Urges Congress", *Reuters*, 21 November, http://www.reuters.com/article/2011/11/22/us-usa-debt-defense-panetta-idUSTRE7AL05220111122 (accessed 26 November 2011).

Allen, J. (2011b) "S & P Spurs Blame Game", *Politico*, 6 August, http://www.politico.com/news/stories/0811/60794.html (accessed 21 October 2011).

Allison, G. (2010) "Nuclear Disorder", *Foreign Affairs*, January/February.

Allison, K. (2007) "Gates Warns on US Immigration Curbs", *Financial Times*, 8 March, p. 7.

Altman, R. C. and Haass, R. N. (2010) "American Profligacy and American Power: The Consequences and Fiscal Irresponsibility", *Foreign Affairs*, 89(6), November/December, 25–34.

Anderson, S. (2011) "40 Percent of Fortune 500 Companies Founded by Immigrants or Their Children", *Forbes*, 19 June, http://www.forbes.com/sites/stuartanderson/2011/06/19/40-percent-of-fortune-500-companies-founded-by-immigrants-or-their-children/ (accessed 3 January 2011).

Anderson, S. and Platzer, M. (2006) *American Made: The Impact of Immigrant Entrepreneurs and Professionals on US Competitiveness*, p. 6. Arlington, TX: National Venture Capital Association.

Antle, J. (2011) "Rick Perry's Humble Foreign Policy", *Politico*, 1 September, http://www.politico.com/news/stories/0811/62431.html (accessed 21 October 2011).

Appleby, J. and Carty, S. (2005) "Ailing GM Looks to Scale Back Generous Health Benefits", 23 June, http://www.usatoday.com/money/autos/2005-06-22-gm-healthcare-usat_x.htm (accessed 24 March 2011).

Armitage, R. and Nye, J. (2007a) "The US-Japan Alliance: Getting Asia Right Through 2020", *CSIS Report*, http://www.cfr.org/publication/13071/csis.html (accessed 1 July 2009).

Armitage, R. and Nye, J. (2007b) *CSIS Commission on Smart Power: A Smarter, More Secure America*. Washington, DC: The CSIS Press.

Asian Development Bank (2009) *Energy Outlook for Asia and the Pacific*, October, Manila: ADB, http://www.adb.org/Documents/Books/Energy-Outlook/Energy-Outlook.pdf (accessed 9 March 2012).

Association of Southeast Asian Nations (2004) "ASEAN Plan of Action for Energy Cooperation 2004-2009", adopted by 22nd ASEAN Ministers on Energy Meeting, Manila, Philippines, 9 June, http://www.aseansec.org/pdf/APAEC0409.pdf (accessed 9 March 2012).

Association of Southeast Asian Nations (2009) "Member Countries", http://www.asean.org/74.htm (accessed 9 March 2012).

Attkins, C. and Hodge, S. (2005) "The US Corporate Income Tax System: Once a World Leader, Now A Millstone Around the Neck of American Business", November, No. 136, Washington, DC: Tax Foundation, http://www.taxfoundation.org/files/sr136.pdf (accessed 2 March 2011).

Auerbach, A. J. and Gale, W. G. (2011) "Tempting Fate: The Federal Budget Outlook", June.

Babones, S. (2011) "The Middling Kingdom", *Foreign Affairs*, September/October.

Bacevich, A. (2010) *Washington Rules: America's Path to Permanent War*. New York, NY: Metropolitan Books.

Bacevich, A. J. (2002) *American Empire: The Realities and Consequences of U. S. Diplomacy*. Cambridge, MA: Harvard University Press.

Bacevich, A. J. (2005) *The New American Militarism: How Americans Are Seduced By War*. Oxford, NY: Oxford University Press.

Bacevich, A. J. (2008) *The Limits of Power: The End of American Exceptionalism*. New York, NY: Metropolitan Books.

Backhouse, R. (2010) *The Puzzle of Modern Economics: Science or Ideology?* Cambridge: Cambridge University Press.

Bailey, M., Elmendorf, D. and Litan, R. (2008) "The Great Credit Squeeze: How It Happened, How to Prevent Another", 16 May, Washington, DC: Brookings Institute, http://www.brookings.edu/papers/2008/0516_credit_squeeze.aspx (accessed 7 March 2011).

Baker, G. (2007) "The Wall Street Slide", *The Magazine of International Economic Policy*, Spring, 26–82, http://www.international-economy.com/TIE_Sp07_Baker.pdf (accessed 31 March 2011).

Balakrishnan, R. and Tulin, V. (2006) "US Dollar Risk Premiums and Capital Flows", IMF Working Paper No. 06/160/, June, Washington, DC: International Monetary Fund.

Baldwin, R. (2006) "Globalisation: The Great Unbundling(s)", 20 September, Finland: Economic Council of Finland Prime Minister's Office, http://www.unescochair.uns.ac.rs/sr/docs/baldwin2006Globalisation.pdf (accessed 26 March 2011).

Baldwin, R. E. (2008a) "Managing the Noodle Bowl: The Fragility of East Asian Regionalism", *The Singapore Economic Review*, 53(3), 449–478.

Baldwin, R. E. (2008b) "Multilateralizing Regionalism: The WTO's Next Challenge", *VOXeu.org*, 29 February, http://www.voxeu.org/index.php?q=node/959 (accessed 9 March 2012).

Barnes, J., et al. (2011) "China Takes Aim at US Naval Might", *The Wall Street Journal*, 4 January, http://online.wsj.com/article/SB10001424052970204397704577074631582060996.html (accessed 6 January 2011).

Barnett, T. P. M. (2004). *The Pentagon's New Map: War and Peace in the Twenty-First Century*. New York, NY: G.P. Putnam's Sons.

Barnett, T. P. M. (2009) *Great Powers: America and the World after Bush*. New York, NY: G.P. Putnam's Sons.

Barro, R. (2009) "Government Spending Is No Free Lunch," *The Wall Street Journal*, 22 January.

Bast, A. (2011) "Pakistan's Nuclear Surge", *Newsweek*, 23 May.

Baumol, W., Litan, R. and Schramm, C. (2007) *Good Capitalism, Bad Capitalism, and the Economic Growth and Prosperity*. New Haven, CT: Yale University.

BBC News (2006) "US Military 'At Breaking Point'", 26 January, http://news.bbc.co.uk/2/hi/4649066.stm (accessed 15 April 2011).

BBC News (2010) "China Faces Growing Gender Imbalance", 11 January, http://news.bbc.co.uk/2/hi/8451289.stm (accessed 9 March 2012).

BBC News. "In Depth Report: The Future of Kashmir", http://news.bbc.co.uk/2/shared/spl/hi/south_asia/03/kashmir_future/html/ (accessed 9 March 2012).

Becker, G. (2008) "Is America in Decline?" *The Gary Becker and Richard Posner Blog*, 3 August, http://www.becker-posner-blog.com/archives/2008/08/is_america_in_d_1.html (accessed 16 April 2009).

Becker, G. (2010) "Slow Economic Growth Is a Crucial European Problem", *Gary Becker and Richard Posner Blog*, 30 May.

Beckley, M. (2011). "China's Century?: Why America's Edge Will Endure", *International Security*, Winter, 36(3), 41–78.

Beinart, P. (2006) *The Good Fight: Why Liberals – and Only Liberals – Can Win the War on Terror and Make America Great Again*. New York, NY: HarperCollins Publishers.

Beinart, P. (2010) *The Icarus Syndrome: A History of American Hubris*. New York, NY: HarperCollins.

Bennett, B. (2011) "Obama Administration Reports Record Number of Deportations", *The Los Angeles Times*, 18 October, http://articles.latimes.com/2011/oct/18/news/la-pn-deportation-ice-20111018 (accessed 21 October 2011).

Bergen, P. and Tiedemann, K. (2011) "Washington's Phantom War", *Foreign Affairs*, 90(4), July/August 2011, 12–18.

Bergsten, C. F., Gill, B., Lardy, N. R. and Mitchell, D. (2006) *China: The Balance Sheet: What the World Needs to Know Now about the Emerging Superpower*. New York, NY: Public Affairs.

Bergsten, F. (2006) "Falling Dollar Saga Still Has a Long Way to Go", *Financial Times*, Debates Economists Forum, 6 December, http://blogs.ft.com/economistsforum/2006/12/falling-dollar-html/#axzz1m1Ud01ly (accessed 10 February 2012).

Bergsten, F. (2007a) "China and Economic Integration in East Asia: Implications for the United States", in *Policy Briefs in International Economics*, pp. 1–9. Washington, DC: The Peterson Institute for International Economics, http://www.iie.com/publications/pb/pb07-3.pdf (accessed 12 December 2009).

Bergsten, F. (2007b) *Speech on Toward a Free Trade Area of the Asia Pacific*, given at the Joint Conference of The Japan Economic Foundation and Peterson Institute for International Economics on New Asia-Pacific Trade Initiatives, 27 November, Washington, DC. http://www.iie.com/publications/papers/paper.cfm?ResearchID=233 (accessed 1 July 2009).

Bergsten, F. (2009) "The Dollar and the Deficits: How Washington Can Prevent the Next Crisis", *Foreign Affairs*, 88(6), November/December, 20–38.

Bergsten, F. (2010) "Submission to the USTR in Support of a Trans-Pacific Partnership Agreement", 25 January, Washington, DC: Peterson Institute for International Economics, http://www.piie.com/publications/papers/paper.cfm?ResearchID=1482 (accessed 9 March 2012).

Bergsten, F., et al. (2006) *China: The Balance Sheet What the World Needs to Know Now about the Emerging Superpower.* Washington, DC: The Peterson Institute for International Economics and the Center for Strategic and International Studies.

Bergsten, F. C. (2008) *China's Rise: Challenges and Opportunities.* Washington, DC: Peterson Institute for International Economics.

Bernanke, B. (2005) *Speech on Global Saving Glut and the US Current Account Deficit*, 10 March, given at the Sandridge Lecture, Virginia Association of Economics, Richmond, VA, http://www.federalreserve.gov/boarddocs/speeches/2005/200503102/default.htm (accessed 10 February 2012).

Bernanke, B. (2007a) *Speech on Global Imbalances: Recent Developments and Prospects*, 11 September, given at Bundesbank Lecture, Berlin, Germany, http://www.federalreserve.gov/newsevents/speech/bernanke20070911a.htm (accessed 17 February).

Bernanke, B. (2007b) *Speech on the Level of Distribution of Economic Well Being*, 6 February, given at the Greater Omaha Chamber of Commerce, Omaha, NE, http://www.federalreserve.gov/newsevents/speech/Bernanke20070206a.htm (accessed 14 March 2011).

Bernanke, B. (2008a) *Speech on Financial Regulation and Financial Stability*, 8 July, given at the Federal Deposit Insurance Corporation's Forum on Mortgage Lending for Low and Moderate Income Households, Arlington, VA, http://www.federalreserve.gov/newsevents/speech/bernanke20080708a.htm (accessed 3 March 2011).

Bernanke, B. (2008b) *Speech on the Challenges for Health-Care Reform*, 16 June, given at the Senate Finance Committee on Health Reform Summit, http://www.federalreserve.gov/newsevents/speech/bernanke20080616a.htm (accessed March 29 2011).

Bernanke, B. (2011a) *Speech on Global Imbalances: Links to Economic and Financial Stability*, 18 February, given at the Banque de France Financial Stability Review Launch Event, Paris, France, http://www.federalreserve.gov/newsevents/speech/bernanke20110218a.htm (accessed 10 February 2012).

Bernanke, B. (2011b) *Speech on the Near- and Longer-Term Prospects for the US Economy*, given at the Federal Reserve Bank of Kansas City Economic Symposium, 26 August, Jackson Hole, Wyoming.

Bernstein, J. (2010) "Nukes for Sale", *The New York Review*, May.

Bertaut, C., Kamin, S. and Thomas, C. (2008) *How Long Can the Unsustainable US Current Account Deficit Be Sustained?* http://www.ssc.wisc.edu/~ mchinn/Bertaut_Kamin_Thomas.pdf (accessed 10 February 2012).

Bertelsmann, S. (2006) "World Powers in the 21st Century", in *Who Rules the World?: World Powers and International Order Conclusions from an International Representative Survey*, pp. 1–29. Berlin: Bertelsmann Stiftung.

Bhagwati, J. (1989) " 'Is Free Trade Passé After All?' Text of the Acceptance Speech on the Occasion of the Award of the Bernhard Harms Prize at the Kiel Institute, Germany, on 25 June 1988", *Review of World Economics (Weltwirtschaftliches Archiv)*, 125(1), 17–44.

Bhagwati, J. (1994) "The US and the World Economy", *Journal of International Affairs*, 48(1), 279–285.

Bhagwati, J. (1995) "US Trade Policy: The Infatuation with Free Trade Agreements", *Discussion Paper Series 726*, New York, NY: Columbia University.

Bhagwati, J. (2008) "The Selfish Hegemon Must Offer a New Deal on Trade", *Financial Times*, 19 August.

Bhagwati, J. (2009a) "Obama Must Fight the Protectionist Virus", *Financial Times*, 4 February, http://www.ft.com/cms/s/0/3efdc764-f2ca-11dd-abe6-0000779fd2ac. html (accessed 1 July 2009).

Bhagwati, J. (2009b) "Obama Must Fight the Protectionist Virus", *Financial Times*, 4 February, http://www.ft.com/cms/s/0/3efdc764-f2ca-11dd-abe6-0000779fd2ac. html#axzz24yZrS1yh (accessed 1 July 2009).

Bhide, A. (2006) "Venturesome Consumption, Innovation and Globalization", in: Joint Conference of CESifo and the Center on Capitalism and Society, Venice, 21–22 July.

Bhidé, A. (2008) *The Venturesome Economy: How Innovation Sustains Prosperity in a More Connected World*. Princeton, NJ: Princeton University Press.

Biersteker, T. J. (1990) "Reducing the Role of the State in the Economy: A Conceptual Exploration of IMF and WorldBank Prescriptions", *International Studies Quarterly*, 34(4), December, 477–492.

Bijian, Z. (2005) "China's 'Peaceful Rise' to Great Power Status", *Foreign Affairs*, September/October.

Bilmes, L. and Stiglitz, J. (2008) *The Three Trillion Dollar War: The True Cost of the Iraq Conflict*. London, NY: W. W. Norton & Company.

Blair, D. (2005) "Impact of China's Emergence on the Asia Pacific Region", in: Panel of the Brookings Institution's launch of the China Initiative, 20 September.

Blair, G., et al. (2011) "Pakistan's Middle Class Extremists", *Foreign Affairs*, 11 July.

Blinder, A. (2006) "Offshoring: The Next Industrial Revolution?", *Foreign Affairs*, 85, March/April, 113–128.

Blinder, A. and Zandi, M. (2010) "How the Great Recession Was Brought to an End", 27 July.

Bloomberg News (2008) "China's Earthquake Candor Contrasts with Tibet Media Clampdown", 14 May.

Bloomberg News (2010) "China's Air Pollution Worsens after Economic Growth Rebounds from Crisis", 27 July.

Bloomberg, M. and Schumer, C. (2007) *Sustaining New York's and the US's Global Financial Services Leadership*. New York, NY: New York City Government, http://www.nyc. gov/html/om/pdf/ny_report_final.pdf (accessed 31 March 2011).

Blumenthal, M. (2006) "Mystery Pollster", 27 February, http://www.mysterypollster. com/main/2006/02/rasmussen_dubai.html (accessed 12 November 2011).

Boese, W. (2005) "Key US Interdiction Initiative Claim Misrepresented", *Arms Control Today*, July/August.

Borger, J. and Watts, J. (2009) "China Launches Green Power Revolution to Catch up on West", *The Guardian*, 9 June, http://www.guardian.co.uk/world/2009/jun/09/ china-green-energy-solar-wind (accessed 9 March 2012).

Boskin, M. (2004) "The Economic Agenda: A View from the US", *Review of International Economics*, 18 May.

Bosworth, B. and Collins, S. M. (2008a) "Accounting for Growth Comparing Indian and China", *Journal of Economic Perspectives*, Winter, 22(1), 45–66.

Bosworth, B. and Collins, S. M. (2008b) "Accounting for Growth: Comparing China and India", NBER Working Paper No. 12943, February.

Bradford, J. (2008) "Shifting the Tides against Piracy in Southeast Asian Waters", *Asian Survey*, XLVIII(3), May/June, 473–492.

Bradford, S., Hufbauer, G. and Grieco, P. (2006) "The Payoff to America from Global Integration", in Bergsten, C. F. (ed.), *The United States and the World Economy: Foreign Economic Policy for the Next Decade*, pp. 65–109. Washington, DC: Institute for International Economics.

Bradley, B. (2008) *The New American Story*. New York, NY: Random House.

Bradsher, K. (2009) "For East Asia, Crisis Prompts a Rethinking of Dependence on Exports", *International Herald Tribune*, 5 March, http://yaleglobal. yale.edu/content/east-asia-crisis-prompts-rethinking-dependence-exports (accessed 12 September 2009).

Bradsher, K. and Krauss, C. (2012) "Pressed By US, Asian Countries Look for Ways to Reduce Purchases of Iranian Oil", *The New York Times*, 6 January, http://www.nytimes.com/2012/01/07/world/middleeast/amid-pressure-on-oil-iran-plans-new-round-of-military-exercises.html?hp (accessed 6 January 2012).

Brandt, L. and Zhu, X. (2010) "Accounting for China's Growth", *IZA Discussion Paper* No. 4764.

Branstetter, Lee and Lardy, Nicholas (2006) "China's Embrace of Globalization", NBER Working Paper 12373, July.

Bremmer, I. (2009a) "State Capitalism Comes of Age – The End of the Free Market?", *Foreign Affairs*, May/June.

Bremmer, I. (2009b) "State Capitalism and the Crisis", *McKinsey Quarterly*, July.

Bremmer, I. and Gordon, D. (2011) "An Upbeat View of America's 'Bad' Year", *The New York Times*, 27 December, http://www.nytimes.com/2011/12/28/opinion/an-upbeat-view-of-americas-bad-year.html (accessed 6 January 2011).

Brender, A. and Pisani, F. (2010) *Global Imbalances and the Collapse of Globalized Finance*. Brussels: Center for Policy Studies, https://www.dexia-am.com/NR/rdonlyres/6EDAB882-A034-4413-8BBD-9EF867606E68/0/Global_Imbalances_final_consolidated_v2.pdf (accessed 10 February 2012).

Brilliant, M. (2007) "A Free Trade Area of the Asia-Pacific: An Idea with Merit, But Is It Feasible", *Brookings Northeast Asia Commentary*, Number 11, September, http://www.brookings.edu/opinions/2007/09northeastasia_brilliant.aspx (accessed 11 January 2012).

Brilliant, M., Hiebert, M., Reis, R. and Waterman, J. (2009) "Economic Opportunities and Challenges in East Asia Facing the Obama Administration", February, Washington, DC: The US Chamber of Commerce, http://www.uschamber.com/sites/default/files/international/asia/files/2009_econopp_eastasia.pdf (accessed 29 June 2009).

Broad, W., Markoff, J. and Sangar, D. (2011) "Israeli Test on Worm Called Crucial in Iran Nuclear Delay", *The New York Times*, 15 January, http://www.nytimes.com/2011/01/16/world/middleeast/16stuxnet.html (accessed 27 March 2011).

Broad, W., et al. (2010) "Iran Fortifies Its Arsenal with the Aid of North Korea", *The New York Times*, 28 November.

Broda, C. and Piero, G. (2009) "The New Global Balance: Financial De-globalisation, Savings Drain, and the US Dollar", *VOX*, 22 May, http://www.voxeu.org/index.php?q=node/3596 (accessed 10 February 2012).

Brooks, D. (2011) "The Mother of All No-Brainers", *The New York Times*, 4 July, http://www.nytimes.com/2011/07/05/opinion/05brooks.html?_r=1 (accessed 29 February 2012).

Brooks, S. G. and Wohlforth, W. C. (2008) *World Out of Balance: International Relations and the Challenge of American Primacy*. Princeton, NJ: Princeton University Press.

Brooks, S. G. and Wohlforth, W. C. (2009) "Reshaping the World Order: How Washington Should Reform International Institutions", *Foreign Affairs*, March/April.

Brown, E. and de Kock, G. (2012) "Central Banks Cushioned EUR's Decline in 3Q 2011", *FX Pulse*, Morgan Stanley, 5 January.

Brown, S. (2003) *The Illusion of Control*. Washington, DC: Brookings Institution Press.

Brown, S. (ed.) (2012) *Transnational Transfers and Global Development*. New York, NY: Palgrave MacMillan.

Brown, Stuart and Haas-Wilson, Deborah (1990) "Centrally Planned Economy Vulnerability to Antidumping Action", *Comparative Economic Studies*, Winter, XXXII(4), 1–27.

Bryce, R. (2008) *Gusher of Lies: The Dangerous Delusions of "Energy Independence"*. New York, NY: Public Affairs.

Brzezinski, Z. (2012) "Balancing the East: Upgrading the West", *Foreign Affairs*, January/February, http://www.foreignaffairs.com/articles/136754/zbigniew-brzezinski/balancing-the-east-upgrading-the-west (accessed 9 March 2012).

Buchanan, P. (2011) *Suicide of a Superpower: Will America Survive to 2025?* New York, NY: Thomas Dunne Books.

Buchanan, P. J. (2002) *The Death of the West: How Dying Populations and Immigrant Invasions Imperil Our Country and Civilization*. New York, NY: St. Martin's Press.

Buiter, W. (2009) "Should Central Banks Be Quasi-fiscal Actors?", *Financial Times*, 2 November, http://blogs.ft.com/maverecon/2009/11/should-central-banks-be-quasi-fiscal-actors/#axzz1WT1mGpKs (accessed 18 October 2012).

Bumiller, E. (2009) "Gates Says US Army Will Grow by 22,000", *The New York Times*, 20 July, http://www.nytimes.com/2009/07/21/world/21military.html (accessed 22 July, 2009).

Bumiller, E. and Shanker, T. (2011) "War Evolves with Drones, Some Tiny as Bugs", *The New York Times*, 19 June, http://www.nytimes.com/2011/06/20/world/20drones.html?pagewanted=all (accessed 22 July 2009).

Burleigh, M. (2012) "Iran Tests Missile as US Tightens Sanctions", *AFP*, 1 January.

Burns, S. and Kotlikoff, L. (2005) *The Coming Generational Storm*, Boston, MA: MIT Press, January.

Bush, G. W. (2008) "Statement by Bush on Anniversary of Proliferation Security Initiative", *The White House*, 28 May, http://www.america.gov/st/texttransEnglish/2008/May/20080528143618eaifas0.8662989.html

Businesswire (2011) "Asian Growth Provides Opportunity to Attract Capital Flow through Regional Exchanges", 17 October, http://www.businesswire.com/news/home/20111017006948/en/Asian-Growth-Opportunity-Attract-Capital-Flow-Regional (accessed 19 January 2012).

Bussiere, M., Fratzscher, M. and Gernot, J. (2005) "Productivity Shocks, Budget Deficits and the Current Account", ECB Working Paper Series No. 509, August, Frankfurt: European Central Bank.

Buszynski, L. (2009) "Russia and North Korea: Dilemmas and Interests", *Asian Survey*, 49(5), 809–830.

Buzan, B. (2004) *The United States and the Great Powers: World Politics in the Twenty-First Century*. Cambridge and Malden, MA: Polity Press.

Caballero, R. (2006) "On the Macroeconomics of Asset Shortages", NBER Working Paper Series. Cambridge, MA: National Bureau of Economics Research.

Caballero, R. (2009) "A Global Perspective on the Great Financial Insurance Run: Causes, Consequences, and Solutions", *VOX*, 23 January, http://voxeu.org/index.php?q=node/2827 (accessed 17 February 2012).

Caballero, R., Farhi, E. and Gourinchas, P. (2006) "An Equilibrium Model of 'Global Imbalances' and Low Interest Rates", *CEPR Discussion Papers* No. 5573, March, London: Center for Economic Research.

Campbell, J. and Shapiro, J. (2009) "The Afghanistan Index", June 24, http://www.brookings.edu/foreign-policy/~ /media/Files/Programs/FP/afghanistan%20index/index20090624.pdf (accessed 23 July 2009).

Carpenter, T. G. (2003) "Uncooperative Pakistan Rates Less US Aid", *Newsday*, 10 July.

Carroll, R., et al. (2009) "Moving Forward with Bipartisan Tax Policy", *A New America Foundation*, 12 February.

Carter, A. (2007) "How Washington Learned to Stop Worrying and Love India's Bomb", *Foreign Affairs*, 10 January.

Cavallo, D. and Diaz, F. (2011) "China's Dilemma: Higher Inflation or Deflation of Exportables", *VOX*, http://www.voxeu.org/index.php?q=node/6116 (accessed 17 February 2012).

Cavallo, M. and Tille, C. (2006) "Could Capital Gains Smooth a Current Account Rebalancing?" *Federal Reserve Bank of New York Staff Report* (237), January, New York, NY: FRBNY.

CBS News Poll Database (2011) "Obama Presidential Approval Rating", 6 November, http://www.cbsnews.com/stories/2007/10/12/politics/main3362530.shtml?tag=contentMain;contentBody (accessed 30 November 2011).

CBS News/New York Times Polls (2011) 25 October, http://www.cbsnews.com/8301-250_162-20125251/cbs-news-nyt-polls-10-25-11/?tag=mncol;lst;3 (accessed 30 November 2011).

Center for American Progress (2009) "Fact Sheet on Proposed Fiscal Year 2010 Defense Budget", 9 April, http://www.americanprogress.org/issues/2009/04/fact_sheet_defense.html (accessed 23 July 2009).

Cette, G. and Bourkès, R. (2007) "Trends in "Structural" Productivity Levels in the Major Industrialized Countries", *Economics Letters*, 95(1), 151–156.

Chandler, M. (2009) *Making Sense of the Dollar: Exposing Dangerous Myths about Trade and Foreign Exchange*. New York, NY: Bloomberg Press.

Chantrill, C. (2011) "US Government Debt", 20 July, www.usgovernmentdebt.us/ (accessed 2011).

Chazan, G. (2010) "Asia Taps New Russian Oil", *The Wall Street Journal Online*, 18 February, http://online.wsj.com/article/SB1000142405274870439880457507153142799787.html (accessed 28 March 2010).

Chen, D. and Mintz, J. (2011) "New Estimates of Effective Corporate Tax Rates on Business Investment", *Cato Institute Tax & Budget Bulletin*, February, http://www.cato.org/pubs/tbb/tbb_64.pdf (accessed 2 March 2012).

China Daily (2010) "Fleet Nears Somalia", 8 March, http://www.chinadaily.com.cn/china/2010-03/08/content_9552917.htm (accessed 28 March 2010).

Chinn, M. and Frankel, J. (2008) "The Euro May Over the Next 15 Years Surpass the Dollar as Leading International Currency", *The National Bureau of Economic Research*, April.

Chinn, M. and Ito, H. (2008) "Global Current Account Imbalances: American Fiscal Policy versus East Asian Savings", *Review of International Economics*, 16(3), August, 479–498.

Choi, J. (2009) "Measuring Progress Using the Drivers of Prosperity", in: The 3rd OECD World Forum on "Statistics, Knowledge, and Policy", Korea, 27–30 October, http://www.oecd.org/dataoecd/54/36/44098483.pdf (accessed 21 March 2011).

Chomsky, N. (2003) *Hegemony or Survival: America's Quest for Global Dominance.* New York, NY: Henry Holt.

Chua, A. (2007) *Day of Empire: How Hyperpowers Rise to Global Dominance – And Why They Fall.* New York, NY: Doubleday.

CIA (2011a) *CIA World Factbook China*, https://www.cia.gov/library/publications/the-world-factbook/geos/ch.html (accessed 5 January 2012).

CIA (2011b) *CIA World Factbook Russia*, https://www.cia.gov/library/publications/the-world-factbook/geos/rs.html (accessed 5 January 2012).

Cirincione, J. (2010) "A New Non-Proliferation Strategy", *International Conference on Nuclear Technology and Sustainable Development*, Center for Strategic Research of the Expediency Council, 5–6 March.

Clarida, R. (2009) "With Privilege Comes...? Global Perspectives", *Pimco*, October, http://www.pimco.com/EN/Insights/Pages/With%20Privilege%20Comes%20Clarida%20Oct%202009.aspx (accessed 17 February 2012).

Clarke, R. (2009) "War from Cyberspace", *The National Interest Online*, 22 December, http://www.nationalinterest.org/Article.aspx?id=22340 (accessed 17 April 2010).

Cline, W. (2005) *The United States as a Debtor Nation*. Washington, DC: Peterson Institute for International Economics.

Cline, W. (2009) "Long-Term Fiscal Imbalances, US External Liabilities, and Future Living Standards", in Bergsten, F. (ed.), *The Long-Term International Economic Position of the United States*, pp. 11–34. Washington, DC: Peterson Institute for International Economics.

Clinton, H. (2010) *Remarks at Press Availability*, given at National Convention Center at Hanoi, Vietnam, 23 July, http://www.state.gov/secretary/rm/2010/07/145095.htm (accessed 9 March 2012).

Clinton, H. (2011) "America's Pacific Century", *Foreign Policy*, November, http://www.foreignpolicy.com/articles/2011/10/11/americas_pacific_century (accessed 11 January 2012).

CMS Medicare Board of Trustees (2008) "National Health Expenditure Projections 2008-2018", Washington, DC.

CMS Medicare Board of Trustees (2009) "The 2009 Annual Report", Washington, DC, 12 May.

CMS Medicare Board of Trustees (2011a) "The 2011 Annual Report", Washington, DC, 13 May.

CMS Medicare Board of Trustees (2011b) "National Health Expenditure Projections 2009-2019", Washington, DC, September.

CNN (2008) "Nuclear Threat from Terrorists Rising, Ex-Senator Says", 10 September.

CNN Opinion Research (2008) 26–29 June, http://i2.cdn.turner.com/cnn/2008/images/07/01/july1noon.pdf (accessed 14 October 2011).

CNN Transcripts (2011a) "CNN National Security Debate", 22 November, http://archives.cnn.com/TRANSCRIPTS/1111/22/se.04.html (accessed 29 February 2011).

CNN Transcripts (2011b) "Full Transcript CNN Western Republican Debate", 18 October, http://transcripts.cnn.com/TRANSCRIPTS/1110/18/se.05.html (accessed 21 October 2011).

Condon, S. (2011) "Obama: 'We Welcome China's Rise'", *CBS News*, 19 January, http://www.cbsnews.com/8301-503544_162-20028958-503544.html   (accessed 8 October 2011).

Confessore, N. and Kocieniewski, D. (2012) "For Romenys, Friendly Code Reduces Taxes", *The New York Times*, 24 January, http://www.nytimes.com/2012/01/25/us/politics/romneys-tax-returns-show-21-6-million-income-in-10.html   (accessed 4 February 2012).

Congressional Budget Office (2005a) "An Analysis of the US Military's ability to Sustain and Occupation in Iraq: an Update", 5 October, http://www.cbo.gov/ftpdocs/66xx/doc6682/10-05-05-IraqLetter.pdf (accessed 27 March 2011).

Congressional Budget Office (2005b) "Corporate Income Tax Rates: International Comparisons", *CBO Paper*, Washington, DC: Congress of the United States, http://www.cbo.gov/ftpdocs/69xx/doc6902/11-28-CorporateTax.pdf (accessed November 2011).

Congressional Budget Office (2009a) "A Preliminary Analysis of the President's Budget and an Update of CBO's Budget and Economic Outlook", Washington, DC, March.

Congressional Budget Office (2009b) "The Long-Term Budget Outlook", Washington, DC, June.

Congressional Budget Office (2010) "Federal Debt and Interest Costs", 14 December, http://www.cbo.gov/doc.cfm?index=11999 (accessed 31 December 2011).

Congressional Budget Office (2011a) "An Analysis of the President's Budgetary Proposals for the Fiscal Year 2012", Washington, DC, April.

Congressional Budget Office (2011b) "2011 Long-Term Budget Outlook", Washington, DC, June, http://www.cbo.gov/sites/default/files/cbofiles/ftpdocs/122xx/doc12212/06-21-long-term_budget_outlook.pdf (accessed 25 February 2012).

Congressional Budget Office (2011c) "Long-Term Implications of the 2012 Future Years Defense Program", Washington, DC, June.

Congressional Budget Office (2012) "The Budget and Economic Outlook: Fiscal Years 2012 to 2022", Washington, DC, January.

Congressional Research Service (2011) "China's Holdings of US Securities: Implications for the US Economy", 26 September, http://www.fas.org/sgp/crs/row/RL34314.pdf (accessed November 26 2011).

Congressional Research Service (CRS) (2009) "Defense: FY2010 Authorization and Appropriations", 15 July, http://assets.opencrs.com/rpts/R40567_20090715.pdf (accessed 27 March 2011).

Cooper, R. (2005a) "Imperial Liberalism", *The National Interest*, 79, 25–34.

Cooper, R. (2005b) "Living with Global Imbalances: A Contrarian View", *Policy Briefs in International Economics*, Number PB05-3, November, Washington, DC: Institute for International Economics.

Cooper, R. N. (2005) "Whither China?" June, mimeo.

Corden, W. (2011) "Global Imbalances and the Paradox of Thrift", *Policy Insight* No. 54, April, Washington, DC: Center for Economic Policy Research.

Cordesman, A. (2007) *Salvaging American Defense: The Challenge of Strategic Overstretch*. Washington, DC: CSIS Press.

Cordesman, A. (2009) "Is the Afghanistan-Pakistan Conflict Winnable?" *Center for Strategic & International Studies*, 29 April, http://csis.org/print/5292 (accessed 31 July 2009).

Cornwell, S. (2010) "Update 2 – US Congress OKs Sanction on Iran's Energy, Banks", *Reuters*, 24 June, http://www.reuters.com/article/2010/06/24/nuclear-iran-congress-idUSN2414825120100624 (accessed 30 October 2011).

Corsetti, G. and Muller, G. (2005) *Twin Deficits: Squaring Theory, Evidence and Common Sense*, October, Washington, DC: Center for Economic Policy Research.

Cost of War (2011) "Eisenhower Study Group", 21 July, www.costofwar.org (accessed 2011).

Coughlin, C., Pakko, M. and Poole, W. (2006) "How Dangerous Is the US Current Account Deficit?", *The Regional Economist*, St. Louis, MO: Federal Reserve Bank of St. Louis.

Coulson, A. (2005) "A Fair Comparison: US Students Lag in Math and Science", *Education Report*, 11 April, http://www.educationreport.org/pubs/mer/article.aspx?id=7036 (accessed 28 March 2011).

Council on Foreign Relations (2007) "US Capital Markets' Competitiveness: Challenges and Choices" (transcript), *McKinsey Executive Roundtable Series on International Economics*, 15 May, New York, NY, http://www.cfr.org/economics/us-capital-markets-competitiveness-challenges-choices-rush-transcript-federal-news-service/p13340 (accessed 20 March 2011).

Council on Foreign Relations (2009) "US Immigration Policy Independent Task Force Report", 8 July, http://www.cfr.org/publication/19743/broken_immigration_system_risks_serious_damage_to_us_national_interests_warns_cfr_task_force.html (accessed 5 November 2009).

Council on Foreign Relations (2011a), "Education and US Competitiveness" (transcript), *CFR Expert Roundtable*, 21 November, New York, NY, http://www.cfr.org/united-states/education-us-competitiveness/p26559 (accessed 2 March 2012).

Council on Foreign Relations (2011b) "Education Reform and US Competitiveness" (transcript), *CFR Expert Roundtable*, 12 September, New York, NY, http://www.cfr.org/education/education-reform-us-competitiveness/p25816 (accessed 2 March 2012).

Council on Foreign Relations (2011c) "US Trade and Investment Policy", *Task Force Report*, September, New York, NY, http://www.cfr.org/trade/us-trade-investment-policy/p25737 (accessed 2 March 2012).

Cowen, T. (2011) *The Great Stagnation: How America Ate All the Low-Hanging Fruit of Modern History, Got Sick, and Will (Eventually) Feel Better*. New York, NY: Penguin Group.

Cox, M. (2001a) "Whatever Happened to American Decline? International Relations and the New United States Hegemony", *New Political Economy*, 6(3), 311–340.

Cox, M. (2001b) "The New Liberal Empire: US Power in the Twenty-First Century", *Irish Studies in International Affairs*, 12, 39–56.

Cox, M. (2001c) "Introduction", in Cox, M., Dunne, T. and Booth, K. (eds.), *Empires, System and States: Great Transformations in International Politics*, pp. 1–16. Cambridge: Cambridge University Press.

Cox, M. (2007) "Is the United States in Decline – Again? An Essay", *International Affairs*, 83(4), 643–653.

Cox, M., Ikenberry, J. and Mann, M. (2004) "An Exchange on American Empire", *Review of International Studies*, 30(4), October, 583–653.

Coyle, P. and Samson, V. (2009) "The Proliferation Security Initiative: Background, History, and Prospects for the Future", *Center for Defense Information*, 9 May.

Crincione, J. (2007) *Bomb Scare: The History and Future of Nuclear Weapons*. New York, NY: Columbia University Press.

Crook, C. (2011) "Washington Is Drowning America", *Financial Times*, 24 July, p. 9.

Curcuru, S., Dvorak, T. and Warnock, F. (2007) "The Stability of Large External Imbalances: The Role of Returns Differentials", *International Finance Discussion Paper* 894 (April), Washington, DC: Federal Reserve Board of Governors.

David, P. (2003) *Zvi Griliches on Diffusion, Lags and Productivity Growth ... Connecting the Dots*, 17 October, Paris, France: CarrJ des Sciences, Ministère de la Recherche, http://www-siepr.stanford.edu/papers/pdf/02-45.pdf (accessed 29 March 2011).

Davis, S. J., et al. (2006) "War in Iraq versus Containment", NBER Working Paper No. 12092, March.

De Jonquieres, G. (2006a) "The Critical Skills Gap", *Financial Times*, 12 June.

De Jonquieres, G. (2006b) "To Innovate, China Needs More Than Standards", *Financial Times*, 13 July.

De Santis, H. (2005) "The Dragon and the Tigers: China and Asian Regionalism", *World Policy Journal*, Summer, 23–36.

De Santis, H. (2012) "The China Threat and the "Pivot" to Asia." *Current History*, 111(746), 209–215.

Dean, M. K. (2007) "ASEAN+3 or ASEAN+6: Which Way Forward?" *WTO-HEI*, 10 September, http://www.wto.org/english/tratop_e/region_e/con_sep07_e/kawai_wignaraja_e.pdf (accessed 20 April 2012).

DeLong, B. (2010) "Radio Discussion with Tom Keene February 4", *Blooomberg Surveillance*, 4 February, http://www.bloomberg.com/podcasts/surveillance/ (accessed 29 March 2012).

DeParle, Jason (2012) "Harder for Americans to Rise from Lower Rungs", *The New York Times*, 4 January.

Department of Defense (2010) "Nuclear Posture Review Report", April, http://www.defense.gov/npr/docs/2010%20nuclear%20posture%20review%20report.pdf (accessed 9 March 2012).

Department of Defense (2011) "Department of Defense Strategy for Operating in Cyberspace", http://www.defense.gov/news/d20110714cyber.pdf (accessed 1 February 2012).

Department of Foreign Affairs and Trade (2010) "Australia Imposes New Broad-Ranging Sanctions against Iran", Australia, 29 July.

DeVol, R., Klowden, K. and Bedroussian, A. (2009) *North America's High-Tech Economy: The Geography of Knowledge-Based Industries*. Santa Monica, CA: Milken Institute.

Dew-Becker, I. and Gordon, R. (2006) "The Slowdown in European Productivity Growth: A Tale of Tigers, Tortoises and Textbook Labor Economics", in: National Bureau of Economics Research, NBER Macroeconomic and Productivity Workshop, Cambridge, MA, 20 July 2006, http://facultyweb.at.northwestern.edu/economics/gordon/nber_SI_percapita_060803.pdf (accessed 4 March 2011).

Dew-Becker, I. and Gordon, R. (2008) "Europe's Employment Growth Revived After 1995 while Productivity Growth Slowed: Is It Coincidence?" 15 April, http://www.voxeu.org/index.php?q=node/1058 (accessed 4 March 2012).

Dillon, S. (2010) "Many Nations Passing US in Education, Expert Says", *The New York Times*, 10 March, Section A, p. 21.

Dinan, S. (2011) "Obama to Deport Illegals by 'Priority'", *The Washington Times*, 18 August, http://www.washingtontimes.com/news/2011/aug/18/new-dhs-rules-cancel-deportations/?page=all (accessed 21 October 2011).

Dobson, W. (2009) "Why the Shift of Economic Gravity to Asia Is Not a Power Shift", *The Globalist*, 21 October.

Dollar, D. (2007) "Asian Century or Multi-Polar Century?" World Bank Policy Research Working Paper 4174, March.

Dombey, D. (2007) "Director General's Interview on Iran and DPRK", *Financial Times*, 19 February.

Dominguez, K. (2009) *International Reserves and Underdeveloped Capital Markets* (pdf). Cambridge: National Bureau of Economics Research, http://www.nber.org/public_html/confer/2009/ISOM09/Dominguez.pdf (accessed 18 February 2012).

Doms, M. (2005) "IT Investment: Will the Glory Days Ever Return?" in *Federal Reserve Bank of San Francisco Economic Letter*, Number 2005-13, 17 June 2005, pp. 1–3, San Francisco, CA: FRDSF.

Dooley, M. and Garber, P. (2009) "Global Imbalances and the Crisis: A Solution in Search of a Problem", *VOX*, 21 March, http://www.voxeu.org/index.php?q=node/3314 (accessed 18 February 2012).

Dooley, M., Folkerts-Landau, D. and Garber, P. (2003). "An Essay on the Revived Bretton Woods System", Working Paper No. 9971, September, Cambridge: National Bureau of Economics Research.

Dooley, M., Folkerts-Landau, D. and Garber, P. (2004) "Direct Investment, Rising Real Wages and the Absorption of Excess Labor in the Periphery", NBER Working Paper No. 10626, July, Cambridge: National Bureau of Economics Research.

Dooley, M., Folkerts-Landau, D. and Garber, P. (2005) "Savings Gluts and Interest Rates: The Missing Link to Europe", NBER Working Paper No. 11520, July, Cambridge: National Bureau of Economics Research.

Doyle, M. (1986) *Empires*. Ithaca, NY: Cornell University Press.

Drezner, D. W. (2009). "Bad Debts: Assessing China's Financial Influence in Great Power Politics", *International Security*, 34(2), Fall, 7–45.

Dudley, W. (2010) *Speech on the US Financial System: Where We Have Been, Where We Are and Where We Need to Go*, 8 February, given at the Reserve Bank of Australia's 50th Anniversary Symposium, Sydney, Australia.

Duhigg, C. and Bradsher, K. (2012) "How the US Lost Out on iPhone Work", *The New York Times*, 21 January, http://www.nytimes.com/2012/01/22/business/apple-america-and-a-squeezed-middle-class.html?_r=2&pagewanted=1&hp (accessed 27 January 2012).

Dulton, S. (2011) "Polls Show Longtime Support for Tax Hikes on Rich", *CBSNEWS*, 12 October, http://www.cbsnews.com/8301-503544_162-20119267-503544.html (accessed 12 November 2011).

Dunaway, S. (2009) "Global Imbalances and the Financial Crisis", *Council Special Report No.44*, March, New York, NY: Council on Foreign Relations, http://www.cfr.org/economics/global-imbalances-financial-crisis/p18690 (accessed 3 March 2012).

Easterly, W. (2002) *The Elusive Quest for Growth: Economists' Adventures and Misadventures in the Topics*. Cambridge, MA: MIT Press.

Economy, E. C. (2007) "The Great Leap Backward?" *Foreign Affairs*, 7 September.

Edwards, S. (2005) "The End of Large Current Account Deficits", NBER Working Paper 11669, September, Cambridge: National Bureau of Economics Research, http://www.nber.org/papers/w11669.pdf?new_window=1 (accessed 18 February 2012).

Eichengreen, B. (2005a) "Sterling's Past, Dollar's Future: Historical Perspectives on Reserve Currency Competition", NBER Working Paper No. 1136, Cambridge, MA: National Bureau of Economic Research.

Eichengreen, B. (2005b) "Global Imbalances and the Lessons of Bretton Woods", *FRBSF Economic Letter 2005-32*, 25 November, San Francisco, CA: Federal Reserve Bank of San Francisco.

Eichengreen, B. (2006) *Global Imbalances and the Lessons of Bretton Woods*. Cambridge, MA: The MIT Press.

Eichengreen, B. (2011) *Exorbitant Privilege*. New York, NY: Oxford University Press.

Eichengreen, B. (2011). *Exorbitant Privilege: The Rise and Fall of the Dollar and the Future of the International Monetary System*. Oxford: Oxford University Press.

Eichengreen, B., Park, D. and Shin, K. (2011) "When Fast Growing Economies Slow Down: International Evidence and Implications for China", NBER Working Paper, March.

Eland, I. (2004) *The Empire Has No Clothes: US Foreign Policy Exposed*. Oakland, CA: The Independent Institute.

El-Erian, M. (2008) *When Markets Collide: Investment Strategies for the Age of Global Economic Change*. New York, NY: McGraw Hill.

El-Erian, M. (2009) "A New Normal", *Economic Outlook*, May, http://www.pimco.com/EN/Insights/Pages/Secular%20Outlook%20May%202009%20El-Erian.aspx (accessed 24 March 2011).

Engel, C. (2009) "Exchange Rate Policies", Federal Research Bank of Dallas Staff Papers No. 8, November, Dallas, TX: Federal Research Bank of Dallas.

Enright, M. (2005) "China and Its Neighbours 2005", *Asia Case Research Centre*, The University of Hong Kong.

Erceg, C., Guerrieri, L. and Gust, C. (2005) "Expansionary Fiscal Shocks and the Trade Deficit", International Finance Discussion Paper 2005-825, January, Washington, DC: Board of Governors of the Federal Reserve System.

Erdbrink, T. (2010) "Cleric calls on Iran to take U.S.-led sanctions seriously", *The Washington Post*, 14 September, http://www.washingtonpost.com/wp-dyn/content/article/2010/09/14/AR2010091403790.html (accessed 6 September 2012).

Etzioni, A. (2011). "Lessons of America's 'Decline' ", *International Journal of Contemporary Sociology*, 48(2), October, 173–187.

European Nuclear Society (2012) "Nuclear Power Plants, World-Wide", 2 February, http://www.euronuclear.org/info/encyclopedia/n/nuclear-power-plant-world-wide.htm (accessed 8 March 2012).

Faiola, A. (2009) "China Worried About US Debt: Biggest Creditor Nations Demand a Guarantee", *The Washington Post*, 14 March.

Fallows, J. (2010) "How America Can Rise Again", *The Atlantic*, January/February, http://www.jmhinternational.com/news/news/selectednews/files/2010/01/201002 01_20100101_Atlantic_HowAmericaCanRiseAgain.pdf (accessed 9 March 2011).

Fan, C. C. (2005) "Modeling Interprovincial Migration in China, 1985–2000", *Eurasian Geography and Economics*, 46(3), 165–184.

Farrell, D. and Grant, A. (2005) "Addressing China's Looming Talent Shortage", October. Chicago: McKinsey & Company, http://www.mckinsey.com/Insights/MGI/Research/Labor_Markets/Addressing_chinas_looming_talent_shortage (accessed 3 March 2012).

Fatás, A. and Mihov, I. (2009) *The 4 I's of Economic Growth*, INSEAD Business School for the World, http://faculty.insead.edu/fatas/wall/wall.pdf (accessed 20 March 2011).

Federal Insurance Deposit Insurance Corporation (FDIC) (2011) *Failed Bank List*. Washington, DC: FDIC, http://www.fdic.gov/bank/individual/failed/banklist.html (accessed 4 March 2011).

Federal Open Market Committee (2009) "Minutes of the Federal Open Market Committee", 11–12 August, http://federalreserve.gov/monetarypolicy/fomcminutes 20090812.htm (accessed 1 March 2011).

Federal Reserve (2011) "Credit and Liquidity Programs and the Balance Sheet", 6 July.

Federal Reserve Bank of San Francisco (FRBSF) (2009) "The Outlook of Productivity Growth: Symposium Summary", *FRBSF Economic Letter*, San Francisco, CA: FRBSF, http://www.frbsf.org/publications/economics/letter/2009/el2009-11.html (accessed 18 October).

Fehr, H., Jokisch, S. and Kotlikoff, L. J. (2005) "Will China Eat Our Lunch or Take Us to Dinner? – Simulating the Transition Paths of the US, EU, Japan and China". The Institute for Economic Development Working Papers Series dp-151. Department of Economics, Boston University.

Feickert, A. and Chanlett-Avery, E. (2011) "Japan 2011 Earthquake: Department of Defense Response", 22 March, Washington, DC: Congressional Research Service, http://fpc.state.gov/documents/organization/159781.pdf (accessed 14 January 2012).

Feldstein, M. (2005) "Monetary Policy in a Changing International Environment: The Role of Global Capital Flows", Working Paper 11856, December, Cambridge: National Bureau of Economic Research, http://www.nber.org/papers/w11856.pdf?new_window=1 (accessed 18 February 2012).

Feldstein, M. (2010) "Missing the Target", *The Wall Street Journal*, 20 January.

Feldstein, M. and Horioka, C. (1980) "Domestic Savings and International Capital Flows", *Economic Journal*, 90(358), 314–329.

Feng, W. (2010) "China's Population Density: The Looming Crisis", *Current History*, September.

Fenton, W. (2011) "Cisco Pushes for Lower Corporate Tax Rates", *PCmag.com*, 28 March, http://www.pcmag.com/article2/0,2817,2382703,00.asp (accessed 10 March 2012).

Ferguson, N. (2004a) "A World without Power", *Foreign Policy*, July/August, http://www.foreignpolicy.com/articles/2004/07/01/a_world_without_power (accessed 29 January 2012).

Ferguson, N. (2004b) *Colossus: The Price of America's Empire*. New York, NY: The Penguin Press.

Ferguson, N. (2006) "Reasons to Worry", *The New York Times Magazine*, 11 June, http://www.nytimes.com/2006/06/11/magazine/11national.html (accessed 18 February 1012).

Ferguson, N. (2008a) "From Empire to Chimerica", Chapter 6, in *The Ascent of Money: A Financial History of the World*, pp. 283–340. New York, NY: The Penguin Group.

Ferguson, N. (2008b) *The Ascent of Money: A Financial History of the World*. New York, NY: Penguin Press.

Ferguson, N. (2010) "A Greek Crisis Is Coming to America", *Financial Times*, 10 February.

Ferguson, N. and Kotlikoff, L. (2003a) "Going Critical: American Power and the Consequences of Fiscal Overstretch", *The National Interest*, 73, Fall 2003, 22–32.

Ferguson, R. (2005) "US Current Account Deficit: Causes and Consequences", in: Speech at The Economics Club of University of North Carolina, Chapel Hill, NC, 20 April, http://www.bis.org/review/r050422b.pdf (accessed 18 February 2012).

Fildes, J. (2010) "Stuxnet Worm 'Targeted High-Value IRANIAN Assets' ", 23 September, http://www.bbc.co.uk/news/technology-11388018 (accessed 5 February 2011).

Finn, M. (2010) *Stay Rates of Foreign Doctorate Recipients from US Universities-2007*. Oak Ridge, TN: Oak Ridge Institute for Science and Education, http://orise.orau.gov/files/sep/stay-rates-foreign-doctorate-recipients-2007.pdf (accessed 2 March 2012).

Fish, I. S. (2010) "Kim a Pit Bull for China", *Newsweek*, 22 November.

Fisher, M. (2012) "The Dangerously Unpredictable Foreign Policy of Newt Gingrich", 20 January, http://www.theatlantic.com/international/archive/2012/01/the-dangerously-unpredictable-foreign-policy-of-newt-gingrich/251734/ (accessed 23 February 2012).

Fishman, T. C. (2005) *China, Inc.: How the Rise of the Next Superpower Challenges America and the World*. New York, NY: Scribner.

Foot, R., MacFarlane, N. and M. Mastanduno (2003) "Introduction", in Foot, R., MacFarlane, N. and Mastanduno, M. (eds.), *US Hegemony and International Organizations*, pp. 1–24. Oxford, NY: Oxford University Press.

Forbes, K. (2008) "Why Do Foreigners Invest in the United States?" NBER Working Paper 13908, Cambridge, MA: National Bureau of Economics Research, http://www.nber.org/papers/w13908 (accessed 19 February 2012).

Frankel, J. (1997) *Regional Trading Blocs in the World Economic System*. Washington, DC: Institute for International Economics.

Fratianni, M. (2008) "Resurrecting Keynes to Stabilize the International Monetary System", MoFiR Working Paper No. 1, October, Rome, Italy: Money and Finance Research Group, http://dea2.univpm.it/quaderni/pdfmofir/Mofir001.pdf (accessed 10 February 2012).

Freeman, R. (2005a) "Does Globalization of the Scientific/Engineering Workforce Threaten US Economic Leadership", National Bureau of Economic Research, Inc Series of Working Papers No. 11457. Cambridge, MA: National Bureau of Economic Research.

Freeman, R. (2005b) "What Really Ails Europe (and America): The Doubling of the Global Workforce", *The Globalist*, 3 June.

Friedan, J. (2006) *Global Capitalism: Its Fall and Rise in the Twentieth Century*. New York, NY: W. W. Norton & Company.

Friedberg, A. (2009) "Same Old Songs: What the Declinists (and Triumphalists) Miss", *The American Interest*, 5(2), 28–35.

Friedberg, A. L. (2011) *A Contest for Supremacy: China, America, and the Struggle for Mastery in Asia*. New York, NY: W. W. Norton & Company.

Friedman, B. (2005) "Deficits and Debt in the Short and Long Run", NBER Working Paper 11630, September, Cambridge, MA: National Bureau of Economic Research.

Friedman, G. (2010) *The Next 100 Years: A Forecast for the 21st Century*. New York, NY: Anchor Books.

Friedman, T. (2005) *The World Is Flat*. New York, NY: Farrar, Straus and Giroux.

Friedman, T. (2008) *Hot, Flat, and Crowded*. New York, NY: Farrar, Straus and Giroux.

Friedman, T. L. (1999) *The Lexus and the Olive Tree*. New York, NY: Farrar, Straus and Giroux.

Fukuyama, F. (2004) "Nation-Building 101", *The Atlantic*, January/February, http://www.theatlantic.com/magazine/archive/2004/01/nation-building-101/2862/ (accessed 18 April 2011).

Gabriel, T. (2011) "At Rallies, 2 Candidates Deliver Blistering Attacks on Illegal Immigration", *The New York Times*, 15 October, http://www.nytimes.com/2011/10/16/us/politics/bachmann-and-cain-deliver-blistering-attacks-on-illegal-immigration.html?_r=2 (accessed 12 November 2011).

Galbraith, P. (2006) "The Mess", *The New York Review of Books*, 53(4), http://www.nybooks.com/articles/18771 (accessed 16 April 2011).

Gale, W. G. and Steuerle, C. E. (2005) "Tax Policy Solutions: Restoring Fiscal Sanity 2005: Meeting the Long-Run Challenge", *The Brookings Institution*, Ch. 5, 13 April.

Gallup Polls (2011a) "Presidential Approval Ratings – Barack Obama", http://www.gallup.com/poll/116479/barack-obama-presidential-job-approval.aspx (accessed 30 November 2011).

Gallup Polls (2011b) "United Nation", 2–5 February, http://www.gallup.com/poll/116347/united-nations.aspx (accessed 14 October 2011).

Ganguly, S. (2006) "Will Kashmir Stop India's Rise?" *Foreign Affairs*, July/August.

Gapper, J. (2012) "Innovation drives America's reinvention", *Financial Times*, 3 October, http://www.ft.com/cms/s/0/615af5a4-0c9b-11e2-a776-00144feabdc0.html#axzz2AKFHCHrd (accessed 18 October 2012).

Garber, K. (2009) "America's New Energy Dependency: China's Metals", *US News*, 1 July, http://www.usnews.com/articles/news/national/2009/07/01/americas-new-energy-dependency-chinas-metals.html (accessed 20 October 2011).

Garten, J. (1995) "Is American Abandoning Multilateral Trade?" *Foreign Affairs*, 47(6), November/December, 50–62.

Garten, J. (2005) "Battle of the Asian Summits", *Newsweek*, 20 November, http://www.newsweek.com/id/51236 (accessed 3 July 2009).

Gates, R. (2009) "A Balanced Strategy: Reprogramming the Pentagon for a New Age", *Foreign Affairs*, 88(1), 28–41.

Gates, Robert (2011) *Speech on the Future of NATO*, given at Security Defense Agenda, 10 June, Brussels, Belgium, http://www.defense.gov/speeches/speech.aspx?speechid=1581 (accessed 29 February 2012).

Gavin, F. (2009) "Same As It Ever Was", *International Security*, Winter, 34(3), 7–37.

Gelb, L. H. (2009) *Power Rules: How Common Sense Can Rescue American Foreign Policy*. New York, NY: HarperCollins.

Gentry, W. (2007) "A Review of the Evidence on the Incidence of the Corporate Income Tax", *OTA Paper 101*, December, Washington, DC: Office of Tax Policy Department of Treasury, http://www.treasury.gov/resource-center/tax-policy/tax-analysis/Documents/ota101.pdf (accessed 3 March 2012).

Gereffi, G. and Wadhwa, V. (2005) *Framing the Engineering Outsourcing Debate: Placing the United States on a Level Playing Field with China and India*, December, Duke University: Master of Engineering Management Program, http://www.soc.duke.edu/resources/public_sociology/duke_outsourcing.pdf (accessed 3 March 2012).

Gerrity, M. (2011) "Asia Pacific Markets Dominate Global Commercial Capital Flows in 3Q", 1 December, *World Property Channel*, http://www.worldpropertychannel.com/international-markets/commercial-real-estate/euro-zone-debt-crisis-jones-lang-lasalle-jll-global-capital-flows-report-hong-kong-real-estate-investment-tokyo-real-estate-report-shanghai-property-trends-sydney-commercial-real-estate-5042.php (accessed 19 January 2012).

Gertz, B. (2010) "Chinese See US Debt as a Weapon in Taiwan Dispute", *The Washington Times*, 10 February, http://www.washingtontimes.com/news/2010/feb/10/chinese-see-us-debt-as-weapon/?page=all (accessed 26 November 2011).

Gilpin, R. (1981) *War and Change in World Politics*. Cambridge: Cambridge University Press.

Girma, S., et al. (2009) "Can Production Subsidies Explain China's Export Performance? Evidence from Firm-level Data", *Scandinavian Journal of Economics*, 111(4), 863–891.

Gjelten, T. (2010a) "Chinese Attacks on Google Seen as Cybertheft", *National Public Radio*, 10 January, http://www.npr.org/templates/story/story.php?storyId=122703950 (accessed 10 April 2010).

Gjelten, T. (2010b) "Cyber Insecurity: US Struggles to Combat the Threat", *National Public Radio*, 6 April, http://www.npr.org/templates/story/story.php?storyId=125578576 (accessed 16 April 2010).

Gjelten, T. (2010c) "Cyberattack: US Unready for Future Face of War", *National Public Radio*, 7 April, http://www.npr.org/templates/story/story.php?storyId=125598665 (accessed 17 April 2010).

Goldberg, L. (2011) "The International Role of the Dollar: Does It Matter If This Changes?" *Federal Reserve Bank of New York Staff Reports*, October, New York, NY: NYFRB.

Goldin, C. and Katz, L. (2008) *The Race Between Education and Technology*. Cambridge: Harvard University Press.

Goldstein, M. and Lardy, N. (2005) "China's Role in the Revived Bretton Woods System: A Case of Mistaken Identity", IIE Working Paper No. WP 05-2, Washington, DC: International Institute of Economics.

Goldstein, M. and Lardy, N. (2006) "China's Exchange Rate Policy Dilemma", *American Economic Review*, 96(2), 422–426.

Goldstein, M. and Lardy, N. (2008) *Debating China's Exchange Rate Policy*. Washington, DC: Peter G. Peterson Institute.

Goldstein, M. and Lardy, N. (2009) *The Future of China's Exchange Rate Policy*. Washington, DC: Peter G. Peterson Institute.

Gordon, B. (2011) "The Trans-Pacific Partnership and the Rise of China", *Foreign Affairs*, 7 November, http://www.foreignaffairs.com/articles/136647/bernard-k-gordon/the-trans-pacific-partnership-and-the-rise-of-china# (accessed 9 March 2012).

Gordon, R. J. (2010) "Revisiting US Productivity Growth over the Past Century with a View of the Future", *National Bureau of Economic Research*, March, http://www.nber.org/papers/w15834 (accessed 3 March 2012).

Gorman, S. and Barnes, J. (2011) "Cyber Combat: Act of War", *The Wall Street Journal*, 31 May.

Gourinchas, P. and Rey, H. (2005) "From World Bank to World Venture Capitalist: US External Adjustment and the Exorbitant Privilege", in Clarida, R. (ed.), NBER Conference on G7 Current Account Imbalances: Sustainability and Adjustment, Newport, RI, 1–2 June 2005. Chicago: University of Chicago Press, Chicago.

Grady, R. (2007) *Is US Losing Its Standing as the World's Financial Superpower?* Remarks at Milken Institute Global Conference, Los Angeles, CA, 23 April, Sant Monica, CA: Milken Institute, http://www.milkeninstitute.org/events/gcprogram.taf?function=detail&eventid=GC07&EvID=839 (accessed 15 March 2011).

Gravelle, T. (2010) "What Makes 700 Million Adults Want to Migrate?" *Gallup Survey*, 18 February, http://www.gallup.com/poll/126065/Makes-700-Million-Adults-Migrate.aspx (accessed 1 February 2012).

Greenhalg, S. (2003) "Science, Modernity and the Making of China's One-Child Policy", *Population and Development Review*, 29(2), June, 163–196.

Greenspan, A. (2003) *Speech on Current Account*, given at the 21st Annual Monetary Policy Conference, 20 November, Cato Institute, Washington, DC, http://www.federalreserve.gov/boarddocs/speeches/2003/20031120/default.htm (accessed 19 February 2012).

Greenspan, A. (2005) *Remarks on International Imbalances*, given at the Advancing Enterprise Conference, London, England, 2 December, http://www.federalreserve.gov/boarddocs/speeches/2005/200512022/default.htm (accessed 2011).

Grim, R. (2008) "Weiner Bill Looks Out for Models", *Politico*, 11 June, http://www.politico.com/news/stories/0608/10997.html (accessed 30 March 2011).

Gros, D. (2009) "Global Imbalances and the Accumulation of Risk", *VOX*, 11 June, www.voxeu.org (accessed 2011).

Gross, B. (2010) "Privates Eye", *Pimco Investment Outlook*, August.

Gruber, J. and Kamin, S. (2005) "Explaining the Global Pattern of Current Account Imbalances", *FRB Discussion Paper* No. 846, 26 November, Washington, DC: Federal Reserve Board.

Gruenwald, P. and Hori, M. (2008) "Intra-regional Trade Key to Asia's Export Boom", *IMF Survey Magazine*, 6 February, http://www.imf.org/external/pubs/ft/survey/so/2008/CAR02608A.htm (accessed 26 February 2009).

Grunwald, M. (2009) "Obama's Budget: Earmarks Aren't the Real Problem", *Time*, 5 March.

Guardian.co.uk (2009) "China Launches Green Power Revolution to Catch up on West", 10 June.

Guidolin, M. and Jeunesse, E. (2007) "The Decline in the US Personal Saving Rate: Is It Real and Is It a Puzzle", Federal Reserve Bank of St. Louis *Review*, November/December 2007.

Gupta, A. and Wang, H. (2011) "Chinese Innovation Is a Paper Tiger", *The Wall Street Journal*, 28 July, http://online.wsj.com/article/SB10001424053111904800304576472034085730262.html (accessed 3 March 2012).

Gupta, V. and Radhika, N. (2005) *Global Supply Chain Management – Best Practices at Li & Fung Limited*. Hyderabad, India: ICMR Center for Management Research.

Haas, M. (2007) "A Geriatric Peace? The Future of U.S. Power in a World of Aging Populations", *International Security*, 32(1), Summer, 112–147.

Haas, M. L. (2007) "A Geriatric Peace? The Future of US Power in a World of Ageing Populations", *International Security*, 32(1), Summer.

Haas, R. (2008) "The Age of Nonpolarity: What Will Follow US Dominance?" *Foreign Affairs*, May/June.

Haass, R. (1997) *The Reluctant Sheriff: The United States After the Cold War*. New York, NY: Council on Foreign Relations.

Haass, R. (2008) "The Age of Nonpolarity: What Will Follow US Dominance", *Foreign Affairs*, May/June, 44–56.

Haass, R. (2010) "We're Not Winning. It's Not Worth It", *Newsweek*, 18 July.

Hacker, J. S. (2006) *The Great Risk Shift: The Assault on American Jobs, Families, Health Care, and Retirement and How You Can Fight Back*. New York, NY: Oxford University Press.

Haghshenass, F. (2006) "Iran's Doctrine of Asymmetric Naval Warfare", *The Washington Institute for Near East Strategy Policy Report*, 21 December, http://www.washingtoninstitute.org/templateC05.php?CID=2548 (accessed 27 April 2012).

Hamm, Steve (2009) "Big Blue's Global Lab", *Bloomburg Business Week*, 27 August, http://www.businessweek.com/magazine/content/09_36/b4145040683083.htm (accessed 15 March 2011).

Hansen, C. (1995) *Swords of Armageddon: US Nuclear Weapons Development since 1945*. Sunnyvale, CA: Chukelea Publications.

Hanushek, E. and Wossman, L. (2007) "The Role of Education Quality in Economic Growth", World Bank Policy Research Working Paper 4122, February, Washington, DC: World Bank, http://www-wds.worldbank.org/external/default/WDSContentServer/IW3P/IB/2007/01/29/000016406_20070129113447/Rendered/PDF/wps4122.pdf (accessed 3 March 2012).

Harlan, C. (2011) "Japan will Take Part in Trade Talks, PM Noda Says", *The Washington Post*, 11 November.

Harris Interactive Polls (2011) "When and Why Should the United States Intervene Militarily", 20 April, http://www.harrisinteractive.com/NewsRoom/HarrisPolls/

tabid/447/ctl/ReadCustom%20Default/mid/1508/ArticleId/759/Default.aspx (accessed 21 October 2011).

Hausmann, R. and Sturzenegger, F. (2005) "Dark Matter Makes the US Deficit Disappear", *Financial Times*, 8 December, p. A15.

Hausmann, R. and Sturzenegger, F. (2006) "U.S. and Global Imbalances: Can Dark Matter Prevent a Big Bang?" Working Paper, November, Cambridge: Kennedy School of Government, Harvard University.

He, Z. (2000) "Corruption and Anti-corruption in Reform China", *Communist and Post-Communist Studies*, 33(2), June, 243–270.

Henning, R. (2009) "The Future of the Chiang Mai Initiative: An Asian Monetary Fund", Policy Brief, Number PB09-5, February, Washington, DC: Peterson Institute of International Economics, http://www.iie.com/publications/pb/pb09-5.pdf (accessed 23 July 2009).

Herberg, M. (2006) "Dire Strait? Energy Security in the Strait of Malacca", Wilson Center. Asia Program Event, 14 November, http://www.wilsoncenter.org/ondemand/index.cfm?fuseaction=home.play&mediaid=7FA82ECB-A160-C2DD-B4BFE5E80B12F128 (accessed 28 March 2010).

Herszenhorn, D. M. (2009) "Obama's Farm Subsidy Cuts Meet Stiff Resistance", *The New York Times*, 3 April.

Higgins, M. and Klitgaard, T. (2005) "Financial Globalization and the US Current Account Deficit", *Current Issues in Economics and Finance*, 13(11), December, Federal Reserve Bank of New York.

Hoffman, Robert (2009) "Comment Oracle Corporation", *Marketplace* podcast, 1 April 2009, minute 12.

Holtz-Eakin, D. (2007) "Equity in the Tax Code", Peterson Institute for International Economics, Washington, DC, 6 September.

Homeland Security Newswire (2011) Businesses Cannot Defend Against Cyber Attacks, Expert Says, 21 March, http://homelandsecuritynewswire.com/businesses-cannot-defend-against-cyber-attacks-expert-says (accessed 29 March 2011).

Horn, H. (2010) "Britain Drastically Cuts Defense Spending", *The Atlantic Wire*, http://www.theatlanticwire.com/global/2010/10/britain-drastically-cuts-defense-spending/22610/ (accessed 20 October 2010).

Hoyos, C. (2009) "Burning Ambition", *Financial Times*, 4 November.

Hubbard, G. and Thornton, J. (2006) *Action Plan for Capital Markets*. Cambridge, MA: Committee on Capital Markets Regulation, http://www.capmktsreg.org/pdfs/ActionPlan.pdf (accessed 24 March 2011).

Hubbard, G. R. and Navarro, P. (2010) *Seeds of Destruction: Why the Path to Economic Ruin Runs Through Washington, and How to Reclaim American Prosperity*. Upper Saddle River, NJ: FT Press.

Hudson Institute (2011) "Index of Global Philanthropy and Remittances 2011", http://www.hudson.org/files/documents/2011%20Index%20of%20Global%20Philanthropy%20and%20Remittances%20downloadable%20version.pdf (accessed 11 March 2012).

Hudson Institute (2012) "The 2012 Index of Global Philanthropy and Remittances", http://www.hudson.org/files/publications/2012IndexofGlobalPhilanthropyand Remittances.pdf (accessed 6 September 2012).

Hufbauer, G. and Grieco, P. (2005a) "The Payoff from Globalization", *The Washington Post*, 7 June, http://www.washingtonpost.com/wp-dyn/content/article/2005/06/06/AR2005060601508.html (accessed 2 September 2011).

Hufbauer, G. and Grieco, P. (2005b) *Reforming the US Corporate Tax*. Washington, DC: Peterson Institute for International Economics.

Hufbauer, G. (2012a) "Why Taxing companies to discourage outsourcing", *Peterson Perspectives: Interviews on Current Issues*, 25 January, http://www.iie.com/publications/interviews/interview.cfm?ResearchID=2032 (accessed 18 October 2012).

Hufbauer, G. (2012b) "Sanctions Are Finally Hitting Iran Hard: Part I", *Peterson Perspectives: Interviews on Current Issues*, 3 October, http://www.iie.com/publications/interviews/interview.cfm?ResearchID=2231 (accessed 18 October 2012).

Hufbauer, G. (2012c) "Sanctions Are Finally Hitting Iran Hard: Part II", *Peterson Perspectives: Interviews on Current Issues*, 4 October, http://www.iie.com/publications/interviews/interview.cfm?ResearchID=2233 (accessed 18 October 2012).

Hummels, D., Ishii, J. and Yi, K. (2001) "The Nature and Growth of Vertical Specialization in World Trade", *Journal of International Economics*, 54, 75–96.

Huntington, S. (1988). "The U.S.: Decline or Renewal?", *Foreign Affairs*, 67(2), Winter, 76–96.

Huntington, S. (1999) "The Lonely Superpower", *Foreign Affairs*, 78(2), April, 35–49.

Huntington, S. (2008a) "The US: Decline or Renewal?" *Foreign Affairs*, 6(2), 76–96.

Huntington, Samuel P. (2008b) "The U.S. – Decline or Renewal?" *Foreign Affairs*, 67(2), Winter.

Huntley, W. (2007) "US Policy Toward North Korea in Strategic Context: Tempting Goliath's Fate", *Asian Survey*, 47(3), 455–480.

Ikenberry, G. (2010) "A Crisis of Global Governance?" *Current History*, 109(730), November, 315.

Ikenberry, J. (2003) "State Power and the Institutional Bargain: America's Ambivalent Economic and Security Multilateralism", in Foot, R., MacFarlane, S. and Mastanduno, M. (eds.), *US Hegemony and International Organizations*, pp. 49–72. Oxford, NY: Oxford University Press.

Ikenberry, J. (2010) "Governing the Globe: A Crisis of Global Governance?" *Current History*, 109(730), 315.

Ikenberry, J. (2011) "The Future of the Liberal World Order", *Foreign Affairs*, May/June, http://www.foreignaffairs.com/articles/67730/g-john-ikenberry/the-future-of-the-liberal-world-order (accessed 9 March 2012).

Ikenberry, J. G. (2002) "America's Imperial Ambition", *Foreign Affairs*, 81(5), 44–60.

Ikenberry, J. G. (2004) "American Hegemony and East Asian Order", *Australian Journal of International Affairs*, 58(3), 353–367.

Institute of International Education (2010) *Open Doors Report in International Educational Exchange*. Washington, DC: IIE, http://www.iie.org/en/Research-and-Publications/Open-Doors/Data (accessed 20 March 2011).

International Monetary Fund (2004) "Public Information Notice (PIN) No.04/99, IMF Concludes 2004 Article IV Consultation with the People's Republic of China", 25 August.

International Monetary Fund (2009) "Fiscal Implications of the Global Economic and Financial Crisis", 9 June.

International Monetary Fund (2011a) "World Economic Outlook Database", April.

International Monetary Fund (2011b) "World Economic Outlook: Slowing Growth, Rising Risks", September, Washington, DC: IMF, http://www.imf.org/external/pubs/ft/weo/2011/02/index.htm (accessed 17 January 2012).

International Monteary Fund (2012) "Fiscal Monitor", 24 January, http://www.imf.org/external/pubs/ft/fm/2012/update/01/pdf/0112.pdf (accessed 28 February 2012).

International Trade Administration (2011) "Tied Aid: What Is Tied Aid?" http://www. ita.doc.gov/td/finance/22.html (accessed 20 April 2011).

Ipsos/Reuters Poll (2011) "Has the US Economy Turned the Corner on the Current Crisis, Is the Worst Yet to Come, or Have Things Stabilized But Not Yet Begun to Improve?" 8 August, http://www.pollingreport.com/consumer2.htm (accessed 1 October 2011).

Irwin, D. (2002) *Free Trade under Fire*. Princeton, NJ: Princeton University Press.

Jackson, B. (2012) "Asia Watch: Rise in Intra-Regional Exports to Help Support Asia as US, EU Demand Slows", Bloomberg, 30 January.

Jackson, J. K. (2008) "Foreign Ownership of US Financial Assets: Implications of a Withdrawal", *CRS Report for Congress RL34319*, 14 January.

Jacobe, D. (2011) "Americans' Economic Confidence Declines Further", *Gallup Polls*, 26 April, http://www.gallup.com/poll/147266/Americans-Economic-Confidence-Declines-Further.aspx (accessed 25 September 2011).

Jacobs, A. (2011) "As Chinese Visit Taiwan, the Cultural Influence Is Subdued", *The New York Times*, 10 August.

Jacobs, E. (2008) "Survey Reveals Voters Wary of Foreign Government Investment", *Reuters*, 21 February, http://www.reuters.com/article/2008/02/21/idUS182920+21-Feb-2008+PRN20080221 (accessed 12 November 2011).

Jacques, M. (2009) *When China Rules the World: The End of the Western World and the Birth of a New Global Order*. New York, NY: The Penguin Press.

Jaffe, M. (2011) "Obama Administration Does Not Brand China as Currency Manipulator", *ABC News*, 4 February, http://abcnews.go.com/blogs/politics/2011/02/obama-administration-does-not-brand-china-as-currency-manipulator/ (accessed 24 November 2011).

Jen, Stephen L. (2006) "The Dollar's Hegemonic Status Will Be Validated", *Global Economic Forum*, Morgan Stanley, 30 January, pp. 24–26.

Joffe, J. (2006) *Überpower: The Imperial Temptation of America*. New York, NY: W. W. Norton & Company.

Joffe, J. (2009) "The Default Power: The False Prophecy of America's Decline", *Foreign Affairs*, September/October.

Johnson, C. (2004) *The Sorrows of Empire: Militarism, Secrecy, and the End of the Republic*. New York, NY: Metropolitan Books.

Johnson, I. (2009) "Foreign Firms Say China Is Growing More Protectionist", *The Wall Street Journal*, 28 April, A8, http://online.wsj.com/article/SB124082482232658755.html (accessed 12 July 2009).

Johnson, S. (2010) "Testimony before the US-China Economic and Security Review Commission", Washington, DC: United States Congress, http://www.uscc.gov/hearings/2010hearings/written_testimonies/10_02_25_wrt/10_02_25_johnson_statement.php (25 February 2011).

Johnson, T. (2010) "Healthcare Costs and US Competitiveness", 23 March, New York, NY: Council on Foreign Relations, http://www.cfr.org/health-science-and-technology/healthcare-costs-us-competitiveness/p13325 (accessed March 29 2011).

Jones, J. (2009) "Many Americans See Stimulus' Costs, Not Benefits", *Gallup Polls*, 18 August, http://www.gallup.com/poll/122372/americans-stimulus-costs-not-benefits.aspx (accessed 14 October 2011).

Jones, J. (2011a) "Americans' Views on Immigration Holding Steady", *Gallup Polls*, 22 June, http://www.gallup.com/poll/148154/Americans-Views-Immigration-Holding-Steady.aspx (accessed 12 November 2011).

Jones, J. (2011b) "Congressional Job Approval Ties Historic Low of 13%", *Gallup Polls*, 16 August, http://www.gallup.com/poll/149009/congressional-job-approval-ties-historic-low.aspx (accessed 30 November 2011).

Jones, J. (2011c) "On Deficit, Americans Prefer Spending Cuts; Open to Tax Hikes", *Gallup Polls*, 13 July, http://www.gallup.com/poll/148472/deficit-americans-prefer-spending-cuts-open-tax-hikes.aspx (accessed 12 November 2011).

Jorgenson, D. and Vu, Khuong (2008) *Projecting World Economic Growth: The Contribution of Information Technology*. San Francisco, CA: Federal Reserve Bank of San Francisco, http://www.frbsf.org/csip/research/200811_Jorgenson.pdf (accessed 3 March 2012).

Judis, J. B. (2004) *The Folly of Empire: What George W. Bush Could Learn from Theodore Roosevelt and Woodrow Wilson*. New York, NY: Scribner.

Kagan, R. (2006) *Dangerous Nation: America's Place in the World, from Its Earliest Days to the Dawn of the 20th Century*. New York, NY: Alfred A. Knopf.

Kagan, R. (2011) "The Price of Power", *The Brookings Institution*, 24 January.

Kagan, R. (2012a) "Not Fade Away: The Myth of American Decline", *The New Republic*, 2 February, 2, pp. 19–25.

Kagan, R. (2012b) "Not Fade Away: The Myth of American Decline", *The New Republic*, 11 January, tnr.com (accessed March 2012).

Kalra, A. (2009) "Students Overseas Business Schools Look to India Placements", *Live Mint*, 27 January, http://www.livemint.com/2009/01/27002136/Students-in-overseas-business.html (accessed 17 March 2011).

Kaplan, R. (2005) *Imperial Grunts: The American Military on the Ground*. New York, NY: Random House.

Kaplan, R. (2009) "Rivarly in the Indian Ocean", *Foreign Affairs*, 88(2), March/April, 16–32.

Kaplan, R. (2010a) "The Geography of Chinese Power: How Far Can Beijing Reach on Land and at Sea?" *Foreign Affairs*, May/June, 22–41.

Kaplan, R. (2010b) *Monsoon: The Indian Ocean and the Future of American Power*. New York, NY: Random House.

Kaplan, R. (2010c) "The Geography of Chinese Power", *Foreign Affairs*, 22 April.

Kaplan, R. D. (2010d) "The Geography of Chinese Power: How Far Can Beijing Reach on Land and at Sea?" *Foreign Affairs*, May/June.

Kawai, M. (2004) "Regional Economic Integration and Cooperation in East Asia", 7 June, Paris: Organisation for Economic Co-operation and Development, http://www.oecd.org/dataoecd/43/7/33628756.pdf (accessed 1 July 2009).

Kawai, M. and Wignaraja, G. (2010) "Free Trade Agreements in East Asia: A Way toward Trade Liberalization?" *Asian Development Bank (ADB) Briefs* No.1, June, Manila: Asian Development Bank.

KCNA (2009) "DPRK Foreign Ministry Declares Strong Counter – Measures against UNSC's 'Resolution 1874'", 13 June, http://www.kcna.co.jp/item/2009/200906/news13/20090613-10ee.html (accessed 9 March 2011).

Keidel, A. (2005) "The Economic Basis for Social Unrest in China", *Carnegie Endowment for International Peace*, May.

Keidel, A. (2007) "China Regional Disparities: The Causes and Impact of Regional Inequalities in Income and Well-Being", *Carnegie Endowment for International Peace*, September.

Keidel, A. (2008) "China's Economics Rise – Fact and Fiction", *Carnegie Endowment for International Peace*, Policy Brief 61, July.

Kennedy, P. (1987) *The Rise and Fall of the Great Powers: Economic Change and Military Conflict from 1500 to 2000*. New York, NY: Random House.

Kennedy, P. (2002) "The Eagle Has Landed: The New US Global Military Position", *Financial Times Weekend*, 1 February, p. 1.

Keohane, R. O. (1984). *After Hegemony: Cooperation and Discord in the World Political Economy*. Princeton, NJ: Princeton University Press.

Keohane, R. O. and Nye, J. (2000) *Power and Interdependence*. Harlow: Longman.

Khanna, P. (2008a) *The Second World: Empires and Influence in the New Global Order*. New York, NY: Random House.

Khanna, P. (2008b) "Waving Goodbye to Hegemony", *The New York Times Magazine*, 27 January.

Kindleberger, C. (1965) "Balance of Payments Deficits and the International Market for Liquidity", *Princeton Essays in International Finance* No. 46, Princeton, NJ: Princeton University.

Kindleberger, C. (1973) *The World in Depression, 1929–1939*. Berkeley, CA: University of California Press.

Kindleberger, C. (1976) "Systems of International Economic Organization", in: Calleo, David (ed.), *Money and the Coming World Order*, pp. 15–39. New York, NY: New York University Press.

Kindleberger, C. (1981) "Dominance and Leadership in the International Economy", *International Studies Quarterly*, 25(2), June, 242–254.

King, N. and Greenberg, S. (2011) "Poll Shows Budget-Cuts Dilemma", *The Wall Street Journal*, 3 March, http://online.wsj.com/article/SB100014240527487 0472800457617674112069736.html (accessed 12 November 2011).

Kirk, R. (2009) "Trans-Pacific Partnership Announcement", Office of the United States Trade Representative Press Office, 14 December, http://www.ustr.gov/about-us/press-office/press-releases/2009/december/trans-pacific-partnership-announcement (accessed 11 January 2012).

Kirkegaard, Jacob (2007) "Offshoring, Outsourcing, and Production Relocation – Labor-Market Effects in the OECD Countries and Developing Asia", Working Paper 07-2, April, Washington, DC: Peterson Institute for International Economics.

Klare, M. T. (2001) *Resource Wars: The New Landscape of Global Conflict*. London: Metropolitan Books.

Kletzer, L. and Bradford, J. (2008) "Fear and Offshoring: The Scope and Potential Impact of imports and Exports of Services", *Policy Brief 08-01*, January, Washington, DC: Peterson Institute for International Economics, http://www.piie.com/publications/interstitial.cfm?ResearchID=880 (accessed 23 March 2011).

Knowlton, B. (2006) "Image of US Falls Again", *International Herald Tribune*, 14 June.

Kohut, A. (2011) "The World Says China Will Overtake America: But Not Many Are Cheering", *The Wall Street Journal*, 14 July, A15.

Koopman, R., Wang, Z. and Wei, S. (2008) "How Much of Chinese Exports Is Really Made in China? Assessing Domestic Value-Added When Processing Trade Is Pervasive", NBER Working Paper No. 14109, June, Cambridge, MA: The National Bureau for Economic Research.

Kose, A., Prasad, E., Rogoff, K. and Wei, S. (2009) "Financial Globalization and Economic Policies", *IZA DP No. 4037*, April, Bonn, Germany: IZA, http://prasad.aem.cornell.edu/doc/research/IZADP.pdf (accessed 19 February 2012).

Kosec, K. and Wallsten, S. (2005) "The Economic Costs of the War in Iraq", *SSRN*, September.

Kotkin, J. (2010) *The Next Hundred Million: America in 2050*. New York, NY: The Penguin Press.

Kotkin, S. (2008) "Minding the Inequality Gap", *The New York Times*, 5 October, Section BU, p. 9.

Kotlikoff, L. (2001) "The Coming Generational Storm", June.

Krauthammer, C. (1990) "The Unipolar Moment", *Foreign Affairs*, 70(1), 23–33.

Krauthammer, C. (2002) "The Unipolar Moment Revisited", *The National Interest*, 70, 5–17.

Krauthammer, C. (2011) "The Grover Norquist Tax Myth", *The Washington Post*, 24 November, http://www.washingtonpost.com/opinions/the-grover-norquist-tax-myth/2011/11/23/gIQAsuJhtN_story.html (accessed 26 November 2011).

Krepinevich, A. (2009) "The Pentagon's Wasting Assets", *Foreign Affairs*, 88(4), July/August.

Krepon, M. (2011) "Pakistan–US Relations", *Speech before the Senate Committee on Foreign Relations*, May 5.

Kroszner, R. (2008) *Speech on the United States in the International Financial System: A Separate Reality? Resolving Two Puzzles in the International Accounts*, 1 September, given at the Central Bank of Argentina's 2008 Money and Banking Conference, Buenos Aires, Argentina.

Kruger, D. and Eddings, C. (2011) "Pimco's Total Return Fund Has 16% in Treasuries", Bloomberg, 3 October, http://www.bloomberg.com/news/2011-10-03/bond-bears-piling-into-treasuries-as-yield-forecasts-cut-by-most-since-09.html (accessed 12 November 2011).

Krugman, P. (1994a) "Competitiveness: A Dangerous Obsession", *Foreign Affairs*, 73(2), March/April, 28–44.

Krugman, P. (1994b) "The Myth of Asia's Miracle", *Foreign Affairs*, 73(6), November/December, 62–79.

Krugman, P. (2010a) "We're Not Greece", *The New York Times*, 13 May.

Krugman, P. (2010b) "Lost Decade Looming?" *The New York Times*, 20 May.

Krugman, P. (2010c) "Taking on China", *The New York Times*, 14 March.

Kupchan, C. A. (2002a) "Hollow Hegemony or Stable Multipolarity?" in Ikenberry, J. (ed.), *America Unrivaled: The Future of the Balance of Power*, pp. 68–97. Ithaca, NY: Cornell University Press.

Kupchan, C. A. (2002b) *The End of the American Era: US Foreign Policy and the Geopolitics of the Twenty-First Century*. New York, NY: Alfred A. Knopf.

Kurlantzick, J. (2005) "The Decline of American Soft Power", *Current History*, 104(686), 419–424.

Kurlantzick, J. (2007a) "Where the War on Terror Is Succeeding", *Carnegie Endowment for International Peace: Commentary*, May, http://www.carnegieendowment.org/publications/index.cfm?fa=view&id=19146 (accessed 12 September 2009)

Kurlantzick, J. (2007b) "Pax Asia-Pacifica? East Asian Integration and Its Implications for the US", *The Washington Quarterly*, 30(3), 67–77.

Kusnet, D., et al. (2006) *Talking Past Each Other*. Washington, DC: Economic Policy Institute.

Kynge, J. (2006) *China Shakes the World: A Titan's Rise and Troubled Future – And the Challenge for America*. New York, NY: Mariner Books.

Lachman, D. (2009) "Despite the Doubters, It's Still Top Dollar", *The American*, American Enterprise Institute Online Magazine, 27 June, www.american.com.

Lal, D. (2004) *In Praise of Empires: Globalization and Order*. New York, NY: Palgrave Macmillan.

Lamont, J. (2010a) "India Offers to Protect China Oil Shipments", *The Financial Times*, 17 February, www.ft.com (accessed 14 January 2012).

Lamont, J. (2010b) "India Offers to Protect China Oil Shipments", *Pakistan Defence*, 17 February 2010, http://www.defence.pk/forums/india-defence/47647-india-offers-protect-china-oil-shipments.html (accessed 9 March 2012).

Lane, Phillip R. and Milesi-Ferretti, G.M. (2008) "Where Did All the Borrowing Go? A Forensic Analysis of the US External Position", IMF Working Paper WP/08/28, February, Washington, DC: International Monetary Fund.

Langewiesche, W. (2005) "The Wrath of Khan", *Atlantic Magazine*, November, http://www.theatlantic.com/magazine/archive/2005/11/the-wrath-of-khan/4333/ (accessed 18 October 2011).

Laqueur, W. (2010) "A Crisis of Wishing", in "What Happened to Europe?" *The American Interest*, 5(6), July/August, 9–10.

Laxton, D. and Milesi-Ferretti, G.M. (2005) "How Will Global Imbalances Adjust?" Appendix to Chapter 1, "Economic Prospects and Policy Issues", *IMF World Economic Outlook*, 68–90.

Layne, C. (1993) "The Unipolar Illusion: Why New Great Powers Will Rise", *International Security*, 17(4), 5–51.

Layne, C. (2006a) "The Unipolar Illusion Revisited: The Coming End of the United States' Unipolar Moment", *International Security*, 31(2), Fall, 7–41.

Layne, C. (2006b) "Impotent Power?: Re-examining the Nature of America's Hegemonic Power", *National Interest*, September/October, pp. 41–47.

Layne, C. (2006c) *The Peace of Illusions: America's Grande Strategy from 1940 to the Present*. Ithaca, NY: Cornell University Press.

Layne, C (2012a) "This Time It's Real: The End of Unipolarity and the Pax Americana", *International Studies Quarterly*, 4 January.

Layne, C. (2012b) "The (Almost) Triumph of Offshore Balancing", *The National Interest*, 27 January. http://nationalinterest.org/commentary/almost-triumph-offshore-balancing-6405 (accessed 26 April 2012).

Layne, C. (2012c). "The Real Post-American World: The Pax America's End and the Future of World Politics", in Clark, S. and Hoque, S. (eds.), *Debating a post-American World: What Lies Ahead?* pp. 41–46. London: Routledge.

Leamer, E. (2007) "A Flat World, a Level Playing Field, a Small World After All, or None of the Above? A Review of Thomas L Friedman's *The World Is Flat*", *Journal of Economic Literature*, 45(1), 83–126.

Leamer, E. (2008) *Macroeconomic Patterns and Stories*. Heidelberg: Springer.

Lee, C. (2010) "President Obama, Dimitry Medvedev Sign Strategic Arms Reduction Treaty", *Politico*, 8 April.

Lee, J. and Shin, K. (2005) *Does Regionalism Lead to More Global Trade Integration in East Asia?* Munich: Munich Personal RePEc Archive, http://mpra.ub.uni-muenchen.de/706/1/MPRA_paper_706.pdf (accessed 17 March 2009).

Lee, Y., Bajoria, J. and Zissis, C. (2011) "The US-South Korea Alliance", *Council on Foreign Relations*, 13 October, http://www.cfr.org/south-korea/us-south-korea-alliance/p11459 (accessed 9 March 2012).

Legatum Institute (2010) *Legatum Prosperity Index Report 2010*. London: Legatum Institute, http://www.prosperity.com/downloads/2010ProsperityIndexFullReport.pdf (accessed 3 March 2012).

Lettow, P. (2010) "Strengthening the Nuclear Nonproliferation Regime", Council Special Report No. 54, *Council on Foreign Relations*, New York, NY, April, p. 3.

Levey, D. H. and Brown, S. S. (2005a) "The Overstretch Myth", *Foreign Affairs*, 84(2), 2–7.

Levey, D. H. and Brown, S. S. (2005b) "The Overstretch Myth: Can the Indispensable Nation be a Debtor Nation?" *Foreign Affairs*, March/ April, 2–7.

Levey, D. H. and Brown, S. S. (2005c) " 'Levey and Brown Reply', A Rejoinder to Brad Setser and Nouriel Roubini, 'How Scary Is the Deficit?: American Power and American Borrowing' ", *Foreign Affairs*, July/August, 198–200.

Levey, S. (2008) "Iran: International Pressure and Economic Crisis", *Woodrow Wilson International Center for Scholars*, 11 December, http://www.wilsoncenter.org/event/iran-international-pressure-and-economic-crisis (accessed 8 March 2012).

Lieber, R. J. (2005) *The American Era: Power and Strategy for the 21st Century*. New York, NY: Cambridge University Press.

Lieber, R. J. (2008) "Falling Upwards: Declinism, The Box Set", *World Affairs*, Summer.

Lin, L. (2009) "Asia's Export-Led Growth Model Is 'Broken,' Roubini Says", *Bloomberg.com*, 7 May, www.bloomberg.com (accessed 1 July 2009).

Lindert, P. (2003) "Why the Welfare State Looks Like a Free Lunch", NBER Working Paper No. 9869, Cambridge, MA: National Bureau of Economic Research.

Litan, R. (2010) *In Defense of Much, But Not All, Financial Innovation*. Washington, DC: Brookings Institution, http://www.brookings.edu/papers/2010/0217_financial_innovation_litan.aspx (accessed 7 March 2010).

Liu, F. (2008) "Asian Regionalism, Strategic Evolution, and US Policy in Asia: Some Prospects for Cross-Strait Development", June, Washington, DC: The Brookings Institution, http://www.brookings.edu/~/media/Files/rc/papers/2008/06_asian_regionalism_liu/06_asian_regionalism_liu.pdf (accessed 9 March 2012).

Lopez-Claros, A. (2006) *The Global Competitiveness Report 2006–2007: Creating an Improved Business Environment*. Geneva, Switzerland: World Economic Forum.

Lowell, L. and Salzman, H. (2007) *Into the Eye of the Storm: Assessing the Evidence on Science and Engineering Education, Quality, and Workforce Demand*, 29 October, Washington, DC: Urban Institute, http://www.urban.org/publications/411562.html (accessed 24 March 2011).

Lucas, R. (1990) "Why Doesn't Capital Flow from Rich to Poor Countries?" *American Economic Review: Papers and Proceedings*, 80, May, 92–96.

Luce, E. (2009) "Obama Urged to 'Make the Case' for Free Trade", *The Financial Times*, 4 August, ww.ft.com (accessed 12 August 2009).

Luck, E. (2003) "American Exceptionalism and International Organization: Lessons from the 1990s", in Rosemary, F., MacFarlane, N. and Mastanduno, M. (eds.), *US Hegemony and International Organizations*, pp. 25–48. Oxford, NY: Oxford University Press.

Lugar, R. (2010) "Expand Nunn-Lugar", *The National Interest*, 29 January.

Lugar, R. G. (2005) *The Lugar Survey on Proliferation Threats and Responses*. Washington, DC: Office of Richard Lugar, http://lugar.senate.gov/reports/NPSurvey.pdf

Lum, T. (2006) "Social Unrest in China", *CRS Report for Congress*, 8 May.

Ma, Q. (2002) "The Governance of NGOs in China since 1978: How Much Autonomy?" *Nonprofit and Voluntary Sector Quarterly*, 31, 305.

MacDonald, B. (2009) "China, Space Weapons, and US. Security Council: Special Report No. 38", *The Council on Foreign Relations*, http://www.cfr.org/publication/16707/ (accessed 13 September 2009)

Mahbubani, K. (2008) *The New Asian Hemisphere: The Irresistible Shift of Global Power to the East*. New York, NY: Public Affairs.

Majumder, S. (2008) "East Asia as Propeller of World Trade", *The Hindu Business Line*, 6 May.

Mandel, M. (2009) "Why Rising Productivity Is Cause for Worry", *Bloomberg Business Week*, 14 May, http://www.businessweek.com/magazine/content/09_21/b4132022776217.htm (accessed 15 May 2009).

Mandelbaum, M. (2005) *The Case for Goliath: How America Acts as the World's Government in the Twenty-First Century*. New York, NY: Public Affairs.

Mandelbaum, M. (2010) *The Frugal Superpower: America's Global Leadership in a Cash-Strapped Era*. New York, NY: Public Affairs.

Mankiw, G. (2010) *Macroeconomics: Seventh Edition*. New York, NY: Worth Publishers.

Mann, C. (2005) "Breaking Up Is Hard to Do; Global Co-dependency, Collective Action, and the Challenges of Global Adjustment", *CESifo Forum*, January, 16–23.

Mann, C. (2006) *Accelerating the Globalization of America: The Role for Information Technology*. Washington, DC: Institute for International Economics.

Mann, C. (2009) "International Capital Flows and the Sustainability of the US Current Account Deficit", in Bergsten, F. (ed.), *The Long-Term International Economic Position of the United States: Special Report*, 20 May, pp. 35–64. Washington, DC: Peterson Institute for International Economics.

Marine Fair (2011) "Important Chinese Ports", http://www.marinefair.com/important-chinese-ports (accessed 9 March 2012).

Markheim, D. (2008) "The Importance of Reviving the Doha Round", *The Heritage Foundation*, WebMemo #2123, 5 November, http://www.heritage.org/research/tradeandeconomicfreedom/wm2123.cfm (accessed 8 July 2009).

Markoff, J. (2005) *What the Dormouse Said: How the 60's Counterculture Shaped the Personal Computer Industry*. New York, NY: Viking Adult.

Markoff, J. (2010) "US Scientists Given Access to Cloud Computing", *The New York Times*, 4 February, Section A, p. 17.

Marsh, P. (2010) "A World To Scale", *Financial Times*, 21 January, p. 7.

Martins, J. and Brackield, D. (2009) "Productivity and the Crisis: Revisiting the Fundamentals", *VoxEU*, 11 July, http://www.voxeu.org/index.php?q=node/3760 (accessed 3 March 2012).

Mataconis, D. (2011) "Debt Deal Reveals GOP Split on Defense Spending", *Outside the Beltway*, 2 August, http://www.outsidethebeltway.com/debt-deal-reveals-gop-split-on-defense-spending/ (accessed 21 October 2011).

Mattoo, A. and Subramanian, S. (2009) "From Doha to the Next Bretton Woods: A New Multilateral Trade Agenda", *Foreign Affairs*, 88(1), January/February, 15–26.

McDonald, M. (2008) "China Confirms Naval Role in Gulf of Aden", *The New York Times*, 19 December, http://www.nytimes.com/2008/12/19/world/asia/19patrols.html (accessed 8 March 2012).

McGrattan, E. and Prescott, E. (2010) "Unmeasured Investment and the Puzzling US Boom in the 1990s", *American Economic Journal: Macroeconomics*, 2(4), October, 88–123.

McKinnon, R. and Schnabl, G. (2004) "The Return to Soft Dollar Pegging in East Asia: Mitigating Conflicted Virtue", *McKinnon Papers*, Stanford, CA: Stanford University, http://www.stanford.edu/~mckinnon/papers/ReturnN.pdf (accessed 19 February 2012).

McKinnon, R. and Schnabl, G. (2006) "Devaluing the Dollar: A critical analysis of William Cline's Case for a New Plaza Agreement", *McKinnon Papers*, Stanford, CA: Stanford University, http://www.stanford.edu/~mckinnon/papers/Cline%20proofs%20JEPM.pdf (accessed 19 February 2012).

McKinnon, R. I. (2010) "Review: China in Africa: The Washington Consensus versus the Beijing Consensus", *Stanford University*, 9 August.

Mead, W. (2007) "Failing Upward: Relax, America Will Survive George W. Bush", *The New Republic*, 22 October, p. 28.

Mead, W. (2010) "American Challenges: The Blue Model Breaks Down", *The American Interest*, 28 January, http://blogs.the-american-interest.com/wrm/2010/01/28/american-challenges-the-blue-model-breaks-down/ (accessed 30 October 2011).

Mead, W. (2011) "America's Play for Prosperity", *The Wall Street Journal*, 30 December, http://online.wsj.com/article/SB10001424052970204464404577118481002593326.html (accessed 17 January 2012).

Mead, W. R. (2004) *Power, Terror, Peace, and War: America's Grand Strategy in a World at Risk*. New York, NY: Knopf.

Mearsheimer, J. (2001) *The Tragedy of Great Power Politics*. New York, NY: W. W. Norton & Company.

Mearsheimer, J. and Walt, S. (2007) *The Israel Lobby and US Foreign Policy*. New York, NY: Farrar, Straus and Giroux.

Meckler, L. (2009) "$318 Tax Hit Proposed", *The Wall Street Journal*, 26 February.

Mendes, E. (2011) "American's Ratings of Their Finances Remain at a Low Point", *Gallup Polls*, 25 April, http://www.gallup.com/poll/147260/Americans-Ratings-Finances-Remain-Low-Point.aspx (accessed 25 September 2011).

Meridith, G. (2007) "Debt Dynamics and Global Imbalances: Some Conventional Views Reconsidered", IMF Working Paper WP/07/4, January, Washington, DC: International Monetary Fund.

Mewbourne, C. (2009) "Emerging Markets in the New Normal", *Emerging Markets Watch*, August, PIMCO, www.pimco.com.

Meyer, J. and Nicholas, P. (2008) "Obama Unveils Plan to Protect US from 21st Century Threats", *Los Angeles Times*, 17 July.

Miller, Matthew (2008) "Obama Doesn't Have to Run as a Liberal", *The Wall Street Journal*, 11 July, http://online.wsj.com/article/SB121573713663744519.html (accessed 3 March 2012).

Miller, Matthew (2009a) *The Tyranny of Dead Ideas*. New York, NY: Times Books, Henry Holt and Company.

Miller, Matthew (2012) "Left, Right and Center", airing on KCRW radio station, California, USA (accessed 14 September 2012).

Miller, Rich (2009b) "Unemployment Confronts Obama Rhetoric with Chronic Joblessness", *Bloomberg Business Week*, 27 September, http://www.bloomberg.com/apps/news?pid=newsarchive&sid=aDx_Srx0Sv8Q (accessed 14 March 2011).

Mills, E. (2010a) "Experts Warn of Catastrophe from Cyberattacks", www.zdnetasia.com, ZDnet, 25 February, http://www.zdnetasia.com/experts-warn-of-catastrophe-from-cyberattacks-62061413.htm (accessed 17 April 2010).

Mills, E. (2010b) "US House of Representatives Passes Cybersecurity Research Bill", www.zdnetasia.com, 5 February, http://www.zdnetasia.com/us-house-of-representatives-passes-cybersecurity-research-bill-62061011.htm (accessed 16 April 2010).

Moffett, D. (2011) "Newt Gingrich on Immigration: Former House Speaker Backs More Moderate Policy than Most Republican Rivals", About.com Guides, http://immigration.about.com/od/immigrationlawandpolicy/a/Newt-Gingrich-On-Immigration.htm (accessed 31 December 2011).

Moniz, D., Kelley, M. and Konaro, S. (2005) "War's Strain Wearing on Army Troops, Tools", *USA Today*, p. 6A.

Montgomery, E. (2009) "Nuclear Terrorism: Assessing the Threat, Developing a Response", *Center for Strategic and Budgetary Assessments*, April.

Moore, S. and Grimm, T. (2008) "This Bud's for Belgium", *The Wall Street Journal*, 3 August, http://online.wsj.com/article/SB121770579562707543.html?mod=opinion_main_review_and_outlooks (accessed 14 March 2011).

Moran, M. (2010) "Q3 2010 Geostrategy Note: Nascent Nukes, Portly PIIGS and the Taliban", *Roubini Global Economics*, 4 August.

Moreau, R. (2007) "Where the Jihad Lives Now", *Newsweek*, 20 October.

Moreau, R. (2011) "The Taliban After Bin Laden", *Newsweek*, 23 May.

Moretti, Enrico (2012) *The New Geography of Jobs*. New York, NY: Houghton Mifflin Harcourt.

Morrison, W. M. (2009) "China and the Global Financial Crisis: Implications for the United States", *Congressional Research Service*, 17 August.

Mullen, M. (2011) "Speech presented at the US Army Sergeants Major Academy at Fort Bliss", Texas, March.

Munchau, W. (2009) "How Toxic Finance Created an Unstable World", *Financial Times*, 24 August, p. 7.

Murakami, T. (2007) "Rules Harm US Fiscal Markets, Report Says", *Washington Post*, 23 January, Financial Section, p. D08.

Mussa, M. (2006) "Discussant Comments", in Caballero, R., Farhi, E. and Gourinchas, P. (eds.), *An Equilibrium Model of 'Global Imbalances' and Low Interest Rates*, BIS Working Papers No. 222, pp. 73–80, December. Basel, Switzerland: Bank for International Settlements.

Nakamura, L. (2001) "What Is the US Gross Investment in Intangibles? (At Least) One Trillion Dollars a Year!", Federal Reserve Bank of Philadelphia Working Paper No. 01-15, www.philadelphiafed.org.

Nankivell, N. (2005) "The National Security Implications of China's Emerging Water Crisis", *The Jamestown Foundation*, 1 September.

Nanto, Dick (2008) "East Asian Regional Architecture: New Economic and Security Arrangements and US Policy", 4 January, Washington, DC: Congressional Research Service, http://www.fas.org/sgp/crs/row/RL33653.pdf (accessed 28 June 2009).

National Coalition on Health Care (NCHC) (2011) *Insurance*, http://nchc.org/issue-areas/insurance (accessed 29 March 2011).

National Foundation for American Policy (NFAP) (2008a) "Talent Search: Job Openings and the Need for Skilled Labor in the US Economy", NFAP Policy Brief, http://www.nfap.com/pdf/080311talentsrc.pdf (accessed 15 March 2011).

National Foundation for American Policy (NFAP) (2008b) "H-1B Visas and Job Creation", NFAP Policy Brief, March, http://www.nfap.com/pdf/080311h1b.pdf (accessed 17 March 2011).

National Foundation for American Policy (NFAP) (2009) "H-1B Visas by the Numbers", NFAP Policy Brief, March, http://www.nfap.com/pdf/0903h1bpb.pdf (accessed 23 March 2011).

National Research Council and National Academy of Public Administration, Committee on the Fiscal Future of the United States Division of Behavioral and Social Sciences and Education (2010) *Choosing the Nation's Fiscal Future*. Washington, DC: The National Academies Press.

National Science Foundation (2010a) *Doctorate Recipients from US Universities*, December, Washington, DC: NSA, http://www.nsf.gov/statistics/nsf11306/nsf11306.pdf (accessed 1 April 2010).

National Science Foundation (2010b) *Science and Technology Indicators 2010*. Washington, DC: NSA, http://www.nsf.gov/statistics/seind10/ (accessed 17 February 2010).

Nau, H. (2001) "Why 'The Rise and Fall of the Great Powers' Was Wrong", *Review of International Studies*, 27, 579–592.

Nau, H. R. (1990) *The Myth of America's Decline: Leading the World Economy into the 1990's*. New York, NY: Oxford University Press.

NBC News/Wall Street Journal Poll (2008) "Do You Think the Fact That the American Economy Has Become Increasingly Global Is Good Because It Has Opened Up New Markets for American Products And Resulted in More Jobs, or Bad Because It Has Subjected American Companies And Employees to Unfair Competition and Cheap Labor?" 7–10 March, http://www.pollingreport.com/trade.htm (accessed 14 October 2011).

NBC News/Wall Street Journal Poll (2010a) "In General, Do You Think That Free Trade Between the United States and Foreign Countries Has Helped the United States, Has Hurt the United States, or Has Not Made Much of a Difference Either Way?", 11–15 November, http://www.pollingreport.com/trade.htm (accessed 24 September 2011).

NBC News/Wall Street Journal Poll (2010b) "In General, Do You Think That Free Trade Between the United States and Foreign Countries Has Helped the United States, Has Hurt the United States, or Has Not Made Much of a Difference Either Way?" 11 November, http://www.pollingreport.com/trade.htm (accessed 24 November 2011).

NBC News/Wall Street Journal Poll (2011) "All in All, Do You Think Things in the Nation Are Generally Headed in the Right Direction, or Do You Feel That Things Are Off on the Wrong Track?", 6 October, http://www.pollingreport.com/right.htm (accessed 14 October 2011).

Newport, F. (2011a) "Americans Favor Jobs Plan Proposals, Including Taxing Rich", *Gallup Polls*, 20 September, http://www.gallup.com/poll/149567/Americans-Favor-Jobs-Plan-Proposals-Including-Taxing-Rich.aspx (accessed 4 November 2011).

Newport, F. (2011b) "Americans Remain Divided on Defense Spending", *Gallup Polls*, 15 February, http://www.gallup.com/poll/146114/Americans-Remain-Divided-Defense-Spending.aspx (accessed 12 November 2011).

Newport, F. and Saad, L. (2011) "Americans Oppose Cuts in Education, Social Security, Defense", *Gallup Polls*, 26 January, http://www.gallup.com/poll/145790/americans-oppose-cuts-education-social-security-defense.aspx (accessed 3 November 2011).

Ng, E. (2008) "Global Financial Crisis Will Hurt China Much More Than the US", *CNReviews.com (CNR)*, 25 November, http://cnreviews.com/china_economy/china_financial_crisis_20081125.html (accessed 28 April 2009).

Nichols, T. M. (2005) "Anarchy, Order, and the New Age of Prevention", *World Policy Journal*, XXII(3), 1–23.

Nicoletti, Guiseppe and Scarpetta, Stefano (2003) *Regulation, Productivity, and Growth: OECD Evidence*, Policy Research Working Paper 2944. Washington, DC: The World Bank Human Development Social Protection Team.

Norrlof, C. (2010) *America's Global Advantage: US Hegemony and International Cooperation*, p. 292. New York, NY: Cambridge University Press.

Nye, J. (1990) *Bound to Lead: The Changing Nature of American Power*. New York, NY: Basic Books.

Nye, J. (2004) *Soft Power: The Means to Success in World Politics.* New York, NY: Public Affairs.

Nye, J. (2011a) *The Future of Power.* New York, NY: Public Affairs.

Nye, J. (2011b) "The Future of American Power", *Foreign Affairs,* 89(6), 2–12.

O'Hanlon, M. (2008) "US Military Check-Up Time", *The Washington Times,* 4 May 2008, available via The Brookings Institute http://www.brookings.edu/opinions/2008/0504_military_ohanlon.aspx (accessed 1 February 2010).

O'Hanlon, M. (2009) *Budgeting for Hard Power.* Washington, DC: Brookings Institution Press.

O'Hanlon, M. and Campbell, J. (2009) "The Iraq Index", The Brookings Institution, http://www.brookings.edu/iraqindex (accessed 23 July 2009).

O'Rourke, K. and Williamson, J. (2001) *Globalization and History: The Evolution of a Nineteenth-Century Atlantic Economy.* Cambridge: The MIT Press.

Obama, B. (2009a) "Remarks by President Obama", The White House, Prague, Czech Republic. 5 April, http://www.whitehouse.gov/the_press_office/Remarks-By-President-Barack-Obama-In-Prague-As-Delivered/ (accessed 8 March 2012).

Obama, B. (2009b) "Text: Obama's Speech to the United Nations General Assembly", *The New York Times,* http://www.nytimes.com/2009/09/24/us/politics/24prexy.text.html (accessed 24 March 2011).

Obama, B. (2011) "Speech presented at George Washington University in Washington", Washington, DC, 13 April.

Obstfeld, M. and Rogoff, K. (2004) "The Unsustainable US Current Account Position Revisited", NBER Working Paper No. 10869, Cambridge, MA: National Bureau of Economic Research.

Obstfeld, M. and Rogoff, K. (2005) "Global Current Account Imbalances and Exchange Rate Adjustment", *Brookings Papers on Economic Activity,* 2005(1), 67–123.

Obstfeld, M., Shambaugh, J. and Taylor, A. (2008) "Financial Stability, the Trilemma, and International Reserves", NBER Working Paper No. 14217, August, Cambridge, MA: National Bureau of Economic Research.

Odom, W. and Dajarric, R. (2004) *America's Inadvertent Empire.* New Haven & London: Yale University Press.

OECD (2008) *Compendium of Patent Statistics.* Paris: OECD, http://www.oecd.org/dataoecd/5/19/37569377.pdf (accessed 17 February 2010).

OECD (2009a) "Indicator C3: Who Studies Abroad and Where", *2009 OECD Data,* http://www.oecd.org/dataoecd/61/32/48631079.pdf (accessed 18 April 2012).

OECD (2009b) *Education at a Glance 2009: OECD Indicators,* 8 September, Paris: OECD, http://www.oecd.org/document/24/0,3343,en_2649_39263238_43586328_1_1_1_37455,00.html (accessed 14 February 2010).

OECD (2010) "China in the 2010s Rebalancing Growth and Strengthening Social Safety Nets", OECD contribution to the China Development Forum, 20–22 March.

OECD (2012) *Country Statistical Profiles,* http://stats.oecd.org/viewhtml.aspx?queryname=18175&querytype=view&lang=en (accessed 19 April 2012).

Office of Management and Budget (2009a) "Budget of the US Government: Fiscal Year 2010", Washington, DC, 26 February.

Office of Management and Budget (2009b) "A New Era of Responsibility", Washington, DC, 26 February.

Office of Management and Budget (2009c) "Mid-Session Review Budget of the US Government Fiscal Year 2010", Washington, DC, 25 August.

Office of Management and Budget (2011) "Fiscal Year 2013 Historical Tables", http://www.whitehouse.gov/omb/budget/Historicals (accessed 12 November 2011).

Official Website of the United States Navy (2011) "The Carriers: The List", http://www.navy.mil/navydata/ships/carriers/cv-list.asp (accessed 15 October 2011).

Olson, M. (1971) *The Logic of Collective Action: Public Goods and the Theory of Groups.* Cambridge, MA: Harvard University Press.

Olson, M. (1984) *The Rise and Decline of Nations: Economic Growth, Stagflation, and Social Rigidities.* New Haven, CT: Yale University Press.

On Point (2012) "Hacking America's Future", 16 February, http://onpoint.wbur.org/2012/02/16/hacking-americas-future (accessed 20 February 2012).

Organizational for Economic Co-operation and Development (OECD) (2006) *Education at a Glance 2006: OECD Briefing Note for the United States*, 12 September 2006, Paris: OECD, http://www.oecd.org/dataoecd/51/20/37392850.pdf (accessed 29 March 2011)

Organization of Economic Co-operation and Development (OECD) (2011) "Aid Statistics, Donor Aid Charts", http://www.oecd.org/countrylist/0,3349,en_2649_34447_1783495_1_1_1_1,00.html (accessed 2012).

Orszag, P. (2011) "The Risks and Rewards of Health-Care Reform", *Foreign Affairs*, July/August, pp. 42–56.

Ottolenghi, E. (2010) "Exposing the Nutrients: How to Improve Enforcement of Sanctions Against Iran", *Foreign Affairs*, 19 October.

Oxford Analytica (2010a) "Innovation Lags in China", 19 March.

Panagariya, A. (2008) "What India Must Do to Modernise", *VOXEU.com*, 15 January, http://www.voxeu.org/index.php?q=node/868 (accessed 4 November 2009).

Pape, R. (1998) "Why Economic Sanctions Still Do Not Work", *International Security*, 23(1), Summer, 66–77.

Pearson Education (2011) "National Voter Turnout in Federal Elections: 1960–2010", *InfoPlease*, http://www.infoplease.com/ipa/A0781453.html (accessed 30 November 2011).

Peoples, S. (2011) "Immigration Debate Intensifies in GOP Race", *Associated Press*, 20 October, http://www.boston.com/news/local/massachusetts/articles/2011/10/20/immigration_debate_intensifies_in_gop_race/ (accessed 12 November 2011).

Peterson, K. (2011) "Tax-Repatriation Holiday Gathers Some Steam", *The Wall Street Journal*, 23 June, http://online.wsj.com/article/SB100014240527023033990457640418376315882.html (accessed 4 November 2011).

Peterson, P. (2009) "Questions American Must Ask on Health Costs", *Financial Times*, 9 August.

Peterson Perspectives: Interviews on Current Issues: Why Taxing companies to discourage outsourcing.

Pettis, M. (2010a) "Is China Turning Japanese?" *Foreign Policy*, 19 August.

Pettis, M. (2010b) "Chinese Consumption and the Japanese 'sorpasso'", Carnegie Middle East Center, 10 August, http://carnegie-mec.org/publications/?fa=41397 (accessed 8 March 2010).

Pettis, M. (2011a) "The Dollar, the RMB and the Euro?" *China Financial Markets*, 12 March, http://www.mpettis.com/2011/03/12/the-dollar-versur-the-rmb-and-the-euro/ (accessed 8 March 2012).

Pettis, M. (2011b) "China's Troubled Transition to a More Balanced Growth Model", *New America Foundation*, 1 March, http://newamerica.net/publications/policy/china_s_troubled_transition_to_a_more_balanced_growth_model (accessed 8 April 2012).

Pew Global Attitudes Project (2007) "World Publics Welcome Global Trade – But Not Immigration", 4 October, http://pewglobal.org/reports/pdf/258.pdf (accessed 12 November 2011).

Pew Research Center (2011) "Question Search: Right Now, Which Is More Important for President (Barack) Obama to Focus on...Domestic Policy or Foreign Policy?" May, http://www.people-press.org/question-search/?qid=1787451&pid=51&ccid=51#top (accessed 11 November 2011).

Pew Research Center for the People & the Press (2007) "What Is Your Biggest Concern about Illegal Immigration? Is It That...It Hurts American Jobs, It Hurts American Customs and Its Way of Life, It Increases the Danger of Terrorism, or It Contributes to Crime?" 30 May–3 June, http://www.people-press.org/question-search/?qid=1683289&pid=51&ccid=51#top (accessed 12 November 2011).

Pew Research Center Publications (2006) "America's Immigration Quandary", 4 April, http://pewresearch.org/pubs/217/americas-immigration-quandary (accessed 12 November 2011).

Pew Research Center Publications (2007) "World Publics Welcome Global Trade – But Not Immigrations", 4 October, http://www.pewglobal.org/2007/10/04/world-publics-welcome-global-trade-but-not-immigration/ (accessed 12 October 2011).

Pew Research Center Publications (2009) "US Seen as Less Important, China as More Powerful", 3 December, http://pewresearch.org/pubs/1428/america-seen-less-important-china-more-powerful-isolationist-sentiment-surges (accessed 14 October 2011).

Pew Research Center Publications (2010) "Public Knowledge: Senate Legislative Process a Mystery to Many", 28 January, http://pewresearch.org/pubs/1478/political-iq-quiz-knowledge-filibuster-debt-colbert-steele (accessed 26 November 2011).

Pew Research Center Publications (2011) "Strengthen Ties with China, But Get Tough on Trade", 12 January, http://pewresearch.org/pubs/1855/china-poll-americans-want-closer-ties-but-tougher-trade-policy (accessed 14 October 2011).

Phelps, E. (2006) "Economic Culture and Economic Performance: What Light Is Shed on the Continent's Problem?" Center on Capitalism and Society Working Paper No. 17, New York, NY: Columbia University.

Phelps, E. (2010) "Radio Disscussion with Tom Keene January 28", *Bloomberg Surveillance*, 28 January, http://www.bloomberg.com/podcasts/surveillance/

Phelps, E. and Tilman, L. (2010) "Wanted: A First National Bank of Innovation", *Harvard Business Review*, 88(1), January/February, 102–103.

Phillips, K. (2006) *American Theocracy: The Peril and Politics of Radical Religion, Oil, and Borrowed Money in the 21st Century*. New York, NY: Viking Adult.

Phillips, K. (2008) *Bad Money: Reckless Finance, Failed Politics, and the Global Crisis of American Capitalism*. New York, NY: Viking Adult.

Pillar, P. (2011) "Terrorism and Civil War in South Asia", *The National Interest*, 24 May, http://nationalinterest.org/blog/paul-pillar/terrorism-civil-war-south-asia-5363 (accessed 9 March 2012).

Pilling, D. (2009) "Asia Will Struggle to Escape Its Export Trap", *Financial Times*, 24 June, p. 13.

Pitsuwan, S. (2008) "A Conversation with Surin Pitsuwan [Rush Transcript; Federal News Service]", *Council on Foreign Relations*, 14 May, http://www.cfr.org/united-states/conversation-surin-pitsuwan-rush-transcript-federal-news-service/p16284 (accessed 12 September 2009).

Pleven, L. and Gold, R. (2011) "US Nears Milestone: Net Fuel Exporter", *The Wall Street Journal*, 30 November, http://online.wsj.com/article/SB1000142405297020 344170457706867048830624 2.html (accessed 23 January 2012).

Pomfret, R. (2007) "Is Regionalism an Increasing Feature of the World Economy?" *World Economy*, 30, 923–947.

Population Division of the Department of Economic and Social Affairs of the United Nations Secretariat (2010) "World Population Prospects: The 2008 Revision Database."

Porter, E. (2008) "Europe Fears a Post-Bush Unilateralism, This Time on Trade", *The New York Times*, 7 June, http://www.nytimes.com/2008/06/07/opinion/07sat4.html (accessed 8 October 2011).

Posen, A. (2008) "Why the Euro Will Not Rival the Dollar", *International Finance*, 11(1), 75–100.

Posen, B. (2003) "Command of the Commons: The Military Foundation of US Hegemony", *International Security*, 28(1), 5–46.

Potter, W. C. and Mukhatzhanova, G. (2008) "Divining Nuclear Intentions: A Review Essay", *International Security*, 33(1), Summer, 139–169.

Powers, R. (2011) "Law of Armed Conflict (LOAC)", http://usmilitary.about.com/cs/wars/a/loac.htm (accessed 2 February 2012).

Pozen, R. (2011) "The Myth of Corporate Tax Reform", *The Washington Post*, 28 September, http://www.washingtonpost.com/opinions/the-myth-of-corporate-tax-reform/2011/09/27/gIQAZine5K_story.html (accessed 4 November 2011).

Pozen, R. C. (2005) "Why My Plan to Fix Social Security Will Work", *USA Today*, 12 June.

Pratap, S. and Quintin, E. (2010) "Financial Crisis and Labor Market Turbulence", 14 September, University of Santa Barbara, http://www.econ.ucsb.edu/about_us/events/seminar_papers/pratap.pdf (accessed 9 March 2011).

Prestowitz, C. (2006a) *America's Technology Future at Risk: Broadband and Investment Strategies to Refire Innovation*. Washington, DC: Economic Strategy Institute.

Prestowitz, C. (2006b) *Three Billion New Capitalists: The Great Shift of Wealth and Power to the East*. New York, NY: Basic Books.

PricewaterhouseCoopers (2010) "Convergence, Catch-Up and Overtaking: How the Balance of World, Economic Power Is Shifting", January, http://www.ukmediacentre.pwc.com/imagelibrary/downloadMedia.ashx?Media DetailsID=1626 (accessed 8 March 2012).

PricewaterhouseCoopers, Hawksworth, J. and Cookson, G. (2008) "The World in 2050 – Beyond the BRICs: A Broader Look at Emerging Markets Growth Prospects", March, http://www.pwc.com/gx/en/world-2050/pdf/world_2050_brics.pdf (accessed 8 March 2012).

Pruitt, B. and Philips, T. (2007) "Kauffman Foundation Study Points to 'Brain-Drain' of Skilled US Immigrant Entrepreneurs to Home Country", 22 August, http://www.kauffman.org/Details.aspx/?id=1020 (accessed 28 March 2011).

Public Radio international (PRI) (2008) "Communication Breakdown: Losing the War on of Ideas", *American Abroad Podcast*, 5 February.

Quindlen, A. (2010) "Follow the Leader", *Newsweek*, 8 February, pp. 22–25.

Quinlan, J. P. (2011) *The Last Economic Superpower*. New York, NY: McGraw Hill.

Quinn, A. (2011) "The Art of Declining Politely: Obama's Prudent Presidency and the Waning of American Power", *International Affairs*, 87(4), 803–824.

Quinnipiac University (2011) "President Is Best of the Worst on Economy, US Voters Tell Quinnipiac University National Poll; Voters Blame Bush over Obama 2-1 for Financial Mess", 14 July, http://www.quinnipiac.edu/x1295.xml?ReleaseID=1624 (accessed 12 November 2011).

Rabinovitch, Simon and Anderlini, Jamil (2011) "Extent of Local Debts in China Laid Bare", *Financial Times*, 27 June, http://www.ft.com/intl/cms/s/0/1e47d528-a092-11e0-b14e-00144feabdc0.html#axzz1xDcXiKBP (accessed 8 June 2012).

Rachman, G. (2011) *Zero-Sum Future*. New York, NY: Simon & Schuster.

Rajan, R. (2006) "Investment Restraint, the Liquidity Glut, and Global Imbalances", in: Conference on Global Imbalances, Bank of Indonesia, Bali, Indonesia, 16 November.

Rajan, R. G. (2010) *Fault Lines: How Hidden Fractures Still Threaten the World Economy*. Princeton, NJ: Princeton University Press.

Ramo, J. C. (2004) *The Beijing Consensus*, May. London: The Foreign Policy Centre.

RAND Corporation (2008) "While China's Regional Influence Grows, US Remains Key Security and Economic Partner in East Asia", *RAND Corporation Press Release*, 17 November.

Rashid, A. (2011) "The Devolution of Pakistan", *The National Interest*, 23 May.

Rassmussen Reports (2006) "Just 17% Favor Dubai Ports Deal", 24 February, http://www.rasmussenreports.com/public_content/current_events/other_current_events/just_17_favor_dubai_ports_deal (accessed 12 November 2011).

Rathus, J. (2009a) "The Ciang Mail Initiative: China, Japan, and Financial Regionalism", *East Asia Forum*, 11 May, www.eastasiaforum.org (accessed 15 May 2009).

Rathus, J. (2009b) "The Ciang Mail Initiative: China, Japan, and Financial Regionalism", *East Asia Forum*, 11 May, http://www.eastasiaforum.org/2009/05/11/the-chiang-mai-initiative-china-japan-and-financial-regionalism (accessed 15 May 2009).

Reinhart, C. and Rogoff, K. (2008) *The Aftermath of Financial Crises*, 19 December, Cambridge: Harvard University Department of Economics, http://www.economics.harvard.edu/faculty/rogoff/files/Aftermath.pdf (accessed 3 March 2012).

Reinhart, C. and Rogoff, K. (2009) *This Time Is Different: Eight Centuries of Financial Folly*. Princeton, NJ: Princeton University Press.

Reinhart, C. and Rogoff, K. (2010) "Growth in a Time of Debt", *American Economic Review*, American Economic Association, 100(2), May, 573–578.

Reinhart, C. M. and Sbrancia, M. B. (2011) "The Liquidation of Government Debt", Working Paper WP 11-10. *Peterson Institute for International Economics*, April.

Ricks, T. (2004). "Wars Put Strain on National Guard", *The Washington Post*, 6 June, A01.

Rivlin, A. and Sawhill, I. S. (2004) *Restoring Fiscal Sanity: How to Balance the Budget*. Washington, DC: Brookings Institution Press.

Roach, S. (2006) "Trade Deficits and Asset Bubbles", *Morgan Stanley Global Economic Forum*, 13 February, www.morganstanley.com (accessed 2007).

Roberts, P. (2004) *The End of Oil: On the Edge of a Perilous New World*. Boston, MA: Houghton Mifflin.

Rockwell, L. (2007) "The Foreign Policy of Ron Paul", a forward in Paul, R. *A Foreign Policy of Freedom: Peace, Commerce, Honest Friendship*. Lake Jackson, TX: Foundation for Rational.

Rodrik, D. (2006) "What's so Special about China's Exports?" *China & World Economy*, 14(5), 1–19.

Rodrik, D. (2008) "The Real Exchange Rate and Economic Growth", *Brookings Papers on Economic Activity*, Fall, Washington, DC: Brookings Institute, http://www.brookings.edu/~   /media/Files/Programs/ES/BPEA/2008_fall_bpea_papers/2008_fall_bpea_rodrik.pdf (accessed 9 March 2011).

Rodrik, D. (2009) *Making Room for China in the World Economy*, December. Cambridge: Harvard Kenned School, http://www.hks.harvard.edu/fs/drodrik/Research%20papers/Making%20room%20for%20China.pdf (accessed 9 March 2011).

Romney, M. (2010) *No Apology: The Case for American Greatness*. New York, NY: St. Martin's Press.

Romney, M. (2011) "Steadfast Alliances", http://www.mittromney.com/policy/foreign-policy/steadfast-alliances (accessed 14 October 2011).

Roubini, N. (2006a) "Orwellian Chutzpah and Doublespeak in the Economic Report of the President: The US Current Account Deficit Becomes the 'US Capital Account Surplus' ", *Nouriel Roubini's Global Economics Blog*, 13 February, www.roubini.com (accessed 2007).

Roubini, N. (2006b) "Will the US Current Account Deficit Close to a Trillion Dollars of Course Foreigners Will Soon Own Most of the US Capital Stock", *Nouriel Roubini's Global Economics Blog*, 22 February, www.roubini.com (accessed 2007).

Roubini, N. (2008a) "The Decline of the American Empire", *Roubini Blog: Global Monitor*, 13 August, http://www.roubini.com/analysis/45701.php (accessed 2 February 2012).

Roubini, N. (2008b) "The Rising Risk of a Hard Landing in China: The Two Engines of Global Growth – US and China – Are Now Stalling", *Nouriel Roubini's Global EconoMonitor*, 4 November, www.roubini.com (accessed 9 March 2012).

Roubini, N. (2009a) "Can Japan Avoid another Lost Decade?" *Forbes*, 23 July, http://www.forbes.com/2009/07/22/japan-deflation-lost-decade-aso-yen-dollar-opinions-columnists-nouriel-roubini.html (accessed 6 November 2009).

Roubini, N. (2009b) "When the Public Debt Rubber Meets the Investors' Anxiety Asphalt", *RGE Monitor*, 28 May.

Roubini, N. (2011) "China's Bad Growth Bet", *Project Syndicate*, 14 April, http://www.project-syndicate.org/commentary/roubini37/English (accessed 8 March 2012).

Roubini, N. and Setser, B. (2004) "The US as a Net Debtor: The Sustainability of the US External Imbalances", NYU, August, revised: November 2004, New York, NY: New York University.

Roubini, N. and Setser, B. (2005) *The Sustainability of US External Imbalances*. New York, NY: New York University, http://www.ifo.de/portal/pls/portal/docs/1/1206797.PDF (accessed 19 February 2012).

Roy, D. (2005) "Southeast Asia and China: Balancing or Bandwagoning?" *Contemporary Southeast Asia*, 27(2), 305–322.

Rubin, R. E., et al. (2004) "Sustained Budget Deficits: Longer-Run US Economic Performance and the Risk of Financial and Fiscal Disarray", *The Brookings Institution*, 4 January, p. 1.

Rushdie, S. (2011) "Pakistan: A Terrorist State", *Newsweek*, 16 May.

Ryan, P. D. (2010) "A Roadmap for America's Future: Version 2.0", January.

Saad, L. (2008a) "Americans See China Crowding Out US as Economic Leader", *Gallup Polls*, 21 February, http://www.gallup.com/poll/104479/americans-see-china-crowding-us-economic-leader.aspx (accessed 14 October 2011).

Saad, L. (2008b) "Congress' Approval Rating Ties Lowest in Gallup Records", *Gallup Polls*, 14 May, http://www.gallup.com/poll/107242/congress-approval-rating-ties-lowest-gallup-records.aspx (accessed 30 November 2011).

Saad, L. (2009) "Americans Remain Critical of the United Nations", *Gallup Polls*, 13 March, http://www.gallup.com/poll/116812/Americans-Remain-Critical-United-Nations.aspx (accessed 24 September 2011).

Saad, L. (2010a) "Americans Back More Stimulus Spending to Create Jobs", *Gallup Polls*, 17 June, http://www.gallup.com/poll/140786/americans-back-stimulus-spending-create-jobs.aspx (accessed 14 October 2011).

Saad, L. (2010b) "One in Three Cite 'American People' as Key US Asset", *Gallup Polls*, 17 February, http://www.gallup.com/poll/126032/One-Three-Cite-American-People-Key-Asset.aspx (accessed 18 October 2011).

Saad, L. (2011a) "Americans Express Historic Negativity toward US Government", *Gallup Polls*, 26 September, http://www.gallup.com/poll/149678/Americans-Express-Historic-Negativity-Toward-Government.aspx (accessed 2 October 2011).

Saad, L. (2011b) "China Surges in Americans' Views of Top World Economy", *Gallup Polls*, 14 February, http://www.gallup.com/poll/146099/China-Surges-Americans-Views-Top-World-Economy.aspx (accessed 12 October 2011).

Saad, L. (2011c) "In US, Slight Majority Now Blame Obama for US Economy", *Gallup Polls*, 21 September, http://www.gallup.com/poll/149600/slight-majority-blame-obama-economy.aspx (accessed 12 November 2011).

Sachs, G., Wilson, D. and Stupnytska A. (2007) "The N-11: More than an Acronym", *Global Economics Paper* No. 153, March.

Sachs, Jeffrey (2011) "Occupy Wall Street and the Demand for Economic Justice", *The Huffington Post*, 13 October, http://www.huffingtonpost.com/jeffrey-sachs/occupy-wall-street-and-th_b_1007609.html (accessed 24 November 2011).

Sanger, D. (2011) "US Said to Turn Back North Korea Missile Shipment", *The New York Times*, 12 June.

Sanger, D. (2012) *Confront and Conceal: Obama's Secret Wars and Surprising Use of American Power*. New York, NY: Crown Books.

Sapir, A. (2006) "Is the Euro Ready for a Global Role?" *Europe's World*, Spring, 56–61.

Schake, K. N. (2009) *Managing American Hegemony: Essays on Power in a Time of Dominance*. Stanford, CA: Hoover University Press.

Scheer, R. (2008) *The Pornography of Power*, June. New York, NY: Grand Central Publishing.

Schott, J. (2008) "The Future of the Multilateral Trading System in a Multilateral World", *Discussion Paper*, Bonn: German Development Institute, http://www.iie.com/publications/papers/schott0608.pdf (accessed 1 July 2009).

Schwartz, N. and Saltmarsh, M. (2009) "Crisis Leaves Europe in Slow Lane", 10 October, Section B, p. 1.

Segal, A. (2010) "China's Innovation Wall", *Foreign Affairs*, 28 September.

Segal, A. (2011) *Advantage: How American Innovation Can Overcome the Asian Challenge*. New York, NY: W. W. Norton & Company.

Setser, B. (2008) "Sovereign Wealth and Sovereign Power", *Council Special Reports* No. 37, September, Washington, DC: Greenburg Center for Geoeconomic Studies at the Council on Foreign Relations.

Setser, B. and Roubini, N. (2005a) "How Scary Is the Deficit? American Power and American Borrowing", *Foreign Affairs*, July/August, 194–198.

Setser, B. and Roubini, N. (2005b) "The Kindness of Strangers", A Reply to Levey, David and Stuart Brown, "How Scary Is the Deficit: American Power and American Borrowing", *Foreign Affairs*, December, Special Edition for the Ministerial Meeting of the World Trade Organization's Doha Round, Hong Kong.

Setser, B. W. (2008) "Sovereign Wealth and Sovereign Power", *Council on Foreign Relations*, CSR No. 37, September.

Shanker, T. (2009) "Stop-Loss Will All But End by 2011, Gates Says", *The New York Times*, 18 March, http://www.nytimes.com/2009/03/19/washington/19gates.html (accessed 23 July 2009).

Sheng, A. (2009) *From Asian to Global Financial Crisis: An Asian Regulator's View of Unfettered Finance in the 1990s and 2000s*. Cambridge: Cambridge University Press.

Shih, Victor (2011) "Guest Post: China's Local Debt Problem Is Bigger than It Looks", *Financial Times*, 28 June, http://blogs.ft.com/beyond-brics/2011/06/28/guest-post-chinas-local-debt-problem-is-bigger-than-it-looks/#axzz1xDatrNxe (accessed 8 July 2012).

Shirk, S. L. (2007) *China: Fragile Superpower*. New York, NY: Oxford University Press.

Shrader, K. (2007) "Suitcase Nuclear Bomb Unlikely to Exist", *The Washington Post*, 11 November, http://www.washingtonpost.com/wp-dyn/content/article/2007/11/11/AR2007111100206.html (accessed 8 March 2012).

Shultz, G. P., et al. (2010) "How to Protect Our Nuclear Deterrent", *The Wall Street Journal*, 19 January, http://online.wsj.com/article/SB10001424052748704152804574628344282735008.html (accessed 8 March 2012).

Shultz, G. P., et al. (2011) "Deterrence in the Age of Nuclear Proliferation", *The Wall Street Journal*, 7 March, http://online.wsj.com/article/SB10001424052748703300904576178760530169414.html (accessed 8 March 2012).

Simpson, J. (2008) "Iraq War Shows Limits of US Power", *BBC News*, 18 March, http://news.bbc.co.uk/2/hi/middle_east/7303985.stm (accessed 31 July 2009).

Singer, P. (2011) "Interview with Tom Ashbrook – The Drone War Goes Global", *National Public Radio*, 11 July.

Sisko, A., et al. (2009) "Health Spending Projections Through 2018: Recession Effects Add Uncertainty to the Outlook", *Health Affairs*, 24 February.

Skinner Monroe, S. (2009) "Clinton's Asia Visit Builds on US Soft Power in Region; Asian Publics Rank US Ahead of a Rising China", *The Chicago Council on Global Affairs Press Release*, 10 February.

Snidal, D. (1985) "The Limits of Hegemonic Stability Theory", *International Organizations*, 39(4), 579–614.

Social Security Board of Trustees (2009) "The 2009 Annual Report", Washington, DC, 12 May.

Social Security Board of Trustees (2011) "The 2011 Annual Report", Washington, DC, 13 May.

Soesastro, H. (2009) "East Asia Must Show Leadership to Keep Trade Free", *The Jakarta Post*, 16 March.

Solomon, J. (2011). "US, France Seek Balance in Mideast", *The Wall Street Journal*, 24 December, http://online.wsj.com/article/SB10001424052970204336104577094500038099554.html (accessed 6 January 2012).

Spector, L. S. (1996) *Tracking Nuclear Proliferation: A Guide in Maps and Charts*. Washington, DC: Carnegie Endowment for International Peace.

Spector, L. S., McDonough, M. G. and Medeiros, E. S. (1995) *Tracking Nuclear Proliferation. Appendix F: Nuclear Supplier Organizations*. New York, NY: Brookings Institution Press.

Spence, M. (2011) "The Impact of Globalization on Income and Employment", *Foreign Affairs*, 90(4), 28–41.

Spence, M., Katz, R. and Lawrence, R. Z. (2011) "Manufacturing Globalization", *Foreign Affairs*, 90(6), November/December, 171.

Srivastava, M. (2009) "Anger Grows in India over US Visa Rules", *Economic Times*, 25 February, http://economictimes.indiatimes.com/Anger-grows-in-India-over-US-visa-rules/articleshow/4189959.cms (accessed 25 March 2011).

Starobin, P. (2009) *After-America: Narratives for the Next Global Age*. New York, NY: Viking Adult.

Sternberg, J. (2012) "China, The World's Greater Fool?", *The Wall Street Journal*, 16 August, http://online.wsj.com/article/SB10000872396390444508504577591063754857288.html (accessed 18 October 2012).

Stiglitz, J. (2011) "The Global 99 Percent", *Slate Magazine*, 4 November, http://www. slate.com/articles/business/project_syndicate/2011/11/occupy_wall_street_and_ the_global_trend_against_inequality_.html (accessed 13 November 2011).

Stiglitz, J. E. (2010) *Freefall: America, Free Markets and the Sinking of the World Economy.* New York, NY: W. W. Norton & Company.

Stiglitz, J. E. and Bilmes, L. J. (2008) *The Three Trillion Dollar War.* New York, NY: W. W. Norton & Company.

Stockholm International Peace Research Institute (2010) "SIPRI Military Expenditure Database", http://milexdata.sipri.org/.

Stokes, D. and Raphael, S. (2010) *Global Energy Security and American Hegemony.* Baltimore, MD: The Johns Hopkins University Press.

Subramanian, A. (2011a) *Eclipse: Living in the Shadow of China's Economic Dominance.* Washington, DC: Peterson Institute for International Economics.

Subramanian, A. (2011b) "The Inevitable Superpower", *Foreign Affairs*, September/October.

Summers, L. (2004a) *Speech on The United States and the Global Adjustment Process*, 23 March, given at the Institute for International Economics, Washington, DC, http://www.iie.com/publications/papers/paper.cfm?ResearchID=200 (accessed 19 February 2012).

Summers, L. H. (2004b) "The US Current Account Deficit and the Global Economy", in: Per Jacobsson Lecture, International Monetary Fund, Washington, DC, 3 October.

Sutter, R. (2008) "Asia's Lagging Leadership", *PacNet* No. 49, 15 September, Honolulu: Pacific Forum CSIS, http://csis.org/files/media/csis/pubs/pac0849.pdf (accessed 9 March 2012).

Sutter, R. G. (2006) "China's Rise: Implications for US Leadership in Asia", *Policy Studies* No. 21, Washington, DC: East-West Center, http://www.eastwestcenter.org/sites/ default/files/private/PS021.pdf (accessed 9 March 2012).

Swiston, A. (2005) "A Global View of the US Investment Position", IMF Working Paper WP/05/181, Washington, DC: International Monetary Fund.

Talmadge, C. (2007) "Deterring a Nuclear 9/11", *Washington Quarterly*, Spring.

Tanner, M. (2011) "Bankrupt: Entitlements and the Federal Budget", *Policy Analysis* No. 673, CATO Institute, 28 March.

Tarullo, D. (2006) "The End of the Big Trade Deal", *The International Economy*, Summer, 46–49.

Taylor, A. (2011) "Debt-Ceiling Deal Means $450B in Defense Cuts", *Associated Press*, 1 August, http://www.military.com/news/article/debt-ceiling-deal-means-350b-in-defense-cuts.html (accessed 21 October 2011).

Taylor, J. and John, C. (2011) "Where Did the Stimulus Go?" *Commentary Magazine*, January.

Tellis, A. J. (2007) "Punching the US Military's 'Soft Ribs': China's Antisatellite Weapon Test in Strategic Perspective", *Policy Brief 51*, Carnegie Endowment for International Peace, http://www.carnegieendowment.org/files/pb_51_tellis_final. pdf (accessed 15 September 2009).

Terror Free Tomorrow (2006) "One Year Later: Humanitarian Relief Sustains Change in Muslim Public Opinion", Washington DC, http://www.terrorfreetomorrow. org/upimagestft/INDONESIA%202006%20Poll%20Report.pdf (accessed 14 January 2012).

The Chicago Council of Foreign Relations (2008) *Asia Soft Power Survey 2008*, http:// www.thechicagocouncil.org/UserFiles/File/POS_Topline%20Reports/Asia%20Soft

%20Power%202008/Chicago%20Council%20Soft%20Power%20Report-%20Final %206-11-08.pdf (accessed 10 May 2010).

The Chicago Council of Foreign Relations (2009) "Implications of the Financial Crisis for Soft Power in Asia", *Special Report*, November, http://www. thechicagocouncil.org/UserFiles/File/Conferences/Soft%20Power/Implications %20of%20the%20Financial%20Crisis%20for%20Soft%20Power%20in%20Asia %20-%20Nov%202009%20Report.pdf (accessed 12 March 2012).

The Chicago Council on Global Affairs (2008) Global Views 2008: Anxiety over Energy, Jobs, and Wealth Shakes America's Global Economic Confidence. Figure 8: Factors in Remaining Competitive, http://www.thechicagocouncil.org/ UserFiles/File/POS_Topline%20Reports/POS%202008/2008%20Public%20Opinion_ Economic.pdf (accessed 12 November 2011).

The Chicago Council on Global Affairs (2010) "Constrained Internationalism: Adapting to New Realities", Chicago, http://www.thechicagocouncil.org/UserFiles/File/ POS_Topline%20Reports/POS%202010/Global%20Views%202010.pdf (accessed 8 October 2011).

The Conference Board (2010) *The Total Economy Database. Summary Statistics 1995–2010.* New York, NY: The Conference Board.

The Conference Board (2011) *The Conference Board Total Economy Database, Summary Statistics 1995–2011.* New York, NY: The Conference Board, http://www.conference-board.org/data/economydatabase/ (accessed 1 March 2011).

The Conference Board (2012) *Total Economy Database: Advanced Economies Show Dramatic Loss in Productivity Edge.* New York, NY: The Conference Board, http://www. conference-board.org/pdf_free/economics/TED2.pdf (accessed 1 March 2012).

The Economist (2007a) "Capturing Talent", 18 August, http://www.economist.com/ node/9645045 (accessed 1 March 2011).

The Economist (2007b) "The Trouble with Migrants", 22 November, http://www. economist.com/node/10193441 (accessed 12 November 2011).

The Economist (2008) "A Surge of Pessimism", 16 October, http://www.economist.com/ node/12437731 (accessed 18 April 2011).

The Economist (2009a) "The Military-Consumer Complex", 12 December, p. 16.

The Economist (2009b) "Lexington: Two Cheers for America", 4 July, p. 30.

The Economist (2009c) "The Long Climb: A Special Report on the World Economy", 3 October, http://www.economist.com/specialreports/displaystory.cfm?story_id= 14530093 (accessed 10 October 2009).

The Economist (2010a) "Reforming European Economies: The Cruelty of Compassion", 30 January, p. 16.

The Economist (2010b) "Testing the Waters", 31 July, p. 32.

The Economist (2011a) "Learning the Hard Way", 3 September, pp. 83–84.

The Economist (2011b) "We Will Frack You", 19 November 2011, p. 34.

The Economist (2011c) "Dreams and Realities: Asia-Pacific Trade Initiatives", 12 November, p. 49.

The Economist (2011d) "Who's Afraid of the Dragon?" 15 October, p. 42.

The Economist (2011e) "The Happening Place: South-East Asian Summitry", 12 November, p. 40.

The Economist (2011f) "Weaving the World Together", 19 November, pp. 72–74.

The Economist (2011g) "Unskilled Workers Struggling to Keep Up with Technological Change", 19 November, p. 84.

The Economist (2011h) "We're Back: America in the Asia-Pacific", 19 November, p. 43.

The Economist (2012a) "Could Asia really go to war over these?", 22 September, http://www.economist.com/node/21563316 (accessed 18 October 2012).

The Economist (2012b) "Crony tigers, divided dragons", 13 October, http://www.economist.com/node/21564408 (accessed 18 October 2012).

The Nation (2010) "Rafsanjani urges Iran not to Dismiss Sanctions as 'Jokes,'" 14 September, http://www.nation.com.pk/pakistan-news-newspaper-daily-english-online/international/14-Sep-2010/Rafsanjani-urges-Iran-not-to-dismiss-sanctions-as-jokes (accessed 9 March 2012).

The Straits Times (2011) "Shanghai Overtake Singapore as World's Busiest Port", 8 January, www.straitstimes.com (accessed 8 March 2011).

The World Bank (2010) *World Development Indicators*. Washington, DC: World Bank.

The World Bank and the Government of the People's Republic of China (2007) "Cost of Pollution in China: Estimates of Physical Damages", Conference Edition, http://go.worldbank.org/FFCJVBTP40 (accessed 2011).

Thorpe, M. and Mitra, S. (2008) "Growing Economic Interdependence of China and the Gulf Cooperation Council", *China & World Economy*, 16(2), March–April, 109–124.

TNS Global (2008) "Asia-Pacific's Top 1000 Brands' 2008 Study", 4 September, http://www.tnsglobal.com/news/news-2057884A240D485B81833B20E2A772D7.aspx (accessed 9 March 2012).

Trans-Pacific Strategic Economic Partnership (2005) "Agreement", 3 June, Washington, DC: Foreign Trade Information System Organization of American States, http://www.sice.oas.org/Trade/CHL_Asia_e/mainAgreemt_e.pdf (accessed 11 January 2012).

Treverton, G. and Jones, S. (2005) "Measuring National Power", National Security Division-RAND, http://www.rand.org/pubs/conf_proceedings/2005/RAND_CF215.pdf (accessed 1 February 2012). Traub, J. (2011) "The Elephants in the Room", *Foreign Policy*, November, http://www.foreignpolicy.com/articles/2011/10/11/the_elephants_in_the_room?page=0,0 (accessed 31 December 2011).

Trichet, Jean-Claude (2006) *Keynote Speech*, 22–23 May, given at the OECD Forum "Balancing Globalization", Paris, France, http://www.oecd.org/dataoecd/51/38/36760320.pdf (accessed 3 March 2012).

Truman, E. (2004) "Budget and External Deficits: Not Twins but the Same Family", unpublished manuscript, June, Boston, MA: Federal Reserve Bank of Boston.

U.S. Energy Information Administration (2011) "Annual US Imports of Other Hydrocarbons/Oxygenates", *Independent Statistics & Analysis*, 28 July, http://www.eia.gov/dnav/pet/hist/LeafHandler.ashx?n=pet&s=mohimus2&f=a (accessed December 2011).

United Nations (2010) "World Population Prospects: The 2010 Revision", http://esa.un.org/wpp/unpp/panel_population.htm (accessed 8 March 2012).

United Nations Food and Agriculture Organization (2012) "Terrastat Database", http://www.fao.org/ag/agl/agll/terrastat/ (accessed 2012).

United Nations Population Division (2012) "On-line Database: Population", http://esa.un.org/unpd/wpp/unpp/panel_population.htm (accessed 8 March 2012).

United Nations Security Council (2008) "Security Council Tightens Restrictions on Iran's Proliferation-Sensitive Activities, Increases Vigilance over Iranian Banks, Has States Inspect Cargo", 3 March, http://www.un.org/News/Press/docs/2008/sc9268.doc.htm (accessed 8 March 2012).

United Nations, Department of Economic and Social Affairs (2010) Population Projections Report, http://esa.un.org/wpp/unpp/panel_population.htm (accessed 7 September 2011).

United State Department of Energy (2012) "Natural Gas Production and Energy Imports 2000–2035", 26 January, http://energy.gov/articles/natural-gas-production-and-us-oil-imports (accessed 18 April 2012).

United States Advisory Commission on Public Diplomacy (2004) "Introduction: Annual Report", The United States Department of State, 28 September.

United States Department of State (2003) "Russia-Iran Nuclear Cooperation", Office of the Spokesman, 31 January.

United States Government Accountability Office (2008) "Comparison of the Reported Tax Liabilities of Foreign and US-Controlled Corporations, 1998-2005", *Report to Congressional Requesters*, http://www.gao.gov/new.items/d08957.pdf (accessed 3 March 2012).

United States Nuclear Regulatory Commission (2011) "Fact Sheet on Uranium Enrichment", 18 October, http://www.nrc.gov/reading-rm/doc-collections/fact-sheets/enrichment.html (accessed 8 March 2012).

United States of America (2002) "National Security Strategy Report 2002". Washington, DC.

United States of America (2005) "The National Security Strategy Report 2005". Washington, DC.

United States Trade Representative (USTR) (2011) "Outlines of the Trans-Pacific Partnership Agreement", November, http://www.ustr.gov/about-us/press-office/fact-sheets/2011/november/outlines-trans-pacific-partnership-agreement (accessed 9 March 2012).

UPI (2010) "Russia Pulls Plug on Arms Deal", 22 September, http://www.upi.com/Top_News/World-News/2010/09/22/Russia-pulls-plug-on-Iran-arms-deal/UPI-49941285186093/ (accessed 9 March 2012).

US Census Bureau (2010) "International Data Base", http://www.census.gov/population/international/data/idb/informationGateway.php (accessed 2011).

US Congressional Budget Office (2008) *How Changes in the Value of the Chinese Currency Affect US Imports*, July, http://www.cbo.gov/ftpdocs/95xx/doc9506/07-17-ChinaTrade.pdf (accessed 17 February 2012).

US Department of Defense (2006) "Wall of Water: US Troops Aid Tsunami Victims", http://www.defense.gov/home/features/2006/2005yearinreview/article2.html (accessed 14 January 2012).

US Department of Defense (2009a) "Annual Report to Congress: Military Power of the People's Republic of China", http://www.au.af.mil/au/awc/awcgate/dod/china_report_2009.pdf (accessed 8 March 2012).

US Department of Defense (2009b) "Budget Request Summary Justification", Washington, DC.

US Department of Defense (2011) *Annual Report to Congress: Military and Security Developments Involving the People's Republic of China*, http://www.defense.gov/pubs/pdfs/2011_cmpr_final.pdf (accessed 9 March 2012).

US Department of Homeland Security (2012) "Secretary Napolitano Announces Deferred Action Process for Young People Who Are Low Enforcement Priorities", 15 June, http://www.dhs.gov/news/2012/06/15/secretary-napolitano-announces-deferred-action-process-young-people-who-are-low (accessed 18 October 2012).

US Department of Labor (2006) *A Chartbook of International Labor Comparisons*, http://www.bls.gov/fls/chartbook/chartbook2006.pdf (accessed 20 March 2011).

US Department of the Treasury (2009) "FY 2010 Congressional Budget Request: Budget Highlights", Washington, DC, May.

US Department of the Treasury (2011) "Resource Center: Treasure International Capital System", 20 July.

US Department of Treasury (2007) "Treasury Conference on Business Taxation and Global Competitiveness Background Paper", 23 July 2007, http://www.treasury.gov/press/releases/reports/07230%20r.pdf (accessed 20 December 2009).

US Energy Information Administration (2011a) "International Energy Outlook 2011", 19 September, http://www.eia.gov/forecasts/ieo/pdf/0484(2011).pdf (accessed 14 January 2012).

US Energy Information Administration (2011b) "World Oil Transit Chokepoints", 30 December, http://205.254.135.7/countries/regions-topics.cfm?fips=WOTC (accessed 6 March 2012).

US Navy (2010a) "US Pacific Fleet Area of Responsibility", 7 January, http://www.cpf.navy.mil/about (accessed 20 February 2010).

US Navy (2010b) "5th Fleet Combined Maritime Forces", http://www.cusnc.navy.mil/command/command.html (accessed 28 March 2010).

US Pacific Command (2011) "USPACOM Facts", http://www.pacom.mil/web/Site_Pages/USPACOM/Facts.shtml (accessed 10 September 2011).

Van Ark, B., Kirsten J., Vlad, M. and Metz, A. (2009) "Productivity, Performance, and Progress-Germany in International Perspective", March, New York, NY: The Conference Board, http://www.conference-board.org/publications/describe.cfm?id=1682 (accessed 7 March 2010).

Varian, H. (2007) "An iPod Has Global Value. Ask the (Many) Countries That Make It", *The New York Times*, 28 June, http://www.nytimes.com/2007/06/28/business/worldbusiness/28scene.html (accessed 11 January 2012).

Vaughan, Martin and Back, Aaron (2011) "Moody's Warns on China's Debt", *The Wall Street Journal*, 6 July, http://online.wsj.com/article/SB10001424052702304803104576427062691548064.html (accessed 8 June 2012).

Vaughn, Bruce (2005) "US Congressional Research Service. East Asian Summit: Issues for Congress", 9 December, Washington, DC: Congressional Research Service, http://www.au.af.mil/au/awc/awcgate/crs/rs22346.pdf (accessed 9 March 2012).

Vine, D. (2009) "Too Many Overseas Bases", *Foreign Policy in Focus*, 25 February, http://www.fpif.org/fpiftxt/5903 (accessed 31 March 2009).

Vira, V. and Cordesman, A. (2011) "Pakistan: Violence vs. Stablility, A National Net Assessment", *Center for Strategic and International Studies, Working Paper*, May.

Wagoner, R. (2005) "Remarks by Rick Wagoner Chairman and Chief Executive Officer General Motors Corporation to the Economic Club of Chicago", *The Washington Post*, 10 February, http://www.washingtonpost.com/wp-srv/nation/documents/wagoner_feb_10.pdf (accessed 30 March 2011).

Walder, A. G. (2009) "Unruly Stability: Why China's Regime Has Staying Power", *Current History*, September.

Walker, P. (2006) "Nunn Lugar at 15: No Time to Relax CTR", *Arms Control Today*, 1 May.

The Wall Street Journal (2011a) "Text of Mitt Romney's Speech on Foreign Policy at the Citadel", 7 October, Charleston, South Carolina, http://blogs.wsj.com/washwire/2011/10/07/text-of-mitt-romneys-speech-on-foreign-policy-at-the-citadel/ (accessed 4 November 2011).

The Wall Street Journal (2011b) "Text of Obama's Speech on Immigration", 10 May, El Paso, Texas, http://blogs.wsj.com/washwire/2011/05/10/text-of-obamas-speech-on-immigration/ (accessed 21 October 2011).

Walt, S. (2011) "What I'm Telling the South Koreans", *Foreign Policy*, October 5. http://walt.foreignpolicy.com/posts/2011/10/05/what_im_telling_the_south_koreans (accessed 16 January 2012).

Walt, S. M. (2005) *Taming American Power: The Global Response to US, Primacy*. New York, NY: W. W. Norton & Company.

Waltz, K. N. (1979) *Theory of International Politics*. New York, NY: McGraw Hill.

Warner, M. (2010) "Examining the Effect of Economic Sanctions on Iran", *PBS News Hour*, 21 September.

Watts, J. (2010) *When a Billion Chinese Jump: How China Will Save Mankind – Or Destroy It.* New York, NY: Scribner.

Wedeman, A. (2004). "The Intensification of Corruption in China", *The China Quarterly*, 180, 895–921, Cambridge University Press, December.

Wei, S. (2010) "The Mystery of Chinese Savings", *VOX*, 6 February, http://www.voxeu.org/index.php?q=node/4568 (accessed 19 February 2011).

Wei, S. and Frankel, J. (1996) "Can Regional Blocs be a Stepping Stone to Global Free Trade? A Political Economy Analysis", *International Review of Economics and Finance*, 5(4), 339–347.

Weiner, T. (2007) *Legacy of Ashes: The History of the CIA*. New York, NY: Doubleday.

Wheeler, W. T. (2009) "Of Pork and Baloney: Obama's Defense Budget", *Counterpunch*, 6 May.

White, Hugh (2011) "Competing for Primacy in Asia", *The New York Times*, 21 November, http://www.nytimes.com/roomfordebate/2011/11/21/does-the-us-need-troops-in-australia/the-us-is-competing-for-primacy-in-asia (accessed 17 January 2012).

White, J. (2004) "Soldiers Facing Extended Tours", *The Washington Post*, June 3, 2004, A01. http://www.washingtonpost.com/wp-dyn/articles/A10961-2004Jun2.html (accessed 23 July 2009).

White, W. (2009) "Some Fires Are Best Left to Burn Out", *Financial Times*, 17 September, p. 11.

Whyte, M. K. (2012) "China's Post-Socialist Inequality." *Current History*, 111(746), 229–234.

Wilder, D. (2009) "The US-China Strategic and Economic Dialogue: Continuity and Change in Obama's China Policy", *China Brief – The Jamestown Foundation*, IX(10), 15 May, http://www.jamestown.org/uploads/media/cb_009_02.pdf (accessed 10 July 2009).

Will, G. (2005) "Comments on ABC This Week", 20 November.

Wines, M. (2007) "Break-In at Nuclear Site Baffles South Africa", *The New York Times*, 15 November.

Wohlforth, W. C. (2012) "The American World Mark III", in Clark, S. and Hoque, S. (eds.), *Debating a Post-American World: What Lies Ahead?* pp. 81–85. London: Routledge.

Wolf, M. (2004) *Why Globalization Works*. New Haven, CT: Yale University Press.

Wolf, M. (2005) "Opening a Three-Part Series, Martin Wolf Looks at Why Beijing Has Enjoyed the Greater Success in Stimulating Growth – And What New Delhi Will Have To Do To Catch Up", *Financial Times* 23 February.

Wolf, M. (2008a) "Emu's Second 10 Years May be Tougher", *Financial Times*, 27 May, http://www.ft.com/cms/s/0/45654f9e-2bfd-11dd-9861-000077b07658. html#axzz1G7k9yJb4 (accessed 9 March 2011).

Wolf, M. (2008b) *Fixing Global Finance*. Baltimore, MD: The Johns Hopkins University Press.

Wolf, M. (2010) "Wen Is Right to Worry about China's Growth", *Financial Times*, 21 September.

World Bank (1993) *The East Asian Miracle: Economic Growth and Public Policy*. New York, NY: Oxford University Press.

World Bank (2009) "World Development Indicators (2009)", http://data.worldbank. org/indicator (accessed 9 March 2012).

World Bank (2010) *Data on Trade on Import Barriers*, updated August, Washington, DC: World Bank, http://econ.worldbank.org/WBSITE/EXTERNAL/EXTDEC/EXTRE SEARCH/0,,contentMDK:21051044~pagePK:64214825~piPK:64214943~theSitePK: 469382,00.html (accessed 29 March 2011).

World Economic Forum (WEF) (2009) *World Economic Forum Business Competitiveness Index 2009–2010*. Geneva: WEF, https://members.weforum.org/pdf/GCR09/ GCR20092010fullreport.pdf (accessed 9 March 2011).

World Economic Forum USA (2009) *The Financial Development Report 2009*. New York, NY: WEF, http://www3.weforum.org/docs/WEF_FinancialDevelopmentReport_ 2009.pdf (accessed 23 March 2011).

World Trade Organization (2008) "Understanding the WTO: Members and Observers", 23 July, http://www.wto.org/english/theWTO_e/whatis_e/tif_e/org6_e. htm (accessed 9 July 2009).

World Trade Organization (2010) *World Tariff Profiles 2010*. Geneva: WTO, http:// www.wto.org/english/res_e/publications_e/world_tariff_profiles10_e.htm (accessed 12 March 2012).

Xafa, M. (2007) "Global Imbalances and Financial Stability", IMF Working Paper, May, Washington, DC: International Monetary Fund.

Xinhuanet (2012) "Iran's Currency Suffers New Depreciation after US Sanctions Iranian Central Bank", 3 January, http://news.xinhuanet.com/english/world/2012- 01/03/c_122526878.htm (accessed 9 March 2012).

Yao, S. (2009) "China Will Learn from Chinalco's Failed Deal with Rio", *Financial Times*, 8 June.

Yeung, H. W. (2004) *Chinese Capitalism in a Global Era: Towards Hybrid Capitalism*. London/New York, NY: Routledge.

Zakaria, F. (2004) "The One-Note Superpower", *Newsweek*, 2 February, p. 41.

Zakaria, F. (2008a) *The Post American World*. New York, NY: W. W. Norton & Company.

Zakaria, F. (2008b) "The Future of American Power: How America Can Survive the Rise of the Rest", *Foreign Affairs*, May/June.

Zakaria, F. (2010a) "Terrorism's Supermarket", *Newsweek*, 7 May.

Zakaria, F. (2010b) "The Real Failed State Risk", *Newsweek*, 19 July.

Zakaria, F. (2011) "China's Not Doing Us a Favor", *CNN*, 14 August, http:// globalpublicsquare.blogs.cnn.com/2011/08/14/why-china-needs-u-s/?hpt=hp_c1 (accessed 26 November 2011).

Zakaria, F. (2012) "Inside Obama's World: The President Talks to TIME About the Changing Nature of American Power", *Time Magazine*, 19 January, http:// swampland.time.com/2012/01/19/inside-obamas-world-the-president-talks-to- time-about-the-changing-nature-of-american-power/ (accessed 28 January 2012).

Zakheim, D. (2011) "Taliban 2.0", *The National Interest*, 1 June.

Zarif, J. (2007) "Tackling the U-Iran Crisis", *Columbia Journal of International Affairs*, 60(2), 73–94.

Zingales, L. (2009) "Capitalism after the Crisis", *National Affairs*, Fall(1), 22–35.

Zweig, D. and Jianhai, B. (2005) "China's Global Hunt for Energy", *Foreign Affairs*, 84(5), September–October, 25–38.

Index

Note: The letter "n" followed by the locator refers to notes in the text.

Printed and bound in the United States of America